OFF THE RA...

'Brendan Ogle's innate sense of fairness led him and his fellow train drivers to challenge some of the most powerful groups in Irish society. His story of the ILDA/Iarnród Éireann dispute raises serious questions about the monopoly position exercised by elements within the trade union movement and about their tolerance of principled dissent. *Off the Rails* is also a tale of disillusionment and discovery, a *Band of Brothers* story sparkling with values of loyalty, integrity and courage.'

– Medb Ruane, journalist

'ILDA and Brendan Ogle's story underlines how far modern Irish trade union leaders have strayed from the principles of the movement's founding fathers. It also suggests that a Faustian pact has been agreed by a handful of powerful trade unionists with the people they are supposed to protect their members from.'

– Paddy Prendiville, editor, *The Phoenix*

'Brendan Ogle is a controversial figure. He is both revered and reviled within the trade union movement. He is a man of fearless conviction, determined loyalty and a formidable opponent. He leads, not from behind a desk, but shoulder to shoulder with those whose sweat and toil he shares. A man with a admirable mixture of integrity and intellect, his recollections on the ILDA strike of 2000 will reignite within the trade union movement debate on sensitive issues such as worker solidarity, inter-union rivalry, power brokering and the role of the media.'

– Don Mullan, author, *Eyewitness Bloody Sunday*

'This is one of the only accounts of an industrial dispute written by one of those who was intimately involved. This book is a great read… It is a fascinating insight into industrial relations and anybody who wants to know how Ireland works should not be without a copy.'

– Mick O'Reilly, Leader ATGWU

'A remarkable book. Not only does it give the inside story of the ILDA/ Iarnród Éireann dispute, but it also offers a penetrating and deeply personal insight into what it is like to be in the eye of a massive media storm. I commend this book for its honesty and detailed description of one of the most bitter industrial disputes in recent Irish life.'

– Michael O'Toole, journalist, *The Star*

'A compellingly interesting, humorous, entertaining and cuttingly honest account and read of the birth pains of a modern train drivers' collective that coalesced into the Irish Locomotive Drivers Association. Mr Ogle's writings reveal his obvious passion and dedication as both train driver and a union man working to protect the interests of train drivers as well as forging a process aimed at improving broader industrial relations harmony both within union and employer echelons and beyond.'

– Keith Harris, journalist, newsmedianews.com

'An original picture of industrial relations in a state company having indeed gone off the rails.'

– Gerald Flynn, Group Industrial Correspondent,
Independent Newspapers.

'A valuable account of the good, the bad and the indifferent that can take place in the trade union movement.'

– Mick Rix, General Secretary, ASLEF

Off the Rails

THE STORY OF ILDA

Brendan Ogle

CURRACH
PRESS

First published in 2003 by
CURRACH PRESS
55A Spruce Avenue, Stillorgan Industrial Park, Blackrock, Co Dublin

www.currach.ie
www.offtherails.org

Cover by Space
Cover photographs by Photocall Ireland
Origination by Currach Press
Printed in Ireland by ColourBooks Ltd, Dublin

ISBN 1-85607-906-6

Acknowledgements

The author and publisher gratefully acknowledge the permission of the following to use material in their copyright: the *Irish Examiner, The Irish Times,* Newspics, Keith Heneghan at Phocus, Photocall Ireland, Derek Speirs and the *Sunday Tribune.*

Every effort has been made to trace copyright holders. If we have inadvertently used copyright material without permission we apologise and will put it right in future editions.

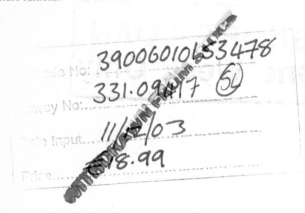
Copyright © 2003, Brendan Ogle

NORMA SMURFIT LIBRARY
NATIONAL COLLEGE
OF IRELAND

WITHDRAWN FROM STOCK

CONTENTS

SHORT LOAN
One Week Only

Dedicated to
Pauline, Dara and baby Kate

PREFACE

To sin by silence when we
should protest makes cowards
out of men.
            – Ella Wheeler Wilcox

Words mean a lot. At least some of them do.

'Normal'.

That word described me perfectly. Brendan Ogle, the eighth born of nine children to Bobby and Moira into a working class area in Dundalk. At school I was clever enough when I wanted to be but not exceptional. Average. 'Normal'. And a bit lazy. I didn't excel at sport either. Sure I could kick a ball or run a race and in certain company I could look quite good. Normal company. But then an O'Hanlon or a Staunton would appear and I became an also-ran.

I did normal things too. I left school too early, starting drinking too early, found myself on the dole too early and took the boat to England just in time. All of that was normal for a lad from Marian Park, or Fatima, or Cox's Demesne or Muirhevna Mor in Dundalk of the mid-eighties. Engineering plants, where I had my first real job, were collapsing and the shoe factories had gone. The breweries were still going strong but even they couldn't provide enough work for everyone. London beckoned. Once there the normality continued. Kilburn, building sites, hangovers. Irish people who were the salt of the earth and some who were... well, not the salt of the earth. I loved it and hated it. Hated the loneliness (even though there were dozens of us) and loved 'the craic'. All 'normal'.

It got cold on the sites in winter so I got a job on the railway. That was good. I met decent people. Line managers who treated workers with respect, with dignity. Even a cocky guy from Dundalk like me. And I worked with colleagues of all colours and creeds. Who cared? Certainly not me. Great men. Union men. First it was the National Union of Railwaymen (NUR) and then it was the RMT. They did normal things. When a dispute arose between management and workers they defended the workers. When a strike was called – and there were several – workers didn't pass pickets or do another's work. It was so normal I never even questioned it. A union official condoning strike breaking? I was as likely to meet a tyrannosaurus rex.

I still came home though. Time and family and the call of home. And so to Irish Rail. It was different. Regimented. I didn't mind that. There's nothing wrong with a bit of discipline. I joined the union I was told to join. SIPTU. After a year or so of cleaning toilets and checking tickets and greasing points I was selected to become a driver as long as I was prepared to move to Athlone or Dublin. I choose Athlone. And still nothing extraordinary. Nothing abnormal. Ups and downs yes, and good times and bad times but such is the stuff of life. All perfectly normal.

Then I encountered an injustice done to my colleagues and I not by our employer, but by our union. Our protector. It was as if my brain couldn't comprehend what had occurred. As if I had to dig deeper to find that it wasn't really an injustice at all. To prove my assumption, my experience, that unions didn't behave this way. So I did. Others did too. And the deeper we dug the worse it got.

It gained a momentum of its own after that. Or at least that's what it felt like. If you are in a club, or a society, or a union and you ask questions, reasonable and simple questions, but get stonewalled for four years what do you do? I leave.

So I left. And others did too. And we formed our own union. One that would do the bidding of its members. ILDA was born.

I still thought this was normal. But it wasn't. Another word. 'Consensus'. In Ireland if you want to put the words 'normal' and 'consensus' into the same sentence I suggest it should read like this:
'In Ireland it is normal not to question the consensus.'

ILDA, by doing nothing other than existing, was questioning, even challenging, the consensus.

Suddenly I was threatened with the sack, in dispute with my employer, in the High Court and then locked out of work for three months. And so was everyone else in ILDA. I was no longer 'normal'. Oh no. I was public enemy number one. I was front page news. I was on T.V. Me. The one time normal guy from Dundalk. And they (they being the consensus) were saying things about me. Often loudly but also in whispers. Here are just a few of the loud things. They said I was 'a maverick', an 'elitist', 'selfish', 'militant', 'old fashioned', 'friendless', 'hollow', 'a rebel', 'cynical', 'irresponsible'. And they said I did things too. I 'wreaked havoc', I 'circled wagons', and I was 'holding the public to ransom'. I also took a 'perverse pride in causing hardship' and we had a 'belief that the world is against them'. (I wonder where we could have gotten that from!)

So if that was what I said and what I did I must have been a pretty unsavoury guy right? Well apart from being 'a conman', 'Mr Misery' and 'Dublin's least popular man' I was actually not too bad.

We got the full 'treatment'. So far you have just had a taste of the media stuff. In work it was, still is sometimes, just as bad. If you drive trains at all hours and eat irregularly but you want to join your local gymnasium to keep fit in Westport or Dublin, Irish Rail will deduct money from your pay, add a few bob themselves, and make all the arrangements. Unless you are in ILDA. In which case you can pay your own money and make your own arrangements until you get with the consensus. If you are in ILDA and you break a set of gates on the Waterford line don't expect to see the main road again for three years, or four, or thirty for all we know. But if you are part of the consensus don't worry about it lads. Eyesight test and off you go! We won't even talk about the ILDA man who was sacked for speeding by an alleged five mph on locomotives where you can have three different speeds being displayed in any cab at the same time. In fact let's not talk anymore about Irish Rail at all. You know why? Because they only want what all employers want. Unions that do their bidding at the expense of their members. That's normal.

The abnormalities lie elsewhere.

INTRODUCTION

In 1994, a simple reaction to a happening in our workplace set in train a chain of events that was to have a massive impact on the lives of many of my friends and colleagues. These events are outlined in detail in this book.

This is no academic record, no tome of wisdom to be studied by historians or sociologists. This is my personal record of events that have shaped and filled my life for nine years — events that have seen me, a worker, a train driver, a husband and father, judged, befriended, attacked, praised, suspected, accused and portrayed by many in the national media as a figure of hate. It has been a roller-coaster ride. This is my experience — events as seen through my eyes, heard through my ears and retained in my memory. I believe that my closest friends and allies will recognise in it experiences of their own. Others, however, will view these events from a different perspective and with different feelings. Nevertheless, the events outlined here are fully accurate as regards my own involvement and as seen from my own perspective of them during this time. I hope that the book will be read in that light.

Whatever else has occurred in the past number of years, one thing is clear. I have been privileged to speak for as decent and principled a group of workers as any man could have as colleagues. Those working men faced an alliance that included three government departments, the industrial relations organs of the state, a 'commercial' semi-state company, Ireland's biggest union and, in fact, the entire Irish Congress of Trade Unions, an at-times hysterical media, and High Court and Supreme Court actions. However, a small bunch of train drivers, who always believed that they had right on their side and that their cause was just, stood together in the face of everything that could possibly have been thrown at them. As time pushes on and new changes and challenges face us all, I know that friendships have been forged among ILDA members that are unbreakable and will last a lifetime.

On 25 August 2000, ILDA members marched with dignity to the Labour Court to bring a ten-week work stoppage to an end. En route one of our members approached me. 'Are you disappointed, Brendan?' he asked. 'Do you think we should have done more for you?' It was an emotional day for us all, so I just replied briefly and moved on. But the question shook me. How could I ever be disappointed in the men who stood by us for those ten long, hard weeks — and have stood by us since — or in those who, out of sheer financial necessity, fell by the wayside before the end? All I can hope for is that they too have never been disappointed in me.

SOLD OUT

I don't think that any of the characters involved in what was to become known as the '1994 productivity' could have envisaged the events that would follow the conclusion of that collective agreement. These players included union officials from the Services Industrial Professional & Technical Union (SIPTU) and the National Bus and Rail Union (NBRU), Iarnród Éireann (Irish Rail) management of course, the Labour Court and, eventually, the Irish Congress of Trade Unions (ICTU). The people who lost out as a result of this agreement were Ireland's train drivers, and they certainly could never have imagined what would be the result of their resistance to this agreement.

The basic facts of this contentious agreement are actually extremely simple and straightforward. Nevertheless, the ghosts of railwaymen past demand that I record the details in a comprehensive manner.

Historically, enginemen had a condition of service called mileage. This condition set a maximum number of miles to be worked per day (140), after which a bonus of one hour's pay was paid overtime for every extra fifteen miles worked. Only enginemen had this condition. Signalmen, guards and other staff didn't get paid mileage. And human-resource directors certainly didn't. This condition was a time-honoured one, dating back to the days of steam when locomotives were manned not only by a driver but also by a fireman — hence my usage of the term 'enginemen'. The fireman's role was to ensure that the fires were always able to produce the requisite amount of steam to drive the locomotive. When dieselisation occurred in 1957, the fireman became a museum piece and a figure of railway folklore. Single manning, as it was called, meant that the driver became a lonely figure with sole charge of train movements.

Rail safety is something that we will have occasion to consider in greater depth later in this book. It is interesting to note here though that it was safety concerns that lay behind the introduction of mileage. The concept was introduced at a time when the rail network, unlike now, covered almost every town and village in Ireland, and the system was owned and operated by several competing companies — Great Northern Railways (GNR), Great Western Railways (GWR), Great Southern Railways (GSR) and Dublin Metropolitan Railways (DMR). In order to protect engine crews from excessively long hours of duty, the grandly titled His Majesties Railways Inspectorate (HMRI) insisted on the introduction of this condition in the knowledge that the punitive payments would lead to the rail companies imposing relatively safe work patterns, or rosters, on enginemen.

In this respect, Irish Rail management was right in 1994 to pronounce that these conditions were from the dim and distant past. They were also, as it happens, from a time when Ireland's railways were in their successful and competitive prime, and were managed and operated by people with immense understanding and interest in safe railway operations. While the type of traction used had changed from steam to diesel, and many of the world's railways had technologically advanced to the highest standards, many of Ireland's train drivers still operated trains on a signalling system and track infrastructure that were over a century old. Ireland's mainline network has now been reduced to little more than nine arterial routes from Dublin to Rosslare, Waterford, Cork, Tralee, Limerick, Galway, Mayo, Sligo and Belfast. In 1994, drivers on seven of these routes were forced to work at least some of their day on the very same system which drivers would have worked generations before — even down to the very bolts and fishplates which hold the tracks together. Worse — drivers in depots such as Sligo, Westport and Tralee would spend an entire day on these routes at speeds slower than those possible on steam engines fifty years before. It still takes roughly four hours to get from Westport to Dublin by train — a distance of a mere 165 miles — over an antiquated signalling system, much of which is fit only for a museum.

Thus the human-resource directors of 1994 were telling only half the story when they talked about the need to eliminate 'archaic work practices'. Their determination to impose modern working conditions did not take account of the fact that the very rail infrastructure itself remained 'archaic'. To the public, theirs was a convincing argument. It made sense. And nobody who knew better contradicted it.

Drivers knew that the argument was not that simple. But even if the public didn't understand, the drivers saw little need to worry in the spring of 1994. Their unions — SIPTU and the NBRU — were, after all, headed up by two former train drivers. They understood and would surely ensure that precious conditions were protected, and falsehoods ignored. It all started well. Drivers, with their unique and valuable condition, received public and written assurances from their unions that only they would vote on drivers' conditions. What could possibly go wrong?

Thus it was with confidence that working men left their engines and went to Dublin to 'negotiate' on their own behalf and that of their colleagues. The negotiations lasted a number of weeks, on and off, and produced the now-infamous 'blue book' proposal document, which proposed a number of changes, primarily the elimination of mileage which was to die when the current crop of drivers had retired. Those who wanted a lump sum could actually sell their mileage. It was pretty standard stuff and not unexpected. Everything seemed to be going to plan. A ballot was held to allow the drivers to have their say. Drivers alone voted on the condition which drivers only enjoyed and — across both unions — voted to reject the blue book by a stunning 98 per cent.

However, SIPTU and the NBRU were advised that the blue book would be implemented without agreement in May 1994. Naturally, a strike ballot was held by both unions and endorsed to a man. Notice was served and the clock began to tick. Public statements were made and debates were held. Although the debates were lively, Iarnród Éireann did not engage in any personalised attacks on the union officials involved. Drivers got themselves ready. I recall sitting, as a new driver, in Connolly shed, and being told by all the senior men that this was our chance to 'get a decent basic' — a reference to the pitifully low basic rate of pay drivers enjoyed at the time. There was to be no turning back. Placards were ready and picket duty was arranged. The clock was ticking and democracy was about to be defended. Midnight on Friday approached.

At first, nobody really knew what had happened. Certainly, I didn't. Confusion reigned and talk of a sell-out was rife. Most drivers had heard through the media that the strike was off. But why? As it transpired, the reason was quite rational. Labour Court Chairman Kevin Heffernan (of Heffo's Army renown) had become concerned that all in Iarnród Éireann were not playing as a team. He had used his good offices to intervene just before the starting whistle blew.

And so the men got off their engines and headed to Dublin for further 'negotiations'. After all, we thought, isn't that what the Labour Court is for — ensuring fair play and avoiding damaging disputes where possible? In the event, what emerged from the Labour Court — Labour Court recommendation (LCR) 14417 — achieved the impossible. It made the blue book look good. Some of the best compensations in the blue book — for example, a retiring driver's mileage passing to his replacement if already in the grade — were to be eliminated with the stroke of a pen. I'm sure we weren't the first group of workers to enter the Labour Court having rejected proposals and to emerge with even worse ones, and I know we weren't the last. Yet we were still sure that union democracy would protect us against such injustices, as it had in the past. It was in for an early test.

While mileage was the major condition of service contained in the blue book — certainly as far as drivers were concerned — there were other items too. As a result, the Labour Court took a dim view of drivers alone voting on drivers' conditions. Crucially, the Labour Court recommended a ballot of all Iarnród Éireann workers on drivers' mileage. All workers would get a weekly pay increase that was under £6 if drivers' mileage were eliminated. It was, to us, a shocking recommendation. What of the written assurances of our unions that only drivers would vote on drivers' conditions? We looked to our unions for help. Those of us in SIPTU were in for a bigger shock.

On 18 March 1994, Tony Tobin and Paul Cullen of SIPTU had sent a notice to drivers, advertising a meeting, which contained the assurance: 'The decision of any other grade or group of grades will not affect Locomotive Drivers. Drivers only will decide on drivers' issues, as is the case in other grades also.' To emphasise the point, these words were printed in bold type and even underlined. Nevertheless, one of my clearest recollections of that time is of a senior driver in Inchicore, Mick Murphy, asking Paul Cullen for an assurance that we would get our own vote. Paul's response was that the Labour Court recommendation was actually legally binding and that the union had legal advice that it was legally compelled to ballot everyone. We now know that Paul was incorrect on this point, but at the time we knew nothing. All that men like Mick Murphy knew was trust in their union. Now that union, SIPTU, simply decided to ballot all employees on our conditions, and to couple this with a recommendation for rejection.

Given the eventual ballot result, the decision to recommend rejection might have been significant. However, on the day of balloting, I received a phone call from my younger brother who had just taken up temporary platform work with Iarnród Éireann in Dundalk Station. While carrying out his station duties, he had received a ballot paper requiring him to vote on the intricacies of drivers' mileage. He was understandably confused and approached his SIPTU representative for advice. Vote yes was the advice received. 'But is there not a recommendation for rejection?' he queried.

He was told to vote yes — 'It's the only chance we've got.' He duly voted yes along with most of his workmates. My brother's SIPTU representative was not the only one who didn't heed the recommendation for rejection. Across the country, there were similar tales. I was at work when I heard about the Dundalk incident. I decided to complain to SIPTU. It was the first phone call I had ever made to Liberty Hall. I asked for Tony Tobin, our official, whom I had never met. I was put through to his office. The man who answered introduced himself as Bobby Jolly. I would get to know Bobby quite well later. I asked for Mr Tobin and was told that he wasn't available. I explained that I wanted to make a formal complaint, and Bobby listened. He told me that although the union had recommended rejection, it was up to members to make up their own minds. I countered that my brother, who had no knowledge of the issues involved, had looked for the union's position as a guide, and the position had been misrepresented. Bobby said he would note my complaint.

I also recall buying the Irish Independent on one of the mornings of the ballot. It contained an article citing all the jobs we would lose if we did not vote to accept the Labour Court recommendation. If drivers didn't lose their mileage condition, there would, according to the Independent, be thousands of job losses. The sensationalism, prominence and timing of the story were an early lesson to me on the kind of manipulative journalism with which I was to become familiar.

Given that drivers in SIPTU were outnumbered in the vote by ten to one, it is a credit to the sense of fairness innate in many SIPTU members that the vote was carried by a majority of only eighty-one votes.

Meanwhile, over at the NBRU, the Labour Court recommendation that all staff vote on drivers' conditions had been treated with the contempt it deserved. Peter Bunting, as General Secretary, had promised his drivers a separate vote and now, for the second time, they got it. The result was emphatic. The Labour Court recommendation was rejected by four to one.

Nevertheless, SIPTU had announced acceptance of the Labour Court recommendation and that the deal would now be implemented. Despite the fact that the majority of drivers across both unions clearly rejected the recommendation; despite the fact that both unions had supposedly wanted a rejection; and despite the fact that the Industrial Relations Act 1990 permitted the pooling of votes across unions following ballots in these circumstances, SIPTU had decided that the game was over.

The NBRU had, until this point, played a marvellous game for its members. It had honoured all commitments given, conducted ballots properly and behaved with propriety throughout. But it was now in a very difficult position. It had now rejected a deal that SIPTU had accepted and was moving to implement. That in itself would have placed the NBRU, as the smaller of the two unions, in an uncomfortable position. But there was so much more to it than that.

In 1993, NBRU members were engaged in a strike at Heuston Station in Dublin. This strike involved staff other than drivers. In the ensuing one-day strike, however, services were severely disrupted out of Heuston, and Iarnród Éireann was looking for compensation. This brought the railway company and the NBRU to the High Court when Iarnród Éireann issued a summons (ref. 93/2490) and argued that the NBRU had not conducted its ballot in accordance with the 1990 Industrial Relations Act. The judge agreed and, on 7 April 1993, granted an order of injunction preventing the NBRU from engaging in or promoting industrial action against the plaintiff, on foot of what became known as the 'Cummins case'. So you can see that by the time the mileage issue arose in May 1994 and the NBRU members wanted their union to go on strike, the NBRU was, whether all its members realised it or not, in a bit of a pickle.

The NBRU now found itself isolated from SIPTU on the mileage issue and facing a lone battle with Iarnród Éireann. It is not clear exactly what happened next but the NBRU somehow gave its agreement to Iarnrod Éireann to implement the package its members had rejected by a margin of four to one, without any further ballot of those members. No further ballot would have been legally permissible in any case as the 1990 Act prohibits unions from holding more than one ballot on the same proposal.

Back in SIPTU, many members were enraged by this turn of events, and the union called a general meeting in Liberty Hall to deal with the issue. One Sunday morning, I travelled to the meeting from my home in Dundalk, together with a number of senior drivers. Charlie McMasters was the SIPTU representative for drivers in Dundalk at that time. Charlie was what we would call a 'loco man' through and through. To him and the rest of us who travelled, the idea of SIPTU allowing other workers to vote on our conditions of employment was a sell-out, pure and simple. Charlie expected answers and he was not alone.

The meeting began with the SIPTU Branch Secretary for Transport, Tony Tobin, addressing the meeting. Tony outlined the process which had led to the decision to ballot all workers on drivers' mileage and made it clear that the decision had been taken by SIPTU's National Rail Council — a body of lay members from all rail grades. But several drivers present had spoken to members of the Rail Council who advised that a number of them had not been at the meeting concerned. In addition the fact remained that SIPTU had agreed to an overall ballot on the false basis that the union was required by law to agree with the Labour Court recommendation that all grades be balloted. Many drivers in attendance could not understand how the NBRU was not similarly bound by law, and quite simply wouldn't accept this explanation. Tony was supported by Jack Nash, SIPTU's national industrial secretary, and effectively Tony's boss. I myself remember Jack making an impassioned plea to the members to trust the union. However, the trust was gone.

A number of drivers then spoke to question how the ballot had been conducted. Some complained about ballot papers being left loose in depots and mess rooms (rest rooms) and about the fact that no signatures were sought for completed papers. Others complained about not receiving a ballot paper at all. Some complained about votes allegedly being taken by telephone. Rumours were rife that a bundle of ballot papers had actually been transported to a management office in Heuston Station. Others complained about the fact that the drivers' vote in SIPTU was not combined with the drivers' vote in the NBRU. And others complained about the actions of representatives, as in Dundalk, not encouraging a rejection of the Labour Court recommendation in accordance with the union's supposed policy. It was this complaint that was to lead to my only input to the meeting.

Tony Tobin commented that none of these complaints had been made before the ballot result was known. I stood up and outlined the formal complaint I had made to Bobby Jolly before the count. Tony stated that he had never received the complaint. One final memory I have of the meeting is of Charlie accusing the union of 'gerrymandering'. Jack Nash, a native of Derry took exception to this accusation. He rose and demanded that Charlie withdraw the accusation. Charlie refused and, in fact, repeated it more forcefully. Unknown to me, the battle lines were being drawn. The meeting concluded with Tony telling an amazed gathering that, from midnight that night, mileage was actually being eliminated as a condition of service for drivers. We were asked to leave the building, as the caretaker had to go home.

Some drivers stormed off in disgust, but others stood on the steps of Liberty Hall trying to take in what they had just witnessed. As Charlie was by now central to the discontent, the Dundalk delegation, which included me, found ourselves in a discussion with various other drivers from around the country. It was here that I first met two men who were to play a key role in events that were eventually to lead to the formation of ILDA – Finbar Masterson and Brian Dunphy.

Brian is a senior driver based in Portlaoise depot. A family man with nine children, he is a native of Inchicore and grew up in a railway family surrounded by the famous 'works'. Finbar is a driver based in Westport depot, and has been driving since 1967. He is married with five children. Like Brian, he is a man who takes great pride in his occupation, and is a staunch upholder of the highest standards of performance relating to all aspects of his driving duties. He is among a group of drivers referred to by John Waters in his weekly column in the *The Irish Times* — who once worked as a railway clerk in Claremorris — as 'the godlike men who drove the iron horses along the permanent way, whose skill and sense of calling rendered pathetic the scratching with biros on invoices that was my daily lot'. For both Finbar and Brian, railway working is in the blood and it is hard for those who know either man to imagine him ever doing anything other than driving trains. Both are men of great knowledge and strong conviction, with excellent employment and disciplinary records. They, and others like them, were bound to have difficulty taking in what they had just witnessed at the hands of those paid to represent them. It is ironic that it was men such as these — the most dedicated and committed railwaymen it would be possible to meet — who would become entangled in a chain of events which would see them treated as pariahs, with their family security threatened as they were led through the courts. However, in 1994, all of that was in the future. At this juncture, drivers in both SIPTU and the NBRU simply wanted a forum to follow up on their grievances relating to the loss of mileage and the manner of its demise. For such a forum, drivers were to look to the past.

Train drivers have always had to pass stringent medical examinations on entrance to the grade. In addition, drivers are required to undergo further regular check-ups as they approach their retirement years. Up to 1975, this was of considerable concern to senior drivers who, after years of shift work and very irregular eating habits, found that their blood pressure might be high or that advancing age might be taking a toll on their eyesight or noisy engines on their hearing. Such men ran the very real risk of summary removal from their job, on medical grounds, with no financial recompense available. It was an intolerable position which saw many drivers reaching a state of high anxiety as the railway's chief medical officer summoned them to a medical examination that had the potential to leave their families with no means of support. It was against this background that drivers formed a national locomotive drivers' committee as a pressure group in order to force their unions — then the Irish

Transport and General Workers' Union (ITGWU) and the National Association of Transport Employees (NATE) — to get some sort of insurance scheme with employer input for drivers who were forced out of the grade on grounds of ill-health. Initially, the unions refused to support such a claim. But the drivers decided to act alone, independently of the unions, and called for a one-day work stoppage. By 6 p.m. on the evening of the first stoppage, which had universal support within the grade, CIÉ (Córas Iompair Éireann, which in 1987 split into Iarnród Éireann, Bus Éireann and Bus Átha Cliath) had conceded to the scheme in principle. It took some time to negotiate the details but, since 1975, train drivers in Ireland have had, as a condition of service, a disability scheme funded equally by the drivers and the employer. The scheme, which is the envy of train drivers in many countries, provides drivers leaving the job through ill-health with 100 per cent of their basic pay until retirement age has been reached. Once it was successfully in place, the driver committee disbanded, having achieved its sole objective.

Now in 1994, almost twenty years later, drivers again discussed the idea of establishing such a committee in order to ensure that the interests of drivers were protected. That very day, on the steps of Liberty Hall, while the officials locked up and consigned drivers' mileage to history, drivers exchanged addresses and phone numbers and, once again, vowed to do whatever was necessary to, as one of them memorably put it, 'keep the unions honest'. The irony was that both men who now ostensibly led the drivers within SIPTU and the NBRU, Tony Tobin and Liam Tobin, had been involved with the initial drivers' committee. Now that they were union officials, however, they had other priorities.

National Locomotive Drivers' Committee (NLDC)

I didn't attend the first few meetings of the newly formed NLDC. My driver training was reaching a conclusion and I had now moved to Athlone. With my fiancée, Pauline, still living in Dundalk, most of my time off was spent travelling there by train while we planned our forthcoming wedding.

However, meetings were taking place at various locations around the country. The NLDC was now on the road and had the support of almost the entire grade. It quickly set itself two clear objectives:

- To investigate the manner in which SIPTU and the NBRU had conspired to eliminate mileage, against the wishes of the majority of train drivers, and
- To attempt to ensure that such a thing would not happen again.

Achieving these objectives was no easy task. Train driving is not like many other occupations. The number of depots and the many different shift patterns within each and every one of these depots in a group of about 300 employees makes the achievement of any successful communication or meeting pattern extremely difficult. To say that drivers were not organised in 1994 would be a massive understatement. However, drivers now realised that it was the fact that they were so disorganised as a workforce that had actually allowed recent events to occur. No matter how difficult it was going to be, drivers would have to try to work together from now on. If that meant making sacrifices, then sacrifices would have to be made.

My first meeting of the NLDC was in the East End Hotel in Portarlington towards the end of 1994. I remember some of the drivers who spoke on that occasion. Apart from Finbar Masterson and Brian Dunphy, there was big Noel Cusack, who spoke with passion about what had occurred. I also remember Tom McCarthy, a soft-spoken Dubliner of about my own age, who was Chairman of the NLDC at the time. He was joined by John Courtney, another Inchicore driver. And then there was Tom O'Brien, now a colleague of mine in Athlone. I don't remember all of what was discussed but I remember being sufficiently impressed with the determination and sense of purpose of those present to commit myself to attend more meetings.

I was now a qualified driver in Athlone and it was immediately apparent to me that drivers in Athlone were seriously deflated, disorganised and had low morale. In Athlone, the difficulties in the overall grade where exacerbated by a remarkable preponderance of freight and night work within the depot. This was a legacy that had been handed down over a number of years as daytime passenger job after daytime passenger job had been surrendered to neighbouring depots in favour of longer night shifts that attracted significant mileage payments and increased earnings. In 1994, a driver in Athlone would work late or night shifts up to thirty-five weeks of the year. P.J. Healy was the NBRU representative for drivers in Athlone. I heard stories of how P.J. had spent many years fighting a lone battle for better conditions and jobs in Athlone. However, on every significant vote, P.J. was beaten down. I was not the only new driver in Athlone in 1994. In fact, I arrived at a time when there was a significant influx of drivers into the depot. These were young men with little interest in being out driving all night, every night. They felt that the work should be shared equally between the neighbouring depots, and P.J. at last had some allies.

I had never really considered taking such an active role in trade union matters. While working on the platform in Dundalk and earlier in England, I had been more interested in the joys of being young with a few pounds in my pocket than in challenging the complacency and lack of organisation in trade union branches or sections. But as I prepared to settle down and plan for the future for the first time in my life, I found my priorities changing. The job was in a mess and I, at twenty-seven years of age, had a long road ahead of me. I decided that I would have to play my part and make an effort if I was to expect others to do the same. Initially I did no more than attend meetings and support the senior men of whom I was somewhat in awe. However, I wasn't one for attending a meeting and keeping my opinions to myself. I spoke my mind on any issue that I had an interest in, and I did so with some conviction. In no time at all, I found myself elected the SIPTU representative for drivers in Athlone, working hand in hand with Finbar Masterson, the section secretary, who was based in Westport.

I continued to attend meetings of the NLDC on a more regular basis. Some drivers who attended undertook to write to their respective unions with enquiries into the lead-up to the ballots on mileage. Finbar and others were engaged in correspondence with SIPTU while, among others, Cork driver Gerard Bluett was deputed to write to the NBRU. We would then gather at NLDC meetings and compare the responses received. SIPTU was becoming concerned at some of our enquiries. In order to counteract our activities, the union decided to hold its own short investigation into what had occurred. Early hopes that this investigation would be in any way impartial were dashed when we discovered that the man charged with conducting it was none other than Jack Nash who had played a key role in all the events leading to the elimination of mileage. Jack did produce a report for General Secretary Bill Attley. Even this version of events was forced to concede that telephone voting had occurred in at least one case, and on other issues the procedure applied was less than perfect. The investigation, however, as with many such internal investigations, was minimalist and failed to address many of the key issues at the centre of our concerns.

The NLDC was having none of it. On 11 September 1994, the committee made a number of decisions. One was to procure independent legal advice; opinions were subsequently sought from Tony Kerr BL. Another was that drivers would pay £5 each to contribute towards initial costs. Meanwhile, the decision that drivers from each depot should attend all future ballot counts demonstrated the extent to which trust between members and unions had disappeared. However, the key decision was to make a formal complaint to the ICTU about SIPTU's handling of the entire matter. It was to be a long — indeed an apparently unending — road.

Appeals, More Appeals and No Appeal

NLDC legal advice was a real eye-opener regarding the legal responsibilities of unions to their members. Basically we were quickly disabused of our naive assumption that a union was required by law to ensure that all decisions affecting members were reached in a fair and democratic manner. What we discovered was that technically — legally — officers of a union could enter into an agreement with our employer without any input from the members at all. This came as a major shock to the system. In essence, the general secretary or other official of a union had the power to sign any agreement regarding any member, without the support, authority or even knowledge of the members concerned. Of course, workers wouldn't join unions who habitually acted in such a manner, so union rules were supposedly devised in such a way as to devolve this power down to the members concerned. Supposedly. The only problem with this system was that any failure to apply the rules properly was simply that — a failure to apply rules. And this was not usually a matter for the courts. The entire matter, we were advised, was a matter for complaint within union structures.

But what union structures? The ICTU seemed an obvious place to which to bring a complaint with regard to its largest affiliate, SIPTU. But what of the NBRU? It was, and is, an independent union not affiliated to the ICTU. So when you want to complain about the NBRU, you must complain to the NBRU itself. We were becoming increasingly unimpressed by this union democracy stuff.

Nevertheless some drivers persisted in asking awkward questions within the NBRU, while the rest of us went off to ICTU for justice. And it all started so well. When Finbar Masterson wrote to ICTU Industrial Officer Peter Rigney in October 1994, he got a quick response, asking him to confirm that he had 'exhausted internal appeals mechanisms within his own union'. Finbar was indeed in communication with SIPTU on a number of matters, including a request by him for a full and detailed ballot result from the previous May. The fact that all, or even most, of the drivers had not been advised of the official ballot on LCR 14417 seemed to us to be a remarkable state of affairs. Finbar had written to Tony Tobin on 12 September 1994, stating: 'The delay in this result is causing serious concern among some members and is giving rise to speculation that there is something to hide'. Finbar wanted to see whether or not the result tallied with the number of papers issued, given how the ballot had been conducted. The NLDC was by now in possession of blank ballot papers that had been sent to us from depots after the result had been declared. In fact, we still have some. Finbar wanted to do some calculations to see if the numbers of ballot papers issued and votes cast tallied, but SIPTU was not being very helpful. On 28 October 1994, Peter Rigney wrote to Finbar, telling him that he was also in communication with SIPTU, and advising Finbar that although he was in communication with Tony Tobin and Jack Nash of SIPTU's public services region, he should bring his complaint to the then SIPTU Regional Secretary for the Midlands, Jack O'Connor, in Tullamore. This was a complete cul de sac. As Finbar was later to discover, neither he nor any other driver was in any way connected to Jack O'Connor's region. On 14 December 1994, Finbar again wrote to Peter Rigney, this time alerting him to Jack O'Connor's failure to meet him and to the fact that he had still not received the ballot result from Tony Tobin, seven months after the vote had taken place.

Finbar eventually met Jack O'Connor on 17 January 1995. The

Regional Secretary for the Midlands listened to Finbar and even sympathised and expressed surprise at the fact of other workers voting on drivers' conditions. However, he then told Finbar that he couldn't help. He was the Midlands Secretary and had nothing to do with the railway or train drivers. Finbar would have to start again. So he did. On 25 February 1995, he met his divisional council and put eleven questions to them, namely:

1. Why were drivers not allowed a separate vote?
2. Why were other staff members allowed to vote on drivers' conditions?
3. Was the Labour Court recommendation binding in respect of voting procedure?
4. What law or section of such law was involved here?
5. Did any member of the Rail Council question the format of the ballot paper?
6. Was there any complaint by any member about the ballot paper?
7. Was the NBRU allowed to vote a second time and, if so, was the Labour Court recommendation altered for it?
8. Why was there no aggregate vote with the NBRU? NBRU says it requested this but it was not acceptable to SIPTU. What law or section of law prevented this?
9. How could NBRU drivers vote separately, but not SIPTU drivers?
10. Why did SIPTU abandon its previous stance on votes of mileage?
11. Why had the result of the ballot not been furnished to members in accordance with procedure?

Although this was not an exhaustive list of all the questions arising, it does reflect that the NLDC was finally getting to grips with the variety of issues involved. No satisfactory answers were received following this meeting. We had always felt that SIPTU would not conduct a satisfactory investigation into these murky events. Now we were even more convinced that an independent investigation was required. Nevertheless, Finbar was required by ICTU to refer the matter to the next internal level, the regional executive committee. Incredibly, it would be twenty-two months before Regional Secretary Brendan Hayes would complete his 'investigation' into this matter. Following a meeting between Brendan

Hayes, Finbar Masterson, Dan Renehan, Tom O'Brien and myself, he eventually wrote to General Secretary Bill Attley on 22 November 1996. Brendan Hayes provided a summary of our meeting only. He made no judgements or pronouncements on the various witness statements produced. His report finished with an apology to the General Secretary for the delay, explaining that he had 'been extremely busy in the run up to my conference'. It was now two and a half years since the contested events of May 1994. In that time, we, as SIPTU members, had argued the same points with everybody who would listen, had been sent up cul de sacs, and had come back down again, but still no one had provided any proper answers. We were simply told that everything was above board.

The whole process was taking so long that events were moving on. Brendan Hayes was not the only man who was busy. Iarnród Éireann was busy hiring consultant Leslie Buckley to conduct a root-and-branch investigation into the company to identify savings. However, Mr Buckley was not to be permitted to investigate savings within Iarnród Éireann's top-heavy management. The 'roots' were secure. Any savings would have to come from the same groups targeted in 1994. It was now 1996 and time for another go. Mr Buckley performed his task well and produced a thirty-three-page report which identified almost £1m of savings per page — £30m in total. It later transpired that Mr Buckley's report was actually written by Iarnród Éireann management under Mr Buckley's 'expert tutelage'. With their own positions and restrictive practices secure from his prying eyes, Iarnród Éireann managers were only too happy to oblige.

While all this was ongoing, I had become more and more involved in union activity. Tommy McCarthy had stood down as Chairman of the NLDC and I had been elected to replace him. In addition, I had replaced Finbar as Secretary of the locomotive drivers' section of SIPTU in Athlone and the west. I was becoming familiar with Liberty Hall, union meetings and management. It was at one such meeting in 1995 that I was to have my first encounter with Iarnród Éireann's new human resource guru, John Keenan.

Iarnród Éireann and its recognised unions had, with the help of the Labour Relations Commission, agreed a new grievance and disciplinary procedure booklet. A series of workshops was held around the country, where John Keenan made a presentation to union representatives and management in the various locations. I attended one such workshop in the Shamrock Lodge Hotel in Athlone in 1995. John Keenan explained the manner in which the procedures were to operate. As part of his presentation, he produced figures detailing the number of days lost through industrial action in preceding years. The figures had dropped dramatically and no days had been lost the previous year. John Keenan asked those assembled for their assessment of the factors affecting this progress. The progress had, in fact, been made under the stewardship of John Keenan's predecessor, Austin Kilbride. The situation was, however, about to change. In any event, several theories were advanced. I ventured that I felt it was no coincidence that the fall in industrial action corresponded with the introduction of the 1990 Industrial Relations Act and the fact that unions felt unsure about how now to conduct action and stay on the right side of the law. My theory received support from an unlikely source. Liam Tobin, Assistant General Secretary of the NBRU, said that I was right and that his union had been fined through the 1990 Act despite the fact that its balloting procedures were entirely proper. I was too polite to ask if they'd paid the fine!

The SIPTU enquiries were finally on the desk of the General Secretary. However, by March 1997, we had heard nothing more from SIPTU. Following a call to his office from Finbar Masterson, Brendan Hayes wrote to the General Secretary on 20 March and advised him that Finbar expected 'a response within seven days and feels that he has been extremely reasonable considering the time that has elapsed since the initial complaint was made and the investigation took place.' No response was forthcoming. Finbar eventually travelled to meet the General Secretary on 3 June 1997, three years after the disputed events had taken place. By any standards, it was a remarkable timescale, of tribunal proportions. Having travelled the 170 miles from Westport to hear what the General Secretary of Ireland's largest union had to say on these three-year-old complaints, Finbar sat in reception as Bill Attley called his secretary from home to advise that he was otherwise disposed and wouldn't be coming into the office that day. Not one to give up at this stage, Finbar persisted. On 18 June 1997, he actually had an audience with the General Secretary. Mr Attley was in possession of all the correspondence from Brendan Hayes. He had the witness statements from various other members — many of whom were not drivers — alleging irregularities. However, Bill Attley, even after all this time, had no answers. He believed that none of the circumstances outlined by Finbar should be a cause for concern. The union, he affirmed, had honoured its commitments to its members in every respect. As the meeting ended, Mr Attley suggested that Finbar was the difficulty and that he would not accept any explanation. Finbar's contention that he had received no explanations after over three years of questions was simply ignored. SIPTU's internal complaints procedure had been completed. Or had it?

Prior to Finbar's initial complaint, SIPTU had put in place a members' servicing and complaints procedure. This procedure had been fully approved by the union's governing body, the National Executive Council. However, while all SIPTU officials would have been very aware of it, no train driver appears to have had any knowledge of it whatsoever. And nobody drew Finbar's attention to this formal procedure for dealing with his complaint. Is it an accident that no one saw fit to draw this member's attention to the appropriate machinery? And what would have been the outcome had this procedure been applied?

With the only internal procedure of which we were aware now exhausted, the path was at last clear for ICTU to investigate the matter. On 3 November 1997, the ICTU appeals board received another formal complaint from six SIPTU members, as required by ICTU rules, and an oral hearing was sought. The six were Finbar Masterson, Tom McCarthy, Joseph Maher, Mick Murphy, John Courtney and Tom O'Brien. Among the complaints was an allegation that SIPTU had altered Labour Court recommendation 14417 prior to the ballot in May 1994.

Throughout this period, the NLDC continued to hold regular meetings and update drivers on the lack of progress to date. The manner of the handling of this matter by the unions had not alone failed to deal with the residue of ill feeling and mistrust towards them since 1994, but had added to it significantly. In addition, as the NLDC grew in strength and influence within the grade, a number of other events had occurred which were making a bad situation worse.

The Buckley report had been eagerly seized upon by Iarnród Éireann and turned into a package of work-practice changes called the 'viability plan'. There were actually 'viability plans' for all three of the CIÉ companies — Iarnród Éireann, Bus Éireann and Bus Átha Cliath. As outlined earlier, the Iarnród Éireann plan envisaged £30m in savings. These changes were to be implemented following discussions with the recognised unions, including SIPTU and the NBRU. However, the personnel involved in the drivers' negotiating teams in those unions had changed radically, and so had the mood. Trust in the union leaderships had been virtually destroyed and, against such a background, it was always going to be difficult for officials to bring their members with them and achieve that level of change. However, management took a different view and misread the situation badly. From a management perspective, the 1994 changes had concluded without any industrial action and without any comparable attack on management or clerical grades being called for by any party. Management was entitled to consider the 1994 changes a resounding success, and it did.

Now, emboldened by that experience and confident in the ability of the unions to deliver their members, management again came a-calling with a set of work-change proposals across the board. These changes made the 1994 productivity agreement seem like a stroll in the park. However, in failing to realise that 1994 had, far from deflating drivers, led to a response within the grade that was organised and capable of responding, management made damaging mistakes that set in place a spiral of events that would eventually bring the railway to its knees and fatally damage relations with a key group of its own workers. There were, however, many warning signals that the drivers would no longer be a pushover.

The Programme for Competitiveness and Work (PCW) was the latest in a series of national wage agreements that had operated in Ireland since the mid-1980s. Like the others, this agreement paid basic fixed-percentage wage increases to workers in the public and private sectors respectively. These agreements had benefited workers in Irish Rail regarding their pay increases. The usual 'inability to pay' plea by management to union wage demands prior to these agreements was now redundant in face of the across-the-board type of increases provided for in the agreements. In order to portray the gravity of the situation outlined in the Buckley Report which we now know was written by Irish Rail management, Iarnród Éireann resurrected the old 'inability to pay' chestnut in respect of the latest PCW increase due in October 1996.

Moreover, management did so with a unanimous vote of the CIÉ board which included four worker directors who voted to withhold pay increases from the very workers who had elected them.

The NLDC had decided to attempt to have people elected to the negotiating committees of SIPTU and the NBRU, and had been moderately successful. In addition, a number of disaffected SIPTU members, including myself, had successfully raised a row about the fact that elections to the mighty National Rail Council (NRC) had not taken place for some time. SIPTU was forced into holding elections to the NRC, and new people, including myself, were elected to the council. In truth, the strategy was simple. We would work tirelessly within the unions to 'keep them honest' and responsive to their members. But if they failed, as in 1994, we would act alone through the NLDC if necessary. The NLDC would be our insurance policy.

The unions' reaction to the withholding of the PCW increase was to ballot their members for industrial action and, having achieved a strong mandate, to issue strike notice. Once again, the clock was ticking towards a deadline. A few days before the day for action, the Labour Court, this time under the chairmanship of Evelyn Owens, called the parties together, as in 1994. Predictably, the parties were called upon to suspend any action while the court considered the position. It was estimated that these considerations would take a fortnight. The unions promptly suspended the industrial action using their 'Executive Authority'. A meeting of the NLDC was called. Following the meeting, a press statement was issued. If the company did not agree to pay the PCW increase by the date of the proposed industrial action, the NLDC would call for the workers to go ahead with the dispute unofficially, but legally. I don't know whether the Labour Court made a judgment that such a call would have resounding support in all three companies. If it did, it was right! The Labour Court considerations were fast-tracked and a recommendation was issued within twenty-four hours that CIÉ should pay the money, worker-director opinions notwithstanding. Industrial action had been averted, the workers got their pay increase, and the genie was kept in the bottle — for now.

If the Labour Court and unions were aware of the new emerging landscape, management continued to dwell in Shangri La. The unions were called to a meeting in Inchicore and presented with the viability plan in all its typed and bound glory. Similar meetings took place in the other two CIÉ subsidiaries. The workers' reaction across the board was angry and determined. Realising this, SIPTU and the NBRU decided to hold a series of marches and allow the workers to let off some steam before the negotiations began. On Wednesday, 22 January 1996, workers in the three CIÉ companies were called to arms in Dublin, Cork, Limerick and Waterford. Union notices were displayed and press releases issued. Routes were planned and placards prepared. Both unions were very careful to issue notices pointing out that this was not industrial action. Workers were to attend the marches if they were available and off duty. There were to be no service disruptions.

However, on the day before the proposed marches, solicitors acting for management sent letters to the unions threatening injunctions if they did not agree to abandon the planned demonstrations. The unions immediately agreed and called off the walks. The workers were furious. I was advised of the decision when I received a phone call from Tony Tobin at 4pm the day before the march. Tony tried to explain that the union was worried about legal action. My reaction was not what Tony wanted to hear. I pointed out that the union notices were very clear that services were not to be disrupted. I also pointed out that no injunctions were given or even sought. This was a solicitor's letter, nothing more, and it had been enough to send the unions off scurrying for cover. I was disgusted. I advised Tony that I would assist in doing everything in my power to ensure that the marches went ahead with or without the unions. He was amazed but I don't know how seriously he took the threat at that stage. By 10pm that evening, however, workers in all three companies were organised, and the media, having earlier assured the public that the planned marches were cancelled, were now telling them that they were on again. It was my opinion that the marches were now likely to be bigger than would ever have been the case if solicitors had not written letters and unions had not run off for cover.

In Dublin, 5,000 CIÉ workers marched from Parnell Square to Government Buildings amid Garda escorts and a media circus; other marches took place in Cork and Waterford. It was a phenomenal show of unity and strength from workers acting alone. It was so successful that, in order to save face with its members, one union tried to claim credit for organising it behind the scenes. Very few bought that story! In Molesworth Street, a demonstration was held and letters were handed in at Government Buildings. I was asked to address the gathered workers and media. It was the first major public address I had ever made and I didn't hold back. Having attacked the viability plan, I turned on the unions and questioned their withdrawal from the march. I said that the workers had spoken and shown that they would defend themselves if the unions did not do their job. And I concluded with a call for 'Peter Bunting of the NBRU and Bill Attley of SIPTU to come down from their ivory towers and do the job we pay them to do'. As luck would have it, a news programme was going out live at the time of my speech and carried some of it across the airwaves. It would be headline news in the following day's newspapers. But I wouldn't have to wait until then to get some very different reactions.

Some workers in Dublin Bus had formed an ad hoc pressure group called the Busworkers' Action Group. This group had played a significant role in organising bus workers for the march. After the march, bus workers decided to follow it up with a meeting to discuss how to build on the success of the demonstration. The meeting was in Conway's pub in Parnell Street and I was invited. A few of the lads from Athlone decided that we would go to the pub for lunch anyway. On the way, we were walking up O'Connell Street when we bumped into Tony Tobin. Tony asked us how the march had gone and we told him that it had been a great success. Somebody made a comment that it was a disgrace that the union had withdrawn its support. Tony responded to the effect that this was a very difficult day for him and that he regretted the turn events had taken. A few minutes later, we were in for another assessment of the march. While we sat in Conway's eating our lunch, a figure in a trench coat stood above me. I raised my eyes to see Peter Bunting looking down on me. 'Are you Brendan Ogle?' he asked. When I replied that I was, he said that I was never to attack him publicly again and that he took exception to being compared to Bill Attley. I asked was he finished and he said he was. I said I could not give him the commitment he was seeking and I suggested that he leave and allow me to finish my lunch. He left. In the five years that would pass before I would next meet him, many statements would be made, Peter's own employment position would change radically and we would actually be on the same side, if only temporarily.

I don't know what SIPTU and the NBRU expected to occur when they withdrew support for the proposed march. I suspect that they didn't expect 5,000 of their own members to go ahead with it anyway. In any event, transport workers had demonstrated that they were now capable of independent action if they needed it. But still, management and the unions did not learn anything. No efforts were made to address the dissatisfaction that members felt towards their unions following these events. In that situation, other alternatives and opportunities would be sought.

The Associated Society of Locomotive Engineers and Firemen (ASLEF) had always been a shadow hanging over train drivers' disenchantment with their present unions. This British-based union represents 98 per cent of the United Kingdom's 17,000 train drivers. Until 1969, Ireland's train drivers had been part of that membership. The late Ray Buckton, was ASLEF's last Irish Officer. ASLEF had property and officers based in Ireland, and most drivers seemed very happy with the service they provided. Finbar Masterson was an ASLEF member prior to 1969. He remembers the pride that ASLEF members had in their union. At many meetings, that pride seemed very much at odds with the sense of betrayal we now felt. It was therefore inevitable that someone would eventually formally propose contact with ASLEF. At a meeting in Dublin's Aisling Hotel, in the spring of 1997, Connolly driver Paddy Donnelly proposed that we institute contact with ASLEF. The proposal was passed, and Finbar wrote to London, to the then ASLEF General Secretary, Lew Adams. Letters were followed by an invitation and, in May 1997, the General Secretary of ASLEF addressed a meeting of the NLDC in Dublin. Lew Adams, in common with all ASLEF general secretaries, had been a train driver before being elected to the top job in the union. And as he spoke, it was very apparent that he was a driver. For a start, nobody needed to explain mileage to him. He spoke simply but well and was received like one of our own. Finbar spent a lot of time in Lew's company that weekend, and they became close friends. It was therefore no surprise when Lew invited the NLDC to send a delegation to meet the ASLEF National Executive at its Hampstead headquarters, and even less of a surprise when the invitation was accepted.

The ASLEF National Executive is the governing body of the trade union and it is made up, in its entirety, of lay members (that is, train drivers). It meets in session for one full week per month in London. Train drivers from each of the ASLEF regions leave their drivers' kit bags down and don their suits and ties for the week-long stay in London. There they meet during office hours in the ornate boardroom and decide upon all matters affecting the members of the union. The General Secretary, as the servant of the members, is then charged with carrying out the decisions of the executive and is held accountable to the executive at all times. As a guest, I have personally attended meetings of the executive where the sitting official was called to task for a perceived failure to carry out a particular duty in a satisfactory manner. ASLEF is truly a union that is organised from the bottom up, as opposed to from the top down.

In June 1997, eleven drivers travelled to London on behalf of the NLDC. In addition to my own depot and Finbar's, other depots represented were Connolly, Dundalk, Inchicore, Fairview, Cork, Limerick, Sligo and Waterford. When we got to the Arkwright Road headquarters, we were welcomed by Lew Adams and given a tour of the building. We were introduced to the office staff and photographed for the cover of the ASLEF journal — a photograph that was to cause much consternation in Liberty Hall. We were then admitted to the boardroom and introduced to the executive. I had been selected to speak on behalf of the group and I did so before we left for the formal meeting with the General Secretary.

Lew Adams began the meeting by outlining that ASLEF now viewed its withdrawal from Ireland as a mistake. He outlined the reasons for that withdrawal and how many of them were related to the developing political situation in Ireland in 1969 and the difficult situation ASLEF, as a British union, was experiencing on a day-to-day basis. Both sides felt that it would be mutually beneficial to explore the possibility of ASLEF's re-establishing its Irish operation. It was immediately apparent that the requirement that trade unions operating in Ireland be licensed would pose a difficulty. In operating such a policy, Ireland has one of the most regulated trade union environments in Europe, and all parties were aware of this. Nevertheless, it was felt that it was worth exploring in detail how these regulations operated and what, if any, opportunity existed for ASLEF to re-establish its Irish base. It was at this meeting that we were to be introduced to a name that we would become very familiar with during all the events that would follow. Daniel Spring & Company Solicitors had been retained in Dublin to provide ASLEF with any advice it would require on Irish affairs. When Lew Adams advised us of this, Thomas McDonnell immediately passed me a note outlining that this was the Dublin solicitors firm established and run by Donal Spring, brother of Dick, who was Tánaiste in the Labour/Fianna Fáil government of that time.

In due course, various elements of the media would expend much energy in speculating on the nature of my relations with Donal Spring, and subsequently Fergus Finlay and John Rogers. Whatever the feelings of these men on that speculation, I was always entertained and amused by it. As my own profile and that of ILDA increased over time, there seemed to be a suggestion by some in the media that we were a pawn being used by some kind of Rogers/Finlay/Spring triumvirate, in an effort to either embarrass or undermine the Labour Party or for some other unspecified reason. The reality is that all three are very committed members of the Labour Party, and any future contact with Fergus Finlay or former Attorney General John Rogers was brought about by our professional relationship with Daniel Spring & Company Solicitors, who were, in turn, retained by ASLEF in London, without any input from us and before ILDA was even formed.

It may be as well here to clarify my own political views, such as they are. I was born and reared in Dundalk and am therefore of a broadly nationalist background. Until very recently (2003) I had never been a member of a political party, however, and neither, to my knowledge, have any of my immediate family. I have always believed that the wealth of society should be evenly spread as far as possible and that the socially excluded should benefit from active policies of inclusion with broad-based support. As I have become involved more and more in workers' issues and the labour movement, I have honestly felt that we have been let down by all political parties, most of whom appear only to want power for power's sake and to enrich themselves and their associates in Ireland of the Tribunals. Another reason I had never done so, however, is simply that no party in Ireland reflected by its actions — as opposed to its rhetoric — my views on a wide enough range of issues for me to feel comfortable as a member. The issues that concern me most are issues relating to the empowerment of workers and the working class. None of our major parties have actively pursued any strategic policies in this regard, in my time. In many ways, my perception that the Labour Party has been failing to do so is particularly disappointing but is explained by the closeness of that party with the mainstream and extremely compliant trade union movement. I have already referred to the level of regulation accepted by trade unions in Ireland. It is such that we have more restrictions placed on the operation of unions here than apply in Britain despite almost twenty years of Thatcherism. All of the restrictions and legislation that are in place to restrict trade union activity are there despite the presence in those governments of the Labour Party as a coalition partner that was partly funded by the trade union movement. I believe that the entire labour movement has many questions to answer in this regard and that, for example, the failure of the movement to secure meaningful legislation dealing with trade union recognition, as is now in place in Britain, is an indictment of a movement which has lost its focus and which is, as I say, more interested in power for power's sake than in actually delivering for its natural constituency.

In recent months, I finally joined the Labour Party when Pat Rabbitte became its leader. The reason for this change was twofold. Firstly, I agree with Pat Rabbitte that this country needs a new political dispensation and a break with the old Fianna Fáil/Fine Gael politics of the civil war. Who cares any more? I certainly don't. However, I do care about corruption in our society; I care about the fact that well over 40 per cent of our electorate feel so disenfranchised from society that they won't vote and that, increasingly, our young people view all our political discourse and our politicians as a waste of time and space. That's what happens when you engage in decades of corruption at the very top and do noting but obstruct tribunals and try to spin your way out of it. People aren't stupid. They will either rebel or just switch off. The night Pat Rabbitte was elected Labour Party leader, he sat on the *Late Late Show* and repeated his pledge not to enter into coalition with Fianna Fáil after the next election. I decided to join at that moment. I don't know if Labour can make the difference although so far the signs are quite good. But I do know somebody needs to make a difference.

In 1997, my constituency was train drivers, and if Donal Spring could assist in advancing the cause of my colleagues, I was very happy indeed to accept his assistance and that of ASLEF. However, it wasn't long after our visit to London that it became clear that no easy answers were available to us in relation to licensing ASLEF for a new Irish base. Nevertheless, the reaction to our London trip was immediate and instructive. SIPTU certainly was more than a little bit put out by it. This manifested itself in several ways. In the first instance, we became aware through ASLEF that the British Trades Union Congress (TUC) had received a formal complaint from its Irish counterpart, ICTU, on foot of a SIPTU complaint. I was struck by how quickly the wheels in ICTU had now turned, compared with the organisation's consistent failure to convene a meeting of its appeals board to consider our complaints against SIPTU and, conceivably, resolve the overall difficulty. It was clear that ICTU and SIPTU were more focused on obstructing any attempt by us to join another union than in resolving our difficulties in the current one. It was to be a central theme of our treatment by both of those institutions through several years. In any event, ASLEF was now being asked to explain its actions to the TUC, and was in the process of doing so. However, SIPTU's reaction was not restricted to complaints in Britain.

At this stage, I was the representative of drivers in Athlone, in addition to being an elected member of the National Rail Council. Finbar was also a SIPTU representative. Demonstrating that SIPTU was much more effective in processing complaints against members than in dealing with member complaints against the union, the union levelled charges that we had effectively brought it into disrepute by having the temerity to talk to ASLEF about our difficulties. We were summoned to appear before our Branch Committee. Finbar dealt with the matter through correspondence, but I thought that it would be interesting actually to meet my accusers and see what their problem was, and what evidence they had to support their charges against me. The Branch Committee was chaired by Tony O'Brien, a Limerick-based train driver who had successfully applied to become a supervisor with Iarnród Éireann. His duties to management were added to considerably by his place on the CIÉ board as a worker director. Tony had, in fact, been one of the worker directors who had voted to withhold the pay increase due under the PCW to CIÉ workers — the action which had led to the threatened disruption followed by the hastily issued Labour Court recommendation that the money should be paid forthwith.

The hearing took place in Liberty Hall and Tony produced the ASLEF journal referred to earlier. There on the cover was a picture of the eleven-man NLDC delegation to London, under the headline: 'Irish Eyes of ASLEF'. This was, according to the Branch Committee, clear evidence of my bringing the union into disrepute. I countered that it was simply evidence that we had visited a fraternal organisation in London to discuss matters of mutual concern and interest and that, at least at this point, that was as far as it went. The meeting lasted only a half an hour or so, and I remember Tony, at the point of exasperation, exclaiming: 'It's very difficult to pin you down.' There was, of course, no evidence that I, or anybody else, had done anything other than challenge the manner in which the union had treated its own members, and look for a remedy for that treatment. I had done so publicly and fully in the open, and I took the view that SIPTU itself, by its treatment of us, had done more to bring the union into disrepute than one hundred visits to ASLEF could ever do. Any mention by me of 1994 was met with sighs and statements that that was all in the past. Although the charges against me were not upheld, I left the meeting with dire warnings ringing in my ears. My future behaviour would be 'closely monitored'.

IRRETRIEVABLE BREAKDOWN

Incredibly, three years after the 1994 debacle, ICTU had still failed to convene a hearing of the Appeals Board to consider member complaints against its largest affiliate. In fact, the Appeals Board would, conveniently, never consider the complaints put to it. I, to my surprise, had become very much a part of the SIPTU machine at grass-roots level and was to have some very interesting experiences as a SIPTU shop steward and member of the National Rail Council. Much of my activity would be in the context of Iarnród Éireann's determination to implement Leslie Buckley's viability plan. For drivers, the next year or so was to be a period of learning, of trying to secure change within SIPTU and the NBRU and to make them responsive to the wishes of drivers; ultimately it was a time for acceptance that change from within was impossible, and that another way was required. That acceptance, and the decisions and events that followed, were truly unforeseen and momentous. But first there was SIPTU work to be done.

Conditions

The resistance of drivers to new productivity talks was not based on any wish on our part to hold on to our existing terms and conditions of service. Rather, it was simply based on a fear that any discussions carried out by unions that had not been reformed following 1994, were doomed to end in disaster. Drivers had a very realistic view of our terms and conditions of service — not surprisingly as we were the ones who actually worked them. Locomotive drivers supposedly worked a thirty-nine-hour week like most of the rest of the PAYE sector. The reality was very different. In all mainline depots except Sligo, drivers worked thirty-nine hours spread over a basic six-day week, Monday to Saturday. This worked out as a basic six-and-a-half-hour day. However, that was only the start of it. Six-and-a-half-hour days aren't very practicable when you take into account running a railway with crossing points of trains (i.e. where feight trains 'cross' with passenger trains), delays and other factors, so drivers generally worked up to nine hours a day. And so, a driver's week was in fact a fifty-four-hour week, or it would have been if there had been no Sunday trains. There was a time when there were no Sunday trains. But times have changed. Sunday has increasingly become part of the working week, with students returning to college after a weekend of clothes washing and home cooking; with workers making their way to their Dublin and Cork flats; and with a full calendar of sporting and social events to be catered for. Everything from Knock Specials to the GAA championships, from the Curragh races to steam-train excursions happens on Sundays and at weekends. And the people who had to drive the trains were those who had already driven them for fifty-four hours that week.

No family man leaving a wife and kids at home seven days a week needs to be lectured about their conditions by someone who has never seen a night or a dawn shift in their life. We knew all about watching dawn break while we drove trains trying to keep the sleep out of our eyes. We knew all about long, foggy nights through the Mayo bogs and hills, with nothing for company but a draught and a faulty cab-heater — oh yes, and the poor auld guard shivering in his top coat trying to keep the two of us warm with tea. And we knew about other things too. Now, with many of the freight trains single-manned, we know the terror of hearing a bang on the front of your engine and not knowing what you have just hit. It could be a stupid pheasant (never a clever jackdaw), or maybe a rabbit, or a cat or dog. Or it could be a person. Some poor demented soul who has had enough and thinks the best way out is to stand in front of a 700-tonne train and forget about it. Whatever it is, the routine is always the same — a call to the signalman to tell him you have hit something so that he can stop the trains from the opposite direction, making it safe for you to examine your train. And then off you go. Gloves on, hand lamp shimmering through the darkness, you descend from the engine and steel yourself as you confront the front of your train. Many drivers have seen sights on that locomotive front or under their train that will haunt them to the grave. And since 1994, when they paid us a 20.5 per cent bonus to get rid of the guard, drivers would be all alone in the black of night, hoping that they wouldn't go mad before some emergency services arrived. I always said that they could keep their money and give me back the guard for occasions like that. They call it 'One Under' on London Underground but in Ireland we just call it suicide. Usually. Because they aren't all suicides. Some are horrific, tragic and often simple accidents — a man out walking his dog, kids playing chicken, the crossing keeper closing the gates and cutting it too fine. All have paid with their lives on Ireland's railways in recent times. And there are even worse events than those — for example, a woman in the car with the radio playing while the child opens the gate and then watches helplessly as Mammy drives under a train going at 70 miles per hour.

They tell you it's just a part of the job, and really they are right. But it isn't an easy part. I wasn't driving very long when my train was involved in a fatality in Co. Offaly. It wasn't a suicide but a tragic freak of an accident. In truth, the other members of the train crew had a greater involvement in that particular accident than I had. But it was horrendous. The word from the hospital that the victim had died was followed by sleepless nights and soul-searching. Could I have done anything differently? Braked a bit quicker perhaps? Departed the station slower? Anything? And then several months later, the inquest and the evidence. You're not Brendan Ogle of Irish Rail then — oh no! — just plain Brendan Ogle. They have long since found a rule, a regulation or a bylaw, and the train crew give evidence as citizens. You know then who's responsible for rail safety, and no amount of newspaper propaganda or ill-informed guff from suits or know-all journalists will ever change it. In my case, all of our train crew were interviewed by the Garda Síochána and cautioned. I was actually told that charges were likely to follow against me, and was forced to seek advice. As it turned out, I had done nothing wrong. I just got a garda who, not understanding the intricacies of railway working, treated the accident like a road-traffic accident, and assumed that the driver must be at fault. I was sent off to the station alone to make my statement. No legal advice was offered by Iarnród Éireann. There is no corporate responsibility for train accidents. So be it. I made my statement to the gardaí and I said everything I needed to say. And then the powers that be in Irish Rail wanted me to give them a copy in case I might have said something that might affect them. Well, they didn't get it!

I learned the hard way about the loneliness a driver feels in that situation. The only support of any value offered comes from other drivers and staff members who have been through similar experiences themselves. And then Iarnród Éireann sends you off for 'counselling', if you feel you need a few days off. Any refusal to go and you don't get paid. So some go and some who don't want to go just go back to work and hope to forget about it. And some of the ones who go never come back to work and, if they do, they wish that they hadn't. On my many trips south, there hasn't been one time that I didn't think of that woman and pray for her as I drove through the town where she lived. And all of my colleagues — be they drivers, guards or checkers — would be the same. It's part of the job.

Shift work is also part of the job. Except, in Irish Rail, it isn't deemed shift work — shift work attracts premium payments for work performed at various times, such as evenings and at night. Shift workers on night work are generally paid a higher rate than when they are on day work. In Iarnród Éireann, workers on night work get paid the exact rate of pay applicable to workers on day shifts. In addition, shift workers tend to have holiday entitlements and rest periods that reflect the shift work they perform. This is not the case in Irish Rail. However, because of the 'unsocial hours' inherent in railway working, workers did generally get a premium of one-sixth of their basic pay, as an 'unsocial hours payment'.

First Daggers Drawn

In Athlone, as mentioned earlier, there is an incredible preponderance of night work. It was this issue which was to lead, in 1996, to my first serious involvement in a potential industrial dispute. At the time, I was the representative of SIPTU drivers in Athlone, while P.J. Healy remained the NBRU representative. By that time, Athlone was sufficiently possessed of young drivers determined that the days of conceding all new work or attractive rosters to other neighbouring depots were over. However, the practice of ignoring Athlone drivers whenever new work was available in the West of Ireland had developed over quite a number of years and was now ingrained to such an extent that Athlone didn't even merit consideration. Athlone drivers were determined that that would have to change, and the timetable change of that year presented them with a very pertinent issue with which to begin that change.

Athlone drivers worked an 'early bird' passenger train to Dublin on weekday mornings. Although the train left Athlone around 6.30am, the driver was on duty at 5.30, to start up the engine and prepare it for services by carrying out his checks and tests. The train returned to Athlone in the form of the 16.50 passenger train from Heuston on weekday evenings. The train then stabled in Athlone overnight. In 1996, Iarnród Éireann decided, rightly, that this would have to change. There was demand for an early-morning train from Galway, with a returning train that evening. So the 6.30am train would henceforth leave Galway at about 5.30am, and the 16.50 passenger train in the evening would continue to Galway and stable there overnight to form the 'early bird'.

Drivers in the depots affected — Athlone and Galway — were aware for some months that these changes were proposed. In Athlone, we discussed it at a drivers' meeting well in advance of the change. It was decided that we would look to work the 16.50 extension from Athlone to Galway. As the changes approached, drivers awaited the proposed rosters. In Athlone, we began informing our foreman and inspectors that we expected this new work to come to Athlone. However, Athlone drivers had been passive for so long that it should have come as no surprise when the proposed rosters were produced and the work had gone, as usual, to Galway. This time, however, Athlone drivers were ready and preparing to challenge the decision.

I decided that I needed to educate myself in the intricacies of the 1990 Industrial Relations Act. Since I had been a SIPTU representative, I had often heard workers' demands for some action or other brushed aside by the union on the basis that the union had to be careful about 'the Act'. To me this legislation seemed to take on the character of a chain that had been permanently tied to our union's arms and legs to prevent it from fighting for members' interests. However, now the interests of my members in Athlone were to the fore, and I wasn't about to trust the interpretation of those I believed had screwed up in 1994. So I went off, bought the Act, and found it very enlightening indeed.

My view of the 1990 Act is that it is a Thatcherite piece of industrial relations legislation of which the iron lady herself would have been very proud. However, it didn't appear to me to be the straitjacket that was presented to workers, by their own unions. It was obvious from it that anything workers might do in relation to industrial action was fraught with danger. However, I was satisfied that, within the Act, the basic civil and human rights to which all workers are entitled in relation to the withdrawal of labour were, of necessity, protected as long as the workers concerned did everything strictly by the book.

P.J. and I discussed our strategy. We took the view that the claims of the Athlone drivers would be taken seriously only if we acted as if we meant business — and that meant balloting for action in the event that we were unsuccessful in procuring some new work. A couple of weeks before the proposed changes were implemented and the work was to go to Galway, we called a meeting of all Athlone drivers. Ten of the twelve attended. I remember it was on a June bank-holiday Monday evening. The mess room in Athlone was full, but the train to form the 'early bird' was stabled in Athlone so, suitably enough, we held our meeting in a carriage of the empty train. The mood was determined. We outlined that the District Manager in Athlone at the time, John Mullin, had agreed to meet us the following morning to discuss our dissatisfaction with the fact that the work was going to Galway and to explain why that decision had been taken. We balloted for action in advance of the meeting. Unlike 1994, all drivers who would be affected by any dispute were offered a secret ballot on the proposed action and were required to sign to confirm that they had received an opportunity to vote in a secret ballot. We returned to the mess room to count the ballots and actually got the foreman on duty to witness the short count and verify that the count was accurate. The result was nine to one in favour of industrial action should the rosters be implemented as proposed, with two drivers deciding not to vote. This was the first ballot either P.J. or I had conducted. We hadn't asked for permission from our unions as we knew that such a request, in the circumstances at that time, would be pointless. More importantly, we knew that we didn't need their permission and that we had done everything in accordance with the 1990 Act. We were now ready to meet Mr Mullin.

The meeting was difficult. According to John Mullin, the decision to send the work to Galway was purely a financial one. It was, he said, simply cheaper to work the job from Galway than from Athlone. However, the 1990 Act wasn't the only thing P.J. and I had researched. While I'd been swatting on the delights of Bertie's Thatcherite legislation (Bertie Ahern was the Minister for Labour who introduced the 1990 Act and later went on to be Taoiseach), P.J had been playing with rosters, proposed rosters, possible rosters and calculators. Our calculation was that Irish Rail would save almost ten man hours per week by working the job from Athlone as we proposed. As P.J. would say, we 'held our whisht' while Mr Mullin outlined his figures. We then told him that he was wrong, forcibly, but we didn't produce our own analysis yet. Instead we stated that we were dissatisfied, and the meeting broke up. We went downstairs to discuss the situation. Five minutes later, we were back. P.J. handed the District Manager a white envelope.

'What's this?' was the predictable question.

'You'd better read it,' P.J. replied. We continued to stand while John Mullin read the seven days' notice of industrial action. He enquired whether our unions knew about this and we replied that they didn't but that we were sure it wouldn't take him long to advise them. He told us that we couldn't do this and we replied that we could and we had and we walked out of the room. P.J. was almost euphoric. Nothing had been achieved but Athlone drivers had drawn a line in the sand — a battle line. We awaited the response.

We didn't have long to wait. As we sat in the mess room, discussing the morning's events, the parcel porter entered to advise me that Tony Tobin was on the phone in the parcels office and wanted to speak to me. I lifted the phone, knowing what to expect. Tony asked whether it was true that we had just presented John Mullin with strike notice. I said that it was. Tony stated that the 1990 Act required union sanction for such action and that we were required to ballot. As the union had not provided ballot papers, we were acting illegally. He told me to go upstairs and withdraw the notice immediately. I replied that we did not require union sanction and that we had conducted a secret, and proper, ballot. I then told Tony that if he repeated his accusation that I had acted illegally, he would be dealing with my solicitor and not with me at all. I could tell that he was taken aback. Not alone were drivers defending themselves but Athlone drivers of all people! He acknowledged that what we had done wasn't illegal but said that it was a breach of union rules. I laughed to myself as I was reminded of Tony Kerr BL and his opinion in 1994. Matters such as SIPTU's behaviour in 1994 were not matters for the courts but were simply, at best, breaches of union rules. The circle had turned.

In fairness to Tony, he tried to resolve the problem from that moment on, and he played a part in the final resolution that prevented a dispute. He called me again later that evening and said that he had fixed up another meeting with John Mullin. When we attended, we found that the District Manager was accompanied by Willie O'Connor, a more senior Dublin-based manager. We produced our analysis of the hours involved and boldly stated that it was cheaper for the company to run the train from Athlone than from Galway. Mr O'Connor disagreed and asked John Mullin to explain his figures to us again. He did. We were unimpressed. We asked bluntly whether John Mullin had left anything out. It transpired that in order for the train to work from Galway, a driver not connected directly with this working would have to be kept on duty in Galway for two hours a night longer than would otherwise be the case to prepare the 'early bird' for traffic in the morning. Irish Rail's figures had failed to take this factor into account. When it was included, it proved to be much cheaper to work the train from Athlone. John Mullin admitted that he had mistakenly omitted these hours and Willie O'Connor asked for an adjournment. P.J. and I waited downstairs for about ten minutes before being called back into the meeting. Willie O'Connor acknowledged that the company's calculations were incorrect and that it was cheaper to work the train from Athlone after all. He then told us that while we had been outside, he had called the District Manager in Galway, and asked him to contact the drivers' representative there to 'seek permission' to allow the work to be transferred to Athlone. We argued that, as the work had never actually begun, there was no need to transfer anything. All that was required was to withdraw the proposed rosters and issue new ones with the work allocated to Athlone on financial grounds. In any event, predictably, the Galway drivers insisted that the proposed rosters must be implemented in full and the work allocated to

Galway. Willie O'Connor then explained that he felt that any failure by the company to comply with the wishes of the Galway drivers would lead to a dispute in Galway. This was felt by him to be something to be avoided at all costs, as isolated disputes involving Galway drivers some years previously had made management wary of the men from the west (or had gained the Galway drivers the recognition and deference they sought, depending on your viewpoint). We couldn't believe our ears. The meeting ended inconclusively.

That evening, a number of calls took place between Tony Tobin and myself, and P.J. and Liam Tobin, the relevant NBRU official. The problem was now a serious one. If it wasn't resolved in five days, the new timetable could not be implemented. We were in a strong position. The company had been shown, and had accepted, that the initial award of the work to Galway had not been right. The company needed the new timetable to be implemented in less than a week and we had a strike ballot in place, notice issued and a very buoyant group of drivers behind us. A meeting in Dublin with the manager of Inter-City, Joe Walsh, would be necessary. Joe — now retired — is a man who didn't like negotiating while looking down the barrel of a gun. He wasn't prepared to meet until we withdrew the strike notice. Both the Tobins engaged in a bout of persuasion to get us to withdraw the strike notice. We didn't need to think about it for too long. We agreed to withdraw the strike notice on the basis that, if the discussions with Joe Walsh didn't succeed, we still had our ballot in place, and another strike notice could be issued in minutes. And so we were off to Heuston Station for some talking!

P.J. is a very wily character indeed. A railwayman of great experience, he worked on the African continent for some years while railroads where being laid during a period of investment, and he has some terrific insights into mind-sets. To those who don't know him, he usually portrays a serious and dour persona, but privately he is a man with a mischievous sense of humour. At the time, that sense of humour would often appear during adjournments in meetings or after high-pressure telephone calls from union officials. It would be hard to bluff P.J. or to put him under pressure and, on this issue, we were never under any real pressure. The meeting in Heuston Station was a hoot.

The first business of the day, predictably, was a meeting with Tony and Liam in Heuston, where they tried, over breakfast, to persuade us just to drop our claim. That meeting didn't last long. So then it was down to business. I remember Joe Walsh and John Mullin sitting side by side, and Joe Walsh beginning the meeting by making a statement about how much faith he had in John Mullin's ability to deal with these matters. It struck me that no one had questioned this, and I felt that the fact that Joe Walsh felt the need to make such a statement spoke volumes. I couldn't help drawing parallels with the inevitable downfall of most football managers shortly after a club chairman feels the need to give them a vote of public support. When we actually got down to business, Joe also acknowledged that the figures didn't add up. He had a proposal to make.

Tommy McGuinness was the oldest driver in Athlone and was due to retire in approximately six weeks' time. As with almost every other driver in Iarnród Éireann, voluntary severance prior to retirement, or 'the early' as it was called, was not a realistic possibility. They just didn't let drivers go early, preferring, health permitting, to get the very last mile out of them right up to their sixty-fifth birthday. But Tommy would be given 'the early' if the Athlone drivers agreed to drop their claim. It was a remarkable offer and well thought out. Everyone liked Tommy. He is a pure gentleman, with not a bad word to say about anybody. In addition, many drivers felt that they owed Tommy. Athlone is a relief depot for the entire West of Ireland. This means that Athlone drivers can be sent to Sligo, Galway, Westport, Ballina or, in bygone days, Tuam, to cover for staff shortages in those depots. While this now happened infrequently, in the past it had been a very regular requirement. Tommy was a single man with a love for the horses and a few pints. He lived alone and he was happy to do the relief for his colleagues who might have been married with a houseful of children and for whom a week or a fortnight away from home was a matter of great inconvenience. By offering Athlone drivers the opportunity to get Tommy out a few weeks early with a not inconsiderable lump sum that he wouldn't get if he went to his full term, Joe Walsh knew what he was doing. However, what would transpire spoke as much about the type of man Tommy McGuinness is as it did about the new resolve among Athlone drivers.

Irish Rail wanted an instant decision from us. Joe Walsh and John Mullin wanted P.J. and me to agree to their proposal there and then. That simply was never going to happen. I explained that we were representing drivers in Athlone but that they would have to vote on any proposal. When Joe tried to push a bit more, we said that we weren't there to be pressured and stood up to leave the meeting. Joe asked us to sit back down, and stated that, if we must, we could ask the Athlone drivers, but he wanted a decision by that evening. We would have to leave the meeting straight away, travel to Athlone and convene an immediate meeting of the drivers. We had no difficulty with that but we assumed that the foreman in Athlone, who wasn't concerned with the ins and outs of this issue but simply with drivers working their trains, would have. Phone calls were made by management in Heuston to the foreman, George Behan, in Athlone. The importance of the matter was explained to him and, somehow, by hook or by crook, he managed to get all drivers off to attend a meeting in the Prince of Wales Hotel in Athlone at 5pm. We were ready to go but Joe wasn't finished. He wanted us to give a commitment that we, as their representatives, would recommend acceptance of this proposal to the Athlone drivers. We wouldn't agree to do so. We stated that we couldn't attempt to pressure drivers on such a matter. Instead, we willingly agreed to make no recommendation to the drivers. They would decide to accept or reject the proposal themselves.

When we gathered for the meeting, I explained the morning's events to the drivers, all of whom were in attendance. I outlined the proposal about Tommy's early retirement and the five-figure sum involved. At that point, Tommy stood up. He explained that he was leaving the meeting and that he felt that the drivers should make the decision that they believed was best for the Athlone depot and not for him. As he didn't want to influence the decision in any way, he would not even use his vote. Tommy left. One or two drivers expressed anger that they were in such a position. I explained that this was a decision for the drivers themselves and that neither P.J. nor I would recommend what they should do. We produced twelve ballot papers and set Tommy's unused paper aside on the table. The drivers each had a secret ballot and signed to confirm this. When the papers were counted, the company's proposal was rejected by nine votes to two.

I believe that the proposal was rejected because it had absolutely no relevance to the matter in dispute, which was the working of a train from

Athlone to Galway. The result caused exasperation among union officials and management alike. I went back over to the station with Tom O'Brien to lock up the makeshift ballot box. Just as we were leaving, we bumped into one of the drivers in the station porch. He said that he was one of the drivers who had voted to accept the proposal and that he was disgusted with his fellow Athlone drivers. He felt that Tommy had been betrayed by the men with whom he had worked all his life. I told him that I had spoken to Tommy and that he had accepted the decision fully, and I also told him that, now that Tommy's retirement had been raised, I felt that the Athlone drivers should not accept any settlement that did not see Tommy properly looked after. He wasn't convinced.

The first reaction I got from management, through Tony Tobin, was one of amazement that we could 'betray' Tommy in such a manner. Events would now be allowed to take their course. I told Tony that that was fine and that P.J. and I would re-issue strike notice in the morning. But by that evening, Tony had called me back. He outlined that Joe Walsh was so shocked by our decision that he was coming to Athlone to meet P.J. and myself, and to seek an explanation. He would meet us at 2pm the following day in the Prince of Wales Hotel. P.J. and I immediately endeavoured to speak to all the drivers by phone. We succeeded in getting a mandate to agree to any proposal that got us a share of any new work and saw Tommy get out on early retirement with his lump sum. When the meeting convened the following day, we were joined by the two union officials and John Mullin. Joe Walsh outlined his shock at the previous evening's decision and proceeded to give us a bit of a lecture about how nice a chap Tommy McGuinness was. P.J. saw red and gave Joe a bit of a lecture about why, if Tommy was held in such high regard by the company, Iarnród Éireann was prepared to recognise this only if we let it off the hook on which it had impaled itself.

Daggers drawn, the meeting settled down. Joe asked us what the problem really was. We outlined that the days of Athlone drivers being treated like second-class citizens were over. From now on, we wanted to be considered for any new work in our area, and that process must begin now. The first adjournment of the meeting was called and, when we returned, Joe had a proposal. He was prepared to allow Athlone drivers to work the 16.50 train between Athlone and Ballinasloe. This would provide us with overtime on a roster that also had an added one-person-operated bonus. It would be a share, albeit a minority share, of the new work. And it was accompanied by Joe's assurance that, henceforth, Athlone drivers would be considered for all new work in the area. We asked about Tommy's retirement, and Joe told us that that offer was off the table — it was now one or the other. P.J, turning the tables, promptly reminded Joe about the acclaim that he had bestowed on Tommy earlier. For a moment, Joe looked like standing firm. However, the practicalities of the impending timetable change demanded a solution, and so the deal was done. Tommy went off to enjoy a slightly early retirement with an unexpected lump sum, and the Athlone drivers enjoyed what they considered to be — in the context of what had been occurring in Athlone for so long — a significant victory.

I outline this incident in all its detail because for me it contained so many firsts — my first involvement in the independent use of industrial relations legislation, my first involvement in the issue of strike notice, my first involvement in the exposure of a serious management mistake, my first serious negotiation with Irish Rail, my first part in a successful outcome achieved by unity among drivers, and my first involvement in a direct tug of war with Tony Tobin as my union official. It was not to be the last.

Talks or No Talks

On a national level, the 'viability plan' had by now been about for some time. Threatening — at least as far as employees were concerned — documents had been produced; marches had been called by the unions, and then called off at the first sign of trouble, and had then taken place anyway; and workers had been preparing, across all three CIÉ companies, for the expected onslaught on their terms and conditions of employment. In Iarnród Éireann, drivers were now watching their unions as closely, if not closer, than management. The old adage of keeping your enemies close but your friends closer seemed a very appropriate one for us, as every utterance from the NBRU or SIPTU was examined by the NLDC and its supporters (at this point, almost every driver) for signs of impending treachery.

The political pressure for movement on the £30m savings in Iarnród

Éireann was beginning to build. It was as a result of this pressure that I was to have my first meeting with Mary O'Rourke TD, then opposition Spokesperson for Transport, among other things. This meeting was arranged by a colleague of mine in Athlone Station, local Fianna Fáil Urban District Councillor John Butler. It took place in Leinster House and it was to be my first visit to Government Buildings. I recall very little of the meeting, which was short and took place in one of the meeting rooms just facing the main entrance to Leinster House, other than the fact that I outlined concerns that drivers had with the viability proposals and the fact that unions might be forced into negotiating severe changes in work practices and job losses without the agreement of union members. I remember the future minister declaring the firm belief that Fianna Fáil, and particularly Bertie Ahern, had in trade unions and how they would not allow unions to be sidelined if they could avoid it. I couldn't help wondering if this was the same Bertie Ahern who, in a previous incarnation, had brought forward the anti-union Industrial Relations Act of 1990. In reality, this meeting was no more than one of introduction, and, as I left to go to Liberty Hall and have some real arguments, I wondered if I would meet Ireland's own iron lady again.

There were to be many arguments in Liberty Hall in the lead-up to discussions on the 'viability plan', as it seemed that nobody wanted discussions on this plan except management and our union officials. Drivers were by now so lacking in trust in our representatives that we didn't see how discussions could end in anything but disaster. But among other grades too there was a reluctance for talks. Although we had been the victims of 1994, other grades had watched on from a safe distance. Now, they too wondered what might happen to them now that Irish Rail had all grades — except, of course, the management and clerical grades — in their sights. And so, even getting talks started was a difficult task for management and union officials alike. The defence mechanism of those of us on SIPTU's recently elected National Rail Council (NRC) was to lay down a number of issues that were to be dealt with before any talks could begin. For example, for a number of years, Irish Rail had been failing to fill vacancies when retirements or illness occurred and, as a consequence, had been filling these posts with temporary staff. This was not an issue for drivers as all drivers were, of necessity, permanent staff.

However, as the representative of all staff in the Midlands, I felt responsible to the platform staff and permanent-way staff who had not been appointed, despite having up to ten years' continuous service. So the NRC compiled a list of all staff who had exceeded one year of continuous service, and insisted on their immediate appointment to permanent staff before discussions could begin on anything else. This tactic had two positive effects from our viewpoint.

Firstly, it rectified the disgraceful situation where experienced and, in some cases, very skilled workers were effectively working on a continuous day-to-day basis. In my own area, a number of staff would eventually be appointed through this process, and this was replicated nationwide. Secondly, it put back the dreaded day when we would have to discuss the 'viability plan'. Obviously this process created its own difficulties and problems and no little frustration among management. This frustration led to an interesting ad-hoc meeting between Human Resource Manager John Keenan, Tony Tobin and me. We were involved in a day-long meeting in the boardroom at Connolly Station about a proposed 'suicide policy' for staff involved in such incidents. The day began on a humorous note. As the various representatives awaited the arrival of management in the boardroom, an NBRU representative called John Sinclair was in attendance. John, who would later be involved in a number of tragic suicides, had attended the workers' march to the Dáil mentioned earlier. Close to the barricades outside the Dáil, John had been caught on RTÉ television burning a copy of the 'viability plan' booklet. As John Keenan entered the room, he walked over to John Sinclair and put a new copy of the plan into his hand, saying, 'Here — I saw you lost yours in a fire.'

As we assembled in the North Star Hotel in Amiens Street for lunch later on, I found myself sitting at an empty table when Tony Tobin joined me. A few seconds later, John Keenan entered and asked if he could join us, explaining that he 'wanted to pick Brendan's brains'. He then began not so much picking as interrogating. Basically, John wanted to know why talks on the 'viability plan' had not begun, and he gave me a lecture on the perilous state of the company. After I had suggested a downward review of management pay levels and the removal of some company cars, I asked John whether Tony had explained why talks had not begun. He said that he knew that there were objections from within the NRC, but that he intended to agree a schedule of meetings with Tony in any case. I raised my head from my soup bowl and replied that Tony would attend whatever meetings the NRC sanctioned and no more. I gave a short, blunt lecture about how the union was the members, and how the mistakes of 1994 would not be repeated.

After that, the discussion mellowed somewhat, and turned to political corruption. I made some sweeping comment to the effect that there was no honesty left in Irish politics. John's reply was one that I was to have reason to recall some years later. He disagreed with my observation on the low ethical standards in Irish political life and evidenced his viewpoint with a tale about his 'close personal friendship' with Kildare TD Emmet Stagg, which he believed showed great principle on Deputy Stagg's part. What interested me was that Iarnród Éireann's Human Resource Director was a member of the Irish Labour Party and had connections to Emmet Stagg.

In due course, Irish Rail made temporary staff permanent, and the 'viability plan' came centre stage again. By now, the union officials had had an idea. For a considerable time, workers had been insisting on a five-day working week, as opposed to what was effectively a seven-day working week. In fact, as early as 1995, over 200 drivers had signed a letter addressed to SIPTU and the NBRU, demanding movement on a five-day working week. The letter had been ignored by both unions. I remember being told at the time that petitions were not to be taken seriously as people always signed them because they felt obliged to do so if their colleagues had signed them. Now, however, under pressure from management to get talks going on the 'viability plan', the officials told us that this was not a threat to us but an opportunity to get a five-day week. Almost overnight, the two officials who had for two years ignored the written demand of their members for a five-day week became the champions of a reasonable working week for drivers. At the time of writing, ILDA members who insist on working the five-day week that these unions eventually negotiated are routinely and systematically threatened with the sack without a word of complaint by these champions of drivers' time off. Back in 1996 though, it was a convenient Trojan horse to kick-start talks. Most of the NRC members did not buy into this empty rhetoric easily. At meeting after meeting, we discussed a possible basis for talks with management. Eventually, the finger could hold the dam no longer. It was agreed that the unions would enter talks with management with a number of preconditions.

These talks would not involve discussion of the job-cutting and cost-saving 'viability plan', but would be productivity talks, aimed at securing a five-day week and a big increase in basic pay for all staff — this would ensure that the talks addressed the pay and working-time concerns of staff, as opposed to being just another attack on badly paid and overworked staff by an overpaid, underworked and top-heavy management

Each grade would vote only on elements relating to that grade — this crucial guarantee would eliminate the injustice of 1994 when a bribe, coupled with sheer numbers, had undone a previously united group of workers

No balloting of any grade would take place, and no changes would be implemented until all grades had agreed all changes applicable to that grade — this was included to prevent any of the supposedly less crucial grades from being isolated and unfairly treated. How these preconditions for negotiation survived, or, in two cases, didn't survive, the process remained to be seen.

Thus, the strands of a negotiating process were beginning to emerge. It was at this point that union officials introduced to their members another proposed strand — the negotiations were to be 'facilitated'. Just what this meant was initially unclear to me. Basically, the experienced sages of negotiations, such as those within management and the union officials, made the startling admission that they could not reach agreement themselves, and they did so even before talks began. Therefore, the Labour Relations Commission (LRC) was to provide an 'independent chairman' to 'facilitate' the entire process. This chairman was to be one of the LRC's limited number of conciliation officers. I was quite confused by this. I was new to this game and had the naive impression that agreements between employers and unions should be reached between employers and unions. I understood that that was not always possible and that, following a disagreement between the parties, conciliation was often necessary on points of disagreement. However, here we had a situation where conciliation was apparently required from the outset, before any discussions between the parties were even attempted. I was sure that this would result in even more shadow boxing between the parties than I had assumed would naturally occur in such a process, and that this shadow boxing would now take place on every single point at issue. It seemed to me that anything the parties could agree on, however small, would save time when the admittedly necessary conciliation process was needed. But I was a novice surrounded by experts.

We even had talks about who was going to chair the talks about talks! Some people in SIPTU didn't want this officer and other people in the NBRU wanted that officer and, of course, Irish Rail wanted a different officer again. Eventually, Kevin Foley was appointed as the lucky man.

Working within SIPTU

So, as 1997 began, the 'viability talks' were also about to take off — or perhaps stagger across the starting line would be more accurate. My role in the affairs of SIPTU was becoming more interesting. In addition to my role as a drivers' representative, I was on the NRC, and the NRC sub-committee which was a trimmed-down version of the NRC and attended meetings when numbers prevented the entire fourteen-man NRC from attending; I was also on the SIPTU sub-committee responsible for presenting a policy document on how to treat staff involved in suicides and other fatal incidents. All of this brought me into day-to-day contact with Tony Tobin. On one level, I had a very good relationship with Tony. Certainly we talked about very many issues and shared ideas on difficulties that arose.

One such difficulty Tony had as the union official was the fact that rail workers were represented by various constituent parts of the union and not by one single branch. Before SIPTU had formed, as recently as 1990, railway workers had generally been represented by NATE, ITGWU or the NBRU. When the ITGWU and the Federated Workers Union of Ireland (FWUI) merged to form SIPTU, many NATE members objected to being swallowed up by Ireland's new largest union. NATE, by now a constituent part of SIPTU, was still viewed by some 'NATE men' as their own little republic. While I would have no ideological objection to this myself, and I was in fact a NATE member anyway, the reality was that NATE had long since ceased to be a useful or operable entity in any way whatsoever. Most rail workers within SIPTU were represented by SIPTU's Dublin Transport Branch, while the country members were generally affiliated to the all-but-defunct NATE. Tony was, of course, the official in charge of the Dublin Transport Branch and SIPTU's only official with any reasonable degree of experience relevant to the rail industry. However, many rail workers in SIPTU could revert to their local SIPTU offices around the country under the NATE umbrella when it came to matters such as conferences and voting. My experience was that rail workers in SIPTU were losing out by not acting together through one rail branch. When Tony suggested to me that this anomaly could be tackled, I readily agreed to assist. SIPTU decided to form a 'railway services division', which would be an all-encompassing branch for railway workers in SIPTU. This required the approval of both NATE and the Dublin Transport Branch. The proposals were supported by the relevant regional secretary, Brendan Hayes, and other senior officials. Predictably, the Dublin Transport Branch agreed to the proposals first. I was not surprised by this as I had felt that many of the more experienced members of the Dublin Transport Branch thought that this development was nothing more than an opportunity for them to extend their membership, while retaining control of any important officers' positions in Liberty Hall. I didn't see the NATE members being the tail on the Dublin Transport Branch dog, so I decided that an early marker should be put down to show that we were not just coming along for the ride. It would also give me an opportunity to settle an old score as it were.

A meeting of the NATE division was called in Liberty Hall for a Saturday afternoon in December 1997. There were two items to be voted on. The first was whether the NATE division would agree to amalgamate with the Dublin Transport Branch into the Railway Services Division (RSD). The second was the business of choosing a nominee to support for the position of SIPTU Vice-President. I was one of the people who spoke in favour of the formation of the RSD. One of the major benefits as I saw it of having such a division was that we, as railway workers, would be entitled to hold our own bi-annual delegate conference to decide SIPTU's policies for its railway workers. Although drivers would, of course, be well outnumbered at any such conference, I was convinced that logical argument would win the day on any issues raised, and that SIPTU would then set about implementing the policies that the conference decided upon. I was, as usual, very naive to make either of these assumptions. Nevertheless, in December 1997, I was in favour of such a venture, and was probably as pleased as Tony himself when the NATE members decided to give the old union a decent burial and join the RSD.

So, the meeting turned to consider who the newly formed RSD should back in the upcoming election for SIPTU Vice-President. The drivers' old friend, Brendan Hayes, was in the running for the job. As the RSD was in Brendan's Dublin public-service region, we were expected to support our secretary's candidature. In fact, we were told, just five minutes after agreeing to merge, that the Dublin Transport Branch element had discussed this the previous Tuesday night and had agreed to endorse Brendan Hayes. I got the distinct feeling that we 'culchies' were supposed to nod and accept the wisdom of our new city partners. I, however, saw it differently. I was already concerned that SIPTU was losing touch with its grass-roots membership on many issues. Carolann Duggan, a rank-and-file worker based in Waterford, had decided to run in this election and was campaigning very effectively. A member of the Socialist Workers' Party (SWP), she had pledged that, if elected, she would accept a salary only at the level of her then salary on the shop floor in Waterford's Bausch and Lomb plant. This had successfully focused attention on the salary levels of SIPTU's executive officers, and ultimately led to their taking a substantial — if only temporary — pay cut. This was the type of shop-floor trade unionism that I felt we needed to see much more of. But I had a difficulty — I didn't think that the attendance would support Carolann.

I myself have never been a member of the SWP. I profoundly disagree with their belief that the way to produce change for workers is to agitate within the trade unions in order to make those unions more responsive to rank-and-file needs. Workers, by their very nature, have a limited amount of time and energy available for union activity. I believe that if this limited time and energy is spent fighting within a union bureaucracy, workers lose and employers laugh all the way to the bank. In fact, I believe that union bureaucracies are a cleverly devised means of soaking up worker dissent in order to give employers as free a run as the union fat cats —

whom we were in the process of electing — want them to have.

So I decided that it was neither practical nor necessary to attempt to get Carolann endorsed by the RSD. When the debate began, a number of speakers rose to propose Brendan Hayes as our nominee. After three or four speakers, I rose to speak. I argued that the RSD Branch should support no one in the election but should allow our members a free vote, unencumbered by our recommendations. I argued that our members were intelligent enough to make up their own minds on such issues. When the chairman of the now-defunct Dublin Transport Branch rose to tell me that it had already decided to endorse the Hayes candidature, I wasted no time in telling him that that decision was improper and that it was for those now in attendance, the RSD, to endorse a candidate or otherwise. I made a formal proposal that the RSD nominate no one. John Noone from Galway seconded my proposal, and I was not surprised when several speakers rose to support it. It developed into a clean fight between the former NATE members, who supported my proposal, and the Dublin Transport element, who were in the chair and backed Brendan Hayes. Chair or not, we won. Brendan Hayes — the man who had prevaricated so much over 1994 — failed to get the nomination of the new branch. He also, ultimately, failed to get the job — he came a distant third behind the impressive Carolann Duggan who pushed the successful Jimmy Somers all the way for the vice–presidency of Ireland's largest union.

My First Delegate Conference
The first delegate conference of the RSD took place in the West County Hotel, Ennis, in June 1998. The Athlone drivers' section had four motions down for debate at the conference, and the delegates were Finbar Masterson and I. The two-day conference was to be an interesting affair. Pauline, who I had married in 1995, and I left our eight-month old baby with her maternal grandparents in Thurles before completing the trip to Clare. We got to the hotel the night before the conference began and entered the bar to meet the other delegates. The NLDC was not without a presence at the conference as, in addition to myself and Finbar, John Courtney from Inchicore was there. John is a man with whom, through the NLDC, I developed a very close working relationship at an early stage. He subsequently became the SIPTU drivers' representative in Inchicore

— Ireland's largest drivers' base — and was to be the co-founder of ILDA along with yours truly some months later. John is a quiet man, almost shy to some, but he has an extremely sharp mind and is principled and honest in everything he does. We spent the evening having drinks with John, a friend of his from the works in Inchicore, Martin Maher, and Billy Costelloe, John Noone and their wives from Galway. The final member of our group was Seán Kenny from Ballina. Seán was a train guard in Ballina and, along with John Noone, was a colleague of mine on the NRC. He had an interest in left-wing politics and was the type to cut through a lot of waffle at meetings and just call a spade a spade. He and I got on very well indeed. As I observed some of the guests who were arriving, I realised that the conference was to be interesting that evening. Sitting in a corner, enjoying a few pre-conference drinks, were SIPTU's newly elected Vice-President, Jimmy Somers, and the Chief Executive of CIÉ, Michael McDonnell.

The following morning, the conference began. What immediately struck me was the lack of debate on most of the motions that had been put down. Motion after motion, the proposers would make their way to the platform and use something less than the permitted five minutes in arguing their case. They would be quickly followed by the seconders who would simply state that they were seconding the motion. The chairman, Tony Hogarty, had explained at the outset that those wishing to speak should form a line behind the seconders to save time getting to and from seats. But there were initially no long queues of speakers on motions — in fact, there were hardly any at all. And so it continued. Each motion was adopted by a unanimous show of hands, with little or no debate — until, that is, the conference came to motion 17.

Motion 17 was the first proposal put forward by the Athlone locomotive section. It proposed four meetings per year for the drivers' group in the branch, in order to keep abreast of developments within the grade — no more and no less. As I began to speak to explain the motion, I became aware of a few delegates making a hissing sound within the hall. I continued anyway and spoke about the need for a policy on suicides, the proposed drink and drug testing of drivers booking in on duty, and the need for the RSD to 'know where we are going with these issues'. The motion was seconded by Inchicore, but by now a line — the first one of the day — was beginning to form behind the seconder. The first speaker was a signalman from Maynooth. He made a speech that was such an attack on drivers as almost to fall under the ambit of incitement-to-hatred legislation. But what was disconcerting was not the content of his speech but its tone. He wasn't alone. The line continued to grow, with delegates launching into blistering attacks on train drivers. The situation reached a farcical position when a driver, John Walsh from Waterford, rose and actually opposed the motion. John had been a member of the NRC for many years and I had met him almost as soon as I had become involved in union affairs. He was one of the very few drivers who was opposed to the NLDC and didn't see anything at all wrong with 1994 and the manner of its completion. I viewed John as a 'safe vote' for the union establishment on any issue, and so we were destined to disagree on almost everything. But John was still a driver. To me it was madness that he should oppose the motion.

John's argument was that all grades — and not just drivers — were entitled to four meetings per year. At this stage, others who had not intended to speak in support of the motion felt the need to do so. The queue was long and the atmosphere in the hall had grown quite hostile, to say the least. I was furious. I had put down four motions on behalf of a drivers' branch. Yet only one of the four — this one — related to drivers only. All the others related to all railway workers and, to be honest, the other three were much more substantial motions than this one. I couldn't believe the latent resentment, bordering on hatred, which those in the hall had towards drivers. The chairman diplomatically adjourned the conference for lunch, as much to allow the temperature to cool as out of concern for delegates' stomachs.

I left the room and was immediately approached by Tony Tobin and Bobby Jolly. Tony asked me to 'refer back' our motion. He explained that if it was put to the vote, it might fall and that he would then be disbarred from calling drivers' meetings when he saw fit. I railed against the feelings some other delegates had towards drivers and told Tony that it was becoming increasingly apparent to me that this was not a union in which drivers had any place. I believe that Tony did not at that point understand the significance of what I was saying. Drivers' delegates then held an impromptu meeting in a corridor. They were all there except John Walsh, and they were all livid. I sought advice as to what I would do next. Before the conference reconvened, I approached the chairman and asked him to allow me to address the conference before any other speakers were called. When I spoke, I outlined that I was there as a drivers' representative and that, as such, I was bound and obliged to argue on drivers' issues. I explained that if I had been a signalman, shunter, train guard or ticket checker, I would be arguing their issues. I had no difficulty if signalmen or any other grades also wanted four meetings a year but that it was for them to propose it and not for me. Finally, I explained that I had not come to divide the union and that I was genuinely shocked by the apparent antipathy of some delegates towards drivers. Because of this apparent antipathy, I agreed to refer the motion back to the Branch Committee as requested, and stated that I and other drivers present would take some time to reflect on what had occurred before lunch.

The assembly then actually applauded me as I returned to my seat. From that moment on, any illusions I, or any other drivers present, might have had that we would not have to mind our own backs from now on were dispelled. We, as drivers, had lost out in 1994 — no one else. And other union members who had gained from that debacle just wanted it all buried, forgotten, airbrushed from SIPTU history. Our consistent failure to allow the scandal to die was causing great annoyance and it all came out in Ennis. That isn't to say that there weren't many delegates in other grades who were supportive of the motion concerned. There were. But as we couldn't be sure that we would carry the motion, we decided that I should effectively withdraw it. In any case, we were strong enough on the drivers' committee to get as many meetings as we needed. When withdrawing, I knew that another more substantive motion tabled by the Athlone Drivers' Branch was to be debated later in the conference and was bound to attract major opposition. We were going to push that one all the way and we thought it best to hold what support we had in the conference hall for that motion.

So we waited for the motion to come up. Motion 23, proposed by the Athlone locomotive drivers' section, called for SIPTU to lobby for full tax relief for payments made to workers in essential services for work performed on Sundays or public holidays. In my address, I attacked the record of the trade union movement in delivering real tax reform for its members. In addition, I attacked the Labour Party who had been in the two previous governments — in coalition with Fianna Fáil, and as part of the Rainbow Coalition — and yet had failed to deliver for the PAYE sector. I attributed their recent election losses to that failure. I argued that the work done by transport workers on Sundays and public holidays was an essential public service, and as such, should not be subject to taxation

I was aware that this address, which also called for a higher tax rate for those earning over £100,000 rather than tax amnesties for crooks, implicitly and explicitly criticised the social partners, including SIPTU. Sitting at the top table was Jimmy Somers, the recently elected Vice-President of SIPTU. My address was met with loud applause from the floor. Nevertheless, it was no surprise when Jimmy Somers took to the podium and addressed the motion. He explained that the union leadership understood the frustration behind the motion and my address but that this was not the way to deliver tax reform. He asked that the motion be 'referred back' for consideration. I was determined that this would not happen. The chairman looked to me and I shook my head. Speaker after speaker then spoke, including Tony Tobin, who repeated the call of his vice-president to refer back. I then went to the podium for my two-minute summing up. I refused to withdraw the motion or refer it back and I again criticised the union and social partners for failing to deliver equitable taxation and benefits for PAYE workers. I returned to my seat and the vote was taken. As I recall, it was the only vote at the conference that actually required the participation of the tellers, and, to my delight, despite the strong opposition of officialdom, the motion was passed.

After a speech I made later at the conference, calling for increased investment in public transport, I was approached by the late CIÉ Chief Executive, Michael McDonnell, who complimented me on my speech. He asked whether I had lobbied new Transport Minister Mary O'Rourke on this issue. I explained that I had and he asked that I continue to do so. He also stated that he was concerned even then, in the summer of 1998, for his own position, as he felt under great political pressure. This issue would run and run and eventually come to a very sad and tragic end with Michael McDonnell's retirement and subsequent death. My personal experience of Mr McDonnell when we spoke at the conference, and on a later occasion which will be discussed below, was of a courteous and affable man with an understanding of the issues that badly needed to be addressed in public transport in this country.

There were other motions discussed and passed at the conference, such as the introduction of a members' charter to outline the benefits of membership and report on progress in achieving the union's aims on a regular basis. It is a matter of record that, despite the passing of this motion at conference, neither it nor many other motions, including the crucial one on taxation, were ever acted on by officialdom. This truly was a 'talking shop' in the purest sense.

On the social side, the conference concluded amicably. Having failed to expunge the residual antipathy of many delegates towards their driver colleagues, we took the diplomatic course and allowed the conference to end without any 'blood letting'. Tony Tobin had arranged a trip from Ennis to Spanish Point for the evening of the second day. We travelled via Lahinch, where there was a meal and dancing in a local hotel. Paul Cullen, the influential Connolly-based driver and worker director, sat beside me on the bus, while Pauline sat in front of us with his wife. Paul was known as perhaps Tony's closest confidant. He asked me my views on the conference and the future direction of the RSD Branch. As I outlined my views and ideas, Paul asked me whether I would be interested in becoming the Branch President. He explained that Tony O'Brien was soon to retire and that his co-president, Tony Hogarty, might have difficulty in continuing alone. I was a bit taken aback by the request given my acknowledged role in the NLDC and the day's events, but I undertook to consider the request and discuss it with Tony at a suitable time.

First, however, I discussed it with a number of close friends. They all expressed the view that this 'offer' was being made in an effort to get me to cease my involvement with the NLDC. The following Saturday evening, I called Tony Tobin. He was en route to Waterford when I spoke to him at length. He explained to me that Paul's suggestion had been made with his knowledge and that he would like me to consider taking up this soon-to-become-vacant position. When I asked him why, he listed some general reasons, and also said some complimentary things about me personally, and my involvement in union affairs. I thanked him but explained that I had an involvement within my own grade, and that there were some outstanding matters awaiting resolution. I would have to see them through, including my involvement in the NLDC.

The End of the Line

In truth, events in SIPTU were livening up and I would soon be sliding down their internal popularity scale. The Ennis conference was to be my last SIPTU conference and, although we didn't know it at the time, also the last of many of my driver colleagues. Discussions on the 'viability plan' were now going ahead in a Kildare hotel. Eighteen drivers from SIPTU and the NBRU assembled in the Finnstown House hotel initially in July 1998, before ultimately doing a three-year tour of many fine Dublin hotels — overnights, expenses and meals included — in a supposed effort to save money.

The negotiations were tense and difficult from the outset. This was inevitable with such a lack of trust on all sides. Kevin Foley's attempts to facilitate a quick and focused set of negotiations were frustrated by an agreement between the parties that approximately thirty-three groups would have thirty-three different sets of negotiations. Drivers would be first. There is not much to be said about the talks from the perspective of my involvement other than to say that, by the time we left, they had still not passed first base at Finnstown House. It would be another eighteen months before these talks would produce anything in the form of proposals for ballot. So, what was it that prompted us to leave?

The NLDC objective was to ensure that our union officials carried out the wishes of the elected driver representatives at all times — and not the other way around. When Kevin Foley, management and the officials decided that we, the drivers, should draw up rosters before we had received any realistic financial proposal, the driver representatives — initially all of us — baulked. As drivers, we knew the rail system better than any manager. We knew the crossing points — where, en route, freight trains would 'cross' with passenger trains — and other details as to how the system could be worked with maximum efficiency. It was grass-routes knowledge that was valuable to the highly paid managers charged with saving costs, and their jobs. Why should we surrender this information, show these people how to run their company and roster patterns properly, and then be faced with a derisory pay offer for our efforts?

Management obviously saw it differently. They persuaded Kevin Foley and the Tobins of the logic of our doing the rosters for them (until that point, drivers had never historically produced rosters from scratch for management. Instead, we saw it as our role to drive trains under agreed roster patterns). As the talks drew towards adjournment at the end of a full, tortuous week of blarney in Finnstown House, management and the unions took the view that when we returned the following week, we would agree to do the rosters. That Saturday night, I met with my members in Athlone, and other representatives did likewise in their areas. I received clear instructions that I was not, under any circumstances, to engage in the formation of rosters with management until financial details of all proposals were on the table.

As I arrived at Finnstown House again on Monday morning, the drivers met in the garden of the hotel. Not surprisingly, we were now all of the same mind, and most had received similar instructions to mine. We made our way to the room for negotiations but the LRC chairman was absent. Immediately, the officials and management told us to break up into groups and begin work on the rosters. One by one, the drivers revealed that they had no mandate from their depots to do any such thing. We refused. Log jam. Would it be rosters then money, or money then rosters? And, in the absence of the independent chairman, who could move it forward or reach a compromise? Compromise was not on the Tobins' minds that day. They immediately spoke to some shop stewards, including me, privately; when that produced nothing, they had a quick sojourn with management. Then it began — a six-hour 'beating over the head' session where we talked and talked and talked about doing or not doing rosters. And, one by one, they fell. These drivers, who were good drivers, were leaned on in major negotiations with their own officials and management and, predictably, they fell. By 4 o'clock in the afternoon, only three drivers were still holding to the positions they had begun the morning with. They were John Courtney and Frank McCartney from Inchicore, and myself.

I was fed up now. Four years of working hard to make our officials accountable to the members, and this was what was happening. I was having no part of it and asked Tony Tobin to call me a taxi to the train station. I was going home to explain to my members what had happened

— and sod the rest of them! John and Frank said that they would go too. John was very strong, and Frankie also knew that we would be seen to be right in his members' eyes. As fears of a split loomed, panic set in — not among the officials, but among the drivers themselves. We were asked to sleep on it. I refused. Then John Sinclair called me aside. He suggested that we do the rosters to the best of our ability and hand them to our officials. They would see how well they worked and fitted, and report this fact, but not show the rosters, to management. If management then came up with an agreeable pay-and-conditions package, the rosters would be theirs. We thought about it but could not decide. Did we trust the officials? Could we after 1994? All the others agreed that this was a good compromise. In the end, John asked that we consider it in the morning and we agreed that we would consider it and consult with our members by phone overnight, which we did. We also spoke to the other delegates in our Glenroyal Hotel base. We explained that we didn't want to see any split but that the shots must be called by the members — not the officials.

When we got back to Finnstown the following morning, Liam Tobin immediately opened the session by attempting to set up roster groups. I intervened and said that we should consider the proposal put the previous evening and that I would agree to such a proposal. My members had agreed that this option was a reasonable way forward. Liam Tobin told me that as Kevin Foley had received a commitment (I must have missed it) that rosters would be done, they must be done; and that was it. I was almost speechless and so was John Courtney. Liam Tobin — and Tony didn't disagree with him — was telling me to do what my members had told me not to do. That is not my brand of trade unionism. I was speechless but just about able to call a taxi. John and I were leaving. Frankie McCartney decided to stay.

BITTER RETORT TO A NEW ERA

As John and I left Finnstown House that evening, we knew that our involvement in those talks was more than likely over. What was to happen next, however, was quite another issue. The NLDC was to meet the following Sunday to discuss the ongoing talks. John and I began the task of speaking to friends in advance of that meeting. I consulted Finbar Masterson and Brian Dunphy, along with Kevin Connolly in Dundalk, and others. By the time Sunday's meeting arrived, I had a proposal ready.

On 14 September, the meeting took place, as usual, in Dublin's Aisling Hotel. I addressed the meeting and explained what had occurred at Finnstown House and how the officials of SIPTU and the NBRU had cajoled drivers' representatives down a road that they had not received a prior mandate to travel. I then offered my view that the NLDC had failed in its four-and-a-half-year campaign to make SIPTU and the NBRU more representative of drivers' opinions. I believed that both unions were just as cavalier in their attitudes towards drivers' wishes as they had been with the notorious productivity 'agreement' of 1994. In summary, the NLDC as a pressure group had failed to reform our unions, and it was now time to act if a disaster of monumental proportions was not to befall the grade. I proposed that pressure groups were not enough and that internal reform without external pressure was not going to happen. It was time for that external pressure, and drivers would have to step out alone. I proposed that we disband the NLDC as a pressure group, resign from SIPTU and the NBRU, and form a train drivers' union to be called the Irish Locomotive Drivers' Association (ILDA). John Courtney confirmed the happenings at Finnstown House and seconded the motion.

SIPTU and the NBRU were concerned enough about our leaving Finnstown House to have a keen interest in this meeting. A number of their representatives who had been in Finnstown House were also in the Aisling Hotel and argued against the proposed course. I felt that their views that we should stick with our unions and officials were not held by the majority in the room. However, it was not an easy decision. Ken Fox, a Cork driver who had trained with me, argued that this proposal warranted a proper discussion within the grade. He suggested that this discussion period should last two weeks and that the meeting should stand adjourned until 28 September. All depots would then send a delegation to the re-convened meeting, and the proposal would be discussed and voted on at that meeting. John and I readily agreed to this proposal.

The two-week discussion period within the grade was surprisingly uneventful. The debate was conducted on a depot-by-depot basis and was, possibly for the last time in respect of ILDA, conducted rationally and with respect for all of the views expressed. From the viewpoint of those supporting the formation of ILDA, a number of specific issues had emerged within the negotiating process which were particularly relevant:

- Annualised hours were apparently going to be part of the agreed outcome as far as SIPTU/NBRU were concerned. This refers to a process, used in other industries, of accumulating hours over a period of weeks, months or, usually, years, in order to provide short and long working weeks. Drivers had given no mandate for discussions on such a concept and had, in fact, opposed it at every proposed stage.

- Separate rates of pay were proposed for drivers doing the same work in the same depots, on the basis of seniority. This would divide established drivers from incoming new recruits and sow the seeds for years of ill-feeling, division and dissension within the grade.

- An increase in the working week was expected, from the basic thirty-nine hours to a minimum compulsory contract of forty-three hours up to a maximum of forty-eight hours a week. Although drivers worked excessive hours anyway, the Organisation of Working Time Act 1997 provided for a maximum forty-eight-hour working week from date of implementation in the various industries. We currently worked a thirty-nine-hour week and the NLDC now saw this as an opportunity to reduce that basic to less than thirty-nine and ultimately thirty-five. Instead, SIPTU/NBRU wanted to increase it up to the maximum forty-eight to be permitted in law.

- Roster patterns were being proposed by drivers (not by management), which would see drivers in bigger depots, such as Connolly Station, getting more hours and therefore more money than drivers at other depots because they had greater voting power, while they gave away actual work to neighbouring depots. This problem was so acute that, at one stage, the negotiating committee actually had seven drivers from Connolly on an eighteen-man committee, despite the fact that Connolly was one of thirteen depots affected by the proposals. The 'agreement' was ultimately described by many as 'a Connolly deal for Connolly drivers' with regular lump-sum payments thrown in as sweeteners to Connolly drivers.

- Five- over seven-day working would, if accepted, see Sunday treated as a normal working day in respect of payments, with no additional payment to be made to workers who worked Sundays, despite the fact the Organisation of Working Time Act 1997 specifically requires supplementary payments to be made for all Sunday working.

- Part-time train drivers was John Keenan's bizarre proposal whereby all railway workers would ultimately be trained as drivers but would then return to their various duties and only take to the footplate to provide relief for ill drivers or those absent for other reasons. This proposal failed to take account of the nature of train driving, where experience built up leads to consistent and professional performance. To us, it was clearly the most fundamental of a number of safety concerns that would emerge. It was also a proposal that we would eventually see consigned to the dustbin despite SIPTU/ NBRU agreement to it and misrepresentation of what was actually proposed.

There were, of course, other issues emerging and later to emerge. However, in September 1998, the fact that the issues of 1994 had been ignored and that the unions had not changed and had become more and more arrogant towards their members was as big a difficulty as any other issue. An example of this arrogance had been provided in Athlone in the summer of 1998. Following the suspension of Ciaran O'Dwyer, John Courtney and myself from SIPTU's negotiating committee, my colleagues in the Athlone Locomotive Branch were furious. Several rang Tony Tobin to argue the case for the reinstatement of the three of us; however, Tony Tobin showed no sign of taking these concerns seriously. The members lost patience with this and decided to call a Branch meeting to discuss the matter on 15 August 1998. This meeting proposed a vote of no confidence in Tony Tobin as our Branch Secretary. I, as the local secretary, called Tony and advised him of this. I told him that the meeting would consider such a proposal and that he was invited to the meeting to explain his actions to the members who paid his wages. He declined the invitation to attend. It was the first time that Tony had refused to attend a meeting of his members in Athlone on their request. For most of them, it would be the last. The meeting proceeded, as Tony had been told it would. The issue was seen so seriously that drivers drove to Athlone from Westport, Ballina and Sligo on a Saturday night to discuss the difficulty that had emerged.

Three motions were passed at the meeting. The first was a vote of no confidence in Tony Tobin as Branch Sercretary. It was followed by a motion of no confidence in the unelected interim Branch Committee of the RSD. There was then a motion proposing that an immediate election be held for a democratically elected Branch Committee. It was agreed that I should do and say whatever was necessary to ensure my attendance at upcoming productivity negotiations. It was also decided that annualised hours must not form any part of proposals put to drivers. Finally, it was agreed that I would continue with my appeal against my suspension.

A letter was sent to Tony Tobin, informing him of the proceedings of the meeting. The letter was copied to John McDonnell, Jimmy Somers, Des Geraghty and Brendan Hayes. If we had any expectations that any of the officers who received this notice would now attempt to address the growing crisis, we were, once again, to be disappointed. None of these officers saw fit to investigate these concerns with the drivers involved. If they spoke to Tony Tobin and told him to resolve the problems that had led to this situation, it was not evident from my next meeting with him.

I did ensure my attendance at the 'upcoming productivity talks'. It was at these talks that I next spoke to Tony Tobin. During a lunch break in Finnstown House, the various parties were enjoying the late-summer sun in the garden. Tony approached me with the letter in his hand. In an angry exchange, he crumpled up the letter, stating that its contents were not worth the paper they were written on. I was not surprised. For a considerable time, I had felt that accountability of SIPTU officials to members had been no more than a pipedream. There, crumpled up in Tony Tobin's hands, I saw evidence in support of this belief. The following day, John and I were gone.

Legalities

The NLDC had, of course, been in receipt of legal advice for some time. This advice was quite detailed and technical, but basically the situation was as follows. The operation and management of most state companies, such as Iarnród Éireann, are regulated by an Act of Government — in Iarnród Éireann's case, the Railways Act 1924. These acts legislate for the full organisation of the relevant company including the method of administering its collective-bargaining obligations. Section 55 of the Railways Act 1924 is the section of the relevant Act applicable to industrial relations, and reads:

> 55.—(1) From and after the passing of this Act the rates of pay, hours of duty, and other conditions of service of railway employees shall be regulated in accordance with agreements made or to be from time to time made between the trade unions representative of such employees of the one part and the railway companies and other persons by whom they are respectively employed of the other part.

So, a statutory provision determined how the railway company was to regulate the terms and conditions of railway employees. Our advice, which ultimately was tested and supported in part in the Supreme Court, was that a new union that was 'representative' of relevant employees — in this case, train drivers — could argue that it was entitled, under statute, to negotiate the terms and conditions of such employees. This opened up the possibility that members of a new union in the railway could not, under statute, be denied the right to negotiate their own terms and conditions if that union was 'representative' of those employees — in this case, train drivers. It therefore followed that the possibility existed, and following a Supreme Court decision ultimately issued in the case of ILDA, still does exist, that any agreement negotiated by a process that excludes such employees is, as a matter of statute, unlawful.

In summary, we were fully aware, before ILDA was even formed, that the legalities of forming a new union in the railways were complex. Bertie Ahern's repressive 1990 legislation in this regard will be explored in more detail in discussion of the High Court and Supreme Court phases of ILDA's history. At this point, however, the first thing that needed to be done was for us to become a registered trade union. This in itself was a difficult and time-consuming task.

The registration of trade unions and the regulation of matters such as rule changes for those trade unions are matters controlled by the Registrar of Friendly Societies. This registry is, in fact, a section of the Department of Enterprise, Trade and Employment. Before a union can apply for a negotiating licence or claim 'excepted body' status (an 'excepted body' is a union that is, under a range of tight qualification criteria, excepted from the requirement of holding a negotiating licence — ILDA would later claim 'excepted body' status), it must first of all become a registered trade union. In order to do this, it must submit rules that comply with a raft of legislation, much of which dates back to the 1800s. The rules will then be assessed by the Registrar who, when satisfied, will issue a trade union certificate entitling the body to describe itself as a trade union and to go on to the next stage of seeking a licence or 'excepted body' status. The task of putting together rules for the proposed new union was one that fell to me. In the two weeks between the initial proposal to form a new union and the re-convened hearing to make that decision formally, I produced a document that was the 'Constitution & Membership', or rules, of the new union. It was a trying task, but for guidance I studied the rules of a number of existing unions; I found much in the rules of the Irish Airline Pilots' Association (IALPA — now a Branch of IMPACT) that was particularly useful. In any event, by the time the meeting to decide on whether or not to establish ILDA had re-convened, we had a proposed rule book and legal advice that would be useful in what was to follow.

The Formation of ILDA

On 28 September 1998, the NLDC reconvened to consider whether or not drivers would form their own trade union and cease to be members of SIPTU and the NBRU respectively. As usual, the meeting was attended by delegates from all depots, and the proposal was discussed openly and honestly. All delegates present, without exception, were agreed that SIPTU and the NBRU had not reflected the views of drivers on key issues in the ongoing negotiations. In addition, all expressed suspicion and mistrust of where these unions were bringing drivers in this process. When I spoke to put the proposal formally, I was again supported by John Courtney. On the day, nineteen of the twenty-five present formally resigned from their unions and joined the new association — the Irish Locomotive Drivers' Association (ILDA).

The following day, I rang Tony Tobin to tell him personally that I had resigned from SIPTU. He already knew. The conversation was short and curt. I attended for work in the morning and was soon approached by the local manager's assistant, Brendan Smith, who advised me that there were meetings in Dublin the following day and that all SIPTU and NBRU driver representatives were to attend. I told him that I was no longer the SIPTU representative in Athlone and that I had, in fact, resigned from SIPTU totally.

And then something that we had been waiting for over four years to happen did happen. ICTU wrote to Finbarr giving him a date for the hearing of the complaint against SIPTU after Finbarr and other complainants had left SIPTU to join ILDA. It was incredible. Cynical even. Nevertheless, Finbarr prepared for the hearing. Until, that is, he got another letter from ICTU Assistant General Secretary Tom Wall on 25 November 1998. It read:

> I understand from SIPTU that you are no longer a member of that union. If this is the case the appeals procedures of Congress are no longer open to you.

And that was it. SIPTU had confirmed to ICTU that Finbarr was no longer one of its members, and the appeal could not therefore be heard. We were henceforth to be treated, rightly, as other than members of SIPTU. At least, until it suited SIPTU. In 2001 we joined the ATGWU and it then suited SIPTU General Secretary John McDonnell to complain to ICTU — on 6 March 2001, two and a half years later — that we were actually SIPTU members in arrears. ICTU conveniently ignored its 1998 letter and agreed with SIPTU.

In any event, in September 1998 drivers began to join the new union, ILDA, in some numbers. Within a couple of weeks, over 30 per cent of all the mainline drivers were ILDA members. Although they generally resigned from SIPTU or the NBRU on joining, stopping Iarnród Éireann from paying their money direct from their wages to their now former union would be a long and difficult task. It should have been a simple process. Pro forma letters to Iarnród Éireann were drafted and supplied to new members to be signed. These letters advised the employer that the worker had resigned from the union mentioned and was formally authorising Iarnród Éireann to stop the payroll deductions to that union (Iarnród Éireann was also approached in writing by the ILDA treasurer about setting up payroll check-offs for ILDA members. It ignored the letter. ILDA members then agreed to pay their subscriptions to ILDA by monthly standing order from their bank accounts). Iarnród Éireann replied to each of the letters by asking ILDA members to 'clarify' their request 'in the context' of Iarnród Éireann's 'collective agreements with our recognised trade unions' and by failing to stop the payments in the interim period. I believe that this approach by Iarnród Éireann had two objectives:

- To confuse, frighten or intimidate the member by the use of legalese, and to sow doubts in members' minds regarding their clear entitlements in this matter;
- To begin the process of creating excessive and unnecessary paperwork for the new union and its inexperienced interim officers (ILDA would hold its first Branch Committee elections in November 1998, two months after the union was formed).

Many members were somewhat confused on receipt of these letters but not a single one that we are aware of failed to respond to this management ploy as requested. Management soon began receiving second letters from the members, 'clarifying' their requests. Typically they stated that the member was 'aware that I have a constitutional right to be a member of a trade union or not to be as I see fit. Reluctantly I have now come to the conclusion that I have not received the representation I deserve within SIPTU (or the NBRU as appropriate), and as such I have resigned from that union.'

However, in almost all cases, this still did not suffice. Management now responded with silence — in some cases, an interminable silence that continued for months and even years. Some members wrote more letters threatening management with legal action for breach of the Payment of Wages Act 1991, which requires employers to stop any deductions from an employee's wages on receipt of a written request. This usually, but not always, did the job, and management then finally complied with its legal obligations, and stopped the deductions. Other members took a more direct route. For example, my friend Tom O'Brien received a letter from Tim O'Connor in the human resources office. When Tom called Tim in his office, and demanded an explanation as to why his earnings were being misappropriated by management, he was referred to John Keenan. John initially began to enter into a debate with Tom about the overall position. Tom, however, was having none of it, and demanded that the deductions stop forthwith. They did.

This was just one example of the management response to the formation of ILDA. Two other examples demonstrate the SIPTU/NBRU response. Both occurred early in the initial recruitment campaign. In order to recruit as many drivers as possible, it was necessary for a number of us to travel to various depots and explain our position to our fellow drivers. It had been our intention that we would do this in a calm atmosphere of mutual respect, with any differences being discussed frankly among colleagues. However, the NBRU in Cork had different ideas. The NBRU has fewer than 3,000 members. A union of that size will obviously feel any loss of membership more acutely than, say, SIPTU, with over 200,000 members. It is perhaps not surprising, therefore, that the NBRU was ready to declare war on its colleagues in the new union — a war that has not abated since.

On Saturday, 10 October 1998, Finbarr Masterson, Thomas McDonnell and I drove to Cork in acceptance of an invitation from a number of Cork drivers. John Courtney was travelling by train to Thurles, where we would pick him up. Before we got to Thurles, John called us from the train to say that Liam Tobin, the Assistant General Secretary of the NBRU with specific responsibility for the rail workers within that union, was travelling to Cork, obviously with the intention of attending the meeting. We called one of the drivers who had invited us to Cork and he was genuinely surprised by this. He did mention, however, that NBRU representatives in particular were very edgy in Cork, and that there seemed to be a lot of planning going on behind the scenes for that night's meeting. On arrival in Cork, we had some time to spare, and made our way to the station to test the water. When I entered the drivers' mess room, I was welcomed with warm handshakes from the two drivers present. One of these drivers was Christy Holbrook, an NBRU member. He invited us to sit down and explained that Liam Tobin had arrived and had been shepherded away by a couple of NBRU reps. He explained that he was unable to attend the meeting, his arrangements having been scuppered by arrangements made by the most senior management in Dublin, specifically the Inter-City manager, Joe Walsh, to release some of the more vocal NBRU representatives. Christy was very annoyed at what he referred to as this 'collusion' between management and the unions to destroy our meeting. He then stared straight at me and asked, 'Brendan, do you have a hidden agenda or are you really this interested in drivers?' We had been aware of this 'hidden agenda' guff almost from the outset. The easy thing about accusing someone of having a hidden agenda — and the reason why it is so hard to defend yourself against it — is that it is supposed to be hidden. I had no answer other than to look Christy right back in the eye and assure him that the only motivation anyone involved in ILDA had was trying to give train drivers fair, open and democratic representation. Christy Holbrook is not one to suffer fools gladly which is why I was delighted when he again shook my hand, asked me for an application form and joined ILDA there and then. He would later be the first president of ILDA and would be my friend and confidant until he eventually had to leave the railway through ill-health after the ten-week dispute in 2000.

Buoyed by this success, we took the short walk across the Glanmire Road to the CIÉ Sports and Social Club building for the meeting. The meeting was held in a very small room upstairs. There were thirty-six Cork drivers in total, of whom approximately half were in attendance, which was quite good when you take into consideration those working. Liam Tobin was there, and I sat opposite him. Someone asked why Liam Tobin was in attendance as this meeting was supposedly for drivers only. Brian Wakefield explained that he had invited Liam to be present. A row immediately began. It was a taste of things to come. I commenced my input by outlining the reasons why ILDA had been formed. As I attempted to raise each point, I was heckled by three particular drivers (all NBRU members) and by Liam Tobin. The meeting soon lurched out of control and was reduced to a shouting match when Liam Tobin told the attendance that I was interested in 'management jobs' with Irish Rail. This was a reference to a period I had served as a relief supervisor in the office shortly after my arrival in Athlone. This period had ended when the job in which I was relieving was advertised on a full-time basis and I told the interview panel that I was withdrawing all interest in that job. I returned to full-time train-driving duties forthwith to concentrate on those and my union activity. However, it was clear from this, and other things that were being said, that the NBRU had decided to adopt an approach to ILDA that consisted of personalised invective directed at me. Unfortunately we failed to deal with this approach adequately on the night. After just over an hour, the shambles was complete when a band began music downstairs and nearly blew us out through the roof. The meeting broke up before we could even produce our forms or literature. Later, over a few pints, it became clear that the majority of drivers present were disappointed with the meeting but felt that it had been hijacked by the NBRU with the able assistance of Irish Rail. Another invitation was issued to us on different terms.

Cork was eventually to become an ILDA stronghold, when half of the drivers in Ireland's second depot eventually joined us, making ILDA the biggest drivers' body in that depot. As a result, many of the most significant events relating to ILDA would have a definite Cork dimension, and many of our most committed members would come from Cork. In addition, we would never again respond so incapably to such hijackings.

One of the issues used by the NBRU that night in Cork would become the issue upon which SIPTU would launch its first attack on me as ILDA spokesman. When it came, it was quite nasty and ended only when lawyers became involved. The previous year, around the time when I was sounded out on becoming Branch President of SIPTU's Railway Services Division, SIPTU had advertised in a national newspaper for a panel of candidates from which future vacancies for SIPTU branch secretaries would be filled. I was aware that my successful challenge to the SIPTU leadership on matters such as the taxation issue at the Ennis conference would not have gone down well at the top of the ivory tower. I sought the advice of Tony Tobin, who was supportive of me and suggested I apply. He believed that those in authority in SIPTU were too big to allow past criticisms by me to deflect them from treating my application to join such a panel fairly. I decided I would apply on the basis that, if successful, I would simply be put on a list to be considered further if a definite and suitable vacancy arose. Accordingly, I was required to attend at an assessment in the Great Southern Hotel, Galway. At this assessment, which was attended by over a hundred others and was just one of a number of such assessments held nationwide, I was required to submit written texts on matters relating to trade union affairs and organising. I decided to address the issues honestly and not to attempt simply to write what I thought the reader might like to read. This resulted in my being called for an initial interview. There were two men on the interview panel, one of whom was Des Geraghty. The interview didn't go well and it was clear to me that there were fundamental differences between how Des Geraghty interpreted the role of a modern union in the workforce and how I interpreted it. Although the interview was cordial at all times, it was clear to me that this was one panel on which I would not be finding myself. This was confirmed a short time later by letter from Liberty Hall.

Now, approximately one year later, this episode was to be used against me by the very man who had encouraged me to apply in the first place, Tony Tobin. One morning, I was in Connolly Station in the drivers' mess room when my attention was drawn to a huge notice on the SIPTU notice board. It was at least twice the size of the normal A4 notices, and dominated the glass-fronted notice board. The notice dealt with the formation of ILDA. It did not name me but did say that one of the key people involved in the formation of ILDA had 'recently' applied for a 'job' in SIPTU. The implication was that ILDA was being set up solely because this person had been unsuccessful in his attempts to get that 'job'. The signature at the bottom was that of Tony Tobin. I was absolutely flabbergasted. Despite disagreements with Tony on most issues regarding the union, I had felt that we had a fairly close personal friendship. However, this clear personal attack meant that he fell spectacularly in my estimation; he has not risen since. Neither was I prepared to take this attack lying down.

Tony received a letter from solicitors acting on my behalf. Because he had not actually named me in the notice, the letter outlined that I, and many workers in Iarnród Éireann, were of the view that the circular, which had by now been reproduced nationwide, referred to me. Tony was invited to give a written assurance, within a specified time period, that the circular did not, in fact, refer to me. Failure to do so would lead us to the conclusion that it did indeed refer to me. It was also clear that any repeat of the pernicious innuendo in another circular would immediately be challenged in the courts. The notice was never repeated.

In November 1998, ILDA held its first elections for a Branch Committee. The elections were carried out by a secret postal ballot of our membership, which was then 108 or approximately 40 per cent of all mainline drivers employed by Irish Rail. Christy Holbrook became our first President, with John Courtney from Inchicore his assistant, Brian Dunphy and Gerry Hughes became treasurers and I, with fifty-eight of the votes, became the Secretary. The Branch Committee was completed by the Chairmen of our divisions, Ken Fox — Cork; Dave Healy — Limerick; Tony Collier — Drogheda; Kevin Connolly — Dundalk; Hugh McCarthy — Inchicore; and my friend Finbarr Masterson for the West of Ireland. ILDA had its Branch Committee in place. At this point, our membership had already eclipsed the driver membership of the badly faltering NBRU and was on a par with that in SIPTU. SIPTU and the NBRU were getting ready to hit back. On Tuesday, 24 November 1998, just days after our Executive Committee was put in place, they did.

SIPTU and the NBRU Fight Back

This increase in membership occurred despite the difficulties our members were having in stopping their contributions to SIPTU and the NBRU, and also despite the increasing belief that being an ILDA member was going to be a recipe for some 'special' treatment from management. I myself was to be the subject of some of this 'special' treatment in July 1999, resulting in the first work stoppage involving ILDA, and ultimately leading us to the High Court and Supreme Court. Before that, however, SIPTU and the NBRU had a stoppage of their own in mind.

The haemorrhage of drivers from those unions to ILDA was causing great concern, particularly in the NBRU, which already had a very small membership base to support its bureaucracy. It was apparently decided that something would have to be done to counteract the impression that those unions would not strike. As a result, drivers on the SIPTU/NBRU negotiating committee came up with the idea not to go on strike, but to go sick! And so an 'issue' was chosen to provoke this sick day. The members of the Garda Síochána could not lawfully go on strike, but they had absented themselves from work the previous year on sick leave in what became known as the 'Blue Flu'. In the same way, the media were to dub this escapade the 'Choo Choo Flu'. We in ILDA had a number of problems with such a tactic. Firstly, the supposed issue in dispute (an obscure statement by the Chairman of CIÉ, Brian Joyce) was not an issue that warranted turning on the television news, never mind stopping trains for a day. As the *Evening Herald* stated on the sick day itself: 'It certainly suits them (SIPTU/NBRU) to allow their members out to flex their muscle in a single day protest and regain whatever ground they may be losing to Brendan Ogle.' Secondly, even if there had been a real issue, SIPTU and the NBRU were, unlike us, fully fledged trade unions with negotiating licences and all the protections and rights to strike that go with them. Why didn't they simply ballot their members and do it properly?

Of course, nobody asked for our views. We were not in unions with licences and therefore had no legal protection should we support this madness. We quickly formed the view that this was nothing other than an attempt firstly to address the perception that SIPTU/NBRU would never go on strike (without SIPTU/NBRU actually doing anything as organisations), and secondly to drag us into an action that would leave us unprotected in a legal and employment sense, and at the mercy of our employer.

Accordingly, we approached this issue in a very forthright way, which, in hindsight, while being totally principled, was also politically naive. We slammed our colleagues for their attempts to defraud the state and the travelling public with a lie — that is, that they were sick when they clearly were not. In addition, we slammed SIPTU and the NBRU for refusing to ballot their members and have a proper strike on this supposed issue, and we threatened to work anyway. The result was three or four days of major national publicity with drivers apparently at war with each other, while SIPTU, the NBRU and Iarnród Éireann all hid. The leaders of SIPTU and the NBRU had attempted to extricate themselves from this mess by saying that they had been 'ordered' by their members to leave a meeting room while their members plotted this action. Some leaders!

We did other things as well. On the day before the Choo Choo Flu bug struck down the SIPTU and NBRU members, we called on the minister to intervene and on the unions to repudiate this action. Amazingly, nothing happened. Everybody just watched and let it go ahead. We met in Dublin at 8pm that evening to discuss the position. At that stage, nobody had intervened, heeded or even welcomed our calls for this stoppage to be called off. It was obviously going ahead. We had two simple choices. We could come into work and worsen an already bad situation with our colleagues, or we could stay at home. In the event, following an extremely difficult meeting, we decided to leave the decision to each individual member. The issue, or non-issue, was not something that affected us, and the tactic was disgraceful so we could not support the action. However, if our members, in order to maintain some semblance of a relationship with their colleagues, did stay at home, they were not, under any circumstances, to go sick. They were to take the hit and lose a day's pay for the stupidity of SIPTU/NBRU. They were also to take the risk that Irish Rail would, in fact, come after them for absence from duty. This is what most of our members did on the day. SIPTU and NBRU members rang in sick and even attempted, in almost every case, to claim a day's sick pay. They did not get it.

That evening, RTÉ's Prime Time did a special on the day's events.

Tim Hastings, the then Industrial Correspondent with the *Irish Independent*, forecast that this would be the last stoppage and that the drivers, having 'let off steam', would now revert to talks with the company and conclude them successfully without a further whimper. He was right. They did. Meanwhile, our membership continued to increase.

It took only a few months for ILDA to become the biggest body representing mainline drivers (excluding DART drivers). Initially, we did not concentrate much effort on trying to organise the DART. The issues that had led to the emergence of ILDA were not of much concern to DART drivers in the two depots of Fairview and Bray. In addition, DART drivers had just succeeded in securing their own bargaining unit — separate from their mainline counterparts — for the ongoing negotiations. Initially, for these reasons, the fledgling ILDA concentrated on building support within what was hitherto the bargaining unit for mainline drivers. Now, by the spring and summer of 1999, ILDA had 40 per cent membership within that grade, outstripping both SIPTU and the NBRU.

The registration process with the Registrar of Friendly Societies was, however, taking longer than had been anticipated. Some members believed that this process was being influenced at a political or social partnership level. At that point, however, there was little evidence to support the belief that ILDA was being subjected to such outside influences. However, that was about to change.

The Right to Represent a Colleague

The events that brought about the change arose out of the denial of representation in individual cases on discipline and grievance. For generations, workers in Irish Rail have had the right to be represented by a trade union official or a chosen colleague in matters of internal discipline or grievance. This entitlement reflected various statutory codes of practice drawn up from time to time by government ministers with responsibility for industrial affairs. Although I had lost the entitlement to represent workers as a SIPTU representative, since ILDA had been formed I had continued to represent some as a colleague. On 8 July 1999 — ten months after ILDA was formed — Irish Rail decided that it had a problem with this.

Two of my colleagues — Darragh Brophy and Willie Fitzpatrick —
had ongoing issues of a relatively minor nature where they had both
nominated me to represent them as a colleague. On the morning of 8 July
1999, Willie phoned and told me that he had just received a call from
Brendan Smith who was a senior clerk in the Athlone rail office. Brendan
Smith had advised Willie of the time and date for his hearing but had
further advised him that he could attend with any colleague except
Brendan Ogle. I immediately called Darragh who confirmed that he had
received a similar message, specifying that I — and I alone — no longer
enjoyed the entitlement to represent workers in Iarnród Éireann, as a
colleague. This came as a complete shock. I actually thought that there
had to be some mistake. So I rang Brendan Smith who confirmed that I
no longer had the entitlement to represent workers as a colleague. He told
me that this message had come from the human resources department in
Iarnród Éireann. This was John Keenan's department so I asked to speak
to him. On being informed that John Keenan was out of the country on
holidays, I made the point to Brendan Smith that this entitlement was a
long-standing one that was fully included in our procedures. He told me
that he was simply relaying the message received.

As I drove my train that evening, the full implications of this decision
were beginning to sink in. Not alone were my colleagues' representation
entitlements being denied but I, alone of over 5,000 employees, had been
singled out as the only employee in Iarnród Éireann to be treated in this
way. It was the clearest case of individual discrimination that I could
imagine. Overnight, the words 'anybody but Brendan Ogle' played on my
mind over and over again. The next morning, Friday, 9 July, I called
Brendan Smith again first thing. I again asked him to confirm that I alone
was henceforth to be denied the entitlement to represent colleagues on
matters of individual discipline or grievance. When he did so, I told him
that this was an issue of discrimination and gross victimisation and that,
as it was causing me great annoyance and distress, I wanted it revoked in
writing immediately. I told him that I would be turning up for work at
3pm that day and that I wanted a written withdrawal of this disgraceful
decision at that point. When he asked what would be the consequences of
a failure by the company to provide such a letter, I replied that the
discrimination was so blatantly wrong and improper that I could not

possibly envisage that Iarnród Éireann would maintain its position, as it was clearly some misunderstanding. No threat was made at any time. In finishing the call, Brendan Smith said that he would contact the relevant people but that he could not see my receiving such a letter at 3pm or at any other time. A short time later, I telephoned one of my inspectors, who is responsible for ensuring my fitness for duty — Denis (Dinny) Minogue. Dinny was in Sligo when I called. I outlined the nature of the decision that had apparently been taken, and I told him that I felt as annoyed and upset about it as anybody would in the circumstances. He was as astonished as I was.

When I arrived for work that afternoon, I signed on as normal. My immediate supervisor on duty was Alan Hughes. I enquired of Alan as to whether there was a letter for me. By the look on his face, I gathered that he knew what I was talking about. However, there was no letter. I then produced a letter from my own pocket and handed it to him. It read as follows:

Yesterday, 9 July 1999, I was advised by Mr Brendan Smith in the District Office Athlone that Iarnród Éireann management had decided that I was no longer permitted to act as a representative if nominated to do so by any of my colleagues. Further I was advised that this decision related specifically to me only and that any other staff member could continue to operate in the agreed fashion. It is therefore clear from these remarks that Iarnród Éireann management have decided to pinpoint me for discrimination and victimisation and I feel that no employee of any company should be treated in this way. I am now informing you my employer that this victimisation is upsetting me and causing me undue stress and annoyance. This is completely unnecessary and totally of your making and I am asking that you now rescind the remarks made yesterday and assure me in writing that this discrimination is at an end.

The letter was copied to Dinny Minogue, to Iarnród Éireann's saftety manager, Ted Corcoran, and to my solicitor, Donal Spring, who, fortunately as things turned out, had advised me to make any complaint I had in writing, to prevent any ambiguity arising.

Having presented Alan with the letter, I went into the drivers' mess room next door. Unusually for that time of day, the room was occupied. Martin Kinahan, a driver from Inchicore and an ILDA member, was sitting there in his uniform. As it was totally unusual for a Dublin driver to be in Athlone at that time of the day, I asked Martin what he was working. He replied 'the up Westport' (trains to Dublin are referred to as 'up' trains and trains from Dublin as 'down' trains). In fact, I was scheduled to drive that particular train that day. On hearing this, Martin asked why then had he been asked to come here. I was about to tackle Alan Hughes on this topic when he entered the mess room with my letter in his hand.

Alan asked me whether I was refusing to work my train. I explained that I had signed on duty, had not refused to work anything but that I was obliged as a duty of my employment to advise the company in advance of my working any train when I was upset or feeling similarly disposed. The letter was my written compliance with my duties as a driver. He asked me whether I intended to drive the up Westport, which was now no more than fifteen minutes away. I told him that now that I had fulfilled my obligations in advising the company of my predicament, I did intend to. Alan left the mess room to bring the letter upstairs to local management (Brendan Smith). While he was gone, Martin explained how he had ended up in Athlone. As normal for an Inchicore driver, he had been shunting a cement train in Tullamore, twenty-three miles from Athlone, when he received a call over the train radio from his inspector in Inchicore before 2pm. In this call he was asked to leave the cement train in Tullamore and travel on the 14.00 hrs passenger train from Tullamore to Athlone as 'no driver was available to work the up Westport'. As passenger trains obviously take precedence over cement trains, Martin naturally complied without further question. It had therefore come as quite a surprise to him when I turned up in the mess room.

Alan returned to the mess room a short time later with another more senior inspector, George Behan. George asked me if I was feeling ill. I told him that I had a letter outlining precisely how I was feeling, and I handed him a copy. He began to question me on the letter. I had no intention of entering into a debate on anything so I simply reiterated the contents of the letter. George, having read the letter, looked at me over his glasses. 'So you're upset, are you, Brendy?' he asked.

I replied that of course I was upset — wouldn't he be upset if they were trying to discriminate against him?

George looked at me solemnly and said, 'Well, Brendy, I'm afraid if you're upset I can't let you go with the train.'

I cut him off in his apologies and told him that I understood that he had his job to do and that it wasn't he who should be doing the apologising. He immediately turned to Martin and asked would he drive the train. Martin's response was quick and to the effect that he would not go with the train and that he was disgusted that he had been landed in this situation by his supervisors and management in Dublin. He went off into Alan's office to ring his manager to give him a piece of his mind.

The 'up Westport' duly arrived in Athlone driven by my good friend and colleague, Tom O'Brien. Tom was expecting me to relieve him but was met instead by George on the platform. George asked Tom would he go back up to Dublin again, and Tom enquired as to my whereabouts. George explained the position, to which Tom replied that if I had been upset by discrimination, then so had he. Not alone would he not work this train back up to Dublin, but he would work no further trains any day until this matter was satisfactorily resolved. This obviously presented a real problem. The passengers were detrained off the up Westport and eventually bussed or taken by taxi to their destinations.

By now, all the clerks and supervisors and the station master were congregated in Alan's cramped office. From the point of view of trains stopping and passengers being inconvenienced, the situation deteriorated fairly rapidly. As Tom arrived in the mess room, I explained my situation and Martin did likewise. Tom was furious. George appeared back in the mess room to speak to Martin. As I didn't want to be in any way accused of influencing Martin, I immediately left and made for the relative quiet of the platform. However, I was quickly joined by Martin. He explained that George wanted him to work the now-empty train back up to Dublin, and asked whether I had any objections. I replied that I had not given him any advice to date and that I wasn't going to start now. On this basis, Martin agreed to work the empty train to Heuston. Nevertheless, it was clear that the situation was spiralling out of control.

When the next driver arrived on duty in Athlone to work the 15.55 passenger train to Ballina, I made sure that I was well out of the way. As the sun was shining, the sanctuary of the platform removed me from the many and varied managers and supervisors who were by now milling about. As it was explained to me later, the driver concerned, an ILDA member, signed on as normal but was obviously then advised of what had occurred. The driver concerned was, in fact, Darragh Brophy — one of the workers who had been denied the entitlement to be represented by me in the first place. The result was inevitable. He refused to go with his train. When the train arrived in Athlone, the passengers were again detrained and transported to their destinations by bus or taxi. Half an hour later, another driver appeared in Athlone. By now, the word had spread and there were so many people milling about that he immediately became aware of the circumstances. He too refused to drive. The media were now aware of the disruptions, and radio stations were carrying updates on their drive-time shows. This actually had a negative effect on services, as word spread to various depots and drivers. I was approached by George Behan who advised me that drivers of trains that were to leave Ballina and Westport had become aware of the disruption. He asked me to speak to them. I spoke to them both, in the presence of management, and simply outlined my position. I did not make any comment on disruption or on what I thought they should do. They both refused to work their respective trains.

As the evening wore on, the situation got worse and was in imminent danger of becoming a national stoppage as news naturally spread. I was more concerned with resolving the problem on a proper basis than with any spread of the action. I called Donal Spring to advise him of the circumstances. Donal had had some dealing with Aer Lingus' John Behan — an advisor to Minister Mary O'Rourke — and undertook to ring him. He quickly called back to say that he had spoken to John Behan, who had expressed surprise and no knowledge of the difficulty, but who had undertaken to make enquiries and see if he could help. I don't know if John Behan ever actually got involved, but certainly a dramatic solution was soon on its way. At 9.02pm, six hours after the difficulty had arisen, Brendan Smith appeared on the platform with an envelope. He called me aside and presented it to me. Its contents were short and to the point, and read:

I wish to make it clear to you that you are not and will not be discriminated against or victimised. You will be treated in the same manner and you will continue to have the same rights as any other locomotive driver.

It was signed and dated 9 July 1999. I was delighted. I had a quick word with a colleague who was beside me and immediately made my way to George Behan's office. I told him that I had now received a letter that had effectively rescinded the decision to discriminate against me and that I was greatly relieved at the assurances it contained. George asked me whether I continued to be upset and I answered in the negative. He therefore immediately advised me that he had no problem with restoring me to my driving duties.

Had I begun to believe that Iarnród Éireann would now start to act in good faith, I would have been sadly mistaken. Within a week, the company would score its most serious own goal to date, and begin a High Court action against the drivers who made up the new ILDA Executive. Before that, however, another disruption took place, this time in Cork, on Sunday, 11 July 1999.

Disruption in Cork

This disruption arose when all Cork drivers, the majority of whom were then members of SIPTU/NBRU, decided to utilise their rest day on that date. This followed an alleged non-payment of ILDA President Christy Holbrook, following his attendance as a witness — provided for in agreed procedure — at a serious accident enquiry on behalf of a SIPTU driver. When word of this spread in Cork, all the drivers involved decided to put aside their union allegiances and protest on 11 July 1999. The result was widespread disruption to mainline services in and out of Cork on that date.

The following week, I was working the crazy 2.25am shift in Athlone. This meant going to bed at around 7pm each evening in order to rise at that ungodly hour. On the evening of Thursday, 15 July, my mother arrived by train to stay with us for a few days. She was just in when the doorbell rang. When I opened it, I was surprised to see Brendan Smith standing at the door with a letter in his hand. He was ashen faced. I immediately knew that something serious was going on but foolishly invited him in instead of running him from the door. When we entered the sitting-room, he presented me with the letter and said that he had been 'told to deliver that personally'. It was a long legalistic letter — four full pages in total — and was written by John Keenan, clearly on and with legal advice. Much of the letter detailed 'evidence' that I was 'holding myself out' as a spokesperson for locomotive drivers, and accused me of 'incitement to breach of contract and acting contrary to statute'. Much of the letter's contents were not in dispute. However, the personalised nature of the attack immediately struck me. The letter concluded by seeking 'before Friday 16 July next (this was 7pm on 15 July) your written undertaking to desist...' from encouraging drivers to take part in a possible industrial action 'next weekend', and also an undertaking that I would effectively cease all activity on behalf of ILDA from that date. Finally, the threat was outlined: 'should such undertakings not be forthcoming by Friday the 16th inst. then the Company will immediately institute disciplinary sanction against you and reserves the right to pursue any legal remedy available to it to prevent any further unlawful work stoppages such remedy to include injunctive relief. I await hearing from you as a matter of urgency in any event on or before the 16th July 1999.'

I had asked Brendan Smith to leave when I saw the length of the letter. Accordingly, I read it alone and was stunned by its contents. Before I had time to compose myself, Pauline entered the sitting-room, saw my face, and insisted on reading the letter. It was to be a difficult evening. I attempted to contact Donal Spring but could not do so. I then called Fergus Finlay who was golfing. When I explained the situation to him, he immediately undertook to go home and try to contact Donal himself. Soon afterwards, Donal called me. I composed myself and read the entire letter. It was now after 8pm, just four hours before the deadline set for responding to this letter. He outlined his view that the growth of ILDA had obviously got management very worried indeed. He asked me about a stoppage on 18 July and I told him that there was not to be any stoppage on that date, as the issues in question (Cork and representation at enquiries) had been resolved. Finally, Donal warned me to be careful of my phone and undertook to respond to John Keenan on my behalf the following day. By the time I came off the phone, it was 9pm and I was obviously stressed and unable to sleep much. Accordingly, I did not go into work the following day at all.

The response from Donal Spring, on my behalf, was swift and to the point. It gave the company assurances that there would be no disruption on 18 July, and that neither I, nor any of my colleagues, had breached our contracts of employment, nor had we any intention of doing so. In addition, it confirmed our acceptance that, as ILDA had no negotiating licence, we could not benefit from the immunities of the Industrial Relations Act 1990. However, the letter had a sting in its tail. Following much painstaking research, the letter formally claimed 'excepted body' status under a section of the Trade Union Act 1941. Such status entitles 'excepted bodies' to negotiate the terms and conditions of their members, notwithstanding the fact that they do not hold negotiating licences, if they comply with certain qualification criteria. As outlined in the letter, the qualification criteria applicable were contained in section 6(3)(h) of the Trade Union Act 1941 amended by section 2 of the Trade Union Act 1942 which reads:

Extension of 'excepted body' in section 6 of the Act of 1941.

2.—In section 6 of the Act of 1941, the expression 'excepted body' shall include a body all the members of which are employed by the same employer and which carries on negotiations for the fixing of the wages or other conditions of employment of its own members (but of no other employees).

This claim of statutory negotiating status would have come as a bolt out of the blue for Iarnród Éireann and we were confident that we clearly fell within the legal definition. This definition was ultimately to be the cornerstone of lengthy actions in the High Court and on to the Supreme Court. However, for now it was our hope that the letter would allow us a breathing space in what was becoming a very difficult period. A further missive from John Keenan to me, on 20 July 1999, ensured that all-out war was to be pursued through the courts, causing great, totally unnecessary, and permanent damage to staff relations in Iarnród Éireann. The letter acknowledged the Spring response and even went so far as to acknowledge that 'services operated on Sunday July 18th, without any apparent organised failure to report for rostered duty....' However, this was obviously not good enough. Minds had been made up, so a shift of the goalposts was required. The letter outlined that I and 'other espoused and recorded members of the grouping' would now be sued for damages for 'previous actions'. It was as if management were actually disappointed that no stoppage had taken place on 18 July and had now decided to concoct some other reason to pursue what turned out to be eleven employees through the courts — and not any old court either. When notice of action was formally served, with the assistance of Iarnród Éireann's in-house solicitors, it was in the High Court. The intention could not have been clearer. We were to be destroyed personally and professionally, and if our wives and children were to be affected, so be it. In case there was any doubt, I was also to be pursued through serious disciplinary action within my employment. On 27 July, I received a disciplinary charge, dated 23 July, which demanded a response within seven days and was unlike any of the many other disciplinary charges on which I had represented colleagues in Iarnród Éireann. This advice was astonishing. In essence, Iarnród Éireann wanted it both ways. The disciplinary advice replicated the charges that Iarnród Éireann had said would now be pursued through the courts. It seemed to me that it had become company policy to get me one way if not the other. Not alone were our homes and families under threat, but my job was now in serious question too.

On 28 July 1999, Iarnród Éireann issued a plenary summons. The following day, ILDA formally and finally became a registered trade union. Although my solicitors made it clear throughout that it was inappropriate for Iarnród Éireann to pursue parallel disciplinary and legal actions, Iarnród Éireann, foolishly as it turned out, was not for turning. This left me in a situation where I had to go through the charade of being seen to co-operate with an internal disciplinary action that I and my advisors now knew would ultimately be decided in the High Court in any case. By now, I was in daily contact with Daniel Spring & Company Solicitors, and with Brian Duncan in particular. Brian was unbelievably helpful to me and continually reassured me at darker moments. Nevertheless, the stress was having a serious effect on my family and on me. On 27 August, while awaiting the disciplinary action, I was admitted to Portiuncula Hospital in Ballinasloe, having collapsed at home. I spent a number of days in hospital, and even that became the subject of written correspondence between both sets of solicitors.

When I was discharged, Iarnród Éireann immediately recommenced its efforts to hold the disciplinary hearing. It was my view that, given the uniqueness of the charges and the overall legal context, I was entitled to legal representation at the hearing. Iarnród Éireann, however, repeatedly denied this representation. This was a major bone of contention between the parties and remained unresolved when the hearing actually took place on 30 September 1999. I had called a number of witnesses, including John Keenan, to appear at the hearing. I had called him because I was convinced that it was he who had been instrumental in pursuing the actions — legal and disciplinary — against me. If I was right in this, the action would be shown to be outside procedure, as it should properly have emanated from my immediate supervisor. It was not and is not permitted for any senior manager to vent his spleen against a particular employee and simply to use his subordinates as tools in a disciplinary exercise. I was determined to expose this 'procedure'.

Accordingly, on 30 September 1999, I met with my solicitor, Brian Duncan, my barrister, Cathy Maguire, and with my colleague, ILDA President Christy Holbrook. We discussed the format for the meeting in the full expectation that Brian and Cathy would not be allowed to attend. Nevertheless, we made our way to the station. When we entered the hearing, we found that Gerry Glynn, my accuser, had appointed himself judge. I outlined that I had my legal advisors outside. He refused to allow them to enter the room. I went outside and advised Brian and Cathy that, as expected, they were excluded. They went off to the Prince of Wales Hotel in Athlone to await developments. Having confirmed with Gerry Glynn that all witnesses, particularly John Keenan, were in attendance, I advised him that, in my view, Christy was ill-equipped to represent me on such serious charges, and that therefore I was asking him to remain silent but to write everything down.

I was presented with the 'book of evidence'. This was the first time I had received any documentation to support the charges against me. The book — and it was a book, containing five sections — was made up of correspondence between the parties and a whole series of transcripts of media interviews I had given at various points. These interviews were fairly standard stuff and didn't contain any reference to my calling for the decapitation of management, civil disobedience, genocide or national anarchy. From management's point of view, however, they might as well have. I was expected to answer all five charges based on this volume of documentation, almost on the spot. I immediately noticed a letter from John Keenan to his subordinate, Gerry Glynn, dated 23 July 1999 — which was, of course, also the date of the disciplinary advice — outlining that he had not received the undertakings sought in his letter dated 15 July, which was enclosed. On this basis, Gerry Glynn was induced to set about his action against me.

I was sorely tempted to call John Keenan immediately as a witness. However, I held my patience. I looked for an adjournment to consider the evidence. This is naturally provided for in the procedure. Gerry Glynn responded that he would give me half an hour. I almost laughed out loud. I explained that half an hour was totally insufficient time to prepare a proper response to such a weight of documentation and I would require the fullest time provided for in procedure. I suggested four weeks. He objected and began to ask me questions relevant to the charges. I sat in silence while Christy simply recorded the questions. After a few minutes of this, Gerry Glynn became frustrated and 'advised' me to reconsider my approach. I maintained my silence. He then proposed calling witnesses. I spoke to explain that they were my witnesses and they were for me to call as part of my defence at the appropriate time. As I had been denied time to consider the documentation presented, this was not an appropriate time to call them and I would not do so. He said something about the trouble the company had gone to to have them present and how they might not be so accommodating the next time. I didn't dignify the remark with any comment. Eventually, Gerry Glynn realised that he was going to get nowhere and said that he was adjourning the hearing to take advice.

The battle of wits was to continue for some time yet. On 4 October, I received a letter from Gerry Glynn, stating that he considered my 'request of an adjournment of four weeks to be excessive and, as the process has already been delayed in this case for various reasons [my being in hospital] I am not prepared to tolerate a further delay to this extent. Accordingly, I am proposing to reconvene the hearing on Monday next 11th October in the District Manager's Office in Heuston Station … as far as possible I will arrange to have your requested witnesses available on that date'. However, unknown to Gerry Glynn, the internal process was over.

While all this had been going on in respect to me, correspondence had been flying between Iarnród Éireann's solicitor, Michael Carroll, and our solicitors. In essence, this correspondence contained threats by Michael Carroll of action against us for a variety of spurious reasons, and claims by my solicitors that Iarnród Éireann could not conclude agreements without recourse to ILDA, coupled with a declaration that we would seek an injunction against Iarnród Éireann if the company acted improperly against ILDA or me. If Iarnród Éireann and its solicitor thought that we were bluffing, they were in for a surprise.

My contacts and meetings with Brian Duncan and Cathy Maguire were now almost daily. I will always appreciate the colossal efforts, way above and beyond the call of duty, which Cathy and everyone at Daniel Spring & Company Solicitors gave to us through this extremely difficult time. At a time when many in the legal profession are the butt of cynicism and criticism, I have to record that we received tremendous support and professionalism throughout. I dread to think what might have befallen us if it had been otherwise.

On Friday, 8 October, the last working day before Gerry Glynn's showdown, I boarded the 6.33am passenger train to Dublin to meet with Brian. All our efforts were about to bear fruit. I spent the morning in a rooftop room in the Spring offices on St Stephen's Green, parsing documents that were to make up my first affidavit in the High Court. Just before noon, Brian and I walked the short distance to the family law firm of Mervyn Taylor — the former Labour Party minister — to have the affidavit witnessed by a Commissioner for Oaths. Then, I got a taxi to Heuston Station to catch the lunchtime train home — I had work that evening — while Brian headed off to the High Court with my affidavit. While I was speeding through the pastures of Co. Offaly, Cathy Maguire and John Rogers SC were making their way to the court of Ms Justice Laffoy to seek an interlocutory injunction against Iarnród Éireann, restraining the company from pursuing its disciplinary action against me until all of these matters had been considered in the High Court action that was to follow. Just as the train left Clara station, I received a call from Brian telling me that I had been granted my injunction by order of the

High Court. For that moment, I felt like the King of Ireland. Iarnród Éireann's 'twin track' approach to get me was over. All the facts would now be decided on by the highest court in the land, and my colleagues who had no connection whatsoever with the stoppages of 9 and 11 July 1999 — but who were also being sued — would now have their day in court too. When the train arrived in Athlone, I was delighted to catch a glimpse of Gerry Glynn on the platform. From his pallor, it was clear that he had received the news. The stakes had been upped considerably.

Our advocate, John Rogers SC, had become involved in our case after Gerry Durcan SC had been forced to pull out. A former Attorney General of some renown, John Rogers had been appointed during the coalition government that featured Donal's brother Dick as Tánaiste. Donal had been delighted to secure his assistance with the case, and we had interpreted Donal's efforts to secure him as an indicator of his attachment to the case. None of us had much prior experience of dealing with solicitors, much less junior and senior counsel. At first, we found the various layers and workings of the legal profession cumbersome and unsettling. However, as the meetings wore on and we began to focus on the reality facing us — a High Court action against a state company — we came to appreciate the sheer professionalism and focus of the people with whom we were dealing.

The High Court

Iarnród Éireann, in issuing a law suit against the eleven named individuals who formed the National Executive Council (NEC) of ILDA, had accused us collectively and individually of 'instigating, organising, inciting and promoting industrial unrest' in Athlone on 9 July 1999 and Cork on 11 July 1999. This was a very serious position for us all to be in. We knew that we had done nothing wrong, so we were left with no option but to fight that case and defend ourselves. We received no help. None of our colleagues in SIPTU or the NBRU raised a voice to help us. Initially, none of the worker directors on the CIÉ board volunteered any assistance or protest on our behalf (Bill McCamley did eventually issue a statement, upon direct request from me, but it came too late; the rest of the worker directors refused Bill's invitation to sign it). No one in the government department responsible for Iarnród Éireann — Mary O'Rourke's

Department of Public Enterprise and Transport — saw fit to intervene. The eleven of us were alone save any support a hundred or so other members could lend us.

In addition to myself, the accused were:

- Christy Holbrook (as Christy was the first named defendant, the trial would be formally known as I*arnród Éireann v Holbrooke & Others*) — a married man from Cork with three children
- John Courtney — a single man in his thirties from Inchicore, who lived alone
- Finbarr Masterson — married with five children, and with thirty-five years of seniority in the grade
- Brian Dunphy — thirty-seven years of incident-free driving behind him; married to Nuala with nine children
- Ken Fox — a young Cork driver, recently married
- Dave Healy — Limerick-based driver from a family of railway workers; married to Patricia with a young family
- Tony Collier — Drogheda driver of many years' experience; married with a young family
- Kevin Connolly — Dundalk-based driver; married with school-going children
- Hugh McCarthy — Inchicore-based single driver, with a passion for working and maintaining steam trains and old railways in his spare time
- Gerry Hughes — a single man from Meath who came up through the works in Inchicore before becoming a mainline driver.

These were the men being challenged by a state company; facing impoverishment through a High Court trial; ignored by a minister who claimed a concern for the working people of Ireland; shunned by their colleagues in their hour of need; and whose worker directors, whom we had elected to represent us on the board, colluded to persecute by their inaction.

I am sure that many in Iarnród Éireann and beyond expected at least some of the eleven ordinary family men now being targeted to revisit their decision to support the fledgling ILDA and to run for cover, begging forgiveness. Not for the last time were they to be confounded. I am proud to record that, from the day the first National Executive of ILDA was elected, never, on any occasion, did any of those eleven men shirk or run for cover during their entire three-year term of office. It wasn't easy though and for many of the eleven the first test would be one that many a table-thumper in union halls had failed before— a hit in the pocket.

Even the basic day-to-day running of ILDA at that early stage cost individuals money. For some, this was nothing new. The NLDC was entirely a voluntary body, with no subscriptions collected. Since its formation, contacts with drivers in many locations had had to be maintained, and telephone bills had been paid by those making the call. In addition, any meetings invariably cost those attending a day's pay, in addition to travelling expenses. For some, private cars were pressed into use with little regard to running costs or wear and tear, not to mention inconvenience. Those involved had not continued with this for four years through any lack of conviction. Thus, when ILDA came into being, a unity of purpose was already reaching maturity, alongside a well-developed camaraderie. Once the High Court case became inevitable, it was necessary to broach the issue of money. Initial estimates from legal advisors were that the case might take two days and that a loss might see us sustain costs, all in, of £90,000. Obviously, this was a considerable sum for a new organisation, and there was simply no reserve there to meet it. We were asked to provide £30,000 up front to get the ball moving. Initially, we held an executive meeting in Tullamore to discuss the position. Prior to that meeting a small number of us had had a discussion about how we would raise the required £30,000. We anticipated one particular member having acute problems raising such money, and the intention was to seek lump-sum payments of £3,000 from the other ten. Obviously this was a sensitive matter. When the discussion in Tullamore opened, all present were asked for their suggestions. The first man to speak was the man who we had anticipated would be in difficulty. He said that there were eleven of us and that eleven £3,000s was £33,000. He had already taken out a five-year loan and we would have his £3,000 by the following Tuesday. That was it. No more discussion. The rest of us also undertook to raise £3,000 as soon as possible. My own came from a loan taken out over three years.

A general meeting of ILDA was called at which the overall position was put to the membership. I remember our treasurer, Brian Dunphy, one of the eleven, asking those in attendance to tell us if they thought we were getting in too deep. Nobody at the very well-attended meeting raised a voice. We outlined that the NEC would be coming up with £3,000 per man. We asked for the assistance of the wider membership with the rest. The meeting decided that, over time, each member would endeavour to donate £1,000 and that this, with a membership of 114, would see us over the £90,000 figure, with a bit to spare. It was on this basis that a decision was taken to proceed with our defence against Iarnród Éireann and, moreover, to pursue a counterclaim for recognition as an 'excepted body' with whom Iarnród Éireann, under section 55 of the Railways Act 1924, was compelled to negotiate. Of course, we were all confident that we could win the case against us, but the recognition claim was equally important. In trying to assess our prospects of that case we became familiar with assessments such as 'arguable case' and 'good stateable case'. Overall we felt that, with a fair wind, we could pull off a double victory and gain recognition without ever having to put a picket or protest of any sort on a gate.

From time to time, the case would come up for 'mention' in the High Court. I would always try to be there on these occasions. Initially I found the pomp and ceremony surrounding the court almost intoxicating. It was hard to believe that we, a group of train drivers simply taking a stand against our employer and our unions, were here at all. From time to time, other drivers, not in ILDA, would materialise in court to take in what was going on. If it ever concerned them, they did nothing about it.

And so, in November 1999, we came to a High Court trial. It had happened so quickly because both sides had agreed that an early trial was in their mutual interest. The day before the trial began, we assembled in the Aisling Hotel in Dublin. We would all sit together throughout the court hearing, but beforehand, with eleven of us involved, it felt like a team preparing for some big match. We all recognised that this was a defining moment for ILDA and for us all as individuals. If we won everything possible, recognition for ILDA would have been achieved almost without a shot being fired in anger. If we lost everything possible, not alone was ILDA finished as a union, but we were in dire straits as individuals. And there were numerous possibilities between those two extremes. The last piece of news we received the day before the trial began told us just how determined Iarnród Éireann was to win. It confirmed that Peter Charleton SC, the renowned prosecutor of some of the most prominent criminal cases in recent Irish legal history, was in place as the company's leading advocate; Roddy Horan would simply play a 'supporting role'. If any of us wondered whether someone somewhere in management could be having second thoughts about going down this route, here was confirmation that they were not. The knives were well and truly out!

Day One

The trial was to be longer than expected. A case that was estimated to take two days of court time in fact took seven. The judge who was assigned to the case was Mr Justice Iarlaith O'Neill who, we were advised, was a relative newcomer to the High Court bench. In any event, he showed a keen interest in the case throughout and, through his occasional questioning of witnesses, seemed early on to have a real grasp of the issues at hand. The first of these issues was the question of who the defendants were. Just as it was clearly intended by Iarnród Éireann to pursue us as individuals, we were anxious that ILDA, the union, should be a defendant. John Rogers began the case by arguing that as the eleven defendants formed the actual Executive Council of ILDA, and as the charges related to alleged activities in respect of ILDA, ILDA should be a defendant in the case. Iarnród Éireann argued forcibly against this. However, once the formal certificate of registration of ILDA as a trade union was presented to the judge, he immediately added ILDA as a defendant in the case. This was important to us because, although we were insistent that the charges against us had no basis, nevertheless we were anxious that if wrongdoing were subsequently to be found, it would be found in respect of our activities in ILDA and not as individual citizens. This would have been impossible had ILDA not been a defendant. Now that it was, we could breathe a little bit easier.

As witnesses began to be called, we became engrossed in the case. After initial statements and legal argument, the first witness was John

Keenan. Peter Charleton spent most of the first day with John Keenan in the box. Throughout the day, he backed up his treatment of us by outlining his unbridled dismay at the emergence of ILDA and the perceived threat this brought to Iarnród Éireann. However I felt that his tone and language were confrontational throughout and, from my position in the court, I formed the impression that this was not playing particularly well with the judge. The eleven defendants were seated together along two benches in Court 13, facing the witness box, with the judge seated to our left at the top of the court room. Between us and John Keenan in the box were the various benches for the advocates, and at the rear of the room, to our right, were more public benches. Although this was a civil and not a criminal case, our seating arrangements, although accidental, appropriately made it look and feel like we, collectively, were 'in the dock'. Throughout several hours with Peter Charleton, John Keenan never once wavered. He spoke at length about his 'statutory obligations' to provide services and how we were interfering with this. He told the judge boldly that we had no entitlement to cease to be members of SIPTU or the NBRU, and that, in fact, we were still members of those unions. Only when he was asked for his interpretation of the various trade union acts and the meaning of 'excepted body status' did he begin to answer in a manner that, to us, portrayed a difficulty in understanding the concept of trade unions. As we left the room, I was struck — and gladdened — by how angry John Rogers was at what he had heard. Not so much the content as the tone of John Keenan's evidence seemed to come as a major surprise to our legal team. On the following day, cross-examination would begin.

Some of the lads went home that evening, but Christy, Finbarr and I were staying in Dublin overnight. To pass time, we took a trip on the DART to Dún Laoghaire and just relaxed. It had been quite a stressful day.

The Remainder of the Prosecution Case
When we awoke the following morning, the mood looked set to continue. Unknown to us, *The Irish Times* court reporter had sat through the previous day's evidence, and there was a report in that paper. As it had been John Keenan's day, the piece didn't read very well from our point of

view. However, this would be our day and I looked forward to the day's evidence and reading about it in the following day's paper. Certainly the day's court proceedings went well. Once our Senior Counsel went about cross-examining John Keenan, he immediately began to damage him. With regard to the removal of my privileges in Athlone, John Keenan — the head of human resources — stated that it should never have happened and that workers clearly enjoyed the entitlement to nominate me or any other colleague as a representative on matters of grievance or discipline. He washed his hands of the events in Athlone on 9 July by pointing out that he had been abroad on holidays, and said that when he had been contacted in the evening, he had immediately issued a directive that resolved the matter.

When the questioning turned to our alleged continued membership of SIPTU/NBRU, he was in bigger trouble. It was vital that, after months of media spinning, the court established just how many members of ILDA there were, whether they were also members of any other union and what percentage this was of the total grade. Only when this was done could our qualification as an 'excepted body' be assessed. John Keenan's position was that we were all members of SIPTU or the NBRU. It was also, despite what the court would decide later, to become the position of those unions at crucial ICTU forums and elsewhere. For now, however, Iarnród Éireann was required to put in evidence a list of all mainline locomotive drivers. When the list contained names that none of us knew about, it became clear that this included new recruits and trainees who were not full drivers as yet. They were immediately discounted. The valid total was 265. John Keenan was then presented with 114 applications to join ILDA, 114 copies of letters to SIPTU and the NBRU from ILDA members resigning from those unions, and another bundle of copies of letters to him seeking that payroll deductions be stopped in respect of those ILDA members. It was compelling evidence. John Keenan had brought various lists showing how some of our members still had money going from the payroll to SIPTU or the NBRU. However, that was because Iarnród Éireann had refused, despite the now-documented court evidence, to stop the deductions. This refusal was, in itself, in breach of the 1991 Payment of Wages Act.

John Rogers then produced our membership list and the witness was questioned on why Iarnród Éireann had failed to stop paying money from randomly picked members on the list to unions of which they were clearly no longer members. Then our Senior Counsel turned to the eleven of us and selected some. He asked John Keenan whether or not he accepted that we were now only members of ILDA. John Keenan prevaricated but seemed unable to accept that all of us were no longer members of SIPTU or the NBRU. This was interesting. We were in court accused of breaches of various Industrial Relations Acts following industrial action. Those Acts provide immunities from such legal actions for members of unions — such as SIPTU and the NBRU — holding negotiating licences. ILDA didn't hold a negotiating licence. If we were actually members of SIPTU and the NBRU, we were in fact immune from such prosecutions under the 1990 Act and shouldn't have been in court at all. Moreover, why had neither SIPTU nor the NBRU — who later would claim us all as their members in arrears — turned up in court to stop this nonsense on the basis that we were their members? They had been invited, by our legal team, to attend court and make whatever representation they wished. While the NBRU typically buried its head in the sand and ignored the correspondence, there was a letter on file from Bowler Geraghty & Co. Solicitors, dated 3 November 1999, acting on behalf of SIPTU. It stated blandly: 'I do not see any reason why our client should be joined as a third party'. In other words, SIPTU didn't see any reason why it should say anything about workers — some of whom it would later claim as its 'members in arrears' — being sued by their employer in the High Court.

In any event, John Keenan was now struggling under intense cross-examination from our Senior Counsel. The entire second day and the first half of the third day of the action were in fact taken up with John Keenan looking increasingly ill at ease in the witness box. In addition to his weak evidence on our actual membership of ILDA, and his lack of any evidence that there had been collusion between the eleven defendants regarding the disruptions of 9 and 11 July, there was also the fact that he was forced, reluctantly, to accept that there had been what he described as 'poor communications' between senior management in the lead-up to those incidents. He was putting a lot of weight on a belief that every Iarnród Éireann employee 'waived' their clear constitutional entitlement to associate or disassociate from trade unions as they saw fit when entering into the company's service. The problem with this argument was that there was no evidence of such a waiver in our contracts of employment. In fact, Iarnród Éireann was unable to provide written contracts of employment for us at all. That was because there weren't any. Not only that, but John Rogers SC was able to produce as evidence letters from some of us, in which we had requested these contracts, and they had not been provided. Instead, Iarnród Éireann had produced booklets entitled 'Outline of Contract of Employment'; these booklets had been rejected by the recognised unions, and had not been signed by anybody. Finally, John Keenan's view that the emergence of a new union would inevitably lead to a total breakdown in industrial relations within the company and that we were too small to be 'representative' took a sound pummelling from our Senior Counsel who elicited the fact that the company dealt with thirteen unions, many of which had fewer members than ILDA. In fact, one such union, the Union of Construction, Allied Trades and Technicians (UCATT), had just two members, and yet was fully recognised by the company.

Not that readers of *The Irish Times* who might have been taken with that paper's reporting of the first day's evidence would have known any of this! Once the 'prosecution' evidence had ended, *The Irish Times* didn't report on any of the numerous difficulties encountered by the company's key witness thereafter. Thus, publicly if not in the court, John Keenan emerged undamaged. We would feel the effects of this later when the ten-week dispute occurred and few in the media knew the true background to this landmark action — they simply reported, wrongly, that it would be unlawful for Iarnród Éireann to deal with us.

Once John Keenan had completed his evidence, Iarnród Éireann called several other witnesses. One of them, Timmy Sheehan — the district manager responsible for Cork during the 11 July stoppage — gave truly remarkable evidence. This was the case that had arisen when Christy Holbrook was not paid for attending a serious accident inquiry as a witness for a SIPTU member who had requested his presence. All Cork drivers in all three unions had utilised their rest day in protest. Now, eleven of us were accused of conspiring to organise that stoppage. We were supposedly responsible for thirty-odd SIPTU and NBRU members having taken a day off on this date. There were no witnesses produced to back this accusation. However, the judge was being asked to conclude that Christy had orchestrated the stoppage. In that context, you can imagine the drama when Timmy Sheehan informed the court that Christy had personally asked him to advise all Cork drivers that he, Christy, was not looking for their support and, in fact, wanted them to work on 11 July. Timmy Sheehan volunteered this in evidence to his own Counsel. His honesty on this point was very welcome and praiseworthy. It also virtually destroyed Iarnród Éireann's always spurious case in respect of the Cork incident.

Timmy Sheehan's Athlone counterpart, Gerry Glynn, gave evidence that was notable only for its invective, but Brendan Smith, who had played a key role in the events in Athlone on 9 July, gave altogether more significant evidence. He took the stand before lunch on Day Five and was initially questioned by Roddy Horan BL for Iarnród Éireann. Roddy Horan concentrated in the main on the telephone conversation between Brendan Smith and myself at 9am on the morning of 9 July. In particular, he asked about my response when Brendan Smith had enquired what would happen if I didn't receive a letter restoring my entitlements when I arrived for work that day. As I had been very aware of the possible significance of Brendan Smith's question, I had obviously strenuously avoided any imputation of a threat. Now Brendan Smith seemed to advise Roddy Horan that that indeed was the case. The barrister seemed less than happy with that answer and, as lunchtime approached, he was still skirting around this issue in several ways. When the judge rose for lunch, Cathy Maguire turned to me and said, referring to Brendan Smith, 'That's one honest man.' However, I was looking across at Brendan Smith and Roddy Horan talking and had an uneasy feeling. I needn't have worried however. I had issued no threat and Smith knew it.

The Case for the Defence

Iarnród Éireann called another couple of witnesses including Tim O'Connor (the former TSSA official), who outlined the cost to the company of the two service disruptions of 9 and 11 July. However, by and large, the company's case was over. It was now up to us to conduct our defence. It was clear to us that John Rogers had successfully damaged the prosecution case almost beyond salvation. The Sheehan evidence was

106

crucial to the Cork element, and only Brendan Smith's latter evidence had the potential to damage me. How much weight the judge might put on that in the circumstances remained to be seen. John Rogers was so confident that he intended calling only a very small number of witnesses. To my disappointment I was not to be one of them. Instead, only Brian Dunphy would be called to give evidence. Christy was also expecting to be called because of an issue that had arisen in Cork. When drivers seek a day off — or in this case wish to utilise a rest day — they normally do so by written memorandum. Although the date for the Cork incident was Sunday, 11 July, four memoranda had been received from drivers looking to be off on Sunday, 12 July. Christy's was included in this. To the company this was clear evidence of collusion between the four, but when Christy was asked to explain this in consultation with John, the answer was altogether less spectacular. Four drivers were in the rest room as normal, filling out their memos, and one asked the date. Another wrongly gave it as 12 July. Accordingly, the four used 12 July as the date on their memos. It was as simple as that. John decided it wasn't necessary to call Christy either.

Brian Dunphy was asked by John Rogers to outline where he had been on 9 July and 11 July and what prior conversations he had had with any of the other ten of us that could be seen as conspiratorial. The answers were that he had been at work and had had no such conversations with anybody. Brian was cool and, as usual to anyone who knows him, as honest as the day is long. When Peter Charleton cross-examined Brian, he spent most of his time questioning him on various minutes from meetings we had had, to see if there was evidence of discussions at those that could be relevant to the 9 and 11 July stoppages. Of course, given the spontaneity of those events, there was none. All Iarnród Éireann had were innuendo and spurious supposition.

Although seven days' long in total, the trial was actually spread over three weeks. The last day and a half were taken up with legal argument relating to our counter-claim on recognition and primarily related to the details of the 1941 and 1942 Trade Union Acts. The 'representative' issue was, of course, crucial. With evidence that we had 114 members out of a total group of 265 mainline drivers nationally, the question was whether we qualified as an excepted body within this definition:

2.—In section 6 of the Act of 1941, the expression 'excepted body' shall include a body all the members of which are employed by the same employer and which carries on negotiations for the fixing of the wages or other conditions of employment of its own members (but of no other employees).

Iarnród Éireann made what seemed to us to be spurious arguments on this point, arguing, for example, that we did not comply with the provision that we 'are employed by the same employer' on the basis that article 5 of our constitution stated that, 'Membership shall be open to all Locomotive Drivers resident or employed on the island of Ireland'. As was explained in court, the reason for this wording was that we had some members who were employed by Iarnród Éireann but who were, in fact, resident in Northern Ireland. This was simply a catch-all provision to cover all eventualities. Iarnród Éireann argued, however, that it meant that we could have employees employed by Translink in Northern Ireland, and that therefore all our members would not be employed by the same employer. In evidence, however, it became clear that all parties accepted that we did not, in fact, have any members employed by Translink. However, Iarnród Éireann argued that the 'aspirational' nature of the rule was enough to place us outside the definition of the 1942 Act, despite the fact that it's wording specifically was 'are employed'.

Overall, though, we were happy with the way our defence had gone. As the trial came to a close, Mr Justice O'Neill, as expected, given the length of the action, announced that he would reserve judgment. He gave an indication that judgment might be issued in two weeks. As events would show, this was to prove overly optimistic.

So, we left the court in reasonably high spirits. John Rogers and Cathy Maguire had been superb throughout and we really couldn't have got any more help from our legal team. The judge had followed the case with great interest and the evidence of the various company witnesses had been such that only a token defence had been presented. Even on the recognition issue, we were naive enough at that stage to believe that simple logic and commonsense would win the day.

For our families, however, the next few months would be very stressful ones as some of them had witnessed at first hand in the court the naked antagonism that our employer held towards us. As Mr Justice O'Neill failed to deliver his judgment in the run up to Christmas 1999 and into the new millennium, doubts began to enter our minds as to what was going on, and all sorts of conspiracy theories began to surface. As the early part of 2000 arrived, what was to be a truly momentous year for ILDA and for me began with Iarnród Éireann striding confidently on with its plans as if the High Court did not even exist!

LAW, NOT JUSTICE

'The New Deal for Locomotive Drivers' was the formal title. Here were forty-eight pages of radical reform complete with appendices, Labour Court recommendations regarding elements of the proposals, and clarifications from Kieran Mulvey and Kevin Foley of the Labour Relations Commission. It doesn't sound like a lot, does it? Yet it's hard to imagine the impact that those forty-eight pages would have on our lives, our jobs, Iarnród Éireann as a company, the legal and industrial courts of the land, and the public in general. I have it here in my hand now and the language in which it is written is still as unclear and ambiguous as ever. The core of the booklet is dated 17 May 1999 but the last document that entered the booklet is actually Labour Court recommendation (LCR) 16374, and is dated 11 November 1999, just three days before our High Court action began. The book first came into circulation in January 2000. It is a mish-mash of reckonable periods and rostering periods, minimum agreed hours and maximum agreed hours, planned hours, contingency hours, contingency drivers, standard weeks and average weeks. And that is just on pages six and seven, under the heading, 'Direct Benefits to Staff'. At times I find the text impenetrable. For example: 'Hours agreed per driver in each depot at the date of agreement will be guaranteed for each existing wholetime driver unless negotiated and changed by agreement'. 'What is a 'wholetime driver?' you might well ask? Doesn't it imply the existence of a 'part-time' driver? It couldn't, because we had all been repeatedly told by Iarnród Éireann that part-time drivers were not proposed. A High Court judge was told in detail how the arrangements

110

for these 'contingency drivers' would apply, and the 'New Deal' document had all the details too. However, when we drew attention to them, we, and by extension the public, were told either that our concerns were invalid or that the element we were concerned about — as in part-time driving — wasn't proposed at all.

Part-time (contingency) drivers are included in the 'New Deal for Locomotive Drivers'. Iarnród Éireann was determined to be the first mainline railway company in the world to introduce the concept of part-time drivers on mainline trains. As discussed above, the company proposed that all available staff from the platform, ticket-checking, cleaning and other grades would be trained as drivers — 'fully trained'. Except that the 'New Deal' reduced the term of 'full' training from seventy-two to forty-eight weeks. So, all staff would get a forty-eight-week training programme as drivers. And then the 'contingency' ones would go back to their old jobs — checking, cleaning, signalling or whatever they normally did — until a 'wholetime driver' became unavailable, through illness or retraining, for example. Then the foreman might call in a 'contingency' driver and say, 'Here, I need a driver. Put down your brush, young man, and get up on that 600-tonne train with its 800 bodies of men, women and children and drive it at 100 mph to Cork. Drive like the wind, my boy!' And off he would go. Toot toot!

The above scenario might seem unreal or impossible. Irresponsible and bizarre even? However, this is the plan that had been dreamt up by a whole team of pen-pushers. And any safety concerns we had and raised were dismissed out of hand. This one problem we had with the 'New Deal' overrode everything else. It topped the list. And Iarnród Éireann management apparently had no concerns for the safety of the plan. After all, at the end of the day, if it all went wrong and 'Mr Contingency Driver' derailed his 800 passengers at his 100 mph on a 30 mph maximum curve that he didn't know existed, who would be in the dock facing the manslaughter charge? It wouldn't be Iarnród Éireann management. It would be the driver; it is always the driver's responsibility. As it was at Paddington, at Southall, at Watford Junction, and in Ireland in the 1980s at Buttevant and Cherryville where the unfortunate driver was formally charged and tried for manslaughter.

'Contingency drivers' — a measure opposed only by ILDA in what became the three-month summer lock-out of 2000 — would finally be killed off as proposed by the October 2000 independent safety report of Sedgwick Wharf, London, which would state: 'In our view it would be desirable to avoid combining infrequent driving, limited driving experience and deployment to the more demanding and higher risk driving tasks'. The report would go on to state that these persons should be confined to 'low risk duties' on 'low risk sections of routes'. In other words, part-time drivers on the mainline were out. Sedgwick Wharf would agree with us totally on three of our four safety concerns which had led to the dispute; and it would agree with us partially on the fourth. However, the media would ignore this because when the joint Labour Court/LRC report into the dispute would be published, on 18 December 2000, the Executive Summary would contain no comment on safety. And the media would see no necessity actually to study the report and find the 'facts' other than those presented to them by the report's authors. It is no wonder that many ILDA members still feel a deep hurt and sense of having been betrayed at the hands of the media and public.

At the end of the day, the ten-week dispute of 2000 was successful in identifying safety issues relating to a policy that subsequently was evaluated by Sedgwick Wharf, and found to be unacceptable as proposed. Sedgwick Wharf also provided remedies for these safety concerns. Don't expect to read about them in the papers though!

Nevertheless, in early 2000, Sedgwick Wharf and our dispute were still in the future. At that time, the fact that the issues of the 'New Deal' were about to be balloted on by SIPTU/NBRU was the biggest surprise of all. As we waited into our fourth month, February 2000, for the decision of Mr Justice O'Neill, the continuing concern of our members that judgment had not been issued was added to by the pace at which all parties to the agreement where now moving ahead towards implementation. To us it did not make sense. If our High Court action on recognition were to be successful, the result would be that the entire deal would have to be renegotiated from scratch and we would have to be included in all discussions and future agreements. Obviously in that scenario, the Orange Booklet drawn up between SIPTU/NBRU and Iarnród Éireann would be dead in the water. So why, against such an uncertain background were they pressing ahead with a ballot and a date for implementation (June 2000) rather than simply waiting for Mr Justice O'Neill's judgment? Our more suspicious members immediately jumped to the conclusion that somehow they were 'certain' of the High Court outcome. Such theories abounded. At this stage, I was becoming expert at sorting out one apparently baseless conspiracy theory from another — not through any conviction about the existence of natural justice, but simply in order to maintain my sanity and to be able to sleep at night. Moreover, as the company was obviously pressing ahead regardless of Mr Justice O'Neill's deliberations, we needed to do likewise. Safety was the most pressing place to start.

Contact with the Minister for Public Enterprise

Since my initial meeting with Mary O'Rourke in Leinster House when Fianna Fáil had been in opposition, she had gone on to become the Minister for Public Enterprise and Transport, following the election of the Fianna Fáil/Progressive Democrat coalition in 1997. As she, like me, happened to live in Athlone, this had at first seemed convenient. Technically, I was actually living in the Roscommon/Longford constituency of her party colleague, Seán Doherty, and Fine Gael's Denis Naughten, but I worked across the river in Mary O'Rourke's Westmeath constituency. Moreover, two ILDA members in Athlone were very active and long-term members of the Fianna Fáil machine and knew Mary O'Rourke quite well. Generally if I felt it was beneficial to speak to her or vice-versa, there was no problem in arranging this, and several meetings took place in her home. In fact, the first of these took place on 18 July 1998, before the formation of ILDA, when I provided her with a written submission of our difficulties with SIPTU/NBRU and Iarnród Éireann, in order that she would understand the events that had led to the stoppage of 12 July 1998, a week earlier.

I had a lot of contact with Minister O'Rourke around this time. For example, on 10 July 1998 — two days before the NLDC stoppage — I had been on RTÉ's Morning Ireland in an interview with Kieran Mulvey, Chief Executive of the LRC. The reason for that stoppage was what all drivers at the time felt was a lack of progress on negotiations for a five-day week. No meetings had taken place for many months. Kieran Mulvey, live on air, asked me to call off the stoppage and said that if that happened he would facilitate talks the very next week. After the interview, I immediately contacted the LRC Chief Executive's office to be told that talks would not be available the following week unless Iarnród Éireann agreed. As the media speculated all that morning over the possible impact of a rail stoppage on one of the biggest sporting weekends of the year, I was in contact with Mary O'Rourke, who had ministerial responsibility for Iarnród Éireann. I told her of Kieran Mulvey's on-air offer, which was now not an offer without the company's agreement. She advised me that she had heard the interview herself, and agreed that Kieran Mulvey had been very clear about facilitating talks. She undertook to make enquiries on the matter. I had four conversations with her and her office that day. At the end of eleven hours of telephone conversations, I was left waiting for a phone call from the minister, who was in contact with management. That call never came.

By Saturday morning, the media, reasonably, were looking for clarity on whether there would be a stoppage or not. I spoke to the NLDC committee and announced at lunchtime that the stoppage would be going ahead. Sections of the media accused us of failing to accept Kieran Mulvey's offer. Minister O'Rourke kept her counsel. When I did meet her a week later, I decided to leave nothing to chance, and presented a formal written ten-page outline of the difficulties, their background and how I felt they could be addressed. On 23 July, I received a letter from the minister, thanking me for meeting her and confirming that, 'I have fully read the document you left with me. I hope matters begin to resolve themselves satisfactorily in the next few weeks'.

By February 2000, the problems had moved on to the 'New Deal' but Mary O'Rourke was still minister, Kieran Mulvey was still Chief Executive of the LRC and Iarnród Éireann was still making problems rather than solving them.

The Spring 2000 Ballot

With Mr Justice O'Neill still pondering who should negotiate this and other collective agreements, Iarnród Éireann and its favoured unions went ahead and balloted. Twice. The agreement contained a clear-cut 'opt out clause' on page 39 of the booklet. Under the heading 'Depots Opting Out', it read simply 'should any depot seek to opt out of the proposed arrangements no agreement will be possible'. We in ILDA were naive enough to understand this clause as meaning that each depot had a veto on the proposals. However, we were to discover that, in the world of Iarnród Éireann linguistics, nothing means what it appears to mean. Each depot was to be balloted separately, with specific arrangements initially being made to keep the ballot papers separate so that counts could be conducted on a depot-by depot basis. It is one of the residual lies of this entire episode that ILDA members were offered a ballot on this agreement but declined it.

ILDA members were emphatically not offered a ballot on the 'New Deal for Locomotive Drivers'. Instead, SIPTU/NBRU simply issued circulars to be seen by all staff, inviting us to leave ILDA and rejoin their unions in order to vote on the 'New Deal'. These invitations to rejoin were nothing new. Since ILDA had been formed, its members knew that they could rejoin SIPTU/NBRU at any time and were regularly encouraged by those unions to do so. Sometimes this encouragement took the form of simple verbal requests to individuals from representatives of those unions. On other occasions, it was a formal written invitation to a person, or, as in this case, a notice displayed in the workplace. And throughout, of course, we had the discrimination against ILDA members by management as an added incentive to us to return to management's favoured pen. That ILDA continued to exist and grow against this background is testimony to the vehemence of its members' opposition to SIPTU/NBRU and anger at management tactics.

At the time when this ballot took place, we were awaiting High Court judgment on a seven-day trial that would include findings on whether ILDA was entitled as a matter of law to be recognised. The idea of our disbanding ILDA and returning to SIPTU/NBRU while awaiting such a judgment is unthinkable. In fact, it is my belief that the timing of the ballot can be explained by the fact that Iarnród Éireann and SIPTU/NBRU, far from wanting us to vote, actually wanted to ensure that they balloted at a time when we couldn't possibly rejoin SIPTU/NBRU to vote down the proposals. They knew that if we rejoined them, they would have had no possibility whatsoever of getting the positive ballot result they needed. Even with the ballot being restricted to SIPTU/NBRU, the ballot result was only 112 for and 83, in total, against, and some of those who voted as drivers had actually begun training only the previous week.

So ILDA members did not get a vote, were not offered a vote and had no possibility of voting. But what of those who did vote 'depot by depot'? Even then there were difficulties. The theory was that all ballot boxes were to be sent, unopened, to the LRC. Thereafter the Chief Executive, Kieran Mulvey, would supervise a count of the unopened boxes in the presence of representatives of both SIPTU and the NBRU. As the ballot was taking place over a number of days, speculation was rife within the grade as to how various areas were voting and what the key issues were. For example, in Cork, the proposal that the four roster patterns be amalgamated into one was of particular concern. There were thirty-six drivers in Cork at the time, and eighteen were ILDA members. Of the other eighteen, six were SIPTU members and twelve were NBRU members. Would the SIPTU/NBRU members on the top passenger roster vote against the agreement despite the urgings of their union officials and representatives? The speculation was that they might. And, with each depot having a veto under the 'opt-out clause', even that would, theoretically, be enough to kill the 'New Deal'.

In Dundalk, there were eleven drivers, and nine of them were ILDA members. There was just one SIPTU and one NBRU member. These two men were to vote alone on proposals that Iarnród Éireann insisted would bind all eleven drivers. In other depots, including my own in Athlone, Drogheda and Ireland's biggest depot in Inchicore, ILDA also had a majority, meaning that the drivers not voting would be bound by a decision taken by a minority. And in Sligo, there were five drivers, all but one of whom were ILDA members. Because Sligo had a different work pattern from other depots — they currently worked a five- over six-day week while everyone else in the mainline operated a six- over six — they were given a separate ballot. Or rather he was. This single vote was to be counted separately from the rest and if it was a 'no', a different process of arbitration would be entered into for Sligo alone. By any logical standard, it was a nonsense.

We hoped that Mr Justice O'Neill might put a stop to this. On one occasion, Cathy Maguire went to his chambers and asked for an estimated date for his judgment, given the concern of her clients with developments. Still it didn't come.

The ballot and the count went ahead without us. The closed ballot boxes were being sent depot by depot to the LRC. Except in Cork — so tense were the SIPTU/NBRU representatives as to the result, that they opened the box in Cork. Three days before the count was due to take place, I received a call from one of our members in Cork who alleged that he had seen the ballots counted and that the Cork drivers had rejected the proposals. The opened box was now sent to the LRC. When all the votes had arrived, they were taken to the North Star Hotel for counting. We looked forward to the depot-by-depot count, confident that at least one depot had vetoed the proposals. We were wrong again. At the North Star, all the votes — with the exception of the single Sligo one — were emptied into one pile on a table and counted as a 'job lot', thus rendering the depot-by-depot 'opt-out' clause irrelevant. The result was 112 For, 82 Against. Then the separate 'second ballot' of the single Sligo vote was conducted. It was a 'no'. Sligo had rejected the 'New Deal'.

I, and one or two other ILDA members, were denied access to the actual count but were nevertheless on the hotel premises on the day. Iarnród Éireann and both unions gave media statements heralding this brave new day in industrial relations in Iarnród Éireann. It was certainly that. Never before had almost half a grade of workers been excluded on a ballot on work changes. Never before had depot-by-depot counts become one collective count. Never before had votes from new recruits just training been valued more than the views of drivers some of whom had thirty-five years' experience in the job. It was indeed a new day. And a very stupid and ultimately disastrous one too.

Did Iarnród Éireann and SIPTU/NBRU really think that isolating half of their drivers before decimating their terms and conditions would simply allow change to happen without consequences? Kieran Mulvey, when questioned about that awkward opened ballot box in Cork, put it down simply to the 'inexperience' of those who conducted the ballot. In fact, if you added them up, the total number of years' combined trade union experience actually present for the Cork count would exceed the age of the modern Irish trade union movement itself.

Meanwhile, ILDA had decided to conduct a ballot of our members on the 'opt-out clause'. Depot by depot, of course. And it was counted and independently verified as normal by a member of the Garda

Síochána. The result was predictable but important in dealing with anticipated questions later on. All 114 ILDA members, in every depot, wanted to 'opt out' of the 'New Deal', in accordance with the 'opt-out' clause on page 39 of the proposed booklet.

Thus, while Iarnród Éireann had a 112-83 majority in favour of its work changes, in reality there were 197-112 against. Readers with good memories and mental arithmetic skills may wonder how that gives a total of 309 drivers, when the High Court had just been told, and two months later would confirm, that there were, in fact, just 265 mainline drivers, including probationers. In fact, thirty-eight trainees voted. And who the other six were remains a mystery.

And so, in the spring of 2000, the 'New Deal' was being pushed through — regardless of safety concerns. We felt that it was time for ILDA to take action — not action that would inconvenience the innocent travelling public, but action that would bring attention to the dangers of what was occurring and appeal to the supposed good sense of those with specific responsibility for these matters.

ILDA Action

The ILDA Executive had been discussing the safety implications of the 'New Deal' and had made representations to the minister and the Railways Inspecting Office (RIO) in her department. We had just produced a report for the RIO on rail safety legislation in Ireland, called *Railways Safety Legislation in Ireland — A Time For Change*, which was pivotal in eventually securing major changes in our arcane and outdated rail-safety legislation and in establishing, for the first time ever, a rail-safety commission independent of the company and government. It is a report of which we in ILDA are especially proud, and we felt that the department, at least, knew that we were players when it came to rail safety. So, we had hoped that when we asked people in the department to take account of our safety concerns with the 'New Deal', they would heed us. To our surprise, we got the deaf ear.

As it happened, the department had commissioned a safety audit by Britain's International Risk Management Services (IRMS). This had been published in October 1998, with a further update released in March 2000. This report was described by IRMS officials to the joint Oireachtas

Committee on Public Enterprise & Transport, chaired by Seán Doherty, as the most damning report that this highly respected company had ever had occasion to produce on a railway in the developed world. The initial report identified over thirty 'unreasonable risks' that were to be eliminated over a maximum two-year period. As this two-year period approached, Minister O'Rourke told the Dáil that Iarnród Éireann had addressed all the 'unreasonable risks' identified in the report. However, when the formal two-year audit was actually published in March 2000, it transpired that only four of the unreasonable risks had been fully dealt with, and, in fact, another twelve had actually arisen in the intervening period. The situation was getting worse. Yet we were still treated with scepticism by many who were prepared to believe the regular assurances of Iarnród Éireann's PR department.

For my own part, any hopes I might have had that the minister would appreciate the concern of a group of workers on rail safety had been dashed, when, as a result of growing public concern about rail safety, the Joint Oireachtas Committee on Public Transport had quite properly decided to question the IRMS, the RIO, Iarnród Éireann, another respected consultant Mr A.D. Little, and the minister herself in public session in February 1999. I attended throughout and sat in the public gallery at the end of the room in Kildare House. Ivan Yates TD was the minister's opposite number in Fine Gael at that time. We were quite happy to share any information we might have regarding rail-safety concerns with anyone including Deputy Yates and Minister O'Rourke. In any event, Ivan Yates began to question the minister on the revelation that before the IRMS report was actually released or supposed to be available, she had shown it to a neighbour of hers, Mr Brian Garvey, who held a very senior position with Iarnród Éireann. Ivan Yates then went on to question Mary O'Rourke specifically on the safety of plans to increase maximum daily mileage for drivers from 360 mile to 420 miles, the maximum working day for drivers from nine hours to ten-and-a-half hours and to reduce the training period for drivers from seventy-two to forty-eight weeks. In obvious need of a diversionary tactic, she turned to me and stated that Deputy Yates had obviously received his information from me, adding that I had supplied the information to her too and had been to her house several times and told her that my members would no longer work a seven-day week. Quite what this had to do with the IRMS report is anybody's guess. Rather it seemed to be a clear tactic to move the emphasis from safety to industrial relations, and I was to be the fall guy. I was flabbergasted. Of course I, as a member of the public, was not entitled to partake in the proceedings at all and had no opportunity to respond to this. It got worse as the minister personally referred to me on two further occasions in her final responses.

The following day, I spoke by phone to a number of members of the Committee. They were as taken aback by the minister's 'diversionary tactics' as I had been. I decided to contact John Kissane who was the secretary for the Joint Committee. On 2 March 1999, I wrote a formal complaint, in which I stated: 'To my utter astonishment the minister, in her response, referred to me personally on three occasions. Moreover she did so in a manner which completely misrepresented my views on the topics raised in a forum where I had no opportunity to respond. I consider this misrepresentation damaging and dangerous'. I explained that I felt her comments were an attempt to deflect attention from the very serious questions raised at the committee and requested an opportunity to go before the committee to explain my views and formally correct the record. This opportunity was not afforded me although I was asked to present my written views to the committee for the record.

Safety on Our Railways

It was no surprise therefore when, a year later, with these proposals about to be forced upon ILDA members, the minister had failed to procure any independent safety analysis of the proposals. The IRMS reports had specifically excluded any assessment of 'operational matters' such as the 'New Deal'. For ILDA, it was time to put up or shut up. We could either whistle in the wind about safety in the full knowledge that no one wanted to believe us when our views were assessed against those of a state company and supporting minister, or we could put our money where our mouths were in an effort to give some credence to our sincerely held concerns. We decided on the latter option. In February 2000, we procured an expert independent safety assessment of the 'New Deal for Locomotive Drivers' by the UK's leading independent safety expert, P.G. Rayner. Peter Rayner is vastly experienced in all facets of rail safety, and was deliberately chosen by us because of his senior management, as opposed to trade union, background. He had been Deputy General Manager of the former British Rail (BR) and had investigated serious and fatal rail accidents going back to 1967. In fact, ILDA was very fortunate to secure him at all as he was at that time a key expert witness in the Paddington/Ladbroke Grove rail-crash inquiry. He had previously fulfilled the same roles in the inquiries into the Southall and Watford Junction train crashes.

The Rayner Report is short, concise and damning. It criticises the 'New Deal' proposals and states 'the proposals within the booklet are ambiguous and in my view will lead to greater strain upon the drivers given the type and condition of the infrastructure'. It states that 'the proposals to change and extend drivers' hours and miles should in my view not be implemented without risk analysis of key changes.' On driver training, it found that 'this opinion [risk analysis] applies also to the altered and reduced Driver Training especially so as Driver Training is very much to the forefront of accident investigation at the present time'. The Paddington accident which was then under investigation occurred when a passenger train, driven by a driver who had been fully qualified for only nine days, passed a signal at danger and ran into an oncoming express passenger train, resulting in the loss of thirty-three lives, including those of both drivers. Rayner finished with his view on contingency (part-time) drivers: 'I have particular concern with regard to Contingency Driving arrangements that are, on the face of it, in my view unsafe.'

As all of these proposals had at their origin the notorious Buckley cost-saving report, it was apt that Rayner placed particular emphasis on a finding of the enquiry into the 1988 Clapham Junction train crash. This disaster had been the subject of an investigation by the UK's Lord Justice Hidden. Recommendation 50 of the Hidden Report was that 'Commercial considerations should not be allowed to compromise safety.'

Here Rayner got to the heart of the matter. He identified the use of the term 'business requirements' in the 'New Deal' document as a violation of this principle. This is what made his report so powerful, but also immensely threatening to those who had put all their eggs in the 'New Deal' basket. On 28 February 2000, ILDA formally adopted the Rayner Report and issued a news release which stated that we had unanimously passed a motion that we would not operate new work practices under the heading 'contingencies' as laid out in Iarnród Éireann's 'A New Deal for Locomotive Drivers'. The press release outlined our reasons for passing the motion. It went on the state:

> Although not necessarily legally binding in this jurisdiction the Association considers such a principle [recommendation 50 of the Hidden Report that 'Commercial considerations should not be allowed to compromise safety'] to be fundamental to the safe operating of a modern rail network. It views any breach of such a principle as an act of gross irresponsibility.

The news release concluded:

> In the continuing absence of an independent safety review and implementation body, and a situation where the operating company are solely responsible for all the financial affairs of the company in addition to safety, ILDA commits itself to continue to put the well being of passengers and staff at the very top of its agenda. ILDA repeats its call for the introduction of such a body with new legislation which will empower it to act in the interest of public safety.

The risk analysis that Rayner sought was eventually carried out, first in a minimalist way by Halcrow Rail and, eventually, in a much more meaningful manner, by Sedgwick Wharf, as a result of the subsequent summer 2000 dispute. As a result of the latter evaluation, part-time drivers were dispensed with as proposed and other changes to the 'New Deal' were recommended on issues like Personal Needs Breaks (PNBs) and maximum mileage per day. Most significantly in the long term, new legislation has now been brought forward, following lobbying from ILDA and others, which provides for an independent safety review and implementation body with significant powers to ensure that Iarnród Éireann becomes a truly safe railway.

I say *truly* safe because Iarnród Éireann has consistently portrayed Ireland's railways as the 'safest in Europe'. This is on the rather spurious basis that there has been no multiple fatality accident since the Cherryville Junction disaster in August 1983 when seven passengers died. This accident followed an earlier catastrophe at Buttevant in Co. Cork in August 1980, when sixteen passengers and two staff died. Iarnród Éireann believes that the fact that there has been no similar accident since then entitles the company to be proud of its safety record. IRMS, however, stated that it was apparent that 'there were major shortcomings associated with the data collected and collated by IE (Iarnród Éireann)', while documenting a long list of 'unreasonable risks', before going on to predict that Ireland's railways had the potential for ten train accidents to occur each year, with seven fatalities, unless immediate remedial action were taken. ILDA has always argued that Iarnród Éireann's safety record must be seen in its proper context.

Firstly, it should be realised and stated that railways the world over are recognised as the safest form of land transport. This is not to say, however, that we should be complacent or that any management should take credit for this safety culture. In most cases, it is the inherent nature of the system itself and the diligence of operational employees that contribute most to rail safety. However, when rail accidents do occur, they tend to be particularly horrific, bloody and, in most cases, preventable either by the use of modern equipment or by the elimination of human error through best practice and training and a realisation by management of the potential risk beforehand. In addition, we need to view our record in the context of the number of passenger journeys in Ireland per year relative to other railways. Passenger journeys tend to vary year on year with seasonal factors also leading to variations on a monthly, weekly and even daily basis. Suffice to say that Ireland's railways have fewer passenger journeys in a year than the United Kingdom's rail network has in a day. This one statistic alone puts in context some of the more ridiculous claims that our railways are safer than those in the UK, when we take into account the number of accidents that have happened there in recent times.

Moreover, Britain's railways, pre-Clapham, were wonderfully run and safe forms of public transport. Since that accident in 1988, major accidents have occurred at Southall, Watford Junction, Paddington/ Ladbroke Grove, Hatfield, Selby and Potters Bar, in addition to the King's Cross underground fire, also in 1988, which was caused by a cigarette being dropped on an escalator. Overall, scores of lives were lost in these accidents. With the exceptions of King's Cross and Clapham, all of these accidents took place after privatisation when, it could be argued, the quest for profits fatally undermined Hidden's principle that 'Commercial considerations should not be allowed to compromise safety.' In addition, it has been found that most of these disasters where what we call 'Automatic Train Protection (ATP) preventable'. In other words, had a modern system (ATP) of signal control that brings trains to a stop when an SPAD (Signal Passed At Danger) occurs, been in operation at these locations, all lives lost would have been saved. This system is readily available the world over but is expensive to install. Ireland does not have ATP or any relevant system in operation on its mainline network, although the DART lines (our slowest passenger trains) do have such a system. When you consider that recent statistics (spring/summer 2002) show that comparable incidents of SPADS in Ireland have doubled in the same period in which they have been halved in the UK, it becomes clear that in this country we actually have absolutely no grounds for complacency on rail safety. And when an expert of the calibre of P.G. Rayner sees the need to point out to us the importance of Hidden's defining principle on safety and cost, one might hope that notice might be taken.

Finally, it is well known to employees in Iarnród Éireann that serious rail accidents have been avoided only through sheer good fortune and quick staff reactions on many occasions in the recent past. However, as Iarnród Éireann enjoys immunity from the Freedom of Information Act (FOI), the position is that unless whistle-blowing staff reveal the details of these incidents, the media and public will never know about them. At this stage, many of us in ILDA view rail safety as too crucial an issue for us to be silenced by threats or mud-slinging. Below is a sample list of just some of the incidents that have occurred 'behind closed doors' on our network:

- Doubling in incidents of SPADS
- Passenger train dividing in two parts in Cork Tunnel without anyone in signalling or in the tiny train crew being aware of the incident until the front portion had travelled to Charleville over thirty miles away
- Train running away unmanned from Rathdrum in Wicklow for four miles towards Arklow in direction of oncoming passenger train

- A packed passenger train destined for Galway and a locomotive weighing 82 tonnes coming within 150 yards of a head-on collision on a single line outside Tullamore in Co. Offaly
- A number of deaths and injuries to members of the public at level crossings in Counties Limerick, Roscommon and Westmeath
- The tragic deaths of two staff members engaged in shunting, while working without the most basic radio communication with the driver involved.

When the Rayner report was issued, it was initially taken very seriously. I had noticed that the *Irish Independent's* environment correspondent, Tracey Hogan, had not been behind the door in reporting on safety issues relating to air, road and rail in the months before Rayner's report became available. In particular, he had broken a very prominent story on 20 January 2000, revealing that there was 'a risk of serious derailments while the entire rail network is being overhauled according to a stark warning contained in a confidential Government report'. As a consequence, I called Tracey Hogan immediately we took delivery of the Rayner Report. We had convened a news conference to discuss the report on 17 February 2000 at Wynn's Hotel in Dublin. The Rayner Report was posted to the media, together with an invitation to attend the conference, at which Peter Rayner would also be in attendance. On the previous Saturday morning, I met Treacy Hogan in Kinnegad, and gave him an advance copy of the report.

On the day of the news conference, the *Irish Independent* carried a piece headed, 'Rail drivers' new roster plan unsafe, says consultant'. The piece accurately quoted the Rayner report on the key issues of drivers' hours, mileage, training and, particularly, part-time drivers being unsafe. With regard to the authors of the 'New Deal', Rayner's question, 'Have the decision takers ridden for four hours and more on the footplate, taken a brief non-authorised break, run the engine around and driven back again?' was contained in the article, which also contained the standard platitudes from Iarnród Éireann's PR gurus that the agreement must be safe because it gave us two days a week off. This fallacy was presented and

125

accepted as fact throughout that year. In the first instance, it ignored the reality that if a ten-hour driving day without breaks is unsafe — and it is — it is unsafe in its own right whether the driver works one day a week or seven. Moreover, although the 'New Deal' contained an aspiration for each driver to have two days off, the reality was that there were insufficient drivers available to allow for this, and drivers who insisted on their two days off, as many of our members did in the final analysis, were threatened in writing with the sack if they didn't agree to work their rest days. In fact, many drivers continued to work a six- or even a seven-day week right up the time of going to press (summer 2003) and I know of instances where drivers have not had a single rest day from a forty-eight-hour week contract for three to four weeks.

It was against this background then that we looked forward to the Rayner news conference of 17 February. Our anticipation was heightened by another *Irish Independent* article in advance of the news conference, which told us that Iarnród Éireann would attend the conference to 'confront' Peter Rayner. Of more significance was the revelation in the story that British consultants 'Halcrow Transmark' were now to risk assess the proposals, although the *Independent* confirmed that the assessment 'had not been completed'. The truth was that it had not even begun, and risk assessment had only now become an issue at all as a result of the Rayner Report. Thus began a pattern of ILDA acting as a safety watchdog on Iarnród Éireann in exposing issues such as the company's failure to get serious changes risk assessed prior to completion of a radical new collective agreement — only to be publicly attacked by a management who privately acted to implement whatever remedy had been highlighted, as if the company had intended to do it all along anyway. As with any such arrangement, much embarrassment is caused to management.

As I drove to Dublin Airport to pick up Peter Rayner, I therefore looked forward to Iarnród Éireann's 'confrontation' with him, knowing that the company was, quite simply, out of its depth. To my pleasure, Peter Rayner had been following the reaction to his report through the Irish media on the internet and was pleased that Tracey Hogan in particular, who had broken the story, had reported his findings accurately. As a result, most subsequent reporting was also generally fair and accurate at that stage.

The news conference was well attended by national television and radio personnel and most of the press. I introduced Peter Rayner and explained to those in attendance why, in the absence of any risk assessment from the company or the department, we had decided to fund this report from our own limited resources (in our case, from our own personal pockets) as a result of our concerns. The assembled media seemed quite taken by Rayner and his style. It was immediately apparent that he was not one to sensationalise or dramatise for effect. In fact, his contribution could have been described as understated. However, it was all the more powerful for that. In making observations such as, 'It is sensible to speculate whether the fact there has not been a serious accident is simply due to the scarcity of the service', before noting that planned modernisation and increases in services coupled with additions to the hours and miles driven per day increase the 'collision opportunities quite considerably', Rayner struck a chord of commonsense with everyone in attendance. Iarnród Éireann was not, however, among those in attendance, having been independently advised (through a phonecall to Britain the previous evening) of Rayner's credentials.

Once Peter had performed a number of interviews, he was off on a short hop to Connolly Station. RTÉ's Róisín Duffy had arranged to interview him there against a railway background. Obviously this required the permission of Iarnród Éireann who, we were told, had acceded. Brian Dunphy, our treasurer and a senior member, went off to Connolly with Peter and RTÉ to be welcomed by Barry Kenny at the front door, much to the annoyance of Brian who had just been dragged through the High Court by Barry Kenny's paymasters. While Peter Rayner was being interviewed, Barry Kenny made a comment to Brian to the effect that this negative publicity for the company was unnecessary. Brian answered that someone had to do something with a madness like part-time drivers about to be let loose on the unsuspecting public, but surprisingly Barry Kenny answered that this proposal would never become a reality in any event.

Any feelings that we were making progress, however, were quickly dashed as Iarnród Éireann went on to state publicly, time and again, that this dangerous new concept would be implemented and, for the first time, publicly began to make statements that these 'contingency' drivers were actually required in order to give their 'wholetime' counterparts rest days and proper breaks.

Before Peter Rayner's day in Dublin was complete, he had another appointment. We headed off to Leinster House to meet a number of Dáil deputies who had also received his report. The Labour Party transport spokesman, John Keenan's friend, Emmet Stagg TD, was the one who spent most time with us, greeting us outside before taking us in for a chat and a drink in the Dáil bar. Deputy Stagg and Peter Rayner discussed the latter's report in some detail. The Labour Party deputy admitted to having been taken aback by what the report contained and told its author that his seven-sentence conclusion alone was a major cause of concern to him. He issued a news release that outlined his concern and undertook to table a number of parliamentary questions to Minister O'Rourke on its contents. Following some small talk, Deputy Stagg turned to me and commented on the timing of this report. He told me that had he seen this report before SIPTU had accepted the new proposals, he would have called Tony Tobin, another acquaintance of his, and told him not to ballot until SIPTU, Ireland's biggest union, had made good the proposals on safety issues. Little old ILDA — the 'nobody's child' of the Irish trade union movement — had outflanked the SIPTU machine, of which Emmet Stagg himself was a fully paid-up member, on the key issue of rail safety.

As we drove Peter Rayner to Dublin Airport for his evening journey back to Hampshire, we were content that the day had been successful in at last putting the issue of rail safety on the public agenda. We were determined that until people capable and determined enough to keep it there came along, we would do whatever needed to be done.

Conversations with Influential People

My friend, Athlone ILDA member Tom O'Brien, was doing what he thought best when he called Mary O'Rourke at home one Saturday evening in March of that year. Tom was as passionate a member of Fianna Fáil as you would be likely to meet anywhere. On proud display in his home were photos of people such as Minister O'Rourke's late brother Brian Lenihan — another native of Athlone, of course — and Charles Haughey. As he was chairman of his local Fianna Fáil cumann in Clonown, just outside Athlone in Co. Roscommon, door-to-door canvassing, church-gate collections and party fund-raisers were all part of Tom's existence. In fact, just weeks previously the minister had attended a local dinner dance at which Tom had also been present, and Tom, like other members, had shared a number of dances with the minister during the evening. Although he would not be the type to 'talk shop' on such occasions, Tom considered himself entitled to feel that he knew and could approach Mary O'Rourke on a matter of genuine concern to him — especially when that concern related to the safety of his occupation in a company over which she had ministerial responsibility. And so it was that Tom called the minister to express his concerns about the Rayner Report. He asked her to ensure that Iarnród Éireann proceeded in accordance with Rayner's recommendations for the sake of the safety of rail passengers and staff alike.

Initially the conversation was friendly and the minister said that she had read the Rayner Report but that she also had the IRMS Report. Tom explained that he was aware of the IRMS report but pointed out that, fine report though it was, it did not deal with operational matters relating to drivers. In an instant, the tone of the conversation changed and Mrs O'Rourke attacked Tom for phoning her at home to lecture her on rail safety. Tom explained that he had not intended to lecture her. However, he stated firmly that, as a driver, he was more familiar with the safety or otherwise of his train driving than she — minister or not — could ever be. The conversation finished abruptly. Tom was, and still is, unable to understand Mary O'Rourke's reaction that evening or indeed her attitude to ILDA in the following months. He is no longer a member of Fianna Fáil, and has resigned from the cumann. In the election of 2002, for the first time in his adult life, he did not canvass or assist Fianna Fáil in any way, despite numerous requests to do so.

I also had a conversation with a senior influential figure in the spring of 2000. Mine, with CIÉ Group Chief Executive Michael McDonnell, was more cordial than Tom's with the minister. The opportunity presented itself one morning when I was travelling back to Heuston Station from North Wall, having driven an early-morning freight train from the Midlands. I was on the number 90 bus from Connolly to Heuston Station when it stopped at Tara Street and Michael McDonnell boarded. I hadn't seen him in the flesh since the SIPTU Ennis conference and, although it was only two years since that conference, so much had occurred in the interim that it seemed much longer. I had a feeling that this was the case not only for me. Michael McDonnell had also been the centre of some attention since our last meeting when he had confided that he felt his position was already under some threat. In the meantime, his chairman, Brian Joyce, had suddenly jumped ship and CIÉ had become enmeshed in a very messy cable-laying contract with telecoms operator Esat. It seemed that hardly a week went by without some newspaper or magazine doing a feature piece on the company's wheeling and dealing, and the embattled Mr McDonnell was often the man to whom they went for answers.

In any event, my only meeting with him to date had been extremely affable and I now decided to seize the opportunity to take issue with him on some of what had arisen since. I waited until the bus arrived outside Heuston Station and, while he exited through the front doors, I exited through the centre ones and called to him. By the time he had turned, I was on his shoulder. I gave him my name and told him I'd like to raise an issue with him. He was somewhat startled to be confronted in this way, but forthcoming nonetheless. He referred to our previous meeting and made a jovial comment about my 'being busy since'. I told him that I and my colleagues had found ourselves at loggerheads with our then unions and had decided to exercise our legal and constitutional right to leave them but that his company, for reasons unknown, had taken the gravest exception to this to the extent of suing us in the High Court using taxpayers' money. I then asked him specifically to explain the reasons for that. This was obviously not an encounter for which the chief executive had prepared that day, and in response he concentrated on the difficulties he faced in his position. He recounted the efforts he had gone to since his appointment to try to induce an industrial relations atmosphere within the company that was progressive and more conducive to the commercial needs of the business, and said that the unions involved had consistently frustrated this process. I argued that the High Court action seemed to me to be calculated to do everything other than build good progressive relations with employees. I suggested that a first step in any such process might be to talk with unhappy workers, to which he replied, 'My door is always open.'

My response of, 'Not to me it isn't', was rebuffed by him with an assurance that all employees were equal in his eyes and that if I had any issues I wanted to raise with him, I should write to his office seeking a meeting. I immediately undertook to do so. By this time, we were standing at the glass door that led to the entrance of the offices upstairs in Heuston, so we said our goodbyes. Just as I was walking away, he, jokingly, called 'Oh Brendan, that time I sued you, did I win?'

'No Michael,' I replied, smiling. 'You didn't. Next time, try talking to us instead'.

He returned the smile and left. As it turned out, my later efforts to procure a meeting with Michael McDonnell were unsuccessful and I was never to speak with him again although we did almost meet at close quarters during the summer dispute that year.

Michael McDonnell later left CIÉ and tragically lost his life soon afterwards.

The High Court Judgment

By the time my meeting with Michael McDonnell took place, Mr Justice O'Neill had finally delivered judgment on *Iarnród Éireann v Holbrooke & Others & ILDA*. This defining moment occurred six months after the case had concluded. We were finally put out of our misery on Iarnród Éireann's attempts to render us destitute, and on our union recognition claim. The judgment had taken so long that many conspiracy theories had run among our members and families while we waited. I worked very hard, and against my natural suspicious nature to put such thoughts from my head, but one incident in particular did concern me at the time, and it continues to concern me. As I was used to being asked by members and others, 'Any word of the judge?' I was not surprised when Michael Murphy, a senior ILDA member from Inchicore, approached me on a locomotive in Heuston Station, saying that he had heard a rumour. It was in early March 2000. He told me that a friend of his who was in SIPTU had been told in SIPTU head office in Liberty Hall that the judgment would be delivered on 14 April. I laughed at the idea that anyone in Liberty Hall would have five weeks' notice of a High Court judgment of which the defendants in the case had no knowledge. However, I was not confident enough to let it go without a phone call to Donal Spring. I asked Donal whether there was any word of the judgment and when he said no I asked him to check with the clerk of the court. Another solicitor in his office, Paula Murphy, had been in regular contact with the clerk of the court on this very matter, but now checked yet again. The response was the same. No date for the judgment as yet. We were eventually told the date less than one week before judgment: 14 April 2000. Michael Murphy has naturally been smelling rodents ever since. And quite a few of the rest of us have too!

When I look back now on all of these events, 14 April 2000 is a date that surpasses all others. It was to be truly a defining moment for us, both on a personal level for all eleven individual defendants, and thereafter for ILDA as an organisation. This was reflected by the attendance in court of many family members and by a significant media presence also. The eleven defendants again sat together to the judge's right, while the company representatives mingled with our families and the media on the other benches. None of us had any indication of what the judgment might consist. Mr Justice O'Neill appeared from his back room and simply began to read it. No ceremony, no preamble and certainly no acknowledgement of the time delay in issuing judgment, or the difficulties that the delay had produced. The twenty-two page judgment was thorough and was read in court in full. It began by identifying the three main elements of the case as follows:

1. The case by Iarnród Éireann against the eleven named defendants
2. The counter-claim by the twelfth named defendant (ILDA) regarding recognition
3. The further counterclaim by myself regarding the company's disciplinary action against me and my application for various reliefs in this regard.

Mr Justice O'Neill dealt with the company's case first and this was broken into the separate Athlone and Cork stoppages of July 1999. In issuing judgment on the Athlone stoppage, he stated: 'I accept as a fact that what was communicated by the Plaintiffs on the 6th July of 1999 was that Mr. Ogle could not represent either of these two drivers in any capacity [that is, either as a colleague or a union representative.' He went on to say:

I accept also the evidence of Mr. Keenan and Mr. Glynn that this communication did not represent the considered position of the Plaintiffs on the issue of representation by colleagues at grievance procedure hearings or disciplinary hearings. I accept Mr. Keenan's evidence, and in this regard he was supported by Mr. Glynn, that at grievance procedure hearings or at disciplinary hearings a driver was entitled to be represented by another colleague and that that would have included Mr. Ogle.

He proceeded to find that

...the damage was done by the flawed communication on the 6th July, 1999. There is no doubt that the Plaintiffs conveyed the message that they would not treat Mr. Ogle as entitled to represent a fellow locomotive driver, either as a union representative or as a colleague. In refusing to allow Mr. Ogle represent a locomotive driver as a colleague, they were in breach of the established grievance procedures. Mr. Ogle appears to have been greatly upset by this communication and quite reasonably formed the view that he was being, as he put it later, pinpointed for discrimination and victimisation. To make matters worse, on the 8th July, 1999 Mr. Ogle rang Mr. Brendan Smith to query the matter and was given the same response. The following morning at about 9.30am Mr. Smith received a telephone call from Mr. Ogle. In the meantime Mr. Smith had been on to the Plaintiffs' Human Resources Department in Dublin and the content of the message conveyed to the two drivers the previous day was confirmed to him. Thus when he spoke to Mr. Ogle at 9.30am on the morning of the 9th July, he had nothing new to convey to Mr. Ogle and repeated the content of the message from the previous day. Mr. Ogle was again upset at this.

As we sat listening, we were delighted that the judge was correctly identifying Iarnród Éireann as the source of the confusion that had led to the Athlone stoppage. Moreover he was now upholding, as a finding of the High Court, the basic entitlement of a driver in Iarnród Éireann to be represented by a colleague on matters of individual discipline or grievance. In dealing with the accusation of conspiracy on our part, the judgment explained that:

> As mentioned earlier, Mr. Ogle did not give evidence and neither did any of the other members of the National Council apart from Mr. Brian Dunphy, the fifth named Defendant. Mr. Dunphy struck me as an honest witness and I am inclined to believe him when he says he knew nothing about the Athlone stoppage until late in the evening when he was rung by Mr. Ogle and that he knew nothing about the issuing of the statement of the 16th July, 1999 purportedly on behalf of the National Executive Council. Having regard to Mr. Dunphy's evidence and also the nature of events which occurred in Athlone ... I accept also, that there was no advance discussion or planning of this stoppage in Athlone by the National Executive Council of I.L.D.A.. It would seem to me that the probabilities are that the stoppages which occurred in Athlone on the 9th July were an unplanned event which in all probability arose as a relatively spontaneous reaction to the grievance of Mr. Ogle, a grievance which was only clearly established on the 8th July perhaps not until the 9th July, 1999.

It now appeared to be clear that Iarnród Éireann was to fail in its accusations regarding the Athlone stoppage. He continued, however:

> There is no doubt, in the light of the evidence given by the witnesses for the Plaintiffs, that as of the morning of the 9th July, Mr. Ogle had a genuine grievance. That of course would not have justified him in inducing or procuring a withdrawal of labour by other drivers or engaging in a conspiracy to that effect, having regard to the fact that he was bound by the well established grievance procedures, a fact which was readily acknowledged by Mr. Dunphy in his evidence. I am satisfied on the evidence that the Plaintiffs have not proved as a matter of probability that the Defendants, apart from Mr. Ogle, had any involvement in the stoppage that occurred in Athlone on the 9th July, 1999. Hence no liability for whatever losses were suffered by the Plaintiffs as a result of this stoppage can attach to any of these Defendants.

This paragraph startled me. What did he mean by 'Apart from Mr. Ogle' and 'any of these defendants'? However, I was quickly put out of my impending panic by the very next paragraph.

Insofar as Mr. Ogle is concerned, I am not satisfied that the evidence of his involvement in the events that occurred on the afternoon and evening of the 9th July is of such a persuasive character as to enable me to conclude that he, Mr. Ogle, in the words used by Hamilton J. 'did definitely and unequivocally persuade, induce or procure' the four other drivers who refused to take out their trains in Athlone that day, to break their contracts of employment by so refusing to drive their trains. While it is the case that Mr. Ogle remained at the depot for the duration of the afternoon and evening of the 9th, there is no doubt that for that period of time he continued to have a genuine grievance of a kind that was deeply upsetting to him and would be likely to have been offensive and upsetting to other locomotive drivers who with knowledge of what had happened would undoubtedly have had a great deal of sympathy for Mr. Ogle. In the light of these factors, the evidence of the Plaintiffs fails to tilt the balance of probabilities on this issue in their favour and I cannot conclude that it was probable in the circumstances of that day that Mr. Ogle unequivocally persuaded or induced any of these four drivers to breach their contracts of employment. I am also not satisfied that the evidence of the Plaintiffs in regard to the events in Athlone that day goes so far as to convince me that on the balance of probabilities there was an agreement or combination between Mr. Ogle and these other four drivers or any other individual to advance Mr. Ogle's grievance, a purpose lawful in itself, by the unlawful means of a refusal by these four drivers to drive their trains. I conclude therefore that the Plaintiffs' evidence falls short of establishing any liability on the part of the Defendants in respect of whatever losses were suffered by the Plaintiffs as a result of the stoppages at Athlone on the 9th July, 1999.

And that was it. Game, set and match to us on Athlone. The test in any civil, as opposed to criminal, action of 'the balance of probabilities' had not been met by the plaintiff in this case, despite the fact that I hadn't even been required to give evidence. It was like winning a match without going onto the pitch. Or put another way, the company had failed on its own words and evidence, not mine. I immediately recognised the significance of this for me personally. If a High Court judge had found me innocent of any wrongdoing, and to be entitled to have felt a grievance because of the company's own failed communications, then Iarnród Éireann could not possibly find against me in its own internal kangaroo court. Mr Justice O'Neill had settled the Athlone issue and my own personal disciplinary issue in one fell swoop. He now moved on to the Cork incident of 11 July, and it was Christy's turn to worry.

At the outset, the judge made it clear that he accepted the evidence of both the company's witnesses on this issue — Timmy Sheehan and Dan Sheehan. This was actually good news, as it had been Timmy Sheehan who had given evidence that Christy had told him that he actually wanted other drivers to work in Cork on 11 July and not to utilise their rest day in support of his claim for unpaid wages — a piece of evidence that was specifically referred to in the judgment. Having outlined the background to the case, the judgment simply concluded:

I am satisfied that there is insufficient evidence to connect the Defendants other than Mr. Holbrook, to the events in Cork. Indeed, other than the statement issued on the 16th July, 1999 already referred to, there is no evidence which connects the National Executive Council of I.L.D.A. to these events. I accept Mr. Dunphy's evidence in this regard. He says he knew nothing about the stoppage in Cork until the 12th July when it was all over. I also accept his evidence that there was no discussion of it in advance and that the events in Cork on the 11th of July in the week leading up to it never came to the attention of the National Executive Council. The contents of the statement issued after the event do not convince me that the Defendants named in these proceedings, apart from Mr. Holbrook, had any involvement in the stoppages that occurred on the 11th July, 1999 or in the events during the week leading up to it. On the contrary, the evidence satisfies me that on the balance of probabilities what happened in Cork was a local event confined to the drivers based in Cork. I tend to be reinforced in that conclusion by the fact that out of the forty drivers based in Cork, only eight were members of I.L.D.A., [at the time of the July 1999 stoppage, although we now had 18] and of the four drivers who submitted notes on the 5th July indicating their intention not to work on Sunday the 11th two were not members of I.L.D.A

This now left Christy in the position I had faced just a few minutes earlier. No blame attached to any of the other defendants but was he going to have to carry the can? However, on this issue too, logic would carry the day. Before finalising the Cork incident, the judgment observed the following:

> That brings me to a consideration of whether or not any liability attaches to Mr. Holbrook for his part in the events that occurred. The Plaintiffs' case at its highest point in the evidence of Mr. Tim Sheehan is to suggest that from the conduct of Mr. Holbrook in refusing to work his own roster on the 11th July, there is to be drawn an inference that such conduct thereby persuaded, procured or induced all of the other drivers not to work on Sunday, the 11th July. That the other drivers did not turn up for work on that day is undoubtedly the case. There is no evidence, however, to suggest that Mr. Holbrook engaged in any form of persuasion or cajoling or otherwise put pressure on any of these drivers not to work. Indeed the contrary is the case. It was accepted by Mr. Tim Sheehan that Mr. Holbrook expressed himself as not wishing to have the other drivers support him and that that fact could be made known to the other drivers and indeed there was evidence that the two unions, S.I.P.T.U. and N.B.R.U., issued a statement urging their members to work normally. The evidence does not assist me at all in ascertaining or understanding what form of bond there existed (if any) between Mr. Holbrook and the other Cork drivers or what form of subtle communication (if any) there may have been between Mr. Holbrook and these drivers which could have resulted in all of them staying out from work on that day, a result that could equally have been no more than the expression of a strong sense of loyalty or solidarity built up over many years of common association and not instigated on the occasion by any act on Mr. Holbrook's part.

The judgment then confirmed the outcome with the following emphatic finding:

Whatever it may have been, the evidence does not, in my view, reasonably support an inference that Mr. Holbrook in the words of Hamilton J., as he then was, 'unequivocally persuaded, induced or procured' these other drivers to not turn up for work on that Sunday. I am not satisfied therefore that the Plaintiffs have discharged the onus of proof on them and satisfied me on the balance of probabilities that Mr. Holbrook either induced or procured breaches of their contracts of employment by these other drivers or that he engaged in an agreement or combination with any of them to effect that purpose.

Accordingly the Plaintiffs' claim for damages for the losses that they suffered as a result of this stoppage must fail against all of the Defendants.

At that point, we were on top of the world. I turned to Ken Fox and said, 'Two down; one to go.' Mr Justice O'Neill didn't even pause for breath before moving on to his findings on the issue of recognition and representation. In outlining the background, he succinctly summed up the issue as what constituted a 'representative' union and if ILDA was a representative union, whether or not Iarnród Éireann had a duty to negotiate with us.

In order to ascertain whether we were representative, the judgment needed to define the extent of our membership as a proportion of the overall grade. This necessitated the judge's weighing the written evidence submitted by us against the company's allegations that our members were still members of either SIPTU or the NBRU. On this issue, the judgment cut through all of the management rhetoric, and, to this day, that of ICTU and SIPTU, by observing that:

The Defendants assert that on the evidence there is no overlapping between their membership and membership of the other two unions and that they have 114 members all of whom have resigned from the other two unions. The Defendants have put in evidence copies of letters of resignation on the part of 114 of the members from the two unions and some 20 letters from other members written to the Plaintiffs instructing the Plaintiffs to stop payroll deduction of union dues hitherto paid to either S.I.P.T.U. or N.B.R.U., on the basis of these persons having resigned from those two unions.

The judge continued:

> I accept that I.L.D.A. does have 114 members currently and that all of these have resigned from the other two unions. Thus, as of the trial of the action herein (November 1999), there was no overlapping of membership between I.L.D.A. and either S.I.P.T.U. or N.B.R.U.

This finding was, and is, in itself massively significant. Mr Justice O'Neill had also accepted 265 drivers (excluding unqualified drivers) as the overall relevant membership of the grade. Put simply, the court had found that ILDA had a total of 43 per cent of the grade and that these drivers were members of ILDA and no other union. It meant that ILDA was the biggest of the three unions representing locomotive drivers. How then could ILDA not be representative if both SIPTU and the NBRU with smaller memberships within the grade were? As we listened, we felt that we were within touching distance of the whole ball game. No judge could have argued with our documentation on our membership but the implications of this were massive. Colossal even. Industrial relations in Iarnród Éireann were about to be revolutionised. The 'New Deal' and its four years of negotiations were about to be consigned to the dustbin. The LRC who had assisted the whole process right down to 'facilitating' the ballot and many nay-sayers who argued that it could not be done — that we couldn't succeed — were all about to be proven wrong. And locomotive drivers were about to have, at last, a union to represent them that would truly put their issues at the very top of the agenda. In fact, theirs would be the only issues on the agenda. Sitting in Court 13, I knew all of this. So did the other eleven defendants, now already vindicated and cleared. So did our families. So, most certainly, did management and the assembled media. We awaited justice. But, in the event, we got law. The judgment continued:

> It would seem to me to follow that if agreements negotiated through the process of Section 55 are binding on the workers in the grades affected and cannot be altered save with the consent of unions which represent them, that the unions which purport to negotiate such agreements under Section 55 must have as their members the

substantial majority of the workers in those grades. Up to the time that ILDA emerged all of the locomotive drivers were in either S.I.P.T.U. or the N.B.R.U., S.I.P.T.U. having a preponderance of members. The Defendants say now that the 114 members that they have now exceeds the number of drivers who are in the N.B.R.U. [and SIPTU — author] and hence the Defendants say that they are as much entitled to be considered as 'representative' if not more so than the N.B.R.U. In my view this is to look at the problem from the wrong way. There is no doubt that I.L.D.A. with 114 members are a minority of locomotive drivers albeit a substantial minority. Thus in my view the Plaintiffs are entitled to refuse to negotiate with them on the basis that they are not representative of the broad mass or of a substantial majority of locomotive drivers. The fact that the N.B.R.U. have less members than I.L.D.A. does not gainsay this. The Plaintiffs have a long established policy of dealing with two unions on behalf of locomotive drivers. Until the emergence of I.L.D.A. these unions represented all of the locomotive drivers. In my view, the Plaintiffs are entitled to continue to regard S.I.P.T.U. and the N.B.R.U. as representative of locomotive drivers they between them clearly representing a substantial majority of locomotive drivers and to refuse to regard I.L.D.A. as 'representative' for the purposes of Section 55.

And that was it. He went on a bit more — providing Iarnród Éireann with a declaration that it would be unlawful to negotiate with us as we were not an 'excepted body' by virtue of article 5 of our rules theoretically allowing for membership in other rail companies — but the paragraph above is the essence of the key judgment. We were bigger than NBRU — and SIPTU — but because they were there before us, it didn't matter how many members we had unless we had a 'broad mass' or 'substantial majority'. The fact that they didn't have a 'broad mass' or 'substantial majority' didn't matter. Section 55 of the Railways Act 1924 was nothing more than a first-past-the-post race which rendered anything that happened subsequently irrelevant. We were stunned. Padraig Yeates described it in the following day's *Irish Times* as a 'pragmatic judgement'. What I concluded was that the little uppity train drivers had got to keep their houses while the big powerful suits got to talk and ignore whomsoever they liked.

As we left Court 13 that day, families beside us holding hands and reporters wanting our reaction, I felt anything but happy. The back-slapping among management in the corridors outside showed who the happy ones were.

There are some moments from that day that will last long in my memory. One is of Roddy Horan BL for the company standing up the second Mr Justice O'Neill had stopped reading and demanding all his costs from us. All his costs. Even for the two-thirds of the case — the most time-consuming elements —that he had lost spectacularly. The judge gave him short shrift and made no award of costs. Pragmatic to the last! Another moment that sticks in my memory was when the judge rose and slipped out of court, failing to look in our direction. I had watched him, hoping to catch his eye, wanting to confirm for myself that he really believed what he had just read out. I didn't get a chance. Then outside, my friend, P.J. Healy, had come up to court for the day. He believed that this would be a landmark day for drivers and, although retired, he wanted to be there for it. Now he stood outside with a tear in his eye and anger on his tongue. He grasped my hand and urged me, 'Keep going, Brendan.' Then he left and our legal team left and management left and we stood there looking at each other.

What Next?

We needed somewhere private to regroup and collect our thoughts, so I rang Wynn's Hotel and booked a meeting room. We walked down Abbey Street, hoping that the air would clear our heads. No one said much. When we got inside the room, we just looked at each other. We didn't even have a written judgment yet to read. That would come later. Perhaps it was as well. Donal Spring called in at one stage to tell us that John and Cathy were bamboozled by what they were reading. There was talk of appeals to the Supreme Court. The Supreme Court? Us? The media reported that ILDA had lost and that it was 'unlawful' for Iarnród Éireann to talk to us. I did a couple of interviews and had to fight hard even to get in a mention that we had actually won the bulk of the case. That didn't seem to matter. The fact that a semi-state company had sued its own respected workers and lost miserably was to be erased from the collective media and public consciousness. That wasn't the message that corporate Ireland wanted to hear. Or send. That was no good to the social-partnership consensus. You can't have train drivers taking on a state company in the High Court and winning anything, never mind most of the case. The message was loud and clear. THE LITTLE GUYS LOST. GET THAT? BIG GUYS WIN AND LITTLE GUYS LOSE!

It was as if we were being told, 'Here — have a few pints. Go home and sleep it off and get back on your train tomorrow and shut up! Stay in your rightful place the next time and do what you're told no matter how wrong, illogical, undemocratic, unfair or unsafe.'

No chance!

A CONSPIRACY BEGINS

As a result of the various stoppages, safety issues, and the legal action, I had become a familiar figure in the media. As someone with absolutely no training in public relations, I was initially very nervous when dealing with the media, particularly radio and television. I clearly recall the occasion of my first radio interview in 1997. It was with Pat Kenny on his morning radio show; I hardly slept with nerves the night before, and was unable to eat that day until the interview was over. Over time, however, I became more relaxed and familiar with many of the personalities involved. One notable exception, however, occurred at the end of an interview on RTÉ's *Morning Ireland* on 20 March 2000.

I was on a telephone line from Athlone and John Keenan was in studio with interviewer Richard Downes. I have always felt myself to be at a disadvantage when I am not in studio while an opponent is. The eye contact and body language between presenter and interviewee can be crucial in determining the tone to be taken and when to interrupt or be more forceful in making points. When an opponent has that advantage while I sit at home, I have often felt that the person in studio gets the advantage and generally the last word in any interview. This particular interview was about serious safety concerns and I felt that, throughout the interview, I had exposed flaws in John Keenan's arguments. Just as the interview was ending, however, Richard Downes commented to me that he had never heard me saying anything positive about Iarnród Éireann, and suggested that, in such a buoyant economy, I might consider working elsewhere. I was thrown. I made some remark about looking forward to having something positive to say about Iarnród Éireann in the future, but I felt that the interview had been personalised and that Richard Downes' comment was prejudiced. The following morning, *The Star* newspaper actually editorialised on the subject, demanding that I receive an apology from RTÉ. I myself had already faxed a complaint to the show's editorial team, requesting an apology. After a follow-up letter, I did receive an apology from RTÉ; it accepted that I was entitled to be upset by the comment, and gave me an assurance that there would be no repeat. In later months, I met Richard Downes on a number of occasions and found him — as with most RTÉ journalists — to be fair, balanced and professional at all other times.

This incident apart, I was now becoming quite comfortable in dealing with the media. However, as the summer of 2000 progressed and ILDA turned into *the* story of the summer, that situation would change, and in some — perhaps many — cases, I encountered hostility and bias at the hands of journalists. That would be later, however. For now, we still had legal matters to consider.

The Decision to Appeal to the Supreme Court

In the lead-up to the High Court case, the prospect that we might ultimately end up in the Supreme Court seemed remote. Given our lack of resources, the likelihood of our being there as a result of an appeal lodged by us seemed impossible. As we had initially been quoted a 'worst-case scenario' fee of £90,000, our financial position was already dire. Although we had been victorious in the High Court judgment on many points, including the substantive case mounted by the company against us, the case had gone on for seven days, whereas the pre-case assessment we had received was for a two- to three-day hearing. We had provided £30,000 up front at an early stage and more was now needed. Any hopes spouses in particular had harboured of being able to pay back the loans quickly had vanished. It was now time for ILDA members — other than the initial eleven defendants who had by now been cleared by the court of any specific wrongdoing — to dig deep and raise more funds or leave a considerable shortfall.

It was against this background that consideration of a Supreme Court appeal of *Iarnród Éireann v. Holbrook* [2000] IEHC 47 (14 April 2000) took place. Despite the perilous financial situation, we felt that Mr Justice O'Neill's judgment almost demanded an appeal. In addition to the normal day-to-day telephone discussions about it, a number of formal meetings took place, involving the entire National Executive Council and our legal team of John Rogers SC, Cathy Maguire BL and solicitors from Spring's. John, like the rest of us, was disappointed with the judgment. We discussed the appeal prospects and it was explained to us that, with a judgment of this nature, the outcome was unpredictable. It was accepted that it was unlikely that Mr Justice O'Neill's judgment would survive the rigours of the Supreme Court intact and without alteration, but what the effects of any alteration might be were far from clear.

As our advisors were aware of our financial position, but nevertheless had a specific and natural involvement in the case at that stage, it was agreed that Spring's at least would cover the Supreme Court appeal *pro bono* or on a 'no win, no fee' basis. And so it was decided within the specified time frame that we, little old ILDA, would be fighting our recognition dispute all the way to the Irish Supreme Court. We were asked to provide another £20,000 against outstanding fees for the High Court case before the Supreme Court case could be prepared. With help from some friends, that money too was raised and paid.

It was the position, however, that many members of the executive were disappointed that money was not coming in from the wider membership in accordance with the commitments that we had received at the outset and had passed on to our legal advisors. A small number of our members outside the executive contributed exceptional four-figure sums, without which we would probably have been unable to go any distance at all in the courts. However, in general, the wider membership donated £200 per man at best, with many contributing nothing at all throughout the entire process. Although almost all members made incredible sacrifices, financial or otherwise, later, the fact remains that for fifteen or so members, the sacrifice of ten weeks without pay was made without complaint and in addition to lump-sums of several thousand pounds that had already been provided. Before we would go much further down the legal route though, that summer of discontent would be upon us and donations for legal matters would dry up for good. Before that, however, there were to be a number of significant events.

With Iarnród Éireann pressing ahead with the proposed implementation of the 'New Deal' in June, our members faced the prospect of an uncertain future regarding their terms and conditions of employment. Within ILDA, one thing was clear. The determination of our members to face down a forced implementation of the 'New Deal' was strengthening, not weakening, with each passing disappointment. To us, our objections were natural and substantive. On the industrial relations front, compulsory Sunday and bank-holiday working as proposed was bad enough, but to be expected to stomach it without any premium payments was simply untenable. It seemed to us to be in breach of the Organisation of Working Time Act 1997, where sections 27 and 28 of that act made premium payments for such work compulsory. To us, the company's claim that these payments were 'incorporated' in an 'overall payment package' did not hold water. Add to that the concerns with the proposal that different and disparate pay rates should apply to different drivers doing the same work; that many important and valued link structures be eliminated; and that radical changes in roster patterns be forced in without any discussion with us — together with an array of other proposed changes — and the potential for trouble was obvious. When this was all capped by serious safety concerns, the picture becomes complete.

It should be noted that in this list of contentious issues, with the exception of premium payments for Sunday and bank holiday payments, there was no mention of money. I feel that this is a point that has not been sufficiently acknowledged throughout the whole sorry saga that was to follow. Here were a group of workers heading into one of the longest and most traumatic industrial disputes in recent years — a dispute that would have a colossal effect on them and their families — and money was absolutely and unequivocally not the issue. The dispute that followed was about a conviction and belief by those workers that they had been wronged in the past and were being wronged again now. Their sense of injustice could not be bought off. On the contrary, they would have to stand by out of work while their colleagues in SIPTU and the NBRU were induced, financially and otherwise, to do their work. The sole aim of Iarnród Éireann seemed to us to be simply to break the belief, spirit and conviction that made ILDA possible. Perhaps the fact that money could not simply be thrown at the workers involved ultimately made what followed even more difficult to resolve.

Following the High Court judgment, however, we were still focused on preventing such a scenario from occurring. The very first thing we did was to amend Article 5 of our constitution from 'Membership shall be open to all Locomotive Drivers, male or female, resident or employed on the island of Ireland' to read 'Membership shall be open to all Locomotive Drivers employed by Iarnród Éireann (Irish Rail) or its successor.' This amendment was carried out following legal advice that it was what was needed in order to comply with the High Court judgment. It specifically restricts membership to Iarnród Éireann employees, thereby clearly complying with section 6(3) of the Trade Union Act 1941.

The change was carried out following a full ballot of all members in April 2000, almost immediately after the judgment, and was submitted to the Registrar of Friendly Societies for ratification on 3 May 2000. It was formally ratified by the Registrar and a confirmation certificate was issued on 2 June 2000. In the lead-up to that date I had been in almost daily contact with the registry, imploring them to pass the amendment before 5 June. Monday, 5 June 2000 was the initial date that Iarnród Éireann had fixed for the implementation of the 'New Deal'. High noon! When the registry — a section of the Department of Enterprise, Trade and Employment — acted so quickly in passing the amendment, we in ILDA read it as a definite sign that 'people who matter' had determined that there was to be no summer rail strike and that space was being created for a solution in the interest of all. We were wrong.

While all that was going on, we also held a conference of our members — the first since ILDA's formation. It took place at Horse and Jockey in Co. Tipperary, and the beautifully renovated but intimate hotel and facilities there were ideal for a grouping of our size. The conference was held over two days — 30 April and 1 May 2000 — and was a resounding success on a number of fronts.

ILDA's First Conference

In the lead-up to the conference, the NEC circulated a confidential questionnaire to every member, asking them key questions on the sort of issues that were coming to the fore. The questionnaire took the form of a series of statements with which members recorded their agreement or disagreement. The responses were collated and presented to the conference in booklet form and on a series of slides for discussion. Some of the responses to the questions were extremely strong and set the tone not alone for a very determined conference but for the action that would follow just six weeks later. For example, one of the statements put to the members was: 'I should be able to have any Sunday I need off in an exceptional family or social circumstance'. This proposition was agreed with by 98 per cent of respondents. On the statement, 'Only full time train drivers should be permitted to drive trains', 94 per cent of respondents agreed. The questionnaire was quite comprehensive and, taken with the strength of feeling expressed at the conference and the unity of purpose apparent, it certainly contributed greatly to enhancing the confidence of the ILDA leadership in articulating the views of ILDA members when that became necessary soon afterwards.

The conference included an overnight stay and a meal and social attended by wives and girlfriends. This provided us all with an opportunity to relax and have a laugh. On a more serious note, though, the conference received some coverage from the national media. Unfortunately, Padraig Yeates, the specialist industrial relations correspondent with *The Irish Times*, was unable to attend. However, a Limerick-based freelance journalist, Keith Harris, was attending the conference, and, to our delight, *The Irish Times* accepted his offer of copy. I felt that it was important that a serious newspaper would report that we were conducting our business in a serious manner, and that it would be better to have a respected journalist present to witness the debates at first hand, than simply to rely on news releases. The result was a more accurate piece of reporting of the conference than we could have expected in any other circumstances. The article, which appeared in *The Irish Times* on 2 May, under the heading 'Largest Train Drivers' Union Rejects Iarnród Offer Overwhelmingly' reported the fact that we were considering legal action to prevent the 'New Deal' from being implemented in contravention of its own opt-out clause, concluding:

> The conference ratified the rejection of the agreement reached between Iarnród Éireann and SIPTU and the NRBU to change train drivers' working conditions. A five-day working week and the right to

have a pre-determined number of weekend days free were also the subject of major concerns expressed by the majority of ILDA members.

I had received some assistance with the conference questionnaire from a man who had introduced himself to me the previous year and who, to my initial concern, had been none other than a previous regional secretary with SIPTU. Martin King had contacted me with regard to some research he was doing into the relationships between workers and their unions. He had done similar research in other companies such as Ballygowan and the banking sector, and explained that he would like to set up a study into train drivers and their relationships with all three unions. The research would ask union members agreed questions about their views of, confidence in, and relationships with their respective unions, and compare the results. As I was perfectly happy to find out through academic research what our members thought of us, I immediately agreed to put the proposal to a meeting of the NEC. Martin had resigned from SIPTU —coincidentally in 1994 — and had been studying and doing consultancy work since. He had been following ILDA's development closely. Some weeks later, however, he telephoned me to explain that SIPTU was not as keen to find out what its members thought of it as we were with our members. SIPTU was even less keen that we would find out, through shared research, what its members thought of it; the National Rail Council had apparently rejected Martin's overtures out of hand. He had had even less success with the NBRU who hadn't even afforded him the courtesy of a meeting. Martin was disappointed by this, but readily offered assistance when I was putting together our own bit of research into our members' views. Moreover, I had made another contact who would be of some help to ILDA and to me as time and circumstance wore on.

And so, with the conference over, and a strong sense of unity amongst our members, our Supreme Court appeal about to be lodged, and Iarnród Éireann preparing for the implementation of the 'New Deal for Locomotive Drivers', the scene was set for a truly remarkable chain of events in all of our lives.

But as with most 'wars', first there was the 'phoney war'.

The Phoney War

Although all the evidence told us that Iarnród Éireann was serious, some of us in ILDA still had difficulty in believing that the company was going to try to force in the agreement on 5 June. Had the company not been listening to our members or taking notice of our increasing ranks and our clear determination not to be bullied into these changes without discussion? Did Irish Rail bosses really think that all they had to do was pick a date and time for implementation, and all our resistance, concern and unity would just collapse? As the days passed, towards the 5 June 'kick off', the company played its ace card, the one that had served Iarnród Éireann so well on every other occasion — the tried-and-trusted lump-sum pay-off.

Although the 'New Deal' provided for pay increases for most drivers based on a flat thirty-nine-hour week, the reality was that many drivers had worked regular sixty- to seventy-hour weeks prior to its implementation. The 'New Deal' would therefore represent a real 'loss of earnings' to these drivers, and the Labour Court had helpfully provided for this 'loss of earnings', in Labour Court recommendation 16347. It is important to emphasise that the money concerned was simply a standard 'loss of earnings' formula, paid only to employees who would incur a loss; it was in no way a reward for working new conditions, or made up as any part of the payments for working those new conditions. In the case of ILDA, approximately fifty of our then 130 members qualified for this payment. I didn't qualify as the 'New Deal' to which I was so opposed actually provided me with quite a significant wage increase, not a loss. Iarnród Éireann would later try to portray this payment, without much success, in quite a different light.

Labour Court recommendation 16347 kindly provided qualifying drivers — about one-third of the total nationally across all three unions — with a loss-of-earnings formula that paid them up to £20,000 lump-sums in extreme cases. In reality, the sums were generally much lower than this headline figure and they were paid out in two parts — one before implementation of the 'New Deal', and one to be paid in December 2000 as a 'Christmas bonus' (workers in Iarnród Éireann, at least operative workers, receive no standard Christmas bonus). We were concerned that payment of this money to some of our members would be used to tie us into the 'New Deal'. In fairness to our members, none of them wanted it. In fact, some SIPTU and NBRU members didn't want it either. We decided that it would be necessary to do everything we could to stop Iarnród Éireann from paying it out. However, as most of our members were paid by credit transfer direct to their bank accounts, we realised that this would be difficult. So, in addition, we began correspondence ourselves, and through our solicitors, that would clearly and publicly demonstrate that we didn't want the money. Accordingly, I wrote to Irish Rail on a number of occasions, instructing management that this 'loss of earnings' money should not be paid. As usual, our letters were ignored. In addition, and 'to be sure to be sure', our solicitors also wrote to Iarnród Éireann's solicitors on our behalf. This correspondence clarified firstly that Irish Rail should not pay the monies to our members as we would be challenging the 'New Deal' through our Supreme Court appeal. However, it also warned that if the company ignored our instructions and insisted on paying the monies anyway, and if we were ultimately successful in procuring negotiating status through the court, we would reserve the right to keep the monies.

That, of course, is exactly what happened. There followed the bizarre situation of workers trying to give management back money that they didn't actually want. On occasion, this reached almost farcical levels when Finbarr Masterson, for example, got a cheque made out for the amount and handed it into management in Westport who then posted it back to him and refused to accept it. In Cork, one of the very few remaining drivers still paid in cash actually refused to draw his wages until the loss-of-earnings money was withdrawn from it, prompting a surreal stand-off with a bemused wages clerk determined to give him money he wouldn't take. If ever anything could illustrate that the upcoming dispute was not about money, these almost comical incidents do so in the clearest terms.

The absurdity of the situation was compounded months later when we had returned to work following the most bitter of disputes, and actually about to work the 'New Deal'. Management then refused to pay the second half of the earnings to many qualifying ILDA members. In fact, to this day, some ILDA members have still not been paid these payments. It is truly ironic that when our members were refusing to work the 'New Deal', management insisted on paying this money, but when we were reluctantly starved back to work and forced to work it, management then refused to pay out the rest. And in possibly one of its most mind-boggling decisions ever, management acted thus with the approval of the Labour Court. But that was all for another day!

And so, 5 June approached and all the pieces were in place for a spectacular showdown. In the lead-up to the planned implementation, Iarnród Éireann issued a most confusing missive, ostensibly telling workers that payroll changes would commence from 5 June but that work conditions would not be changed until 18 June 2000. Or was it the other way around? It was so brilliantly ambiguous that nobody could tell and confusion reigned amongst members of all unions. ILDA members, however, were having none of it. As far as we were concerned, 5 June was the date for implementation of changed work practices, unless someone clearly told us otherwise. Then, dramatically, on 3 June, Iarnród Éireann made the following statement in a letter to SIPTU and the NBRU: 'On and from the pay period commencing Monday June 19th the new pay and conditions will apply'.

The Eleventh Hour

The NEC had met on 31 May to consider the impending crisis, and had decided to schedule an extraordinary general meeting for the afternoon of Sunday, 4 June, to afford members the opportunity to decide how to approach any attempted change in their working conditions the following morning. The meeting, which was held in the Aisling Hotel in Dublin and was the subject of a fair degree of media attention, was very well attended and necessitated a last-minute move to the hotel's biggest function suite. RTÉ wanted to interview me for television before the meeting and recorded interviews with many of the members about the 'New Deal' also. The anger was palpable, and I think the assembled media quickly became as aware of that fact as we had been for some weeks. When Christy Holbrook, as President, opened the meeting, we put Iarnród Éireann's ambiguous letters to the floor and debated their possible meanings, without any clear consensus. What was crystal clear, however, was that if the 'New Deal' was implemented the following morning, not one person in that room was going to work it.

The debate quickly turned to tactics for dealing with this reality on the basis that, unless we got clarity, we were taking the worst-case scenario and dealing with it. In considering tactics, a number of issues arose. For a start, there is no set 'book-on' time for train drivers at any depot. Individual drivers book on individually at different times throughout the day, afternoon, evening and night, in well over a dozen depots throughout the state. It isn't like a shop, office or factory where all the protesting workers could assemble at the same time and simply not work or mount a picket. In our case, the first driver on duty would report at Inchicore Depot, alone, at 00.01 hrs on 5 June 2000, June bank holiday Monday. Thereafter, his 129 fellow ILDA members could be booked on at any time that day in any one of thirteen separate depots. How could we organise this and ensure that members, although isolated, remained unified and strong? How would the company and the foremen on duty react? Would they send each driver home and hope that somewhere the chain would break? Would they allow us to sit it out and await the next driver to turn up and join the protest? If so, how would this work as members of SIPTU and the NBRU arrived to work the agreement while we sat there idle? Would drivers be suspended as had happened in 1994? Was there the potential for trouble and discourse amongst different drivers in different depots? And would the company have a unified national policy in place at all or would each scenario differ on a depot-by-depot basis, causing confusion and division?

As the only real union in Ireland without a negotiating licence, ILDA found itself in a unique position. We could not legally ballot our members for a strike. We could not place pickets on our workplaces. We enjoyed no legal immunity for any such strike action and, still reeling from their defeat on those issues in the High Court, none of us doubted that Iarnród Éireann was just waiting for us to make a mistake. Any opportunity to drive the nail home in court the next time would be seized upon by our employer. How we handled this would be crucial. Our protest at our treatment would, of necessity, be just that — a protest, a withdrawal of labour. We were walking a legal and industrial relations tightrope.

All of these matters were considered by the meeting but with particular focus on our colleagues in other unions and their reaction to us. Relations with our SIPTU and NBRU colleagues had not totally disintegrated at that stage. In some cases, relationships among drivers had been forged through years of working together and would not easily be broken. There was also a sense of unreality about the whole situation. I believe that many SIPTU and NBRU members believed that we would back down or that there would be some intervention, some fudge. None of them were in the Aisling Hotel on 4 June though. None of them understood the months of pent-up anger we felt at our isolation in the workplace, and our sense of betrayal by our colleagues — not for their disagreement with us but for having allowed our entitlement to hold our views to be trampled on in their name. Ultimately, as far as many of our members were concerned, our colleagues were, whether they knew it or not, responsible. The drivers' union that they had all seemed to want so much but had not had the courage to join was now under attack, and they were standing by, letting it happen. The longer the meeting went on, the hotter the atmosphere in the room became. After over an hour of discussion, Tom O'Brien from Athlone got to his feet with the only proposal he felt was appropriate in all the circumstances.

Although a native of Athlone, Tom had begun his driving career in Limerick and worked the south of Ireland routes extensively. Now back in Athlone, he was also well known to all of our west of Ireland, Midlands and Dublin-based members. In his mid-thirties with ten years' seniority, he was both experienced enough to have the respect of our older members, and young enough to share bonds with our younger and newer members. And he was a man who spoke from both the heart and the head.

Tom addressed the meeting and asked whether or not our members wanted to continue to work as they had been working for months. Did they want to continue to be pariahs in their own place of employment? Did they respect a management who apparently thought nothing of the standards we held so dear? Did they want to work with colleagues who looked upon us as people with no rights; a different class of workers to be used, abused and then, when we said stop, ignored? And were we not, in fact, being forced from our employment by default? 'Constructive dismissal' is the legal term used when a worker is treated so badly within his or her employment as to be left with no option but to resign. Wasn't that what was happening to us? By the very fact of having our working conditions decided on by a minority within our grade, without even the courtesy of an individual — never mind a collective — consultation, was

Iarnród Éireann not really telling us to get out? It was powerful stuff. Stirring stuff. And when it was concluded with a formal proposal that we all resign, en masse, and declare ourselves 'constructively dismissed' from our positions with our employer, I nearly fell off my chair. Not because I didn't think that Tom was serious. I bloody well knew that he was. But because in that room, in that atmosphere, at that precise moment in time, I was worried that his proposal might actually be passed. I would have liked to have had some time to consider all the permutations and possibilities. There was, after all, a lot in what Tom was saying. But if somebody seconded that proposal, we were bound by rule to put it to a vote. There and then. Christy was in the chair and sitting directly on my left. He also realised the dangers of the situation and, having exchanged a few whispers with me, he called an adjournment for half an hour, and suggested to the members that they use the time to reflect on the seriousness of the proposal that had just been tabled.

As I left the room with Christy, drivers began to discuss their individual positions. I walked out of the 'hot house' atmosphere and straight into a media scrum. The media had been waiting, and immediately assumed that the meeting was over when we exited. I was asked for our decision, and explained to the assembled journalists that the meeting had been adjourned at the point when a proposal had been made for us to resign from Iarnród Éireann en masse. Theoretically Irish Rail could be down almost half its train drivers by tea-time.

Even on a Sunday afternoon, on a bank holiday weekend in mid-summer, a shock wave went through the assembled media. It was then that I learned just how helpful some journalists could be in certain circumstances. Padraig Yeates was in Westmoreland Street and reporting events for *The Irish Times*, and Eilis Brennan was the RTÉ reporter present. While Eilis told me that RTÉ was in contact with John Keenan at his home to tell him the news, Padraig was on the telephone asking me just how serious the situation was. I explained that unless the position was clarified, a dispute the following morning was now inevitable, and mass resignations were also a distinct possibility.

The hotel had kindly provided me with an office and typing facilities. However, at this point, it provided more of a sanctuary than anything else. I spoke to some people by phone — journalists mostly; also Fergus

Finlay and Martin King; and then to Padraig Yeates again. He had spoken to John Keenan and he had seemed worried — surprised and concerned as much for us as for anything else, I was told. I wondered. But, in any case, John Keenan was prepared to talk. Padraig was offering his number and I was writing it down. This was new. Now at the point of complete and irrevocable breakdown, the man who had sued us wanted to talk. I got ready to dial, and then put the phone down again. RTÉ was on the other line, saying that John Keenan was on his way to Montrose to give a live interview on the 6.01 news. RTÉ believed that we would get the clarification we were waiting for and the crisis could be averted. I folded up the yellow Post-it with his number on it, and put it in my pocket. I decided not to call for now but to keep the number anyway. Then Padraig Yeates was back on. John Keenan knew that I had his number and was waiting for my call while he traversed the city bound for live TV. I decided to leave him sweat. Leaving my sanctuary, I headed off back to the meeting to tell the members that 'clarification' might be provided on the 6.01 national TV news. Then I asked hotel staff for assistance in moving the ninety to a hundred drivers present to a room with a television. Tom's proposal would have to wait a little while longer.

As all the drivers packed into an upstairs room, the news coverage of the impending dispute began with pictures of us entering the hotel four hours earlier. Following footage of interviews with me and some of the members, the focus turned to John Keenan for his response — live, supposedly. But it wasn't. I had just received a call telling me what John Keenan had said. And so we waited as he explained in clear language that there would definitely be no changes in our work practices the following morning, or indeed until at least 19 June. The latest letter to SIPTU and the NBRU was, in fact, the letter that most closely described the true position.

That was more or less it. There was some debate when members pointed out, rightly, that John Keenan had not dealt specifically with the payment issue. It wasn't a real problem though. Drivers are paid two weeks in arrears so, even if new payments were somehow applied through the payroll, we had the insurance of knowing that we couldn't possibly receive them until the week after 21 June, by which time we would either be in dispute, or a resolution would have been offered. Once this had been talked through, those members who could still catch trains home made a dash for their stations while others made alternative arrangements. Before I could do either, there was the media to be dealt with and a formal news release to be drafted and issued. The statement was strong. Having outlined our difficulties with the plan and provided P.G. Rayner's contact details, it went on to complain that we had been 'victimised, intimidated, discriminated against and threatened with legal action by a tyrannical employer led by egotistical management who lack any real or cohesive vision of the future for Ireland's rail network and its Locomotive Drivers.' And if Keenan was ambiguous on payment, ILDA was not. In referring to the 19 June letter, our press release continued:

Although typically ambiguous this letter clearly demonstrates in written form for the first time that the implementation of the pay and conditions elements of these proposals have been postponed to 19th June to coincide with proposed implementation of rostering arrangements. ILDA confirm that all members will work normally for current pay until June 18th when this meeting will be reconvened. This Union does not seek any 'retrospective' payments after June 19th with regard to duties performed between June 5th and 19th 2000. All payments should be in line with current pay rates as of today's date and existing agreements. ILDA do not consider any unsolicited payments which are not wanted or sought to in any way bind us to this ridiculous and unworkable agreement. This meeting will reconvene on Sunday 18th June 2000. In the meantime we hope Iarnród Éireann, The LRC, politicians and the press will behave responsibly and ensure that no further crisis ensues.'

The statement received national exposure. All media correctly interpreted the evening's events as simply opening up a two-week window of opportunity to prevent a real crisis on the national railway in mid-summer. A two-week breathing space had been bought at the eleventh hour. And we were sure that lessons would be learned. Sure too that any complacency within Iarnród Éireann regarding the limits to which our members would go to maintain their rights would now disappear and that SIPTU and the NBRU would do whatever they could to prevent the grade from fracturing right down the middle in what would obviously be an extremely divisive and dangerous dispute. And finally, we felt confident that politicians, including Minister O'Rourke, would ensure that all possible avenues would be utilised now to keep the trains running and Ireland's tourists on the move.

Window of Opportunity?

The following morning's *Irish Times* provided the first hint that all was not well. I was livid when Padraig Yeates, who had been so helpful, reported the afternoon's events thus:

> The threat to train services has receded following a dramatic about-face by the Irish Locomotive Drivers'Association (ILDA). Shortly before 8.00 last night the association issued a statement instructing members to work normally this morning. Only three hours earlier the executive secretary of the ILDA, Mr Brendan Ogle, had said that up to 70 members were planning to resign rather than accept new working conditions proposed by Iarnród Éireann.

'About face?' Where? If there had been any pullback it certainly hadn't been on our part. Further down, the article made much of Iarnród Éireann's statement that there had been no contact with ILDA. It didn't say that it was I who had decided not to contact John Keenan on this one occasion when he was awaiting and wanting contact. But I was becoming used to the media and the ways in which articles could be written. That wasn't my immediate concern. What was of much more importance was that the 'two-week window' had begun with an apparent retrenchment by Iarnród Éireann as soon as it was off the initial hook. There was not the slightest hint that lessons had been learned. I resolved to wait and see for a number of days, hoping that this was just an example of the media adopting their own angle. But I feared it wasn't.

And so I waited through the first week in June for something to happen. Anything. Nothing did. There was no intervention from the state's 'sophisticated industrial relations machinery'; no contact with the Department of Transport; and certainly no approach from management. I got frustrated, annoyed and angry in turn. I spoke to our members and considered planning simply for all-out war and to hell with them! But when nothing had still occurred by Thursday, 8 June, I asked my close confidant, Thomas McDonnell, to call in for a chat. I explained to Thomas that I felt we had an obligation to do everything humanly possible, however distasteful, to avert this crisis. The fact that others might shirk their responsibilities could not excuse our doing the same. Our objective was to represent our members' interests but avoid this dispute if at all possible. I convinced Thomas that it was time that we made contact with John Keenan. And so I sat down in my hallway and dialled his mobile telephone number. And he answered.

The conversation was surprisingly cordial. He agreed that it might be beneficial to explore how we could move forward. He also offered the opinion that a 'line of communication' between us would be useful although he was concerned about the security of such a line. He expressed concern that Joe Meagher might find out about it.

Joe Meagher is a man of whom most of the people who followed the ILDA dispute through the media would have little or no knowledge. He is, in fact, the Chief Executive of Iarnród Éireann. His role throughout the entire ILDA business from formation to court to disputes and the shenanigans after we had joined the ATGWU has always been unclear. What is clear though is that he was John Keenan's boss, although John Keenan was the very public face of management. I have always had a nagging suspicion, however, that Joe Meagher might deserve a lot more than a single token paragraph acknowledging his existence.

Anyway, when John Keenan expressed himself concerned about Joe Meagher, I assumed that he must be even more formidable than John Keenan. Quite frankly, though, I didn't believe for one minute that John Keenan would attend a meeting with me without the knowledge of Joe Meagher. I just wanted to explore every avenue and if that meant meeting John Keenan alone and face to face, then so be it. We agreed to meet the following Wednesday night — 14 June 2000 — in Kinnegad, exactly half way between Athlone and Dublin — neutral ground. That would leave just three full days before our reconvened meeting on Sunday, 18 June. That surely would be D-Day with no place to run or hide for anyone — no more second chances or escape hatches. Surely John Keenan knew that too!

As I drove to Kinnegad on the evening of 14 June, I had many reservations. My previous dealings with John Keenan had not been pleasant, as we have seen. I almost turned back. But it wasn't about me or my sensitivities or feelings. This was bigger than that. Our members were not for turning and we had to try to find a solution to the threatened dispute, sooner or later. And if that meant, metaphorically speaking, supping with the devil, then that is what had to be done.

We were to meet in Harry's of Kinnegad at 7.30pm and I was there on time. However, John Keenan had been delayed. When I phoned him, he asked me to drive as far as Enfield to meet him. It was almost 8.30 when the conversation finally got underway in Flaherty's of Enfield. It was to continue until 11.45pm. Everything relevant was discussed and the conversation varied widely in tone and content. When we were discussing the development of ILDA, he caught me off guard with a compliment. He said that he had been impressed by the manner in which we had conducted ourselves through the media on occasion and that he saw how drivers would be attracted by ILDA's forthrightness and radicalism. He even conceded, to my amazement, that if he had been a train driver, he would have joined ILDA himself! I think we both began to relax a bit as he talked a bit about his family background in the labour movement. That brought me on to an old bugbear of mine — how could a supposed 'labour man' sue workers in the High Court? Initially he simply shrugged his shoulders, unwilling to debate the perceived contradiction, but then he admitted that those tactics had been totally pioneered by himself and that he, in his own words, 'had to take responsibility for that'. This was something that we had all assumed as his performance in the witness box had hardly been that of the reluctant aggressor, but the candour of his admission was nonetheless startling. There was, however, no apology; as confessions go, it was hardly contrite!

Eventually we turned to the 'New Deal' and its upcoming implementation. I emphasised the strength of our members' feelings, while he explained the determination of the company to see the deal in, before comparing us to 'two trains heading towards each other at top speed on a single line'. On Sunday there was going to be a head-on collision and neither of us knew what the outcome would be. I was somewhat surprised by this. Was he telling me that the company had no contingency plans for the upcoming 'collision'? If that were the case, I concluded on the spot that we were in more trouble than I had thought. I countered that if two trains are headed for a collision, it is up to someone — anyone — to pull some points and signals to re-route one or both of them. I was there to meet him to see if we could pull some points or re-route us all away from disaster. He smiled and asked me whether I had any ideas.

We had talked about the factors motivating the SIPTU and NBRU members and had agreed that money was the major factor. Certainly time-off wasn't, as there were not enough drivers to provide rest days at that point. I suggested that we could look at the overall scenario and put a number of elements together to provide a solution. Basically, my idea was that Iarnród Éireann would tell SIPTU and the NBRU that its initial safety assessment – prompted by the Rayner report - had suggested further and more prolonged investigation — as it turned out, that assessment would ultimately be required in any case. This would mean that these investigations would prevent the 'New Deal' from being implemented for a number of months — the summer tourist season. As a gesture of good faith, the company would agree to frontload implementation of the pay element of the proposals forthwith, thereby defusing most of the anticipated SIPTU/NBRU angst. ILDA would undertake to make no public comment and to continue to work throughout. In addition, we — together with Iarnród Éireann's legal team — would undertake to do everything in our power to ensure the earliest possible Supreme Court hearing of our appeal (this hearing eventually took place in November 2000). The ultimate safety validation would be presented only after the Supreme Court decision, thereby, theoretically, removing from the agenda of any future dispute any uncertainty over the legalities of union-recognition issues. By then, more drivers would also be trained, providing for more rest-day relief; the courts would be out of the equation; all safety issues would have been finally dealt with; and the situation would be a lot more fluid and more conducive to a relatively peaceful changeover of conditions. Even if a dispute did then happen, at least it would not be in peak summer season and at the busiest time of the year.

This proposal provided Iarnród Éireann with quite a lot in terms of tying everybody into the 'New Deal', on the basis that all drivers would immediately be accepting monies for eventually working its provisions. In addition, it would mean that if a dispute were necessary, it would occur at a much more suitable time for the company in commercial terms. It would also provide the benefit to all parties of dealing with the safety concerns in a comprehensive manner and bringing finality to that issue before any possible dispute. And finally, it provided for the Supreme Court case on recognition to be concluded; the Supreme Court findings were obviously going to be pivotal in deciding whether or not ILDA could practically continue without a negotiating licence.

I had discussed the possibilities of such a proposal with a small number of close members and associates. They had all agreed that it had at its core a real attempt to put together an interim solution that took account of the positions of all parties and attempted to take the heat out of the developing crisis. Moreover, they felt that if Iarnród Éireann met it even a quarter of the way, no dispute would be necessary or would follow. John Keenan's immediate response, however, was negative and disconcerting. He dismissed the idea that there could be any delay to the implementation process, and seemed to me to be certain that the company could deal with any consequences. I tried to explore how the company might intend to do that, but direct questions failed to elicit any response. I concluded that either the company had no contingency plans or John Keenan was hiding them well.

The conversation turned to a possible further court action and I decided that I needed to be clear on my position on this. I told him that I accepted that he had to manage the situation, but said directly that if he attacked my wife and family again, that would be personal, not professional, and that there would be only one winner at that stage. I suppose it could have been construed as a threat, and perhaps it was. In the context of his acceptance of responsibility for the previous court action, it was possibly uncalled for. But being sued by our employer was and is a really sore point with me. Even the slightest hint of a repeat was going to meet with only one response.

In any event, the meeting finished as it had begun — cordially. John Keenan had not given a definitive response to my proposal, and promised to sleep on it. We agreed to speak again about it by telephone before close of business on Friday, the last working day before our general meeting and implementation. However, as I drove home, I knew deep down that the meeting had been a failure and would produce nothing useful. It was my opinion that John Keenan was not looking for a way of avoiding confrontation, and all the meetings and telephone conversations in the world wouldn't change that one fact. What I didn't know, however, was that by the time I next spoke to him, I would be in possession of information that was of such a nature that John Keenan's response to it would prove conclusively to any reasonable observer that Iarnród Éireann was not in the solution business.

Then, out of the blue, the very next day — Thursday, 15 June 2000 — I received the letter that I had feared would never come. On 1 June 2000, before the initial stand-off, I had referred to the Labour Relations Commission Iarnród Éireann's failure to address difficulties through procedures with us. In my post on that afternoon, I received a formal invitation from the LRC to attend a 'conciliation conference' under the auspices of the Commission's Chief Executive, Kieran Mulvey. The letter also said that a similar invitation had been issued to the company. I was delighted and relieved. At last, the state's industrial relations machinery was acting in the interests of workers and the public alike. It was the way it should be. I spoke to a number of our members on the phone and they were as relieved as I was. Having managed to find a two-week window of opportunity, and having watched 75 per cent of it just disappear, I now felt a weight being lifted from my shoulders.

I phoned John Keenan, but he said that he had received no corresponding letter. It later transpired, however, that Iarnród Éireann had received an invitation from the LRC but that John Keenan apparently had not been made aware of it! I also spoke to a number of journalists and we immediately welcomed this intervention and confirmed that we would attend conciliation. Then, in an effort to escape the cabin fever of my 'office', I picked my daughter up early from the crèche and took her for a treat in McDonald's. Just as I was leaving McDonald's, however, my phone rang. It was Niall Mooney of the *Irish Examiner*. He told me the staggering news that the LRC had withdrawn its invitation to conciliation. I drove home faster than I should have and tried to call Ray Magee, the LRC's Director of Conciliation. He was unavailable, and no one else could tell me what was going on. It was the next day, Friday, 16 June 2000, before my fax machine kicked into action. A few short seconds later, there it was before my eyes: the Director of Conciliation of the

LRC's signature on a letter telling me that the offer of state-sponsored conciliation on the eve of a national rail dispute had been 'an administrative error'.

The letter stated that the LRC could facilitate only 'recognised' trade unions. I had a sense of barriers being placed in the way of any possible solution by person or persons unknown. The LRC had sat on our referral from 1 June to 13 June before responding. It had sent letters to both parties. In that fortnight, ILDA, Iarnród Éireann and the prospects of a major national rail dispute had seldom been out of the news. It had been discussed in parliament. Dire warnings had been issued by us, and others, about the potential fall-out if third-party intervention did not take place by the second seemingly unalterable implementation date of 18 June. And after two weeks of sitting, watching, reading and assessing, the state's industrial relations machinery had issued an invitation to conciliation 'by accident'?

On the same day, Friday 16 June, I was advised of the existence of a statutory code of practice (SI 146/2000) that could avoid the dispute. In the same telephone conversation, I was told by a friend, who had received the information from a contact in a government department, that a senior SIPTU figure had demanded the withdrawal of the offer to us. The person in the department had been so shocked by this and by the manner in which it had been handled by the LRC, which comes under the auspices of the Department of Enterprise, Trade and Employment, that they had decided to bring the existence of the recently implemented code of practice to our attention through a mutual contact.

Before the day was out, I would have further experience of such strange behaviour across a wide section of bodies, including the company, the LRC and two separate government departments. The misleading nature of Ray Magee's statement that the LRC dealt solely with 'recognised' unions was about to be exploded. In the previous weeks, the minister responsible had changed the code under which he, Kieran Mulvey and everyone else at the LRC operated — and in a manner that actually fully included ILDA. In fact, the LRC itself had been the author of the new code. Things were about to get murkier and murkier.

Statutory Instrument (SI) 146/2000

Not a very attractive heading is it? In fact I would forgive you if you looked at that heading and decided to skip to the next chapter. That would be a mistake though because although the title SI 146/2000 has a ring to it to induce sleep in the most afflicted insomniac, the reality is that not alone was it the key to preventing and later resolving this dispute, but it also led to a most spectacular and long-running episode of evasiveness and moving of goal-posts by agencies at the very heart of government and beyond. It is worthwhile therefore to spend a little bit of time explaining its origins.

Readers may remember the SIPTU/Ryanair dispute at Dublin Airport over SIPTU's claimed right to represent baggage handlers employed by the low-cost airline. And anyone who had an interest in flying to or from Dublin Airport on Friday, 21 February 1998, most certainly will. The remarkable events of that day occurred as a result of Ryanair's customary and predictable refusal to negotiate with unions. In this case, thirty-nine baggage handlers had decided to join SIPTU, who, along with most unions, had become increasingly concerned by the failure of many 'blue-chip' employers to engage in collective negotiations with trade unions — that is, to recognise them. With Ireland's uniquely low levels of corporation tax within the European Union, many employers from overseas had moved here and had set up procedures for dealing with workers that excluded unions. Interestingly, when SIPTU decided to flex its muscles on this issue and face down an employer, it chose an Irish one, Ryanair. And even more interestingly, it chose thirty-nine baggage handlers, most of whom had short service with the company and were hardly the most powerful group of workers with which to launch such a crucial battle on this crucial issue.

On Friday, 21 February 1998, SIPTU was busy effectively blockading Dublin Airport. However, by that evening — publicity achieved and reputations enhanced (for now) — it was back to Liberty Hall on a promise of an 'investigation' by the Labour Court. The union was in retreat and its members, on whose backs it had all taken place, were hopelessly exposed. The result was predictable — most of the baggage handlers eventually lost their jobs or left them. The dispute did, however, put union recognition in its proper place at the top of the agenda of the wider labour and union movement. In fact, as the social partners met to discuss the next partnership agreement, there were what seemed earnest mutterings from within ICTU that there would be no deal unless the thorny recognition issue was finally addressed. A few state dinners later and Partnership 2000 (P2000) was in place and ready for the printers, with a promise included that a 'high-level group' comprising employers' representatives from the Irish Business & Employers Confederation (IBEC), senior 'high-level' trade unionists and mandarins from the Departments of the Taoiseach, Finance, and Enterprise, Trade and Employment would deal with the union-recognition issue. At the time, Mary Harney was Tánaiste and Minister for Enterprise, Trade and Employment. The immodestly named 'high-level group' was to meet to draw up ways of dealing with the union-recognition issue. And they did meet. Lots of times. And they drew up plans. Lots of plans. And one element of those plans was Statutory Instrument SI 146/2000, signed by Mary Harney as the relevant minister on 26 May 2000. Just in time for the ILDA dispute.

Industrial Relations in Ireland is, in essence, a voluntary arrangement between employers and unions. Nobody can be compelled legally or constitutionally to talk to anyone unless there is a specific statutory basis for such an arrangement in a specific company. Instead, a whole series of voluntary arrangements are entered into and supported by voluntary codes of practice and statutory bodies such as the Labour Court, Labour Relations Commission and Rights Commissioners who generally 'assist' in the resolution of disputes between willing participants, rather than impose solutions on parties they have summoned before them. As a commonsense system, it has much to recommend it when participation by all parties is agreed to. However, if Michael O'Leary and Ryanair choose not to deal with SIPTU, that is their freely made choice and there is little or nothing that can be done about it. SIPTU may huff and puff and threaten to blow Ryanair's house down; the Labour Court may helpfully find that baggage handlers in Ryanair deserve a pay rise; but nobody can force Ryanair into negotiations or solutions.

It was this fact that presented so many difficulties for unions such as SIPTU. Any non-participation in negotiations, conciliation or arbitration by an employer left unions with a stark choice — stop moaning or enter into a dispute. Perhaps SIPTU had hoped that blockading Dublin Airport would provoke such a public and government outcry that Michael O'Leary would immediately be brought to his knees. It didn't work. There was indeed a public outcry — a massive one. And SIPTU bore the brunt of it, at least for a short time. But it was long enough for the 'high-level' group to be established and for SIPTU to return to the inner circle of social partnership.

The high-level group met almost thirty times in total. One might have expected a set of guidelines to be produced that finally forced employers to recognise and take account of the constitutional right of citizens to associate and join a union of their choosing — guidelines that took on board the provisions of Article 11 of the European Convention of Human Rights which allows every worker to join or form a trade union for the protection of their interests. Instead, the group looked at the details of the statutory codes of practice for dealing with individual grievances or matters of discipline, not union recognition — what the baggage handlers' dispute had supposedly been all about! These codes provided statutory guidelines of best practice to be applied to workers and employers who needed procedures to use in matters of grievance or discipline only. In fact, the Labour Court would later confirm that the codes set the minimum standards to apply to procedures of this nature. The code of practice that was in being when the high-level group sat went under the title of 'Code of Practice on Disciplinary Procedures Statutory Instrument (SI) No. 117 of 1996'. Under the heading of 'General Principles' the code, at paragraph 4, defined an employee representative as an 'authorised' trade union or a colleague of the employee's choice. In other words, employees facing a disciplinary charge had a statutory right under the code to representation by a colleague of their choosing or an 'authorised' trade union. But Ryanair was refusing to 'authorise' SIPTU. And countless other employers did likewise, with SIPTU and other unions losing out. Therein lay a major problem for the trade unions. And so it was changed. On 20 May 2000, Code of Practice on Disciplinary Procedures Statutory Instrument (SI) No. 117 of 1996 was revoked and replaced by the new Code of Practice on Grievance & Disciplinary Procedures Statutory Instrument (SI) 146 of 2000. Significantly, the code was extended to deal with worker grievances but the really significant change concerned the definitions of a worker representative. Again under the heading of General Principles, and again under paragraph 4, it is stated:

> 4. For the purposes of this Code of Practice, 'employee representative' includes a colleague of the employee's choice and a registered trade union but not any other person or body unconnected with the enterprise.

That was it. With a stroke of her ministerial pen and the stamp of her ministerial seal, Mary Harney, as Minister for Enterprise, Trade and Employment, had made SIPTU, Mandate, AEEU, ATGWU, TEEU and sixty-five other registered trade unions 'employees' representatives' under the statutory provisions of the code — whether Michael O'Leary liked it or not. And ILDA was included too. The minister might have forgotten us when she signed the new code. Likewise the mandarins in the high-level group when they discussed a new code, and the Chief Executive of the Labour Relations Commission when he drew it up. But on Friday, 16 June 2000, on the eve of a national rail dispute that now seemed unavoidable, someone somewhere in government buildings did remember ILDA and the recently implemented new code. That person had read in the morning papers about the impending dispute and knew of the LRC's supposed 'administrative error', and felt that the code was relevant. It was the solution we had been searching for. All our members' grievances with the 'New Deal' could now be addressed individually and those individuals could be represented, under the statutory code, by ILDA, the registered trade union.

By the time I actually had the document in my hand, it was almost lunchtime and I tried to call John Keenan. I eventually got him just after 2pm In the meantime, I had contacted our solicitors who immediately recognised the potential significance of this document and began to work on some letters. When I got through to John Keenan after lunch, I was initially a bit excitable and he couldn't understand what I was on about. I calmed down and began again. As I continued to explain to him how the code had come to be changed and what it meant, he became almost silent. I began to get the feeling that this was not a call he had expected, or wanted. The conversation ended with him expressing great scepticism about any prospect of a resolution but undertaking to investigate the matter and get back to me.

His response on the phone, together with the fact that we were now only three hours away from the official close of business on the last working day before the 18 June deadline, convinced me that I should act quickly. I immediately began to write a series of letters to relevant parties, pointing out the change to the code of practice. Firstly I wrote to John Keenan, telling him formally in writing what I had just told him on the telephone, and concluding:

> Therefore, and with effect from the date of the Statutory Instrument, 26.05.00, the Company is in breach of the obligations imposed on it by S.I. 146/2000, in that you are continuing to refuse to entertain our representations. You are now being formally requested to comply with the terms of the Instrument, and your confirmation to this effect will obviate both the consequences of failure to comply, and reference of the matter directly to our legal advisors.

The letter was faxed to his office and the fax receipt retained.

I also wrote to Mary O'Rourke and to Mary Harney, contacting their offices first to obtain their direct fax numbers and requesting that my letters would be brought to the attention of both before they left their offices that evening.

The letter to Mary O'Rourke, the minister to whom Iarnród Éireann was supposedly accountable, was similar to that to John Keenan, also pointing out the existence of the code, how it applied to ILDA, and how Irish Rail was in breach of it by refusing to deal with us. It concluded:

> We are now formally to request that you take steps to seek and ensure that Irish Rail comply with the terms of the Instrument, to obviate both the consequences of a continuing failure to comply, and consequent reference on the matter directly from our legal advisors.

The letter to the Tánaiste began by pointing out to her, as the minister responsible for the LRC, the difficulties that the withdrawal of that body's invitation to conciliation had presented. It also pointed out the relevance of SI 146/2000 before concluding:

> We are now formally to request that you take steps to seek and ensure

that Irish Rail comply with the terms of the Instrument, to obviate both the consequences of a continuing failure to comply, and consequent reference of the matter directly to our legal advisors. In this regard, the position of the Labour Relations Commission, the authors of the Code of Practice, is inexplicably called into similar high relief. In this particular regard, we would ask that you investigate the cause and source of this 'administrative error', correct the situation, and facilitate this registered trade union with its right to represent its members' grievances and help prevent the impending industrial relations disaster.

Both letters were faxed to the direct numbers I had been provided with and fax receipts retained.

I followed these letters up with a missive to the LRC's Director of Conciliation, Ray Magee, in which I said that the 'unfortunate administrative error', to which he had referred in his fax, had 'heightened greatly an already inflamed atmosphere in this dispute which you have been aware of since 1st June 2000.' I concluded:

In relation to the current position of the Labour Relations Commission please be advised that whereas it may have been the practice in the past only to deal with 'recognised' Unions where they exist, the LRC are not currently acting in compliance with their statutory obligations regarding statutory instrument No. 146/2000, section 4 paragraph 4, since the 26th May 2000. This supersedes previous legislation as you are aware. In this regard ILDA is a registered Trade Union by decision of the Registrar of Friendly Societies dated 29th July 1999 and 2nd June 2000. I have referred this matter to our legal advisors.

Before 5 p.m. that evening, both ministers, the LRC and John Keenan had also received letters from Daniel Spring & Company Solicitors, acting on our behalf. These letters confirmed our status as a registered trade union, and outlined our new entitlements under the statutory code of practice. Having formally drawn attention to our status, all letters pointed out the opportunity that had now been presented to the addressees to avoid a dispute, and called on each of them, respectfully, to act accordingly.

I had spent whatever time I had to spare during the afternoon briefing media personnel on the new developments. I spoke to RTÉ's then Industrial Correspondent, Peter Cluskey. He had a detailed knowledge of all aspects of industrial relations and was immediately able to grasp the potential significance of the new SI 146/2000. While I was busy writing and faxing, he was making phone calls in an effort to assess how the various parties were responding to this new development. It seemed to me that they were all taken by surprise by the unearthing of SI 146/2000 in the context of this dispute, but I was fully satisfied that ILDA, together with our solicitors, had done everything humanly possible to avoid any dispute. If it meant that our members' grievances had to be dealt with individually, then so be it. It might be a little cumbersome, but it was a much better solution than a rail dispute during the summer months. There was nothing to do now but sit back and await developments.

I was actually quite relaxed by now — relieved that we could all be saved from the industrial relations abyss. I was also extremely grateful to the anonymous civil servant who had drawn our attention to SI 146/2000 that morning. A solution now seemed inevitable.

As Friday evening passed, however, my phone remained silent save for a few media enquiries and the usual plethora of calls from anxious members. Saturday, 17 June 2000, was extremely quiet — unnervingly so. I received no call from either the Department of Transport or the Department of Enterprise, Trade and Employment. No statements emanated from the LRC telling us that our meeting the next day was unnecessary, and outlining the means by which it intended to implement its new code of practice. And no mysterious third party was sent to us, offering their services as an honest broker. Most significantly of all, John Keenan was unavailable. I attempted to contact him by mobile on several occasions in the latter half of the day, but without success. As Saturday evening fell, I was a busy man — busy planning for a general meeting and preparing a report for our members on all that had happened.

I simply could not believe it. ministers, management and the Chief Executive of the LRC were all away, presumably enjoying the weekend weather, while a national rail dispute loomed before us. And a solution sat on all their desks. I had the fax receipts to prove it. I still have them! Perhaps the conventional wisdom among, or advice received by, the people that matter was that we weren't serious, that we would inevitably collapse in a heap at the first sign of trouble and run up to our locomotives with our new part-time driver colleagues, to drive trains for ten, eleven or twelve hours. If that was their advice, it was poor — nay, pathetic — advice. All we wanted was equality, parity of esteem with our colleagues, and observance of a statutory instrument by a minister who had signed it less than three weeks earlier. Instead we got silent phones, buried statutory instruments and invitations that became administrative errors. And they got the inevitable rail dispute. I could have told them that. I did tell them that. But they wouldn't listen. *C'est la vie!*

The events of Sunday, 18 June 2000, were ultimately inevitable. We had a large, well-attended meeting. There were questions from the media as to whether there would be 'a strike', and assurances from ILDA that we would neither 'strike' nor have new conditions rammed down our necks without so much as the courtesy of a consultation, never mind a negotiation. And then we went home. I could go on and on about the speeches and the passion, determination and anger, resentment and fully justified paranoia about what could possibly be going on behind the scenes to explain what we had just outlined to our members. But there's no need. Anyone who needed proof that the people that matter had called it all wrong, again, and that ILDA members would stand firm got it the next morning, in spades. What they didn't get, across most of the network, was trains. The only surprise to us was that everyone else seemed surprised.

We felt that a conspiracy had begun, and, as a result, so had a three-month long national rail dispute.

LOCKED OUT

Monday, 19 June 2000, was the first day of a work stoppage that was to last exactly ten weeks in total and to span the three busiest months of the year for Ireland's tourism industry, and consequently potentially the three biggest months for Iarnród Éireann in terms of passenger traffic. The ten-week lock-out would be the longest uninterrupted such dispute in Ireland for many years. It occurred, and was allowed to occur, in what is supposed to be a responsible, commercial semi-state transport company, during peak season. Moreover it occurred in a country that has what we are led to believe is the most sophisticated industrial relations conciliation and arbitration machinery in Europe or anywhere else. Yet, on 19 June 2000, the much vaunted Labour Court, Labour Relations Commission and Rights Commissioners might as well not have existed at all.

For me, the dispute began at 2am on that Monday morning with a phone call from a slightly intoxicated railway worker, who was not a driver, but who was apologising, unnecessarily as it happened, for his own perceived failure to do more, through various committees that he sat on in SIPTU, to prevent the impasse. A few hours later, just before 6am, I had a phone call from a journalist with Independent Network News (INN), requesting an interview for an early-morning news programme on what she described as major disruption to the early-morning services. I decided to get up at that stage and had soon begun a pattern of media interviews and members' consultation that was to continue unabated for the entire summer.

It should be borne in mind that until this point we were unclear as to

173

what format the dispute would actually take. We were determined not to go on strike at all for a number of reasons. In the first instance, without the necessary negotiating licence, formal strike action would clearly be unlawful. Of equal importance, however, was the fact that our members wanted to work and would, in fact, ultimately remain available for work at all times throughout the upcoming dispute. Our difficulty was the imposition by our employer (without agreement or consultation with our members) of radical new work practices. We were, however, prepared and available to continue to work our existing and agreed conditions until all outstanding issues had been resolved in whatever manner became possible, be that SI 146 or any other means. Moreover Iarnród Éireann had specifically allowed two depots — Portlaoise and Sligo — to continue to work these very same existing conditions.

In order to assess the position nationally, I began to ring members in some of the bigger depots, such as Inchicore and Cork, where drivers would have been presenting themselves for duty at a variety of times since midnight. In all cases, the same pattern emerged. Drivers had reported for work as normal but had not been allowed by management to book on duty. Sometimes they had been prevented from doing so by very senior management who, unusually for such ungodly hours, were out of bed and in attendance. Train drivers book on for duty by signing a log or register. This signature has a legal significance in that it is a statement by the driver that he is fit to take up duty in accordance with his rules (properly rested, free from the influence of drink/drugs, and so on). The signature is then further endorsed by the driver's qualified supervisor, and this signature represents an acceptance that the supervisor has seen the driver and that he is fit for work. In rule, no driver may take up duty, take possession of his driver's kit or even attempt to enter a driver's cab until this register has been signed and endorsed. However, on this particular morning, management had different ideas. As drivers reported for work, the 'sign-on books' had been removed by management. Instead, ILDA members were met with an inquisition that, generally, went something like this:

Driver: Where is the sign on book?

Manager: Before that, will you work the 'New Deal'?

Driver: I don't know anything about it. Why didn't you discuss it with me before now?

Manager:	There are new rosters. Will you work them?
Driver:	I don't even know what they are.
Manager:	I can't let you sign on until you give me a commitment to work the new rosters.
BL:	That is a matter that you should take up with my registered trade union. I am available to work existing agreed rosters while you do so.
Manager:	In that case, I cannot let you sign on.

Of course, these exchanges varied slightly from case to case. Some conversations would have been more terse, others more polite. On one or two occasions, the supervisors were even apologetic. But the relevant content was the same in all cases. And the net result was that 128 ILDA members were prevented from booking on duty, by virtue of their physical means of doing so (sign-on book) having been removed. In order to gain access to it, they would have to give commitments that management knew they could not give.

My first direct involvement came early that morning with a call from my colleague, Darragh Brophy, at the station in Athlone. When Darragh reported for duty, the Athlone sign-on book had been removed and he was confronted by District Manager Gerry Glynn, who had travelled especially from Galway and had taken the chair of the foreman, George Behan. When Darragh refused to work the rosters, he went into the drivers' mess room and called me. I drove in, entered the station and asked the district manager what was going on. He explained that no driver was being allowed to book on duty until he agreed to work the new rosters and conditions. I offered the view that this was unnecessary and assured Gerry Glynn that we would continue to work our agreed conditions until matters were resolved. The district manager said that this was not good enough. By now, the morning news shows were giving maximum coverage to the disruption. I sat in the car park at Athlone station and switched on RTÉ's *Morning Ireland,* just in time to hear comments about the disruption the 'strike' was having on services. I called the newsroom on my mobile phone and was immediately put through to studio where I explained, live on air, how our members were being prevented from taking up duty, and that they were available to work the same conditions as drivers in Sligo and Portlaoise were being allowed to work. This wasn't a strike — it was a lock-out.

As the day wore on, the pattern of denying workers the right to book on duty was repeated, member by member. Each member then took his place in his mess room to await developments, in the knowledge that he would not be paid and that there were trains that should be moving and were not moving.

The first couple of days were actually low-key affairs after the initial public surprise at the level of disruption, but there were some things that happened that would cause divisions that have never been healed. One such incident took place in Athlone depot itself. The 'early-bird' train from Galway to Dublin was rostered to be driven by a Galway driver to Athlone, where it would be taken up by an Athlone driver who would work the remainder of the train to Dublin. The 'New Deal' proposed to change this and have the Galway man working it through to Heuston Station. Naturally, Athlone drivers in ILDA were anxious to retain this working in their depot. There was nothing unusual about this conflict. These issues arise year in and year out, and are usually resolved amicably following discussion. For as long as the issue remains unresolved, it is the custom and practice that the existing train rostering continues until agreement is reached — that is, the status quo remains. This is indeed what happened on Monday 19 and Tuesday 20 June 2000 with the Galway to Dublin 'early bird'. As a result, the train was driven to Athlone by the Galway driver, as normal. The Galway driver got off in Athlone, and, when no Athlone driver was available to work it to Dublin, the train went no further.

However, another element of this working was about to rear its ugly head. Back in 1994, while drivers nationwide were getting used to through-working from terminal to terminal, management had given the four Galway drivers a letter assuring them that they would be required to work only one train per day — the 15.25 passenger service ex. Galway — through to Dublin. This meant that although many drivers had been working all trains from Cork to Dublin and back for the six years prior to the dispute, the Galway drivers had been having it somewhat easier, thanks to the written dispensation they had elicited from management back in 1994. The 'New Deal' now provided an opportunity to make some cash from these letters. In fact, page 38 of the proposal document specifically stated: 'A special situation arises in the case of Galway drivers, where a particular written agreement exists. This will be dealt with exceptionally.' However, to the obvious annoyance of some of the Galway drivers, that provision of the 'New Deal' had not been acted upon by management since its insertion in the proposals in May of 1999, thirteen months earlier.

All four recipients of these letters had been members of the NBRU. Since 1994, another Galway driver had been recruited who had no letter but was also a member of the NBRU or SIPTU on all occasions. He could be required to work through to Dublin on any occasion. No Galway driver had ever joined ILDA. Now, with their ILDA colleagues prevented from working and therefore not being in receipt of any wages, and with Iarnród Éireann anxious to resume full services on at least one route, the Galway drivers saw their chance. On the evening of 20 June, the second day of the dispute, a senior manager travelled from Dublin to Galway to speak with a representative of the Galway drivers. At the meeting, it was was agreed that each letter-holder would receive a £10,000 lump-sum payment as 'compensation' for surrendering his letter. Not only that, but the fifth driver who had no letter was also paid compensation for giving up something that he didn't even have. In total, management paid out more than £40,000 of taxpayers' money to buy back these letters and to keep a non-letter holder on side — and this in a company that supposedly had to save £30,000,000 just to survive. From the following morning, the Galway drivers continued to work the 'early-bird' service to Dublin, driving past their Athlone colleagues and thereby carrying out their work during an industrial dispute. For completeness I must record here, however, that one of the Galway drivers was off ill during all of these shenanigans and, as he remained off ill throughout most of the ten-week ILDA dispute, he did not, at any time during the dispute, carry out what we considered to be our work.

When all the details of this incident emerged, it created terribly bad feeling between ILDA members and the Galway drivers. It is one of my core beliefs that a trade unionist should not pass a picket of another worker, in any situation. However, I do readily concede that ILDA, although clearly a trade union, did not have formal pickets during this dispute. In fact, for the first two days of the dispute, our members simply sat idle in their mess rooms, out of sight. I also fundamentally believe, however, that no worker should carry out the work of a colleague who is engaged in a trade dispute, whether there are pickets or not. To do so can only fatally undermine whatever protest or struggle a colleague may be involved in and give succour to management. No SIPTU or NBRU member passed an ILDA picket during this dispute because there were no pickets. In addition, many SIPTU and NBRU members studiously ensured that they carried out only their own duties at all times, often having to resist management tactics such as trying to run timetabled trains as special trains, by changing a train's schedule or identification to disguise the fact that it was a train that would otherwise have been worked by an ILDA member. I do not blame management for engaging in such tactics — management has an obligation to ensure that as many trains operate as possible. Neither do I resent SIPTU or NBRU members who worked their own jobs. If they felt that the 'New Deal' was beneficial to them, and they were not confronted with pickets, they were, in my view, fully entitled to do their own work.

Many SIPTU and NBRU members, however, went further, and, like the Galway drivers once they had surrendered their letters, performed our work throughout the dispute. As a trade unionist, I have no hesitation whatsoever in labelling as 'scabs' those workers who carry out the work of colleagues who were engaged in a trade dispute. To do otherwise would be to subvert and deny the founding principles of the Irish, and indeed global, trade union movements. That is something I will not do in order to be politically correct. The definition of a scab in my dictionary is 'An employee who works while others are on strike; a strike breaker' or 'A person hired to replace a striking worker'. On the basis that SIPTU and the NBRU considered us to be on strike, and lashed us on any occasion that we described our situation as a lock-out, their members who did our work must, by this clear definition, be scabs. In my opinion, any driver who drove any ILDA member's train between 19 June and 28 August 2000 performed the same act as the Thatcherites who broke Britain's miners, or the supporters of William Martin Murphy during the Dublin lock-out. Sometimes you just have to call a spade a spade.

Dáil Debate

The second day of the dispute also saw an emergency debate on the floor of parliament, with heated exchanges taking place between Transport Minister O'Rourke and various opposition TDs. Fine Gael's Olivia Mitchell, Nora Owen and Jim Higgins tackled the minister on the level of disruption, its causes and what she was doing to aid the situation. The minister, as she would do throughout the entire dispute, chose to hide behind the High Court judgment, using it as a reason for doing nothing. Never once did she acknowledge that the ILDA rules had been amended by the registrar to comply with the judgment. Nor did she make any effort to ensure the continued running of the trains over which she had ministerial responsibility — something she could have done had she chosen to use SI 146/2000 in each individual case. However, Deputies Owen and Higgins (the latter having replaced Ivan Yates as Fine Gael spokesman on these matters) in particular were having none of it. Deputy Owen asked the minister to 'clarify the content of SI 146/2000, section 4, paragraph (4) of which refers to a "registered trade union".' She also asked if a 'mistake' might have been made in the statutory instrument in the use of the word 'registered' rather than 'authorised'. When the minister stated that no mistake had been made with the wording of the Statutory Instrument, Deputy Owen asked directly: 'Is ILDA a registered trade union in the meaning of the word "registered"?'

The minister was finally forced to confirm: 'The Irish Locomotive Drivers' Association is a registered trade union under friendly societies legislation. It is not a trade union with negotiating rights.' The minister was correct. But as Deputy Owen had correctly deduced, negotiating rights or not, our status as a registered trade union, allied with SI 146, allowed us to pursue the individual grievances of our members through individual case taking, not collective negotiations. It would be bizarre to think that an experienced minister like Mary O'Rourke would be unable to grasp the clear, and dispute-resolving, distinction, especially given the letters that she had received on this matter from ILDA, and separately from our legal advisors.

The debate raged on. Jim Higgins got to his feet:

Does the minister agree it is appalling and untenable that Iarnród Éireann refuses to enter into dialogue with the Irish Locomotive

Drivers' Association when it represents 132 of the 280 drivers, which is 47%? If that figure were taken with the drivers from the other two unions which rejected the proposals of Iarnród Éireann, it represents a clear majority of drivers who are opposed to the deal being forced down the throats of the locomotive drivers.

Does the minister agree it is an extremely responsible job to drive approximately 800 people at speeds of up to 100 miles per hour? The lives and limbs of up to 1,000 people are in one's sole care? In that context, does the minister agree it is folly and irresponsible for an employer to flatly ignore the majority of people who do that responsible job and refuse to even enter into dialogue with them? Does she further agree it is incredible that until September 2001 drivers will be required to work up to ten and half hours per day for seven consecutive days, driving distances of up to 420 miles per day? Is the minister concerned about safety? Will she listen to the people who drive these locomotives and who will have to carry the responsibility should these long hours take their toll and cause an accident which could have devastating consequences?

Is the minister aware that the Labour Relations Commission invited the Irish Locomotive Drivers' Association to talks but then said the invitation was an administrative error? Is it not clear from the minister for Enterprise, Trade and Employment's directive, SI No. 146 of 2000, that ILDA is a registered trade union and Iarnród Éireann is obliged to negotiate with its members?

Does the minister agree it is Stalinist for an employers' organisation to ruthlessly reject the concerns of drivers who do such a responsible job, to refuse even to speak with them and direct that they accept provisions with safety implications about which they have serious reservations which are supported by independent authority?

At last, in an almost empty Dáil chamber, someone was addressing the real issues. The minister responded, 'The Labour Relations Commission has informed me that an administrative error was made in writing the letter. I accept that is the case.'

Deputy Higgins' response, however, was quick and to the point. He replied: 'No, they were got at.'

The minister tried to move away from this territory by detailing all the supposed benefits of the disputed agreement. Bizarrely she was supported in this by Emmet Stagg, who seemed to have forgotten his concern over the Rayner Report just two months earlier. Perhaps if ILDA were ever able to afford to bank roll the Labour Party, as SIPTU does, a cosy alliance might be formed with us too. However, for now, Fine Gael (hardly a party workers in this situation historically expected support from) were on their own when it came to holding the minister responsible to the Dáil.

Minister O'Rourke was sitting next to the Tánaiste, Mary Harney. The Fine Gael TDs had the bit between their teeth:

When the caucus with the Tánaiste is over — I can understand why there might be a little miscommunication between the two because there is such patent contradiction here — will the Minister deny that up to September 2001, train drivers can be required to work a seven day week in a row and a ten and a half hour day? Does the Minister agree that the High Court has not prohibited Iarnród Éireann from discussing or having a dialogue with the Irish Locomotive Drivers' Association? It has not prohibited this. Therefore, according to the Tánaiste's statutory instrument, it is obliged to do so because it is a registered trade union, which has been clarified.

Before the minister got a chance to respond, Deputy Higgins revisited the very kernel of the LRC/ SI 146 debacle:

Is the Minister for Public Enterprise aware of reports that the Labour Relations Commission was subjected to pressure, after issuing an invitation to the Irish Locomotive Drivers' Association to meet it, to withdraw the invitation?

Significantly, the minister — having been forced to confirm that we were a registered trade union — did not answer the question.

While the debate threatened to peter out with Deputy Stagg making gags (I hope they were gags) about trade unionists like me being shot under Stalinist or Trotskyite regimes (I cannot argue definitively with Deputy Stagg on this point as he is obviously better versed in the tactics of Stalin and Trotsky than I am), Nora Owen had the final word and ended the debate with a question that summed up the Government position succinctly: 'Is the minister saying a statutory instrument is unlawful?'

The Media

While all of this was taking place at the close of Day Two, I was on my way to RTÉ in Donnybrook to partake in a live radio interview on the dispute to date. En route, I received a call from one of our Cork members who told me that SIPTU members were planning to place pickets on the gates to Kent Station in Cork the following morning. I was informed that the reason for this was related to ongoing difficulties between SIPTU and NBRU members in Cork, most of whom were not drivers, but that our members would not be passing any pickets. I accepted this immediately. Whatever difficulties we had with SIPTU, the idea of a group of our members passing a SIPTU picket at any time was not one I wished to countenance or would support. Nevertheless when I discussed this with my travelling companion, Thomas McDonnell, we immediately agreed that this development, if it transpired, would add a further interesting aspect to the dispute and create further difficulties for management and the SIPTU leadership.

When I arrived at RTÉ, I was shown into the canteen where I immediately met with former *Irish Independent* Industrial Correspondent Tim Hastings. Tim was now working in the Industrial Relations faculty at University College Dublin (UCD). He had been invited, as an 'independent expert', to take part in the live discussion on the rail dispute. We discussed the dispute loosely while awaiting the arrival of John Keenan for Iarnród Éireann. The debate was aired in the 10pm discussion slot to be hosted on that evening by Emily O'Reilly. To be honest, the debate was poor enough with both sides signalling that they were digging in and Tim basically telling listeners that this dispute had been a long time coming and might not be easily solved. My attempts to focus on the failure of various parties to use SI 146/2000 to move the situation forward were not really successful and much of the debate centred on the varying merits of our respective safety reports.

As the debate ended, I was anxious to depart without having to engage in any significant discussion with John Keenan. I was determined not to divulge anything about the following morning's possible developments in Cork, as I had formed the view during the debate that he had no knowledge of any additional impending difficulty. As a consequence, Thomas and I exited the building immediately. As we drove towards Martin King's house to discuss developments over late-night coffee, we came to the conclusion that a trip to Cork the following day looked inevitable. In addition, we discussed how we might resolve what we considered to be a growing problem. The debate with Emily O'Reilly had been too low key for our liking and we were struck by the apparent general acceptance that the dispute might be a protracted one. In fact, as we reflected on that day's media activity, we concluded that interest had been well down on the previous day. Part of the reason for this surely lay in our members being confined to their mess rooms, out of sight of management, the public and the eyes of the media. The dispute was lacking in a visual impact that ultimately would focus media attention and therefore engender the necessary public pressure to force a resolution. But what were we to do when we couldn't legally picket? We were faced with something of a conundrum. Events the following day, however, would solve that particular problem!

SIPTU members did indeed place SIPTU pickets on entrances to Kent Station from dawn on the morning of 21 June 2000. They were the first pickets to be placed on any workplace during the period of the ILDA dispute, and the irony of their being SIPTU pickets was lost on nobody. Our members telephoned me from Cork early that morning and told me that they would be supporting their SIPTU colleagues' pickets. They also felt that this was a positive development in that it would focus more attention on the dispute. It is also fair to say that they were relieved to be out of their mess room with an opportunity to explain their position to members of the public directly and through the media. Indeed, the media immediately now focused most of their attention on Cork. As Brian Dunphy — our treasurer and one of our most senior members — and I prepared to drive to Cork, we were advised by our president, Christy Holbrook, that the SIPTU and NBRU leaderships and management were flying to Cork to talk to their members to try to get the SIPTU pickets called off.

You didn't have to be a genius to realise that the dispute had, or was about to, take a dramatic turn for the worse. I explained the position to my family and packed my bags for the drive to Cork. We hadn't got very far — around Birr in Offaly, as I recall — before Christy called to tell me that the SIPTU dispute had been resolved and that SIPTU members had removed their pickets. We now had a choice — return to the station in Cork and risk being out of sight and out of mind, or escalate the situation by some legal means other than picketing. I spoke to most of our Cork members on my mobile phone and it was agreed that our members would get buckets and write 'ILDA LOCK-OUT' on them, and would collect money at the gate. This would have two purposes. Firstly, any monies collected would come in very handy for workers who would soon not be in receipt of any wages, and for an organisation with virtually no resources. Secondly, and more importantly, these 'bucket collections' would provide us with a visible presence at the gate of the workplace. This would allay the growing feeling of helplessness our members were experiencing hidden away in dingy (especially in Cork) mess rooms. As our Cork members began to get organised, we stopped for lunch in Mitchelstown and took the opportunity to make calls to other depots and talk about similar protests.

None of our members needed to be told the importance of not being obstructive to passers-by, be they passengers or other workers, while carrying out our protests and collections. Nevertheless, by early afternoon on the third day of the dispute, our members had a very visible presence outside the main entrance of each station, and the dispute was entering a new, highly visible, phase. As we arrived at Cork, it was lashing rain. Outside the Glanmire Road entrance, under large umbrellas, many of our members were gathered, in high spirits, with buckets at their feet. They received Brian and me with warm handshakes, and the feelings of unity and solidarity were immediately palpable. If we were going to have to do this the hard way, at least we were in it together.

I spent the afternoon in Cork, talking to members and reading the transcript from the previous night's Dáil debate. As I spoke to the growing number of journalists reporting on the escalating dispute, I was struck by their failure to grasp the issues in dispute, and the possible means of their resolution, in the detail that the Fine Gael opposition had in the parliamentary debate with the minister responsible. Rather than ask them to put these questions to Iarnród Éireann and Minister O'Rourke, I decided to start publicly seeking a live TV debate on the issues. Three days in, and already I felt that the only way the questions would be properly put would be if I was given the chance to ask them myself. I didn't get my debate. At least, not at that stage. But it was clear that we were going to have to evaluate how to deal with the media and, more importantly, react to their coverage. It was hard-hat time.

Looking back on the media coverage of ILDA, I am at once annoyed, frustrated, amused and thankful to the scribes and journalists with whom I have had dealings over a five-year period. What I have learned is that journalism has, like every other profession, a very mixed bag of people making a living from it. There are fair people and unfair people; busy people and very, very lazy people; people with an axe to grind or a particular agenda, and those who go to great lengths to achieve balance in everything they do. It has been my pleasure and bad luck to have had to deal with all types of journalists during my term as ILDA Secretary and spokesman. Throughout, I have endeavoured, insofar as was possible, to treat all those contacting me fairly, and to give of my time without complaint. I believe that every journalist with whom I dealt was provided with enough material to enable them to fulfil their obligations to report on ILDA, our members and me in a balanced and fair manner.

I grew up, like many people, with an idea that if something was reported on the TV or radio news, or in the *The Irish Times, Irish Independent,* or *Irish Press,* then it must be true. I had lost any trust I might have had in tabloid newspapers having watched a documentary on the Hillsborough football disaster and the manner in which one tabloid in particular, *The Sun,* reported on that tragic event and its aftermath, and the added grief suffered by bereaved families and those injured as a result. I now wonder how many people involved in incidents, disputes, politics or anything else newsworthy have been judged unfairly by me, as a result of what I have seen or read about them in the media. I believe that I now have a greater understanding of the media and how it works, or in some cases doesn't work, and the varying agendas at play for some of those who work in it. Having suffered personally from baseless allegations about having a 'hidden agenda', it is not my intention here to make similar allegations about others. However, there are some things that, if someone dealing with the media realises them, do help to explain what might otherwise remain unexplained about the coverage received.

From an early stage, I was aware of the history linking some of those who opposed the emergence of ILDA in the trade union movement and some of those who reported on it in the media. As we came under increasing media pressure and criticism, knowledge of who our opponents' friends were within the media stopped me from going mad at times. Within a few decades, the Official IRA (or 'stickies', as its members were known) had turned to political means to achieve a united Ireland, and transformed itself into Sinn Féin the Workers Party, which, in time, had shortened its name to the Workers Party, then becoming Democratic Left, and more recently had merged with the Labour Party. While politicians such as Proinsias de Rossa, Pat Rabbitte and Eamon Gilmore have all been members of one or all of these parties down through the years, and have made lives for themselves in politics, other former members made their way in the trade union movement and some have careers in journalism. These people invariably continue to have perfectly legal and proper dealings with each other now through their various occupations. Nevertheless much of the most critical coverage we received could not be explained by a decades-old shared affiliation. Some of it was just plain daft, over the top or simply lies.

To begin with, however, I think that anyone involved in industrial relations must have a realistic view of the type of media coverage they can or might receive. The stark reality is that we are all consumers and, as consumers, we understandably get very annoyed when we are inconvenienced by a withdrawal of an expected, or even a necessary, service. As a result, I was always a little amused when I would hear a worker argue against a dispute because it didn't have 'public support'. My view is that if a group of workers — no matter how badly treated by management — is going to wait for 'public support' before taking part in industrial action, then nobody will ever take industrial action. It is a source of amusement to me also that during a dispute 'public support' — which generally does not exist at all — is often described by the media as 'ebbing away' or 'waning', often in bold headlines, in a clear attempt to demoralise the disputing workers. The ILDA Executive always counselled our members not to read the newspapers if they found themselves annoyed by what they read, and instead to focus their attention on any live debates that might take place on radio or television. 'Don't live this dispute in the media' was a phrase our members became used to hearing from me and other members of the NEC. Only live debates are free from the editors' pens or the reporters' prejudices, and can be used much more effectively and accurately by the participants to get their central points across. I always felt that we would do very well in live debates and that our members should listen to, and in fact take part in and be available for, as many of these as possible.

In terms of the amount of media coverage received, the dispute of 2000 went through a number of phases. The first day attracted a great deal of coverage, but, as time went on, this diminished greatly for a period. One week in, I was actually very concerned at the lack of media coverage of the dispute. News release after news release received little or no coverage, and all the follow-up calls in the world seemed to achieve nothing. I even spoke with news editors about the paucity of the coverage as I began to feel that there might have been a news embargo on us in some quarters. The last thing I, or our members, wanted was to be locked out of work indefinitely and to be simply forgotten about or ignored. However, then something happened that turned the lack of coverage of the dispute on its proverbial head and made ILDA, Ogle and even the colour of my walls, what I ate for lunch and every detail of my personal background front-page, back-page and features-section news across the board. The media know it as the 'silly season', a four- to six-week period from the end of June to mid-August when the Dáil rises, courts close, tribunals adjourn and everything that normally features in our media just stops, leaving a raft of journalists with nothing to talk, write or report about. In the summer of 2000, ILDA filled the 'silly-season' vacuum. And — boy, oh boy! — did we get media coverage? In keeping with the season, much of it was silly.

It began with a feature article on me in the *Sunday Tribune*, written by Richard Oakley. Each week the *Tribune* does a 'profile' piece on someone in the news at the time, which is supposedly a lengthy cover piece, usually accompanied by a caricature drawing of that week's 'victim' and a small 'CV', typically outlining no more information than the name of the subject, his or her age and why they are in the news. During the dispute, Richard would call me every Friday or Saturday during the dispute, and was a journalist with whom I always thought I got on fairly well. So I was surprised one Sunday morning during the dispute when I saw a news article on page 4 of the *Tribune* (stating, wrongly, that the LRC was 'to meet striking rail union') end with the words 'Brendan Ogle profile, page 21'. Curious as to whether or not the LRC had committed yet another 'administrative error' and issued an invitation to us, I tried not to choke on my toast while thumbing my way to page 21.

The headline described me as 'The man who has turned the train crisis into a war of words' and told me in the highlighted text at the top of the page that 'public sympathy for the train drivers is ebbing away rapidly'. I moved swiftly to the first line to be told that 'Brendan Ogle must be feeling very isolated this weekend'. Now feeling totally alone in the world, I scanned the page for evidence of my 'isolation' or of the fact that I, and not someone else, had turned the 'crisis into a war of words'. The article didn't touch on any of the issues involved in the 'New Deal' at all — not a single issue in a full-page article. Silly season, you see! Instead, people like John Keenan, a nameless SIPTU 'former shop steward' and other nameless 'researchers' on media shows all slagged me off for everything from my Dundalk accent to using the 'impenetrable' SI 146 (a three-line sentence in a statutory instrument signed by a minister), and for a perceived 'failure to compromise' with anyone. Even my 'logical method of argument' fell foul of the journalistic pen on this occasion. As I pondered whether I should henceforth adopt an 'illogical method of argument' (it certainly hadn't done others in the dispute any harm!) I read how an RTÉ 'vox pop' had also found people critical of me and how this was 'unusual for Ireland where people tend to be instinctively on the side of workers in a dispute'. Was the reader actually expected to believe that if RTÉ turned up at a train station with a microphone and approached passengers who could not get to work because there were no trains as a result of a dispute, that those passengers would be 'instinctively' on the side of the workers in dispute? I actually found the article quite entertaining!

I highlight this article of the many for a number of reasons. Firstly, its prominence in that paper was indicative of the fact that the ILDA dispute had become the only game in town as far as many members of the media were concerned. The article was also written without giving me any opportunity to respond to any of the points raised or to any of the anonymous persons who supposedly supplied the information that made it up. In fact, ILDA did not have a single quote in either of the prominent and large articles in the *Tribune* on that day. And finally, the article was also very personalised indeed and did not even attempt to deal with a single issue involved in the 'New Deal'. In fact, it was an exact reflection of the public relations approach adopted by Iarnród Éireann throughout the dispute and beforehand.

Upsetting Telephone Calls

On three occasions during the dispute, I was forced to change my telephone number. On each occasion, this followed a barrage of mostly abusive phone calls at every hour of the day and night from anonymous persons. On most occasions, words such as 'bastard' or threats such as 'We're coming to get you' would be yelled down the phone before the caller hung up. On other occasions, people would want to know our side of the dispute, while outlining the inconvenience they had suffered. And on a number of occasions, callers would listen and end up wondering why they had not read or seen in the media what I had just told them. On every occasion, I endeavoured to find out where the caller had got my number. Most of them willingly told me that they had called Iarnród Éireann to complain, only to be given my phone number, coupled with a suggestion that they call me. I got so fed up with this that I actually said to one such caller, 'You got this number off Iarnród Éireann', before she had told me. This threw the lady into something of a panic as she denied furiously, for whatever reason, that this had been the case, before outlining how she had got my mobile number from directory enquiries. When I told her, honestly, that the number she had called was actually registered in my wife's maiden name, she simply told me to 'Fuck off' before hanging up abruptly.

These incidents pale into insignificance, however, when considered against information I received from two journalists in March 2000, three months before the dispute had begun at all. I was having a quiet night in one Friday when a journalist from a national newspaper called me and asked whether I knew Barry Kenny, Iarnród Éireann's PR guru. I replied that I had crossed swords with Barry over the airwaves on a number of occasions but had never actually met him and so didn't know him on a personal level at all. To my horror, the journalist told me that he had met Barry Kenny that day and had been given what the PR man called a 'press briefing' about me. During this briefing Barry had questioned my political orientation and motivation. The journalist had been troubled by this and had decided that it was fairer that I be put in the picture about what had been said. I was truly stunned. I knew the journalist fairly well and knew him to be a quality journalist. This revelation, coming from him, shook me to the core. What to do about it though was quite another matter.

Ten days later, I received another call on my private line in my home in Athlone. My home actually contained two separate telephone lines with different telephone numbers. One number was, at least at that point (March 2000), for strictly private use and was known only to a very small numbers of contacts and friends. No journalist had it and it was, of course, ex-directory. My other line was the ILDA line upstairs that was available to everybody. Anyway, I had just returned form work at 4.00pm on this day when my private phone rang. I answered it, expecting a close contact or friend, but was immediately confronted by a strange voice belonging to a journalist identifying himself as being from a national daily newspaper. My first question, before he could even explain why he was calling, was to ask him how he got hold of my private number. He told me that he had got it from a contact of mine whom he had called earlier in the day. At that stage, I was totally perplexed. Who was giving out my private number to journalists, and why? I decided to let the journalist explain. He told me how that morning he had spoken to Iarnród Éireann's Barry Kenny, from whom he had received a 'briefing', during which Barry again questioned my political beliefs and orientation. The journalist had then sought me out in order to advise me of what had been said and, having failed to contact me on my mobile telephone (at that point, I was driving trains), had successfully managed to get my private number. I had been hoping that the previous incident had been isolated, but here was evidence of another effort to blacken my good name in journalistic circles in Dublin.

No wonder I was getting such bad press!

Personalised Attacks

Three years on, I am as upset as I was back then by the overtly personalised nature of much of the coverage of all matters relating to ILDA. I have in my hand a newspaper headline I have picked at random from the time. It reads, 'Ogle's men taking us for a ride'. I don't recall any newspaper headlines during the teachers' or nurses' disputes saying, 'Lennon's men and women are taking us for a ride', or 'Doran's masses taking patients for a ride'. I don't recall Des Geraghty or any other representatives of workers being targeted by such personalised headline writing. It hardly ever happens. But where ILDA was involved, to personalise and attack me as an individual was somehow acceptable. That was totally wrong for various reasons. In the first place, it was wrong because it failed to recognise that, in some ways, I was no different from any other spokesman for any other group in the country. I was elected to speak on behalf of people. I don't know exactly why I was treated so differently by many commentators, but some facts are undeniable.

There was much too much comment about the fact that I hailed from Dundalk. Time and again, my border origins were referred to, almost imperceptibly in isolation, but, on reflection, there was a definite pattern. Moreover, some journalists did a lot of digging. Paul Colgan of *The Sunday Times* spent a day talking to people I had known back home and visiting old drinking haunts of mine in Dundalk. I heard about this when a former drinking mate, to whom I hadn't spoken in six years, called to tell me that peculiar questions were being asked about me. I called Paul Colgan and he confirmed that he was writing a feature piece about my background in the town that many journalists in the 1980s described as 'El Paso'. To be fair, the piece actually confirmed that *The Sunday Times* had unearthed nothing sinister during its investigations but it also acknowledged that questions had been raised, and the paper's interest in delving into my past in the first instance was significant as far as I was concerned.

So what was going on? As outlined above, two journalists had been honest and principled enough to inform me of Iarnród Éireann's efforts to blacken my name in March of that year. Readers can judge for themselves whether they were the only journalists approached with this nonsense. And nonsense it is. I have never, ever, had any involvement whatsoever with criminal or subversive elements in Dundalk or elsewhere. I have never been in any trouble with the Garda Síochána in my life – at least I hadn't until this dispute. Throughout the dispute, I thought the best approach when this particular line raised its head in any form was to ignore it. However, it is appropriate for me to correct the record formally now. I believe that working-class people throughout this island — Catholic, Protestant and dissenter — have much more that unites us than divides us. Problems such as poor housing, lack of employment opportunity, financial and social barriers to quality education, and health care are problems that are common to people in West Belfast, East Belfast, Marian Park in Dundalk and Ballymun in Dublin. These are the real endemic ills that afflict such communities — the inequality in the distribution of wealth and opportunity throughout society. That is why our jails are filled with people from areas where neglect and social inequality are rampant, and not with people from the more affluent areas of our towns and cities. Instead of providing tax amnesties for the criminally rich and corrupt, and financial inducements and benefits of every possible type for those in society who need them least, at the expense of those who need them most, if we could focus our resources fairly, we might actually remove the sense of isolation, frustration and despair that leads people to express themselves only through violence or crime. We might achieve a real peace and sense of inclusion and justice among today's youth, thereby ensuring a better future for us all. That is not to say that cultural and religious difference can or even should be eradicated. On the contrary, I think a mature society at peace with itself could acknowledge and celebrate such differences. Why not? I might be a Celtic-supporting nationalist from Dundalk but I have much more in common with a train driver from East Belfast who marches on 12 July than with an Iarnród Éireann suit.

It is strange for a working-class lad to be reading about himself in newspapers. Certainly I didn't recognise the person portrayed by the media in summer 2000 as the Brendan Ogle I know. In the end, I concluded that many in the media simply didn't want to portray the real me, the real ILDA or the real issues in dispute. It was to be spin instead of substance; attack instead of debate; lies instead of truth. And I believe that the reason for this was that the outcome was preordained. We had to lose

ILDA members and their families march on Dáil Éireann to hand in a letter of protest to Mary O'Rourke, Minister for Public Enterprise on 29 June 2000.
© Aidan Crawley, Photocall Ireland

Members of ILDA marching to the Labour Relations Commission in Dublin on 29 June.
© Alan Betson, *The Irish Times*

With P.G. Rayner at a press conference in Buswell's Hotel, Dublin,
1 July 2000.
© Derek Speirs, *Sunday Tribune*

ILDA members Donal Tobin, Mike Fitzsimons and Kieran Brett on
picket duty at Kent Station, Cork.
© Newspics

Carmel Masterson blocking the Westport to Athlone rail line in protest at the treatment of her husband Finbarr.
© Keith Heneghan, Phocus

Kevin Gough, Mick Baneham, Gerry Heffernan and Barry Humphreys, locomotive drivers from Inchicore, on picket duty at Dublin Bus Donnybrook depot on 9 August 2000.
© Billy Higgins, *Irish Examiner*

ILDA members picket Heuston Station as their dipute with Iarnród
Éireann approaches the end of its seventh week.
© Paul Sharp, Photocall Ireland

With Chris Holbrook, President of ILDA, at a meeting of ILDA
members in Dublin on 14 August 2000, at which a ballot was held on
the Labour Court recommendations.
© Alan Betson, *The Irish Times*

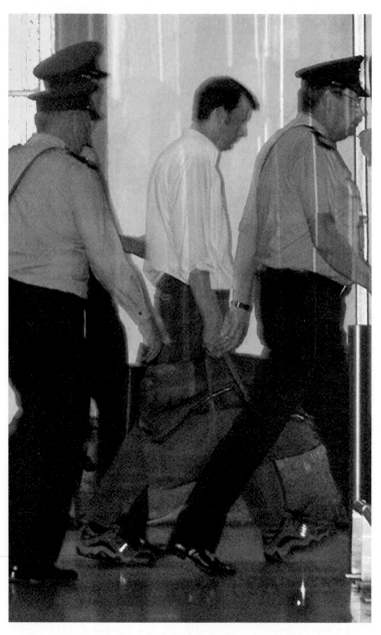

Being removed by gardaí from the CIÉ boardroom at Heuston Station
on 23 August 2000.
© Alan Betson, *The Irish Times*

Speaking to the press at the gates of Kevin Street Garda Station after
being released from custody.
© Alan Betson, *The Irish Times*

Facing the media outside the Labourt Court after the summer 2000
lockout was called off, 25 August 2000.
© Billy Higgins, *Irish Examiner*

With Jimmy Kelly and Mick O'Reilly of the ATGWU arriving at an
ICTU meeting in Parnell Square, Dublin to discuss the May 2001 rail
strike.
© Joe Dunne, Photocall Ireland

because someone, somewhere had decided that that was the way it had to be. And I don't mean someone in Iarnród Éireann either.

A Conspiracy?

On its own we had the company beaten up a stick. What other company could close down its business for three months and lose £15m because it wouldn't talk to 130 of its workers? None. Because no shareholder would stand for it. Not in Virgin Trains, GNER, Scotrail, Connex or any other railway run as a commercial business. Yet in Iarnród Éireann, the shareholder said, 'No problem. How much more money do you want to break these 130 train drivers who you tell us are a such a threat — another £5 million? Another three weeks? No problem, sir.' The shareholder in Iarnród Éireann is the government on behalf of the state's citizens. So the government of the day bankrolled a state railway company in an avoidable and unnecessary dispute, at great expense to the taxpayer, workers, customers and, ultimately, to the company itself. Why? Was it because someone argued that they had given the government fifteen years of wage restraint and it was pay-back time? That it was time for a favour to be returned by allowing a 'social partner' to pursue its own vendetta against ILDA at the expense of taxpayers?

We came to the conclusion very early on that for our opponents this dispute was not about the 'New Deal' at all. It had all been allowed to get out of control and become something much bigger than that. It was about breaking ILDA — destroying us. And the media, government, trade union social partners, industrial relations organs of the state and Iarnród Éireann were all working together at some level to achieve that single unachievable aim. So, having come to this conclusion, we put our hard hats on and just waited to see how long, and how far we could go, and how long, how far and how much they were prepared to waste to pursue this insane agenda. It was to be a long roller-coaster ride.

Disruption of Services

As the dispute settled down, with ILDA members holding buckets and placards, we were able to evaluate the varying levels of disruption nationwide. The busy routes from Dublin to Cork and the tourist areas around Killarney and Tralee were devastated. Our strong and determined membership in Cork was added to by the not inconsiderable support of SIPTU members there. Although these workers did not join us at the gate, they certainly refused to do our members' work and, periodically throughout the ten-weeks, disputes would emerge among those working that would also have a further detrimental effect on services. The majority of NBRU members in Cork, on the other hand, did any work that they were asked to do in addition to their own. This wasn't enough, however, to provide any reasonable service to or from Cork and Cobh. Interestingly, ILDA had no members among the three drivers located in Tralee who supposedly serviced Kerry. However, Kerry drivers were utilised for much of the dispute in working services usually operated by Cork drivers. In effect, management sacrificed Kerry and the South West. Yet, even with the assistance of the Kerry drivers, most Cork services operated only from Dublin to Mallow and back, with bus transfers in between. Elsewhere in the South, services were much better on the Wexford and Waterford lines where ILDA members were thin on the ground.

Around Dublin, our big membership in Inchicore meant large-scale disruption to Heuston services, but most Connolly services survived thanks to 'the Connolly deal for Connolly drivers'. After the initial few days, Galway services, now operated by drivers in possession of their lump-sums, were almost unaffected, but elsewhere in the West of Ireland, service provision was dire. Finbarr Masterston found himself on the gate at Westport for the first time in his thirty-three years of driving, and his driving colleagues in Westport in SIPTU did not operate services either. Although some sort of service did operate from Ballina, the big Mayo towns of Westport and the county town, Castlebar, had no service for almost the entire dispute. Further north, the ILDA members in Sligo, although not involved in the 'New Deal', did not operate many services either on the notorious Sligo line. Finally, the depots of Dundalk and Drogheda were hammered as a result of the strength of ILDA there. This did not affect the Enterprise from Connolly to Belfast, which is operated exclusively by drivers from those terminal depots, but commuter and freight services from the two Louth towns suffered badly.

Overall, Iarnród Éireann, reasonably in its view, tended to concentrate what drivers were available on passenger services as opposed to freight trains. This meant that freight customers had their services affected disproportionately to the number of drivers actually in dispute. While this prioritising of passenger services is mirrored in overall company policy regarding freight, it is perhaps sad that in a country with such an inadequate road infrastructure, freight traffic by rail is so far down the priority list of those controlling what passes for traffic policy in Ireland.

Tactics

Back at the front, however, the Thatcherite tactics that were to be used to try to break ILDA were getting into full swing. For example, as the first weekend of the dispute arrived, unsubstantiated accusations that ILDA members were making abusive phone calls to other drivers were coupled with newspaper speculation that ILDA and its members could be sued by passengers as a result of the dispute. The absurdity of some of what was going on was emphasised by an incident in the car park of Cork Station. Iarnród Éireann stated that a young clerk working in the offices there had had the brake pipe of her car severed, allegedly by an ILDA member. Our members in Cork, many of whom knew the woman involved, were furious that such an accusation would be made, and we decided to get to the bottom of it. Accordingly, two of our members paid a visit to the Garda station in McCurtain Street in Cork, where they were told that a report had been made but that there was no crime suspected and no suspicion whatsoever attaching to any member of ILDA or to any other employee. However, the fact that our management could even suggest that any of our members would indulge in such activities was an early indicator of just how embittered some of those who had allowed the dispute to happen had become, now that the dispute had occurred and ILDA had not dissolved at the first sign of difficulty.

On a personal level, I returned home for the first weekend of the dispute and spent as much time as possible quietly reflecting on what had emerged. Over the weekend, I was able to sort through all the media bull, hysterical allegations and bitter words and again try to bring some focus to how we might actually resolve this dispute. Two things appeared to be clear. Firstly, the other unions were more focused on enticing their members to do our work — with only mixed success — than they were on creating any space for a resolution. Running a scabbing operation was obviously not a policy aimed at peace and reconciliation in the workplace and, if any opportunity arose to try to put an end to such tactics or at least talk them through, I felt that we should take it. Secondly, the LRC had failed our members and acted with great duplicity. How a state agency, whose sole reason for being is to provide for conciliation between disputing parties in cases such as this, could stand by and do nothing was absolutely beyond us in ILDA. As Week Two began, I decided that we would try to refocus on reaching a position where the LRC would do its job and, just as importantly, would be allowed to do it.

We refocused on the reasons, at least as presented to us, why the LRC had not provided conciliation to date. The correspondence that we had received from that body initially claimed that it could not provide conciliation because we were not a 'recognised' trade union. Yet many disputes arise between employers and unions who are not recognised by those employers, particularly in the private sector. The LRC was not set up as a statutory body simply to offer conciliation to parties who have friendly arrangements with each other or full recognition arrangements. This was finally exposed by SI 146 as the nonsense it was. Now, with the code of practice in our pockets, it was time to pay the LRC a visit.

I had another reason for wanting to make contact with the LRC. Just before I had left Cork to spend the weekend with my wife, I had given an interview to a prominent journalist who had expressed amazement that we were still locked out five days in. He was able to tell me that Kieran Mulvey of the LRC had sought preliminary legal advice regarding his obligations under SI 146 and that it seemed that he did indeed have to afford us the normal facilities as a registered trade union. He was scheduled to get more detailed advice at the start of the following week and, the journalist told me, Kieran Mulvey had said that if his preliminary advice were confirmed, he would intervene. This was good news but not altogether surprising. We too had sought and got a formal legal opinion from John Rogers SC, which clearly outlined not alone how our rule change placed us within the ambit of the High Court declaration, but also, more importantly in the short term, how SI 146 clearly provided for us to receive full facilities from the organs of the state, including Iarnród Éireann, as a registered trade union. As we were anxious to emphasise this point — and naive enough still to believe that there might be people in these organisations who would ensure that proper provisions such as this were used — we had taken the exceptional stance of providing copies of this legal advice to both ministers and, through Mary Harney's office, to Kieran Mulvey himself.

Thus the weekend was not one of gloom as we awaited Kieran Mulvey's confirmation of his initial legal advice and an invitation to formal conciliation. While we knew that employers did not of necessity have to accept such invitations, we could not imagine Iarnród Éireann, a semi-state company. refusing, or being allowed to refuse, such an invitation. And so we waited. On Monday, 26 June, we waited. And on Tuesday, 27 June, we waited. And journalists anxious to report every development waited. RTÉ's Peter Cluskey stood outside the LRC office with the actual code in his hand, telling national news viewers that this document could lead to a resolution of the dispute. But still no move came. We began to make our legal advice widely available in an effort to build up some momentum behind this issue. We publicly called upon Kieran Mulvey, Mary Harney or Mary O'Rourke to outline what advice they had received on the code and their varying obligations under it. We were met with a stony silence. And so we decided to act.

On Thursday, 29 June, ILDA members assembled outside Lansdowne Road DART station and began a march to the LRC on Haddington Road. A news release issued by us before the march described what was planned as 'a low-key, peaceful and dignified demonstration by the ILDA at the failure of relevant authorities to utilise the avenues and frameworks available to resolve this dispute in the public interest.' In fact, over eighty ILDA members were joined by their wives and children, many pushing buggies or prams, on a demonstration that had a Garda escort throughout its meandering route through Dublin's afternoon traffic. In their hands, members held individual letters to be delivered by each individual in attendance. Colleagues who couldn't travel to Dublin for the march had letters handed in on their behalf that were signed on the widely accepted 'p.p.' basis, with their permission of course. All letters outlined that ILDA was a registered trade union in accordance with the new code of practice and that its individual members were entitled to have their grievances heard and addressed, initially through conciliation, with arbitration through the Labour Court to follow if necessary. The media also came along for the walk, following the lengthy march throughout. It was a warm balmy day, and with many of our members wearing sunglasses, photographs would appear the following day that made the march look not unlike a scene from the film, *Men in Black!* The mood was amiable as ILDA members and their families mixed with the media. We arrived at the LRC, and I went in with Finbarr Masterson and Brian Dunphy to ask for Kieran Mulvey. He was 'unavailable'. The letters, all of which were addressed to him as chief executive, were therefore handed in at reception while cameras flashed. And then we began walking again. A longer walk this time to Kildare Street and the separate offices of Mary Harney and Mary O'Rourke, Ministers for Enterprise, Trade and Employment, and Public Enterprise and Transport, respectively. A letter presented by me to Mary Harney at that time outlined the full legal and statutory basis for a resolution to the dispute. It may be beneficial to readers to include the full text of that letter here.

Letter to Tánaiste and Minister for Enterprise, Trade and Employment — 26/6/00

Dear Ms. Harney

I refer to a letter from Mr. Vickers, your Private Secretary, dated 21.06.00, in reply to my letter to you dated 16.06.00. In it he raised a number of points on your behalf. I should like to respond as follows:

1). Firstly he has misleadingly named the High Level Group as the 'High Level Group on Individual Representation'. In fact it was constituted under paragraph 9.22 of Partnership 2000, and functioned as, the 'High Level Group on Recognition of Unions and the Right to Bargain' under the auspices of the Department of the Taoiseach. The High Level Group was established in response to trade union demands in respect of union recognition. Its first report, dated December 1997 was rejected by the trade union movement. Following this the Irish Congress of Trade Unions (ICTU) eventually, and without reference to its membership, relinquished its long standing demand for a legislative basis for trade union recognition and instead accepted the Code of Practice route in March 1999. It was in this context that a number of codes of practice were to issue from your department.

2). S.I. 146/2000, is one of these codes of practice. As far as the trade union movement was concerned at the time, it was specifically designed to enable unions to take cases for members in establishments which would not recognise these trade unions. Instead of a system like the recently enacted British legislation entitling unions to be recognised, Irish unions settled for an ability to process individual cases to the LRC and Labour Court. That certainly was the understanding then, unless the minister has changed her interpretation since.

3). This particular Code of Practice, prepared by the LRC, which you as Tánaiste signed on 26.05.00, defines, for the purposes of the Code of Practice, an 'employee representative' as including a 'registered trade union'. It does not say a 'registered trade union with a negotiating licence' nor a 'registered trade union which the employer recognises', nor does it say a 'registered trade union which has excepted body status'. ILDA is a registered trade union and as such falls firmly within the S.I. 146/2000 definition. Further it will remain within said definition for the period from 26.05.00 to the date of any change in the definition which you contemplate.

4). Since the 130 individual members of ILDA have various individual grievances with the 'New Deal for Locomotive Drivers' — a deal in which they were neither individually nor collectively consulted — they have informed me that they wish to have their individual grievances dealt with under the terms of the Code of Practice S.I. 146/2000. The fact that Iarnród Éireann negotiated terms with two unions (SIPTU and the NBRU) does not, nor could not, remove the obligation from this employer to consult with, and seek the agreement of, other individual drivers who were not members of either of those two unions. Significant contractual changes were being made by the employer. In this case the employer acted wrongly in forcing those changed terms of employment on employees who had not been engaged by the employer in any form of consultation, regardless of whether they were members of ILDA, or any other Union, Society or Association.

5). An employer's responsibility to its employees when making contractual changes is not diminished because the employer sought and obtained the agreement of unions not connected with the balance of its employees in the category in question. At the very least, it is also a case of the most appalling inept management practice. Is it any wonder that over 48% of the locomotive drivers have individual grievances? The grievances may all be remarkably similar, but they are nonetheless, individual. Individuals were confronted with new work practices when they presented themselves for work in the customary fashion on 18.06.00. And as you know, their response was individual in nature.

6). As regards the issue of collective negotiations, ILDA is a Registered Trade Union. It does not have a negotiating licence. It is open to Iarnród Éireann to take up the 'excepted body' possibility, in the event that it wishes to have collective discussions with ILDA to resolve this situation. They have chosen not to, but to facilitate maintaining this resolution option for Iarnród Éireann, we have amended our constitution fully in line with Mr Justice O'Neill's judgment and pursuant to section 6(3)(h) of the Trade Union Act, 1941 as amended. The Registrar of Friendly Societies has accepted and approved this amendment, and the appropriately issued certificate confirms this fact. There is now no legal impediment to Iarnród Éireann taking the 'excepted body' route to talks.

7). As regards the LRC, they drafted the Code of Practice for the Tánaiste, which she signed on 26.05.00, as S.I.146/2000. The LRC seems to have failed to fully appreciate the new role it wrote for itself under the terms of S.I. 146/2000.

8). I am to respectfully suggest that you consult the office of the Attorney General on the foregoing, if you doubt the veracity of what I have set out. In addition, Section 43 of the Industrial Relations Act, 1990, also identifies the Labour Court as an additional source of opinion for you, should you so desire. I will await the outcome of your consultations with these bodies on these matters, at your earliest convenience given the urgency of the matter.

This is the ninth day of this unnecessary dispute. It will not be resolved without dialogue. I can only speculate on the dynamics that are preventing a resolution. We have attempted to keep open the 'excepted body' route, as indicated above. In addition, we have identified the S.I. 146/200 option, even though it may be slightly more cumbersome, nonetheless it remains an avenue if all the parties are willing to avail of it. It is in this context that I would respectfully suggest that you might decide to be more proactive in helping the travelling public, the company and the drivers who clearly do have grievances, in identifying methods and avenues in which a solution can be found, rather than having your Private Secretary issue curt three paragraph letters which seek to erect additional obstacles to resolution. I regret to say your approach, thus far, has been anything but helpful.

One might have thought that such a letter would have prompted the Minister for Trade and Employment to reconsider her approach and to respond to all of the serious issues outlined. We awaited a response but our letter seemed to leave the minister stuck for words. On 5 July 2000, we received a response from Mr Vickers in his capacity as Private Secretary to the Tánaiste. It contained thirty-two words if you include the Dear Mr Ogle bit. Here it is:

Dear Mr. Ogle,
I wish to refer further to your letter dated 29 June. An Tánaiste has asked me to state that she does not propose to intervene in the current dispute.

I call it the 'fuck-off letter' but I'm quite sure Tánaistí don't use such language. It might be more honest if they did but, in any case, I got the message and so did our members, their wives and children.

We continued our walk across the city, this time to Liberty Hall, the spiritual and traditional home of Irish trade unionism, but now a place that I would argue houses only a very poor imitation of the principles espoused by Larkin and Connolly. On arrival at Liberty Hall, a small ILDA delegation entered the SIPTU headquarters and met with SIPTU General Secretary John McDonnell. We handed a letter to him that called upon SIPTU to do anything positive it could to resolve the dispute, concluding:

> I am calling on you as General Secretary of S.I.P.T.U. to consider whether your Trade Union has done everything it can to facilitate a resolution to this dispute in the public interest. In addition I am asking you to consider honestly, and privately, whether your union or individuals within it have sought to prevent resolution to this dispute. I am asking you and your organisation to ensure that no impediment is placed by you to prevent this Trade Union from exercising its democratic, constitutional and statutory entitlement to pursue the concerns and grievances of its membership.

Our belief that people within SIPTU were preventing a resolution to the dispute was thus put directly to the General Secretary of Ireland's biggest union. He responded to these specific charges by outlining that he was personally not aware of any efforts by anybody in SIPTU to interfere in the dispute, and I believe that he was telling the truth.

As we left Liberty Hall, we crossed the street to address our members and the still-assembled media. I was careful not to stand next to the Connolly memorial erected to honour one of the fathers of Irish trade unionism, not because I didn't think it appropriate — in fact, I felt that our members were standing up for and protecting true trade union values — but because I simply didn't want to give anyone a further stick with which to beat us or an opportunity to sneer at us. After a short address, we left to await a helpful response from those to whom we had presented the letters. It was as well we didn't decide to hold our collective breaths while waiting.

The Labour Relations Commission Response

Instead of welcoming the individual referrals of the issues in dispute and using its own code of practice to bring the dispute to a conclusion, the LRC wrote back to each of our members and told them that they would have to take up their grievances with the company in the first instance. The LRC also questioned the fact that the letters of some of our members — those who couldn't make it to Dublin for the march — had been signed on their behalf. The implication was that this somehow made them invalid or they had been signed by agents of the KGB or something — this from an organisation that has sent me a complete file of letters almost all of which have been signed on the self-same 'signed on behalf of' basis. While our members pondered the best way of taking up their individual grievances with the company, up popped Iarnród Éireann on the national airwaves, conveniently, telling all and sundry that the only way to take up grievances was to end the dispute, go back to work and take up any grievances with the 'New Deal' while they were working it. So the LRC's role in assisting the end of this dispute simply extended to telling our members to end it, take up their grievances within their employment and stop sending awkward letters that called on the Commission to fulfil its statutory functions in dispute resolution.

The SIPTU Response

Following our meeting, SIPTU's General Secretary summoned the other senior officials in Ireland's largest union to his office, gave them a lecture on the legacy of Connolly, Larkin and union solidarity in general, called an end to their disgraceful scabbing operation and offered olive branches to our members that would smooth the waters and help create a climate where resolution was possible. Well, actually, he didn't. SIPTU remained silent, the scabbing continued, our members' attitudes hardened and the situation continued to deteriorate.

Eamon Dunphy and the IFI Story

Brendan Ogle was by now becoming headline news and most of the headlines weren't good. Faced with a complicated collective agreement and a difficult and complex history, some in the media did what they do best — ignored the issues and focused more and more on personalities. I was getting used now to the cameras clicking wherever we went, and to the posse of microphone-holding reporters looking for today's headline. I continued to try to be helpful, to the point of naivety. For example, I agreed to have a photo taken by an agency who wanted it for use in the Sunday papers. I drove with the photographer to the old railway line in Athlone and I posed here, there and everywhere — looking across the Shannon, under the well-known landmark of the Shannon bridge, in the old station and, finally, standing between two tracks in my suit, looking like I owned the bloody place. No public relations advisor would have allowed it but I just did it. It never even dawned on me how it would look until I saw it. Lesson learned.

I did other silly things too as far as the media were concerned. Eamon Dunphy had a show on radio at the time. I preferred to listen to Navanman, to be honest, but in the mid-1990s, at least in the early stages, there was something interesting and refreshing about Dunphy's 'direct' style of interviewing. So I tuned in whenever I could, eventually noticing that the broadcaster could be direct, confrontational, insulting, but not always, and not to everyone. My personal experience began when I was driving to Portarlington on 24 June to pick up Brian Dunphy for our latest round of meetings and I listened to *Morning Ireland*. On this particular morning, they had a new take on the ILDA dispute — unless it was resolved quickly, it would cost jobs and they wouldn't necessarily be railway workers' jobs. Irish Fertiliser Industries (IFI) was in trouble and its Arklow manager, Bill Flood, was on air outlining the details of a developing 'crisis'. The semi-state company needed our trains to transport its lethal ammonia cocktails in safety away from roads between its Arklow and Cobh plants. Unless this cargo could be guaranteed twice a day, four or five days a week, the plants could not operate and would close. It was the first that I or anyone else in ILDA had heard of it. I wrote down Bill Flood's name and title and resolved to ring him when I got to Dublin.

Brian and I had booked a room in Buswell's Hotel — directly across from Leinster House, and the favoured watering hole of many of its TDs and Senators — and we had invited as many of our elected representatives as possible to meet us, listen to us, help us, seek explanations from us, or whatever they liked, before they adjourned for their holidays and left the nation's railways to rot in the summer sun. We got a fairly good attendance at the meeting. Throughout the day, more than twenty TDs popped in to discuss with us the dispute itself and the breaking story of IFI. To my surprise, when I raised the issue of IFI with one Fianna Fáil TD, he told me not to be too concerned about it, pointing out that the minister responsible for the semi-state company was none other then the Minister for Public Enterprise and Transport — Mary O'Rourke herself!

In any event, I decided to call IFI's Bill Flood. I called him from the lobby in Buswell's Hotel just after lunchtime. He was friendly and welcoming of my call and he outlined the concerns he had for his plant and his employees. He explained that ammonia supplies had almost dried up and that unless IFI got some through by rail, then disaster beckoned. I accepted what he told me at face value and immediately offered to go to his plant and speak with him, his board, his workers or anyone at all to explore whether or not there was any way of getting supplies through despite the dispute. He thanked me for the offer and said he would speak to some people and get back to me. I gave him my contact numbers and returned to the room to meet the latest group of TDs.

In the following days, we in ILDA relied on the media to tell us about the developing crisis at IFI. To be frank, some of our members weren't convinced that this was a real crisis at all. IFI had been struggling as a business for almost twenty years and this was just the latest in a long line of crises. In addition, our members knew, because our members drive the trains, that IFI generally closed down for two weeks each year during the summer-holiday season so that essential maintenance and cleaning work could be carried out on the plant that dealt with such dangerous chemicals. Was this just the normal summer shutdown or was the situation really more serious?

As the days passed, the newspapers, radio and TV coverage seemed to confirm our worst fears. The plants were to close on Friday, 7 July, for good. It was over for IFI, and ILDA was to blame. Enter Eamon Dunphy. His show, *The Last Word,* wanted me live in studio on the day of the closure. I knew what was coming as I drove up to Dublin and prepared for the oncoming attack. My mobile phone rang en route. It was the Chairman of Wicklow County Council, Pat Doyle. Mr Doyle was naturally upset about the situation in Arklow and the loss of so many jobs. In the absence of any outside efforts to help, he had planned a series of meetings for the following day, Saturday, 8 July, in the county offices in Wicklow Town. He invited ILDA to attend. I accepted and assured him that if it were possible for us to do anything at all, we would. He said that Iarnród Éireann and the other unions would also be there. He had even set up a suite of separate rooms so that those who didn't want to meet face to face wouldn't have to. The meetings would commence at 2pm.

Eamon Dunphy was unaware of this when I arrived in his studio. As the interview progressed, he was gradually moving up to top gear. Fathers were going home to their children that evening with their last pay packet to tell their families they had no jobs. What had I to say to those children? How could I explain how my members and I had cost their fathers their jobs? I explained that we had been available to help if we could but that it was hard to help when nobody would talk to you. I then outlined the Wicklow County Council initiative and said that I hoped — believed — that, with equal good will on all sides, we could get IFI back in production. Eamon Dunphy pulled back but interestingly asked me to speak to him again on Monday after the Wicklow meetings. I left Today FM and immediately began working on ideas for the following day.

Firstly we chose our delegation. We expected a media presence and fuss and we didn't want to play politics with the situation. A small team would suffice — myself, Brian Dunphy, and Christy Holbrook — secretary, treasurer and president, respectively. I spoke to our members in Inchicore, Connolly and Cork. They were the depots from which the ammonia trains were worked. These were the men who would need to co-operate with any plan to get ammonia moving. Assurances were received. ILDA members would not be found wanting if the only problem was moving ammonia from Cobh to Arklow and back.

Saturday was a beautiful sunny day. I drove to Portarlington to pick up Brian and then we took the stunningly scenic route over the Wicklow Gap and down to Wicklow Town. On the way, I took a call from a newscaster at Today FM. He was checking that we were going to Wicklow and, in passing, told me that Eamon Dunphy's interview the previous evening was the talk of the place — he had gone over the top and would look silly on Monday.

We found the county building easily and early — too early to be put off by the empty car park. Christy hadn't arrived yet and we didn't want to be sitting alone in a car park while managers, county councillors and rival trade unionists arrived with media in tow. We arranged to meet Christy for a coffee in town and returned together about ten minutes before the meetings were set to begin. This time, the empty car park sent us a very different message. Something was going on and it wasn't meetings as arranged in the Wicklow County Council buildings. The next two hours explained everything. All the people who we had been told we would be meeting were actually meeting elsewhere — in Connolly Station in Dublin. Sometime that morning, Iarnród Éireann, SIPTU, NBRU and IFI representatives had agreed not to go to Wicklow but to try to hatch their own method of transporting ammonia, and to exclude our members. We didn't even get a phone call to tell us of the change of venue and that we were no longer invited. To be fair, Pat Doyle apologised profusely and said that it had been taken out of the hands of the County Council. I accepted then, and still do, that he had no part in what took place. It was clear to us that Iarnród Éireann wanted to use the IFI crisis to 'persuade' more SIPTU and NBRU members to do our work. Solving the IFI situation was not the main objective. Breaking ILDA was. Once again, typically, neither objective was achieved. Why don't people just talk?

Eamon Dunphy was prepared to talk and, on his show on 10 July, he did talk. One might have expected him to have Iarnród Éireann or SIPTU or the NBRU on to explain why they hadn't gone to Wicklow. Instead, he had me on to explain why I did go and how I found nobody else there. His response? 'Is it your position that you'll have to settle the strike before you lift the threat of these people being permanently unemployed. Is that your position?' he asked. I explained that it was not our position but that I was not, under any circumstances, going to outline for the first time, live on his show, what our members were prepared to do. Eamon Dunphy, however, took a different tack. He wanted me to tell SIPTU and NBRU members to drive the trains of our members who were locked out of work. He asked: 'Are you prepared to put people permanently on the dole when you're supposed to be a working man yourself, supposed to be a trade unionist?' Not content with the SIPTU and the NBRU scabbing operation as it was, Eamon Dunphy wanted me actually to organise it for them. Against my own members. I worked hard to keep my cool and succeeded. Not so my interviewer. As I outlined how we had been available to prevent this crisis for ten days before IFI closed, and how we could work to explore a resolution with representatives of the IFI workers, he exploded: 'So you wanted them to negotiate for you. You're a conman, you're a conman; you don't tell the truth.'

At that point I had done interviews with all of Ireland's top newscasters and commentators. I did many more afterwards. Many of those interviews had been tough, probing and aggressive. But how was I supposed to react to being called a conman, live on national radio, to over 100,000 listeners? I reacted by finishing the interview, holding my temper, and cautioning him about the nature of his attack on me.

I was doing the interview by phone from Brian Dunphy's house in Portarlington as we were en route to meetings in Limerick and Cork later that evening. The following day, a meeting had been arranged between ILDA and IFI workers in Cork, at their request. Brian had kindly left me alone in his sitting-room to concentrate on the interview, while he and his family listened to the show on radio elsewhere in the house. After I had put the phone down, Brian entered the room. My immediate reaction was to feel slandered and libelled by this attack that had called my honesty, character and integrity into question in the most vitriolic way and without justification. And then I began to get angry. How dare he? I thought of our members and their wives struggling to pay that month's mortgage. I called my own wife, hoping she hadn't been listening. She had. It was a difficult call. She was worried about me and I was worried about her. And I was off down south and wouldn't be home for days. As we drove towards Portlaoise, I did the only thing I could think of doing. I called my solicitor, Donal Spring. Donal hadn't heard the interview, but Brian had been taping it, and we played it back to him over the phone. He immediately contacted *The Last Word*, which was still on air, and sought a withdrawal and apology for the libel. It never came.

When Eamon Dunphy came back on air the following evening, he had SIPTU's Noel Dowling lined up to support him in putting the boot in further. The SIPTU representative explained that his members were going to work but were doing the 'traditional' thing of not doing our members' work, before going on to tell listeners that this dispute could close IFI permanently and was not simply a matter that would last a number of weeks. Eamon Dunphy then went on to tell listeners that

Brendan Ogle — not ILDA, not our members, not P.G. Rayner, but Brendan Ogle alone — was the only person in or connected to Iarnród Éireann with a problem over safety. According to him, I was 'responsible for the plight of the workers in Arklow and other workers in Cork', and he encouraged Noel Dowling to 'do your best to resolve this and take Mr Ogle on'. Even Noel Dowling — the man known by some within Liberty Hall as 'the enforcer' — had to pull back from that and tell Eamon Dunphy that it was 'not a question of taking people on'.

The attack got a considerable reaction from many who had heard it. Those close to me were angered by it. Eamon Dunphy began to get messages from listeners and, almost to a man or woman, they were critical of him and his comments. The only positive thing that can be said about Eamon Dunphy's behaviour with regard to me was that he read out many of these comments that were critical of him. Iarnród Éireann didn't miss its opportunity either. The following morning, I did an interview on Cork's 96FM where John Keenan regurgitated Dunphy's comments, saying that he regretted that my unpopularity had prompted such words. The clear message was that if only we would go back to work, people would stop calling me names.

Over the entire three months of media frenzy, this Eamon Dunphy interview hurt more than any other criticism. I cannot look at the man on television now without reaching for the remote control. I didn't sue him because ultimately my legal advice came down to this — Eamon Dunphy, Today FM and its parent company would fight. They would enjoy, even relish, the fight and its ensuing publicity. If they lost, they lost. They would pay but would get full value for their efforts. However, if I lost, there would be no consolation prizes for me. There would be my own legal bill and theirs and they would be substantial — easily in six figures, and we were talking old Irish pounds here. In a nutshell, I was advised that I had about a 60 per cent chance of defending my name successfully in court, and a 40 per cent chance of financial ruin for my family and me. At the end of the day, I am a family man and a train driver. I am the guy down the road who works nights, has a mortgage and car loan, a credit card, a wife and child, with bills to pay. And I'm not going to take a 40 per cent chance of destroying my family. Eamon Dunphy, Today FM and their advisors knew this. Little guys get libelled and big guys don't. The injustice of it still eats at me.

Interestingly the same presenter found himself emerged in controversy in the summer of 2000 when he supported Roy Keane in the stance he took at the World Cup in Saipan amid a media storm. As the Keane story ran and ran and Eamon Dunphy got more and more excited throughout the episode, so too did the media frenzy intensify, and the commentator came under the spotlight in a big way. This obviously impacted upon him severely and he took to commenting in public on the effect the frenzy was having on his family. Thanks to him and others, my own wife and family knew very much how they would have felt.

Something else that caused annoyance at the time were some of the public relations stunts pulled on our members and on me by Iarnród Éireann's public relations team. Just like Margaret Thatcher during the miners' strike in 1984/5, Iarnród Éireann spent thousands of pounds on adverts in the national dailies, feeding the public a constant diet of misinformation. Just like Thatcher with the miners, scabs were portrayed as men of principle, taking the proper line against 'the enemy within'. Just like Thatcher with the miners, Iarnród Éireann tried to portray honest working men — men like Finbarr Masterson and Brian Dunphy — as thugs and bullies. And just like Thatcher, Iarnród Éireann and the right-wing factions of the media turned personal. The *Evening Herald* slaughtered ILDA in general and me in particular. Later in the dispute (and only when what passes for Dublin's transport system was affected), that paper produced an edition that had six full pages on ILDA and me, with a far-from-complimentary front-page photograph of me. Now I may not be built like the side of a barn and I'm no Russell Crowe, but if the photograph of me on the front page of the Evening Herald on 3 August 2000 and reproduced again in miniature inside is the *Herald*'s idea of an accurate image of me, then I need urgent plastic surgery and I should not be allowed outdoors until I get it, lest children run into their houses when they see me coming, while their dogs hide under cars! And the headline on page 1 read: 'He represents only 100 train drivers, The Courts have rejected his claims. But today this man created chaos for 250,000 Dubliners'. Another headline to yet another story inside described me as 'The Chaos Instigator'. We even got the editorial that evening: 'Stop Ogle holding us to ransom' it screamed. Anyone who had braved the front-page photo and got inside that far could read how 'anarchy' was being created by 'Brendan Ogle's irresponsible and self-serving tactics'. Self-serving? I had by then been without any income whatsoever for two-and-a-half months. The tactic was clear: Break Ogle and you break ILDA.

And then there was the *Daily Mirror* — once the workers' daily in the UK. Accompanied by a colour version of the awful picture used in the *Herald*, the headline read: 'Meet Mr. Misery — this is the head of the Union that brought chaos to Dublin'. Under the headline is a picture of about forty yards of a busy Dublin street, with the caption 'Strike action by ILDA kept buses off the streets'. And — I kid you not! — there we have two of Dublin Bus's finest double-deckers clogging up the road. It is funny now, but it hurt at the time. However, with the exception of Eamon Dunphy, the *Herald*, and the *Mirror*, the rest of it was fine — annoying often, sometimes intrusive, perhaps generally not as balanced as we would have liked, but basically attempting to be fair. After all, here were 130 train drivers and the guy from Dundalk with no training, versus a state company, two government departments, the mainstream trade union movement in Ireland, the state's conciliation service and all their PR appendages and hangers on. This was David and Goliath stuff. And David has no complaints at all about the manner in which he was treated by most of the media.

The IFI Solution

On 12 July, two days after my second interview with Eamon Dunphy on *The Last Word*, a delegation of IFI workers and senior shop stewards met with an ILDA delegation in Cork. We met in a hostelry on the outskirts of Cork, called the Viaduct. A big pub with private areas, discreet corners and food served all day long, it became something of a base for us in Cork during the dispute. There were about twenty at the meeting and the delegations were of equal size. An IFI representative in Cork, Tom Morrissey, arranged it. It was also attended by some of the IFI workers who had driven down from Arklow. The first thing they did was explain to us what had happened the previous Saturday. They were some of the people we had expected to meet under the auspices of Wicklow County Council. However, on Friday evening, arrangements were changed and they were led to believe that there was the possibility of a breakthrough with the SIPTU and NBRU members in Cork in relation to working our trains in greater numbers. A meeting was convened involving themselves and their officials (who stayed away from our meeting), Iarnród Éireann and delegates of the SIPTU and NBRU rail workers concerned. The railwaymen from Cork explained that, regardless of any pressure, they wouldn't be working our ammonia trains. The IFI people, realising that they were on a fool's errand, immediately instituted contact with us in Cork. We were only too happy to meet them. We explained our position about not working the 'New Deal' and they accepted it fully. They told us that they viewed us as people defending our rights as workers and said that they did not want us to work the 'New Deal' to save their jobs. They had, down through the years, had their own industrial relations difficulties, and they understood exactly where we where at. We too understood their position and stated that we would do everything we could to help.

We discussed possibilities and it was agreed that the IFI trains, in the exceptional circumstances being presented, needed to be treated differently. We said that we would work them on a 'ring-fenced' basis. This work would be considered neither part of the 'New Deal' nor part of the old terms and conditions. It would be totally without prejudice to our position, or that of the company, on the substantive issue. The only issue that arose was one of payment. We agreed that any money earned by our members on these duties would be put into a central fund and distributed equally to all our members. We were in this together. However, our members would not work for the new rate, even though it was higher than the old one. They wanted only the old, and lower, payment. If Iarnród Éireann had a problem with that, they could do what they liked with the balance. The agreement would deal solely with IFI and could be written or guaranteed by a respected third party, such as Bishop Buckley of Cork who was making it known that he would do everything he could to help resolve the impasse.

The IFI workers were overjoyed. They left us at lunchtime, shaking hands and heading off to bring the good news to their officials and Iarnród Éireann. We, naively, agreed not to discuss with the media what we had offered until the IFI delegation came back to us. During the afternoon, I was repeatedly pressed by the media on what we had discussed with the IFI workers, and each time I said that I couldn't disclose any details but that we were hopeful of a successful outcome. Just after 4pm, Tom Morrissey called me. He explained that the offer had been rubbished by his officials and Iarnród Éireann and that they had gone off to the media. He was angry and upset — his job was on the line, after all. Then at 5pm, I heard the radio news. Mary Harney, the Minister for Enterprise, Trade and Employment, was asked about the offer and she said, bluntly, 'No'. For afters, we had Noel Dowling, whose IFI members were supposedly now out of work, telling Eamon Dunphy how there would be no deal as we wanted it 'signed', and that would be 'recognition'. All he had to offer his members in IFI were the same old tired calls for his railway members in Cork to do our work.

I now smelled rats all over the place. The Tánaiste was prepared to shut down a semi-state company permanently with a bland 'no' when there was a ring-fenced, without-prejudice solution on the table? A SIPTU representative was prepared to tell his IFI members that they were permanently on the dole, without any real effort to deal with the problem? It didn't add up. My mind stopped racing. I called Tom Morrissey back and told him not to worry. I told him that I was convinced that IFI would re-open after the normal two-week closure whether the ILDA dispute was resolved or not. Tom thought that I was being ridiculous. I wasn't. I was right.

There was another week and a half of Eamon Dunphy persecuting his latest victim, and Noel Dowling asking his railway members in Cork to 'put their principles aside and do the right thing'. There were meetings in Cork when the entire Executive of ILDA headed south to meet Bishop Buckley, Labour's John Mulvihill who was Chair of the Council and the Lord Mayor, in the Town Hall while, simultaneously, Messers Mulvey and Pomphrett of the LRC, Iarnród Éireann, Liam Tobin of the NBRU, and Noel Dowling of SIPTU met over the road, still trying to force the majority of their members to do what they were never, ever going to do. This lasted for hours until the bishop, the lord mayor and the councillor got fed up being used (they were supposed to be pressuring us to surrender, I suppose) and broke off, justifiably, with the process. Another day, Tom Morrissey called me to say that Des Geraghty was on his way to Cork and that he would sort everything out. It is a sign of the pressure I must have been under at the time that I reacted badly to this particular call from Tom. Expletives were used. I headed south myself too. But when I got there, Des had already gone back to Dublin after a wasted journey. His members would not do our work.

The following Monday, IFI — tanks cleaned and maintenance carried out — re-opened. There wasn't a word from Eamon Dunphy. The ILDA dispute still had many weeks to run and hadn't, as it turned out, even reached the half-way stage. Throughout the rest of it though, we never heard from or about IFI again. In fact, the next we heard of IFI, Bill Flood or Tom Morrissey was in October 2002, when, over two years later, the whole operation closed for good with the loss of over 600 jobs. This time, the tragedy for the workers was real, and not simply an exercise in manipulation.

NOT FOR BREAKING

And so where does that leave us? Well in terms of timing it brought us into the last week of July 2000 and the dispute into its sixth week. The IFI workers who had supposedly gone home to their children with their last pay packets were miraculously back at work. However, Ireland's railway services continued to chug along in some areas and rot into the ground in others. In addition, all ILDA members were now under severe financial strain and no one who could help wanted to. At this stage, it is worth taking a cold look at what those with the power to help resolve this dispute were actually doing six weeks into a national train strike, and to assess their role in events to date.

SIPTU and the NBRU

To date, no discussions of any sort had taken place between these unions and ILDA, with the exception of the fruitless twenty-minute meeting with SIPTU General Secretary John McDonnell. No behind-the-scenes talks or contacts aimed at looking at issues that could be beneficial to drivers in all three unions had been initiated. Part-time drivers were equally unsafe whether they drove trains previously driven by full-timers in membership of ILDA, SIPTU or the NBRU. Yet instead of discussing such matters, the sole focus of the officials of these unions on their frequent trips around Ireland was to encourage more and more of their members to do the work of ILDA members. Of course, the net effect of this activity was eminently predictable — further polarisation of drivers. It is my view that SIPTU and the NBRU should, early in the dispute, have issued statements simply saying that they did not agree with our view of the 'New Deal' but that it was a matter of conscience for their members whether they supported our protest or not and that they, as representatives of working people, would remain available at all times to do anything they could do to help. In the event, their actions achieved the worst of all worlds in causing further division and bitterness, alienating their own members, especially in places such as Cork, and leading to other disputes. And all for an extremely negligible impact on services, which should primarily have been a concern for management in any case.

Iarnród Éireann/CIÉ Management

The approach of management throughout this period mirrored that of the unions exactly. From the moment when ILDA members were prevented from signing on for duty on 19 June, every action and utterance by management was calculated to break ILDA members collectively and individually. No olive branches were offered and no recourse to common ground was sought. Vitriol was the daily diet meted out to ILDA and me by a plethora of spokespersons. At one point during the dispute, I received the news that Barry Kenny — having lectured us for weeks and months about the democracy of trade unionism — was leaving Iarnród Éireann to go and work in that bastion of trade unionism, Ryanair. Initially, Myles McHugh from Galway was asked to fill Barry's shoes. It was to be a short sojourn. After fulfilling his new public relations functions for a short number of days, Barry was somehow enticed back to Iarnród Éireann. Myles was not in the least embarrassed by his re-assignment back to Galway, and was even reported in the *Sunday Business Post* as describing Barry's sojourn to Ryanair as 'holidays'. From where we were standing, it didn't really matter whose face was on the television that evening or whose voice was resounding over the airwaves. The message was the same — war, war, war. If it wasn't a daily dose of propaganda paid for by tax-payers, in the form of misleading adverts in our national dailies, it was assurances that services would return to this line or that line tomorrow, that ILDA was about to break, that we had no support or that we were all 'mavericks' and 'wild cats' — day after day, week after week, month after month. It hurt.

Many ILDA members had years of trouble-free experience behind them, driving trains 24/7 for their customers. Most never even needed to know the names, never mind job descriptions, of these 'suits'. Now, for the first time in their lives, something — their terms and conditions and safety — meant enough to them to make them take a stand at great cost to themselves. Overnight, the 'suits' emerged from whatever offices they had been hiding in for years to brand these men 'mavericks' and 'wild cats'. All the years of working away diligently; all the foggy frosty nights peering for unlit signals that belonged in the dark ages, to warn of gate crossings that weren't opened; all the phone calls taken at home and the quick dressing and driving into work to cover some unforeseen 'emergency' or other; all the years of night work; all the shifts spent doing their best with crumbling locomotives and rolling stock — all immediately went down the pan as a result of the use of a few sharp words in a few short (in the context of a lifetime of dedicated service) weeks. We have a member in the West of Ireland to whom I spoke over two years after the lock-out had finally ended. I was not that surprised to discover that he had all but forgotten about the boredom of being out of work for ten weeks, had learned to deal with and account for his loss of three months' pay and mortgage money, and was even on better terms with his colleagues who had done his work during the dispute. But what still rankled with him most and was engrained on his memory was the use of the label 'maverick' with regard to him and his fellow ILDA members. No matter what healing time brings to us all, some things will never be forgotten, and some things will most definitely never be the same again.

State's Industrial Relations Machinery

In Ireland, politicians, employers and worker representatives alike are prone to referring to our 'very sophisticated industrial relations machinery'. There are also some employers and workers who believe that this 'machinery' is actually nothing more than a mechanism for a nanny state to interfere in employer/worker relations. However, that is not a debate that I would wish to take part in at this time. Love it or loathe it, this 'sophisticated machinery' is a fact of life for most employers and worker representatives, certainly in the public sector. Without it, they would actually have to deal face to face with each other, reach agreements alone, and make them stick. The industrial relations machinery consists of the Labour Court, the Labour Relations Commission (LRC) and the Rights Commissioners Service. The Labour Court generally works on the basis of referrals made to it under various pieces of industrial relations legislation. It didn't become involved in this dispute until much later than the six-week stage, although, as discussed earlier, it was open at all stages to Mary Harney, as Minister for Enterprise, Trade and Employment, to seek the 'opinion' of the court on our entitlements under SI 146/2000.

The LRC, on the other hand, had been involved in the process throughout. It brokered the 'New Deal' in the first instance. It then 'supervised' the ballot. It wrote the new code of practice, SI 146/2000, bestowing upon itself the clear obligation to deal with ILDA as a registered trade union. It received referrals from ILDA members on all of the issues in dispute. However, for weeks, it failed to issue any invitations to conciliation. The LRC is the conciliation service and the Labour Court is the arbitration service — a two-step approach to industrial peace and harmony. It sounds simple doesn't it? In fact, as the whole system is voluntary in nature, it works only if the parties agree to play ball. Often, one or other party, fearing a likely outcome, doesn't. That wasn't ILDA in 2000 though. We wanted the assistance of these two bodies; we would accept all invitations that arrived. Yet, taxpayers who fund a conciliation service in this country suffered a three-month rail dispute which saw absolutely no conciliation between the parties in dispute at all. None! So what exactly was the LRC doing during this time?

On Saturday, 15 July, during the IFI crisis, I was in Brian Dunphy's house en route home from speaking to some by-now-skint ILDA members when I saw the 6 o'clock news on national television. Kieran Mulvey, Chief Executive of the LRC, was being interviewed against the backdrop of an empty rail line. He said that he had had enough. He told viewers how it had gone too far and this madness must end. I was delighted. I was even more delighted when he made it clear how he was going to back his sentiments up with actions. The LRC was convening meetings in Cork within forty-eight hours — Monday, 17 July, to be exact — to try to resolve this dispute. Anxious to seize the opportunity, Brian and I immediately arranged for the entire ILDA Executive to decamp to Cork so that whatever decisions needed to be taken could be taken without delay or prevarication. I waited for Kieran Mulvey to call me and tell me the time and venue for the showdown. Sure enough, on the road between Portarlington and Athlone, the phone did ring. It wasn't anyone from the LRC though. It was John Mulvihill of Cork County Council, and he wanted the ILDA lads to meet him and Bishop Buckley when we got to Cork.

When Monday arrived, the papers and news shows were full of it. With little news other than the rail dispute, all eyes seemed to be on Cork. En route we discovered that the LRC was taking two conciliation officers. Tom Pomphrett was accompanying Kieran Mulvey to Cork. Liam Tobin was leading the NBRU entourage, and Noel Dowling would be there to represent SIPTU. And of course Iarnród Éireann's John Keenan and Joe Walsh would also be attendance. We had overnight bags with us and were prepared for twenty-four-hour sessions of head banging if required. On our arrival in Cork, a large palatial room at the top of the civic-office building awaited us. However, the interminable delays awaiting others, punctuated only by adjournments between delays, alerted us to the fact that all was not what it seemed to be. John Mulvihill and Bishop Buckley seemed as bemused as us. Could we not just go back to work? Wouldn't it be easier all round?

While we waited for the serious talking to begin, more adjournments took place and it dawned on us that the bishop and the county-council chairman were under pressure. We awaited the arrival of the heavy-hitters from the LRC and prepared to bed down for the night if required, but by now our executive members were discovering that these adjournments were actually being used for telephone conversations between officials for John Mulvihill and the council, and the 'other parties'. There was actually another party taking place, quite separately, and it wasn't in the Cork civic offices. It was, in fact, in the much more appropriate setting of Kent Station, and present were SIPTU, the NBRU and management. And the LRC of course. The LRC representatives were over at the station trying to broker a solution to a dispute between two parties, ILDA and Iarnród Éireann, while one of the parties was stuck a few hundred metres across the River Lee with a bishop and the county council chairman. The closest the LRC got to talking to ILDA was talking to the bishop who talked to ILDA and then popped out again to tell the LRC what ILDA was saying. I didn't know whether to laugh or cry.

Strong words were exchanged between our members as it became clear that Bishop Buckley and John Mulvihill were being hopelessly manipulated by the group over at Kent Station. Bishop Buckley had, of course, acted in good faith throughout, and out of a real concern for the impact the dispute was having on members of his congregation. However, I think he now sensed that he was in an impossible position. Both men explained to us that they were seeking a final adjournment and that they would engage with the Kent Station party and come back to us in one final effort to make progress. We were asked to leave the building for a short time. As we waited across the road, we discussed the turn of events among ourselves. Once again, the only conclusion to which we could come was that they didn't want to resolve the dispute and reach a conclusion acceptable to all sides; they wanted to break ILDA. The rest of the country, our customers, freight business and tourist interests would just have to indulge them in that vain pursuit. They wanted ILDA's head on a plate.

A couple of 7-ups and a mobile phone call later and we were back in the civic buildings again. Bishop Buckley and John Mulvihill outlined to us that they had been led to believe that there was room for manoeuvre and that that was why they had put their good offices at the disposal of the parties. It was now clear to them that there was, in fact, no possibility of discussion, conciliation or any movement whatsoever from the other party, and therefore they were unable to provide us with any further assistance. They regretted this, wished us and our families well and took their leave. We sat in stony silence apart from a few words from me thanking both men for their efforts.

Over at Kent Station, Kieran Mulvey and Tom Pomphrett emerged from what was laughably described in some sections of the media as 'an intensive nine-hour negotiation', with no solution to the dispute. SIPTU and the NBRU yet again urged their members to work ammonia trains voluntarily, and Iarnród Éireann said it would 'review drivers' concerns' if we returned to work, and again stated that it was 'confident' that ammonia trains would be back within twenty-four hours.

As a postscript to this section, it is worth noting that not all citizens are ignorant as to what the LRC should be doing in such circumstances. When the LRC responded to our members' individual letters by failing to offer conciliation, on 4 July, our members outside Athlone Station with their bucket collection received a sum of money from a motorist who pulled up, got out of his car and presented money to our members, explaining that the LRC's response to our pleas for help had led him to believe that we were being stitched up. He supplied his name and address to our members, received a receipt, and wished them luck for the remainder of the dispute before speeding off again.

The Media

Overall, the media coverage of the dispute to date had been extensive, but it still hadn't reached its peak. Apart from the three examples discussed in the previous chapter, the coverage elsewhere was as good as any group of workers in our position could have expected it to be.

There are some articles that stood out as being particularly positive. Fergus Finlay was by now well versed in all aspects of ILDA and the dispute, and his weekly comment piece in the *Irish Examiner* reflected this on more than one occasion. In fact, his coverage of ILDA-related issues had begun much earlier than the 2000 lockout. Following the localised disputes in Athlone and Cork in 1999, Fergus wrote that Iarnród Éireann's actions and communications had led to the problems, and gave some details about the terms and conditions of drivers, and the management culture within Iarnród Éireann. Fergus received some interesting feedback from a number of people about that piece. Apart from the retired drivers with up to forty years' service who wrote to point out to him that their pension was not £54 per week, as he had written, but a measly £38 per week, Iarnród Éireann also reacted to the piece. Furiously. The result was a lengthy and very prominent reply to Fergus's article, by John Keenan, in the *Examiner* of 30 July 1999. In the first eight lines, he talks about 'characteristic misinformation' and 'misrepresentation', and refers to the 'self styled Irish Locomotive Drivers Association' as a 'maverick group'. He finishes by telling Fergus Finlay off for criticising the company's procedures for treatment of staff involved in rail fatalities, and promises that 'an agreed company/trade union procedure on this issue will shortly be published'. In fact, this matter had been outstanding since I had ceased to be a member of the SIPTU sub-committee that produced a report on this issue before I had left that union in September 1998. Ten months later, an agreed policy had still not been 'published'. When I raised this with John Keenan in a subsequent telephone call, he told me that he had been too busy dealing with 'unofficial industrial action' to get around to the matter. However, when the next disruption took place — a full eleven months later, in June 2000 — the policy had still not been published. It is now autumn 2003, over four years since the *Examiner* promise that 'an agreed company/trade union procedure on this issue will shortly be published' — and there is still no sign of it.

However, getting back to the media coverage of the dispute, on 23 June 2000, the *Examiner* produced a full-page article featuring both John Keenan and me, outlining our respective viewpoints; it reflected the balanced view of the *Examiner* to the events that were unfolding. The paper was so balanced in fact that one day the editorial supported our call for talks to resolve the dispute and another day was highly critical of us and didn't! On balance, though, we had no complaints about Ireland's third national daily.

The Irish Times, on the other hand, was a mixed bag. Padraig Yeates used his experience to great effect and even appeared as an 'expert' on RTÉ on occasion, giving his view of events. The *Times* also allowed me my own piece early in the dispute, which was effective in getting our point across; and we received supportive comment pieces from two journalists whom I respected greatly as a reader but had never spoken to or known in any way — John Waters and the late Dick Walsh. There was also an article from another columnist in *The Irish Times*, which I thought was hilarious although I appreciate that it might not have been the intention of Fintan O'Toole simply to amuse. Fintan was extremely upset about our dispute. Being a thinking man and one of great intellects, he, of course, was able to transcend the mundane concerns the rest of us had about having no wages if you were out of work, or having to walk to work if it was raining and there was no train, or missing hospital appointments, or losing business, or not being able to get to see the three lakes of Killarney in a horse- drawn carriage. Oh no, Fintan's concern about the dispute was that childhood was under attack and he outlined a bleak future where 'little boys will never again dream of becoming train-drivers'! Well I laughed and I laughed, and when I was finished laughing, I laughed some more. And then I thought, 'Stop laughing, Brendan. My god — what if Fintan is right and I just haven't seen the wider picture? Have I been too tied up with nonsense such as members with no wages and rail safety issues to see the bigger picture, the wider issues, the children with their Hornby's? Maybe Fintan is right. Maybe thousands of little boys are out there at this very minute dreaming of being train drivers and we're ruining it all, destroying their childhood innocence.' And then I thought again. It couldn't be that serious in the whole scheme of things.

Over at Independent Newspapers, coverage was mixed also. If the overall balance of the coverage tended, in my view, to be a bit 'statest', that was perhaps understandable from Ireland's biggest-selling daily. My favourite journalist of all, Gene Kerrigan — again a man with whom I had never spoken or had any dealings —wrote a piece in the *Sunday Independent* that slated his media colleagues for their 'demonisation of Brendan Ogle', which he described as a 'media scandal' itself. Gene compared it to the demonisation of the great — at least as far as I am concerned — Tom Darby thirty years earlier. Tom formed and built the National Bus Union that ultimately became the NBRU. He is a legend among many who knew him and his straight-talking approach and refusal to enter into over-friendly relations with management — he used to pay for his own meals at meetings and insisted on sitting with his members and not with the 'suits' — were an example of what I think any representation of workers should be about. Gene went on to state that 'lies' about ILDA were being reported as fact and pertinently asked why the media couldn't handle 'the awkward fact that only 36 per cent of train drivers voted for the new agreement'. The piece finished with the comment that 'standards of reporting and comment have been applied to Ogle which, if applied to Bertie Ahern [Taoiseach] or John Bruton [leader of the opposition] would quite rightly cause uproar'!

Elsewhere in the *Sunday Independent*, we also received support from the pen of John Drennan and, interestingly, that of the Business Editor of Ireland's biggest-selling Sunday newspaper, Shane Ross. His colleague in that section of the newspaper, Martin Fitzpatrick, however, wrote an article on 3 September 2000, in which he offered the opinion that to 'concede' to ILDA would have been to attack the national wage agreement. In fact, of course, the one thing the dispute was not about was money. He went on to report that we had been rebuffed by Kerry Independent TD Jackie Healy Ray, whom, he said we had approached. In fact, the opposite was the case on each point. Reading Martin Fitzpatrick's piece, one found oneself forming a mental picture of hundreds of other little ILDAs out there, plotting to destabilise the state. He concluded with a plea for new regulations to 'make more difficult the registration of a trade union' as 'seven people with a set of rules and a small fee can persuade the Registrar of Friendly Societies that they should set up a union'. Such a move might keep the Irish Business and Employers' Confederation happy, but it would also be a gross infringement of the civil and constitutional right of citizens to join a trade union, not to speak of the provisions in article 11 of the European Convention of Human Rights (ECHR) that citizens can not alone join but form their own trade unions. The excellent *Sunday Business Post* was able to look at the ILDA dispute in its proper context of years of mismanagement of the railway and a failure of the established unions to represent their members, leading to a major problem that affected everybody. Throughout the entire dispute, this newspaper carried the viewpoint of both sides, explaining matters in a non-partisan fashion, and in language that was not sensationalist. Apart from Richard Oakley's weekly phone call, followed by his piece in the *Sunday Tribune*, and *The Sunday Times'* failed attempts to dig up some dirt on me, as detailed in the previous chapter, the rest of the coverage in the Sundays was often scant enough.

The less said about the tabloids, the better. *The Star*, however, did cover the dispute in more detail than others of the genre and in a less hysterical fashion, and it even went to the trouble to quote accurately whatever I might actually say to its reporters!

The Ministers

Mary Harney's bland 'no' to the agreement for working ammonia trains, hammered out by ILDA members and IFI workers, spoke volumes about her role in the dispute, as did the curt reply to the very detailed letter presented to her office and detailed in the previous chapter. Mary O'Rourke's statements and those of her officials will be dealt with in some detail later.

Generally though, the political reaction and behaviour of politicians outside the two departments directly involved provided a number of interesting moments. Throughout the dispute, Jim Higgins TD, as spokesman of the main opposition party at the time, was looking for a means to provide a solution. He seemed genuinely puzzled by the failure of relevant authorities to use instruments such as the new code of practice to broker a settlement, and the vehemence of the comments being made by some of the other parties. Moreover, Deputy Higgins was at the time becoming involved with the investigation of the evolving Mini-CTC scandal where Iarnród Éireann overspent millions of pounds of taxpayers' money on a signalling contract that ultimately fell apart and failed to deliver the promised system on time or remotely near budget. Although Jim Higgins was balanced in his input at all times, balance was not what people opposed to ILDA were looking for. At one stage, early in the dispute, Deputy Higgins attended a discussion meeting on the future of transport in Dublin, where ILDA and its troubles were not on the agenda at all. That didn't prevent his being verbally attacked outside by a SIPTU entourage, the nature of the attack being such that the TD was shocked by the tone and content of what was said to him. It wasn't to be his last shock.

Jim Higgins was a prominent member of the Joint Oireachtas Committee on Public Enterprise and Transport, which was chaired by Seán Doherty, Fianna Fáil TD for Longford/Roscommon, which was my own constituency. This was just one of a number of powerful all-party committees established to focus on specific issues of concern. Obviously a national rail dispute that was now in its seventh week was of major concern to the committee responsible for Public Enterprise and Transport. I had been in contact with Seán Doherty in his capacity as my elected representative — I had actually voted for him and his running mate, Michael Finneran, in the previous 1997 election — but to date he had made no statement or comment or applied any pressure that was in any way useful to resolving the dispute. I was unhappy with this but, as the sixth week rolled into the seventh, my local TD finally gave me an assurance that the Joint Committee he chaired would meet on 27 July, and that ILDA and all other parties would have ample opportunity to put their case to the committee. I had attended meetings of this group as a member of the public before and was very familiar with its method of operation and, as such, I realised fully the benefits of this hearing to us. It would not be possible to overestimate the significance to ILDA of a properly run special meeting of this committee at this stage of the dispute. The committee was open to the public and media when it met and there was bound to be a considerable media presence for this hearing. Those attending — and we were told that officials from the Department of Transport, the company, ILDA, SIPTU and the NBRU would all be invited — would make a preliminary statement and would then be questioned in as much depth as required by any members of the committee who had questions or points to put. After the LRC debacle in Cork the previous week, here finally was a chance to cast aside the bluff and the bluster, to expose the truth and the untruth, the legalities and the illegalities, the procedures available and not available. It would be an opportunity for all parties concerned to be tightly quizzed in depth by experienced politicians from all parties, and in full view of the media! I didn't see how we could lose in this forum.

And so the big day arrived. The venue was Kildare House, a large committee room just across the road from the Dáil, which housed most of the opposition TDs on higher floors. I was there ahead of the 11 o'clock starting time, and was advised of the 'running order'. Department officials would be first in the hot seats, followed by Iarnród Éireann. Then it would be the turn of the unions, and finally Minister O'Rourke would arrive. We were a little put out that SIPTU and the NBRU would be there as they were not in dispute and I didn't see what they would have to offer. However, it was a small price to pay for finally getting our say in a proper forum.

I was joined in the ILDA delegation by our president, Christy Holbrook; vice-president, John Courtney; and by Brian Dunphy, Finbarr Masterson and one or two others. When we arrived, we met the Iarnród Éireann delegation in the hallway. It was made up of John Keenan, Ted Corcoran who was the safety manager, and Joe Meagher. The space was quite cramped and, although the mood was cordial, I think that everyone felt uncomfortable, so there was relief all round when we were invited into the large room for the hearing to begin. Within minutes, the media and public space at the back of the room was packed. The TDs were already in attendance, seated on the left-hand side of a long table, complete with microphones and visual display units for each person. At the top of the table, sitting in front of the Irish flag, were the chairman, Seán Doherty, and the secretary, John Kissane.

I scanned the TDs to see that everyone was there and was immediately struck by two factors. Firstly, I noticed Conor Lenihan TD, nephew of Minister Mary O'Rourke, sitting in the middle of the row of elected representatives. As he was not a member of this committee, I was surprised to see him there. Deputy Doherty explained that Deputy Lenihan was, in fact, a proxy for another committee member who was unable to attend. I was immediately uneasy, though. However, worse was to come. We knew that Jim Higgins of Fine Gael was on top of his brief but the Labour party's transport spokesman, Emmet Stagg TD, was nowhere to be seen.

I was particularly interested to see how officials from the department — very experienced civil servants — would deal with the code of practice issue. However, in the event, all we got was a regurgitation of press releases and statements that the minister had repeated since the dispute had begun —namely, that it would be 'unlawful' for negotiations to take place with ILDA. The next course was served to the Joint Committee by Iarnród Éireann management, and, once again, a full dose of vilification was served, with side orders of untruth, innuendo and propaganda, none of which addressed the key safety issues in dispute. This course was quite a substantive meal in itself and took a considerable amount of time. As I sat at the back of the room, taking copious notes, I was looking forward to the upcoming opportunity finally to put ILDA's case across. I was sure that now that we finally had an even playing field, the true picture could emerge and the misleading advertisements in newspapers and all the public relations spin would be rendered useless by basic facts, commonsense and what I was sure the committee would see as our genuine, sincere and solo efforts to bring this dispute to an end.

His timing was impeccable and it looked to me as if it had been planned with the precision of a military operation. Just as Iarnród Éireann's 'quiet man', Joe Meagher, was ending his very personalised attack on my members and me, Emmet Stagg appeared over my shoulder — obviously a man on a mission — and addressed the Chair. He apologised for his late arrival, saying that he hadn't known that this special sitting of the Oireachtas committee of which he was a long-standing member had been convened. Had he known that this meeting was scheduled, he said, he would have objected. This major issue of national importance was not, according to the Deputy Stagg, a proper topic to be dealt with by this committee at all. He felt it should be dealt with by Iarnród Éireann (of which his friend, John Keenan, was the Manager of Human Resources) and the 'recognised unions' (the largest and most powerful of which, SIPTU, included him in its membership). His late arrival to Kildare House had allowed Iarnród Éireann, preceded by department officials, ample time to regale the committee and assembled media with their version of events. However, he had arrived just before ILDA had time to get out of our chairs and outline our view of events. To my horror, Deputy Stagg then demanded that the hearing be adjourned to consider a proposal he had that no further witnesses (like us) be called and that the rest of the hearing be abandoned. He was supported in this by Minister Mary O'Rourke's nephew, proxy committee member Conor Lenihan.

Committee chairman Seán Doherty, my local TD who had assured me that we would finally get our say at this hearing, agreed to the adjournment and ordered that everybody leave the room to allow the committee to decide how to move forward — or backwards. I felt that it was akin to any of the many tribunals we have in this country hearing evidence accusing people of all sorts and then just adjourning without giving the accused party any opportunity to respond.

And so we stood outside Kildare House while our elected representatives on the Joint Oireachtas Committee for Transport decided whether this national rail strike that was in its seventh week was something important enough for them to consider and whether we were entitled to a right to reply to some of the scurrilous things that had been said about us before Deputy Stagg had switched on the radio, discovered what was going on, and driven to Dublin to call a halt to proceedings. The assembled media were bemused. We were absolutely fuming. I began to tell the assembled media about the link between Emmet Stagg and John Keenan. The assembled hacks seemed amazed. Was I suggesting that the whole thing was contrived?

After a short time, Deputy Jim Higgins came outside to tell us that there had been a bitter exchange among the committee members, but that it had been decided by a majority vote that the hearing would be adjourned and that no more witnesses would be called. As someone who simply wanted the dispute to end — there had now been no trains to parts of his Mayo constituency since the middle of June — Deputy Higgins was disgusted by what he had seen, and expressed himself to be so to me and to the media. He went on national television and radio that evening to outline his views and to ask where a solution to this dispute was likely to come from now. I packed my bags and went home, finally realising that we'd had it. First the invitation to conciliation that became an 'administrative error'; then there was the dismissal of the provisions of a new code of practice, the abuse of a High Court judgment, the manipulation of IFI workers, and now this. Ireland's most powerful political and industrial relations forums seemed, in the era of 'social partnership', to be in a coalition to act as partners to destroy just over a hundred train drivers.

When I got home that evening, emotionally bruised and battered and very angry, I spoke to our legal representatives and wrote a news release, outlining what had just occurred. It was issued the following morning, and offered the opinion that the Joint Oireachtas Committee meeting had been 'a cynical and contrived propaganda exercise choreographed by Fianna Fáil and Labour members of the committee' and that it had been 'designed to assist Iarnród Éireann and the Department of Public Enterprise to further misinform the public about this dispute, its legalities and nuances.' The news release also detailed Deputy Stagg's interests in the matter, which I felt should have been declared 'in advance of his proposal to abort the meeting' — namely, his membership of SIPTU and his friendship with John Keenan, Iarnród Éireann's Human Resouces Manager. The text continued:

> The decision not to allow ILDA to respond to the scurrilous and false comments and references made about it has no basis in what is supposed to be a democracy. Specifically the Department of Public Enterprise public position on our legal status is very much at odds with that detailed fully in private papers procured by ILDA under the FOI from the Department of Enterprise, Trade and Employment. ILDA also made an FOI request to the Department of Public

Enterprise who have refused to co-operate with that request and have supplied no documents to date. That request is now out of time and consequently will be appealed. Many Joint Committee members had every reason to fear what ILDA would have revealed to it yesterday had it been given the opportunity....

Freedom of Information

The Freedom of Information (FOI) Act 1997 was introduced by a rainbow coalition government comprising Fine Gael, Labour and Democratic Left (since merged with the Labour Party) shortly before Fianna Fáil returned to government in coalition with its right-wing breakaway party, the Progressive Democrats (PDs). We now found ourselves confronted by a Department of Transport headed by Fianna Fáil's Mary O'Rourke and a Department of Trade headed by the PD leader, Mary Harney. It struck me that the FOI Act might prove to be a useful tool in finding out what the departments were really thinking about ILDA, our actions and our status as events developed. And so, on 16 June 2000, just days before the dispute began, I wrote to the Freedom of Information officers in both departments, seeking 'sight of/copies of all files, reports, records, commentaries, notes, submissions, letters (sent/received) and responses contained in any departmental storage systems relating to: 'The Irish Locomotive Drivers' Association, and/or Brendan Ogle.'

As the dispute began and continued, we awaited a response from both departments, although from correspondence such as the letters from Minister Harney's department and from repeated public and media comment by Minister O'Rourke, it seemed to be very clear what the views of the departments were. In essence, Mary O'Rourke kept saying to us, to the public and to the Dáil, that she could not intervene as to do so would be 'unlawful' following the High Court judgment issued that April; and because of this, there was no prospect whatsoever of talks with ILDA now or in the future. Over at the Department of Enterprise, Trade and Employment, Mary Harney had effectively ignored the current statutory instrument for seven weeks and had not done or said anything that might have assisted in resolving the dispute. Curt and minimalist letters allied to equally curt and negative answers to media questions on the issue had been her stock in trade throughout. And so we were in no real hurry to get documented evidence of the views held about us by those departments. Their views, at least publicly, seemed crystal clear.

Then, seven weeks into the dispute, a brown envelope arrived in my letter box. It was from the Department of Enterprise, Trade and Employment and, to my surprise, contained documents that contradicted much of what we had heard publicly from the two departments. Nestling among a plethora of newspaper cuttings and letters from ILDA, with responses that we had already received, were several internal memoranda and 'file notes' that contained much information that was totally new to us. This documentation outlined how experienced civil servants had been monitoring ILDA for months, assessing and even predicting our actions, and offering each other advice on how the High Court decision, our rule change and our growing membership affected our current status and might further affect it in the future. And, most startling of all, most of this comment actually agreed with everything that we had been saying about our status. Moreover, it seemed to be very much at odds with the positions taken and statements made by Minister O'Rourke in particular, as outlined above.

Readers will by now be familiar with our rule change in accordance with the High Court decision, and our strong legal advice that this rule change now qualified us as an 'excepted body'. On 20 June 2000, Minister O'Rourke had told the Dáil that to talk to us would be 'unlawful', a view she reiterated to the country's travelling public. Yet now we uncovered a document from Joe McDermott — principal officer in the Department of the Tánaiste — to his counterpart in Mary O'Rourke's department, outlining how the change in ILDA's constitution 'paves the way for it to qualify as an excepted body'. The document was dated 2 May 2000 — seven weeks before Minister O'Rourke's Dáil and public statements. We were stunned. And that wasn't all. The name of another principal officer, Maurice Cashel, appeared on another document which stated that our rule change presented 'a more difficult position to counteract, particularly if membership breaks through 50%. If the ILDA achieves a higher membership than SIPTU and the NBRU it would be difficult to oppose negotiating rights.' Joe McDermott concurred. In another document, he wrote 'it [ILDA] is now quite close to having 50%

of the Locomotive Driver membership. If it passes 50% the argument that it is less representative than SIPTU/NBRU combined falls apart.'

Privately, the most senior civil servants agreed with ILDA about the significance of our rule change, its effect on our status and our membership levels. Privately, they agreed that as ILDA's membership continued to grow, all arguments against recognising it were falling apart. However, publicly it was 'unlawful' to talk to us, and ILDA could never achieve recognition. Despite the ongoing damage to the nation's railway, and the inconvenience and loss being suffered by tens of thousands of people, there seemed to be a determination to turn logic, fairness, procedure, rule, law and the workings of government committees on their heads.

Chambers of Commerce

While all of this was taking place, various groups and affected parties would appear on the nation's airwaves, screens or newspapers, claiming that ILDA was responsible for every possible problem you could think of. In this feeding frenzy it never seemed to dawn on many of them that everything they had been force-fed by Iarnród Éireann's propaganda machine might not actually stand up to close scrutiny. Chief among these 'contributors' were the Chambers of Commerce of Ireland (CCI). Initially this group — which represents business interests — simply outlined the genuine and reasonable concern of its members that they were losing out as a result of the disruption on the national railways. However, as the media interest intensified, the CCI got caught up in the growing hysteria, moving on from outlining the difficulties experienced by its members to actually pronouncing and apportioning responsibility in areas where it had little or no expertise — namely, Iarnród Éireann's industrial relations, collective agreements and rail-safety issues. On 17 July, the *Irish Independent* carried a piece that outlined how 'the country's largest business organization is preparing to sue striking railmen if the train drivers' dispute remains unresolved'. The piece outlined how £3m a week was being lost by business interests as a direct result of the dispute, saying that the CCI 'is prepared to take action in the courts on behalf of its members'. Action against Iarnród Éireann was not under consideration.

Thus began a new aspect to the media coverage of the dispute. From then until near the end of the lock-out, the CCI was never far from the microphones, warning or threatening our members with dire consequences if we didn't immediately succumb to its demands. The following day, the *Independent* went further, and told readers that CCI had actually begun legal action 'against individual train drivers who are members of ILDA in a bid to break the strike impasse'. I tried to respond to this by being polite towards the CCI at all times — at least in public — and simply sympathising with the plight of those suffering losses, while outlining that no one was actually suffering more losses than our members. It didn't work. One particular CCI member, Peter Shanley in Westport, launched a blistering personal attack on Finbarr during an interview on local radio, ably assisted, it must be said, by the interviewer on this occasion. In the interview, Finbarr was repeatedly asked by the questioner to ensure that the SIPTU members in Westport — over whom Finbarr had no control whatsoever — worked the trains out of Westport. Peter Shanley was of the opinion that ILDA was solely responsible for getting trains moving again, and even went so far as to blame Finbarr personally for the fact that Westport trains were not running, and thus for tourism losses, missed chemotherapy appointments and even deaths. In a small town like Westport, Finbarr was naturally distressed about the effect this attack might have on him and his family, even when the dispute came to an end.

Typically each contribution from the CCI ended with the inevitable question from interviewers about whether or not they would be suing us. I was fully aware, however, that our members had no contractual arrangements with members of the CCI individually or collectively. Any contracts that were in being were between CCI members and Iarnród Éireann, not ILDA or its members. Therefore any breach of contractual arrangements was in fact a breach of contract between that CCI member and Iarnród Éireann and, unless the CCI had more money than sense, Iarnród Éireann should have been the one with its lawyers on stand by. But, of course, CCI had no intention of suing Iarnród Éireann for breach of contract. I could never fully figure out whether this whole issue was primarily aimed at increasing the profile of the CCI and its members in small towns like Westport or whether it was a threat to be used to pressurise our members back to work.

In industrial relations, I have always worked on the basis that you must ultimately be prepared to carry out any threat you make. This applies whether it involves walking out of talks, taking industrial action or seeking legal support to protect your employment. As the dispute neared its end, I eventually lost patience in one radio interview and challenged the CCI to put up or shut up. I told the group that if it contacted me, I would supply it with the names and addresses of each of our members and that our members would look forward to receiving any correspondence the CCI would like to send us, from its solicitors or otherwise. That did it. For what remained of the dispute, the CCI became a threat-free zone!

Members' Morale

Up to now, our members had been amazing. Locked out of work over a dispute that could and should have been avoided, that they never wanted and that they, like I, probably believed would be resolved within days anyway, they had watched as one opportunity after another was deliberately let slip by people in authority. They had been forced to go without pay while many, but not all, of their colleagues in SIPTU and the NBRU trade unions did their work, often in addition to their own. One might have expected that by this time, morale would have been low. Commentators began the dispute by swallowing the Iarnród Éireann line that our members would break early, and would capitulate, hook, line and sinker. As week after week passed, however, it became clear to everyone that ILDA members were standing firm. This eventually led to incredulity among some members of the media; several interviews were conducted with ILDA members in their homes by journalists intrigued by the determination and unity we were showing.

My domestic situation was difficult but was being handled magnificently by Pauline with some help from family members. My life had evolved into an endless pattern of meetings and trips around the country, punctuated by media interviews and the constant search for a resolution. At home in Athlone, Pauline worked, looked after our then three-year-old daughter, and tried to keep the wolf from the door. On no occasion did the undoubted pressure she was under evolve into pressure on me to do anything other than what our members and I thought was the best thing to do. Surrender was not on the agenda. Evidence of her support was not needed but the following example makes her position abundantly clear.

One morning, I was packing my bag for my latest trip when a colleague called and told me to switch on 2FM. When I did so, I was more than surprised to hear Pauline speaking to Gerry Ryan on his morning chat show. Those who know my wife will know that she is not a person who would normally volunteer for interviews on national radio. However, in previous days, Gerry's listeners and some invited commentators had been pontificating on ILDA and all its evil deeds. A number of Pauline's work friends had encouraged her to call in and outline how this dispute felt from her perspective. Initially she had simply called to speak to a researcher and correct some point. However, never one to miss an opportunity, Gerry had ended what he was doing, plugged in a phone line, and begun to talk to her live on air. By the time I tuned in, the interview was almost over. Gerry Ryan gently prompted Pauline to find out whether or not she would like to tell us to go back to work, to end this. Pauline's response was emphatic. She would rather starve than see us do something that we couldn't live with. The point had been made.

Other wives and families also saw fit to make their own points at various times. This led to a most remarkable incident on Sunday, 16 July 2000. Since the outset of the dispute, not a wheel had turned on a train or locomotive in Westport Station. Obviously this had had an effect on the tourist industry in that beautiful part of the country and, as outlined earlier, Finbarr had taken a lot of flak locally for taking the stand that he did. Although ILDA had two members in Westport — among four drivers — at the time, one of these was out with a long-term illness. As the dispute evolved, Finbarr would stand alone outside Westport Station in full uniform, with his bucket, protesting. His two friends who were SIPTU members would not pass him, and so no trains had arrived or left Westport since the evening train that had brought Finbarr home from our meeting on 18 June, just hours before the dispute had begun.

On Sunday, 18 July, Iarnród Éireann decided that the empty train that had been standing idle for so long was to be moved to Dublin for use. But who was to drive it? Certainly none of the other Westport drivers would. Obviously with over half of the drivers in Athlone involved in the dispute, options there were few. Before the weekend even began, drivers in SIPTU who were working were approached, but they refused. Although they were working throughout the dispute, they were generally engaged in their own duties. What was now being asked was quite different. However, the only NBRU member in Athlone was prepared to go to Westport and work the train out. But there was another problem. The Athlone to Westport branch was an old single line, with semaphore signals and no direct communication between drivers and signalmen, which would have been essential to a one-man-operated train. In those circumstances, a second man was needed — a guard. On the morning concerned, a guard on duty was asked to accompany this NBRU driver to Westport. A SIPTU member, he had just reported for duty and was technically available to go. However, he refused. The manager on duty was unhappy and warned him that disciplinary action could follow. He still refused and actually booked off duty and went home. Another guard, also a SIPTU member, had just finished his turn of duty. Iarnród Éireann called him at home and he agreed to return to the station and to work the train to Westport with the NBRU driver.

Finbarr was wound up over this. In the heat of battle, the removal of the train from Westport seemed like a significant development. He saw it as his work, or that of his colleagues in Westport who had supported him, and resented anyone from Athlone coming in and acting in this way. He decided that he would go into the station that morning and try to discuss the situation with the man concerned. And so the morning arrived and the two Athlone workers travelled by taxi the 85 miles into Westport to move the train. I called Finbarr at lunchtime to see what had happened. From his tone, I immediately realised that he was upset, although it would only be much later that I would get to hear the full impact that this single issue had on Finbarr. He outlined how he had seen the driver and his guard get out of a taxi, and he had approached them. When Finbarr asked could he have a word, the driver responded with a blank 'no'. Finbarr said that moving the train was 'Westport work' but the driver's response was too blunt to publish and to the effect that nothing Finbarr had to say mattered to him. At that, Finbarr said no more, got into his car and went home, while the crew prepared to move the train. As he explained this to me, I heard his wife, Carmel, in the background say, 'See you later', and a door close. Finbarr, in mid-sentence, said, 'There's my woman gone over now to sit on the line', before continuing on with the conversation.

At first, I didn't take it seriously, but by the time he had finished talking, I had begun to wonder. I said, 'Carmel isn't really gone over to sit on the line, is she?' To my utter amazement, Finbarr responded that she was, that she was upset and that she had gone off with a chair to block the line in an effort to prevent the train from leaving Westport. Finbarr lives in a part of Co. Mayo called Islandeady. It is halfway between the towns of Westport and Castlebar, and only 100 yards or so from the main railway line — a single track that serves both towns and continues on the 165-mile route to Dublin. In addition, there is a gate crossing not far from Finbarr's house. As Finbarr explained how he had been trying to persuade Carmel not to do it just before I called, I realised that he was serious. Carmel Masterson, a mother of five in her mid-fifties, was sitting in the middle of the railway line on a deck chair. I didn't know whether to laugh or cry.

What followed was an incident that will live long in the memory of everyone with any involvement in it. Apparently Carmel presented herself to the gatekeeper, himself a former driver and neighbour whom she knew very well, and told him of her plans. That done, she opened her deckchair and took up position on the sleepers, slap bang between the two running rails of the main Dublin to Westport rail line. Of course, the gatekeeper was obliged to call back to Westport Station immediately and send the railway warning 'obstruction on the line' message. This meant that the train could not leave the station until 'the obstruction' was removed. But Carmel Masterson was going nowhere in a hurry. She sat there for hours. Carmel explained her actions to the *Irish Independent* at the time:

> I never done anything like that in my life. I'm just an ordinary housewife; I stayed at home to rear six children and I worked a little before arthritis took over. But I am absolutely frustrated by the whole set-up. My husband has worked for Iarnród Éireann for 42 years, did double shifts for them and has been a train driver for 30 years. It is absolutely disgraceful what is happening. It really hurt when people in Westport said that it was my husband alone who was responsible for the drop in tourism in Westport over the last few weeks. When I heard Iarnród Éireann had sent another driver down on Sunday to

take out an empty train to Athlone, I said to myself, enough is enough. I made my own protest, my own statement. I went out to Islandeady junction and asked the person at the gates to open them up for me. He did and I brought my chair and sat there for four hours.

Carmel outlined how the Westport stationmaster had asked her to move, adding, 'I refused and then she contacted the acting District Manager John Daly and then the gardaí were called. The gardaí didn't say anything but what the company was trying to do was wrong.'

In fact, Carmel calmly sat on the line for a full four hours, with her newspapers. She politely refused to leave the line and, when the Garda Síochána arrived, she lay down in peaceful protest. The gardaí had some difficulty clearing the line but eventually took Carmel to Castlebar Garda station, where she was cautioned but not charged, and then released. The empty train bound for Athlone eventually did get through, but Carmel's point had been made, and it would be several more weeks before another service left Westport Station.

Carmel's protest caught the public imagination; families of ILDA members around the country sent messages of support to her, and began to ask what they could do to help. Calls were made to radio phone-ins, and letters were sent to ministers and the relevant authorities. Some time later, on 3 August, Carmel and the wives and children of some other ILDA members arrived at the office of the Minister for Public Enterprise and Transport, Mary O'Rourke. Carmel grew up just minutes from the Lenihan family home where Mary O'Rourke was reared. Among those presenting at the department was five-week-old Donna Healy, fifth child of ILDA's Limerick member, Dave Healy. Little Donna had not even been born when the ILDA lock-out began. Dave's wife was just recovering from the birth of the child and did not work outside the home, in any case. At this point in the dispute, the Healys, like all other ILDA families, were feeling the pinch. However, on arrival at the department, the families were told that the minister was on holidays.

Increased Pressure for a Resolution

For almost eight weeks now, ILDA members had stood silently with their buckets, protesting outside their workplaces. They had watched as many of their colleagues in SIPTU and the NBRU — many of whom they had considered friends as well as colleagues — performed their work, before the ILDA members went home without wages, week after week. As the majority of mainline rail services are to and from Dublin — rather than within the greater Dublin area — services between the capital and the west and south were the worst affected by the ILDA dispute. As services north are operated by Belfast drivers not employed by Iarnród Éireann, and because of the strength of SIPTU and the NBRU among drivers at Connolly depot, only commuter and freight services through Drogheda, Dundalk and on to Belfast were hit. The mainline Dublin to Belfast 'Enterprise' service had run as normal throughout. Elsewhere, however, things were dire. Westport Station, for example, hadn't seen a passenger train throughout the entire dispute. Sligo, Ballina and Limerick trains were also severely affected. Most services on the main Dublin to Cork line went only to Mallow with bus transfers the final thirty miles to Cork; and Kerry — Ireland's tourist Mecca — had seen its services decimated.

There is no doubt in my mind that if Dublin services had been affected to the extent of services elsewhere, the dispute would have been resolved long before this point. Some local people decided to try to take matters into their own hands. While Peter Shanley and the Chamber of Commerce Ireland were getting stuck in over in Mayo, a new group sprang up in Kerry solely as a result of the dispute. The Killarney Rail Action Group (KRAG) was a body created to bring pressure to bear for a resolution to the dispute. However, unlike the CCI, KRAG wanted to bring pressure on all parties — Iarnród Éireann, the minister and ILDA. As such, they deserved our respect and got it. The group included politicians, businessmen, trade unionists, hoteliers, and representatives of charitable and community groups in the Kerry area such as the St Vincent de Paul (SVP) society. I first became aware of this group over the August bank holiday weekend. On Sunday 8 August, our executive was holding a meeting in the Tullamore Court Hotel. The meeting had been convened to consider an escalation in the dispute, which had occurred two days earlier.

On Friday morning, 4 August, our members from Drogheda, Dundalk and Dublin brought their protest to the gates of Fairview DART depot in Dublin. In doing so, they had decided that with the seventh week of the dispute drawing to a close, an escalation in the protest was essential. They felt that the Dublin area needed to be targeted to bring renewed focus and pressure to bear on those who had so far failed in their responsibility to help to provide a resolution. The escalation had a considerable effect on DART services. DART drivers were surprised to be confronted by our members, and many of them turned around and went home. We had just two DART members but enough support was won to devastate the morning rush-hour service through Dublin. CIÉ reacted by phoning the Garda Síochána to say that DART drivers were being intimidated and that the 'pickets' should be removed. While gardaí arrived on the scene in minutes, and attempted to move our members on, they ultimately had to explain to management that our members were doing nothing wrong and that they could not be forcibly removed. Our members' behaviour was typical of the good-natured manner in which they had conducted their protests elsewhere for seven weeks. Nevertheless, the message was clear. ILDA members were now willing and able to escalate the dispute if they felt the need to in order to bring it to a conclusion.

As spokesman for ILDA, I was placed in a difficult position by this escalation. I could not publicly support secondary action of this nature without walking into a legal quagmire. Nevertheless, I fully understood — and shared — the frustration of our members. As a consequence, I refused to accept the invitations of interviewers to 'condemn this illegal secondary action'. As far as I was concerned, my first obligation was solely to my members, and everything else came some distance down the line after that.

And so, by Sunday 8 August, ILDA and the GAA hurling championships seemed to be the only news story in town. The media frenzy surrounding the Tullamore meeting had been heightened by reports the previous day that CIÉ was actually considering sacking all ILDA members unless we returned to work. These reports were clearly intended to frighten our members back to work, but, in a volatile situation, they were only ever likely to provoke a hitherto unthinkable counter-reaction from ILDA members. For the first time, I began to hear our members whisper about blocking rail lines, sitting on tracks, and getting arrested and jailed if necessary. Iarnród Éireann must have heard these whispers too because as I got out of my car in Tullamore that Sunday morning, the first journalist to spot and get to me was RTÉ's Deirdre McCarthy. She asked a question about how I envisaged the meeting going and, when I responded by saying that our members were angry and were preparing to face this new threat head-on, she took me aside and told me that Barry Kenny of Iarnród Éireann was assuring the media that no such plan existed or would be acted upon. That was one piece of good news.

I was then handed a copy of the *Sunday Independent* newspaper and asked to comment on an opinion poll in that paper, which had found that 61 per cent of the people polled felt that CIÉ should negotiate with ILDA to resolve the dispute. Even more tellingly, many of those questioned said that they were frustrated by the failure of any outside agency to intervene. This poll — the first and only one of its type during the dispute — provided us with a tremendous boost as we entered our meeting. The outcome of this meeting was inevitable. ILDA reiterated that we 'were available to participate in any reasonable solution to find a resolution', but it was clear at the meeting that the dispute was moving into a new phase and that, in the absence of a solution, further escalation was inevitable.

In truth, the escalation had begun in Limerick the previous week. Fed up looking at SIPTU and NBRU members walk past them, jump on their trains and drive off, our members had decided to act. A group of them got into their cars and drove to a level crossing a few miles outside Limerick. There they mounted a protest in the roadway, effectively preventing the level-crossing gates from operating. The result was a lengthy delay to the Limerick to Dublin passenger train that had just left Limerick's Corbett Station. The gardaí who arrived on the scene saw the protest as a peaceful protest on a public roadway — fully allowed in law. It continued for almost two hours. As I left Tullamore that evening, I knew that I had been unable to offer to our members any hope of an immediate solution and, in that void, further incidents like the Limerick one seemed inevitable. I joined Pauline and our daughter in her parents' home in Tipperary that evening and was just sitting down to dinner when I got a telephone call from Nialas Moriarty of the Killarney Rail Action Group (KRAG). Neily, as he was known, explained that he was the Chairman of KRAG and that the group would like to meet with ILDA. He and some of his members had met with Minister O'Rourke and CIÉ Chairman John Lynch some days earlier. I decided that we would go to Kerry and address these issues head on, in typical ILDA fashion.

The following day, 7 August, was August bank holiday Monday and the dispute was now moving into its most critical phase. Monday's media coverage was extensive. Part of it focused on an intervention by NBRU founder and former General Secretary, Tom Darby. Tom Darby had contacted me a few days earlier and offered to do anything he could to help. It was an offer I couldn't refuse. His almost legendary reputation among transport workers generally, and NBRU members in particular, demanded that I meet him. We met in Dublin's Fairview Inn and spoke for hours. He was distressed by the actions of the union he had built up. It was unthinkable that an NBRU led by him would provide scab labour to management, and he had decided that enough was enough. He was offering to do whatever he could to help. However, while management made complimentary noises about Tom Darby, the reality was that his intervention was causing massive embarrassment to them and the unions — Peter Bunting and the NBRU, in particular.

I spent the following morning preparing for our trip to Killarney to meet KRAG, but was disturbed mid-morning by a phone call from Finbarr in Westport. In other circumstances, Finbarr would have spent most of the dispute on the road with us, but the situation was such that his lonely presence in Westport was vital to ensure that no other drivers from the West would perform his work. This was a difficult position for him to be in but one that he stuck out superbly. On one occasion, a number of our members from Dundalk actually hitched a caravan to their car and drove over to Westport to help. For a number of days, they slept in the caravan and joined Finbarr at the gate when necessary. Anyway, that morning, as I was getting ready to go to Killarney, Finbarr explained that a Ballina driver had been persuaded to come over to Westport and to work the afternoon passenger train to Dublin. Now, on 8 August 2000, a passenger train was to leave Westport for the first time since 17 June.

Finbarr was disconsolate. He was convinced that this one driver would provide the example needed for others in the west and around the country to follow suit, and that effectively the Westport action was over.

In desperation, he decided to take a leaf out of the Limerick members' book and mount a protest at a level crossing. He was joined by an ILDA member from Ballina, Dessie Gallagher, but on this occasion the protest at Garryredmond crossing near Claremorris was ineffective. Finbarr was so down that he didn't really have the appetite for the protest, and the train progressed to Dublin with little delay. As far as Iarnród Éireann was concerned, this was the breakthrough for which management had been waiting. News programmes throughout the country treated this one train leaving Westport as a total collapse of our action, to the extent that I was much more concerned about the effect this incident and the deliberately hyped coverage of it would have on the morale of our members elsewhere. This then was the background against which we were driving south for our meeting in 'The Kingdom' with KRAG. I was accompanied on this trip by Thomas McDonnell and Brian Dunphy, and we were meeting Christy Holbrook in Killarney. Throughout the four-hour journey south, word was coming through to us that our members, particularly in Cork, were extremely worried about the lifting of the 'Westport blockade'. The closer we got to Killarney, however, the more I tried to focus on our meeting with KRAG, Jackie Healy Rae and all.

Jackie Healy Rae was a local TD, who, having failed to secure the Fianna Fáil nomination to run for the party in the 1997 general election, had decided to run as an 'independent'. When he romped home with ease, he immediately formed a four-pronged alliance with three other independent TDs, Mildred Fox from Wicklow, and Harry Blaney and Tom Gildea from Donegal. The fact that Fianna Fáil and the Progressive Democrats could not form a majority government gave the 'gang of four' positions of real power. They were promised packages that would bring money and resources into their constituencies that would never otherwise have been forthcoming; and in return they gave Fianna Fáil and the PDs support in forming a government. I came to feel that what Jackie Healy Rae wanted was to be the man to do what Mary O'Rourke, Mary Harney, Kieran Mulvey, Iarnród Éireann and others hadn't done. He wanted to be the one who ended the dispute.

As we got out of our cars at the luxurious Killarney Park Hotel, where the meeting was to take place, we explained to a large delegation of local and national media personnel that we wanted this dispute resolved even more than the forgotten people of Kerry and the extended area wanted it resolved. There were well over a dozen KRAG members present at the meeting, and each KRAG member present wanted to outline to us how the dispute had affected their business, constituency or interest. It was clear that the dispute was impacting badly on the area, but, as we explained our position, many in attendance began to see that the dispute couldn't be resolved that easily. The rest of the meeting — several hours of it — was spent working on an agreed joint statement. We would acknowledge the genuine upset and loss being suffered by Kerry people, and KRAG would quite willingly say that we had serious issues to be dealt with and call on the relevant authorities to do their jobs. But it wasn't that simple. The statement needed to include reference to the various groups represented by KRAG, and in an agreed order. We just sat there while a miniature turf war took place between some — not all — KRAG members over which grouping or interest had most emphasis in the statement. By 9pm we were starving — we hadn't had anything to eat since leaving Athlone around midday — so sandwiches were ordered and we were shown into a side room. While there, I had a phone call from Fergus Finlay to say that Finbarr Masterson had been on radio with some drivers from SIPTU and the NBRU, and it hadn't gone too well. However, Fergus Finlay had been taking some soundings and thought that there was a possibility of moving the situation on a bit. He thought we were wasting our time in Kerry, and he wanted to know how soon we could get to Dublin. We made arrangements to meet him as early as possible the following evening.

We went back into the meeting room but it was almost midnight before KRAG agreed the final statement. We agreed it too, but by then the media had long gone; nobody carried the statement in any event. I was pissed off. It was now too late for a proper meal at the hotel and we had no accommodation arranged either. Although the tourist industry in Kerry was supposedly on its knees, almost everywhere was booked out. We ended up eating in Burger King and we eventually got accommodation in the Great Southern Hotel, having been turned away at several B&Bs. However, as we walked around Killarney's busy streets at midnight on that evening in the first week of August — like prats with suits and briefcases — we felt so low. We couldn't see where we were going to go to next. The Westport situation had faltered; our members finances' were now getting really bad; and we were beginning to hear an increasing number of tales of particular difficulty relating to a few of them. Throughout the dispute, we had collected small sums of money at the various depots and, rather than distribute this money among all our members, we had focused it on particular areas of concern. But even so, the pressure on some of our members was immense. As if that wasn't enough, the Killarney meeting had been a total waste of time. As I finished my pint in the Great Southern that night, and headed off to bed, I commented to Thomas McDonnell that we needed something dramatic to happen quickly.

It must have been around 8am when I awoke and lifted the TV remote control in my room. I switched on the RTÉ teletext service as I had done on hundreds of occasions over the previous few weeks, but on this occasion, the headline hit me like a bolt from the blue. 'Dublin Bus services hit by wildcat pickets'. I jumped up in bed and read the page. It outlined how ILDA members in Dublin had mounted 'flying pickets' on Dublin Bus garages from early that morning, and how services had been 'decimated'. Apparently Dublin Bus workers had supported our members and refused to take out their buses, leaving the capital city with little or no peak-hour bus service. From my perspective, this was sensational news. The despondency — which I now realised would have been partly fed by fatigue — that had washed over me as I went to sleep was now erased by the need to make phone calls and find out what was happening. I called John Courtney on his mobile. He was outside a bus garage and told me that they had been there since 5am. They had received spectacular support from the Dublin Bus drivers and nothing was moving in or out of the garages. They planned to continue their protest until mid-morning.

When I went down for breakfast, I found the other three already discussing unfolding events. We ate quickly, checked out of the hotel and hit the road for Dublin. The day's events had provoked a renewed media storm. As we headed north, I conducted interview after interview by phone while Thomas drove. The big questions to which the media wanted an answer were when would our members be removing their protests and would the evening bus schedule be free of disruption. I passed on the information I had received from John Courtney that the protests would be removed by mid-morning. By mid-morning, however, John had called me back. Gardaí had turned up and our members were fearful that they might be arrested. However, the Dublin Bus drivers were insisting that we should not withdraw our protests and that if arrests did take place, they would replace our members' protests with pickets of their own. As it was, many of them were accompanying ILDA members outside garage gates with — what I later saw to be — spectacular results.

To be honest, I was delighted with this turn of events. I could tell from the media reaction that what had happened had completely changed the face of the dispute. Very few had given a damn about the suffering in other parts of the country for weeks, but now that Dublin had been hit with a vengeance, the game had changed. I was beginning to feel for the first time that we could now build momentum to force an intervention, or an outright solution. I advised John to do whatever he felt was appropriate and that any statement I made would be to defend our members.

For weeks, there had been speculation and rumour that we were about to hit Dublin Bus. Each new rumour was accompanied by information on how SIPTU and the NBRU were expecting this escalation and had their senior shop stewards prepared to face us down if we approached 'their' garages. We had our own information, and it indicated that we could expect some support from Dublin Bus workers who were as suspicious of their unions as we were. But we hadn't expected anything like this. This was a wipe-out, and it was a massive embarrassment to SIPTU and the NBRU. And then, as if the day hadn't been eventful enough, I got another phone call. This time it was from Finbarr. He outlined how he had reflected overnight on the previous day's events in Westport and had decided to speak to the driver in Ballina who had worked the first train out of Westport the previous day. They discussed the position that Finbarr was in and the driver involved had decided that he would not return to Westport to work that train again. After all the previous day's hype, the 'Westport blockade' was, unbelievably, back on again. I couldn't believe my ears. Just at the point where, for the first time in the dispute, I had become concerned about events and the impact that they were having on the morale of our members, happenings in Dublin and Westport had injected new life into our stand. I knew from other phone calls that our members in other parts of the country from Dundalk to Cork were euphoric at the day's events and were, in fact, planning their own escalation tactics.

As we continued our marathon drive to Dublin, I got a call from Justine McCarthy of the *Irish Independent*. She wanted to do an in-depth feature piece with me for that Saturday's weekend newspaper. The idea was to follow me for a day and to write a fly-on-the-wall piece about what it was like to be involved in this madness. Initially, I was reluctant. I didn't trust many journalists and had never dealt with Justine McCarthy before. I told her I'd call her back later.

When we hit the outskirts of Dublin, it was slap bang in the middle of the evening rush hour. It was a beautiful sunny evening, which was just as well because as we approached Newlands Cross on the Naas Road, we had still not seen a single Dublin bus. We continued into Dublin to the top of Inchicore. Still no buses. In fact, we were near Rathmines — close to the middle of the city — before we met the first, single, Dublin bus of the day. It was incredible.

That evening was spent with Fergus Finlay. He had been speaking to an old friend of his, Phil Flynn. The name had popped up as a possible mediator in the dispute on many occasions since its onset. Although I had never met him personally, he was friendly with Martin King, and I had a good idea about how he operated. He had also worked with Fergus Finlay when they were both trade union officials years earlier and their friendship had been maintained since. I also knew that Phil Flynn had the ear of Mary O'Rourke. It now transpired that both men believed it possible that CIÉ Chairman John Lynch could be induced to send each ILDA member a letter, but not threatening the sack as had been hinted at days before. In fact, these letters would outline conditions, acceptable to all parties, under which our members could return to work. Therefore it was vital that people knew our bottom lines on a number of issues. We spent the evening outlining just that to Fergus Finlay. There could be no part-time train drivers, and personal-needs breaks were a must in longer rosters. Our statutory entitlements relating to working Sundays and public holidays also needed to be upheld. Issue by issue, we went on. In general, it was agreed that the primary focus needed to be on an agreed basis for a return to work. Once that had been achieved and a number of investigative forums established in the short term, other less immediate issues could then be investigated.

I also discussed with Fergus the idea of the *Irish Independent* 'fly-on-the-wall' feature. He felt that I should do it. However, he warned me that while Justine McCarthy was a very good and respected journalist whose copy would not be interfered with, she would reserve the right to use any incident or comment that might occur and that she deemed important to the story. This didn't spook me at all. What could she see or write that would be embarrassing to me? I called Justine McCarthy and agreed to meet her in Athlone the next morning. It would be a big day media-wise. RTÉ was concentrating its current affairs programme, *Prime Time*, around the dispute, and I was making my television studio début live on the show. I had been on *Prime Time* before, earlier in the dispute, but that was a short pre-recorded interview conducted in Heuston Station. This was a much more substantive piece, with lead-in pieces from some of our adversaries, followed by a head-to-head with John Keenan and me, live on air. I was looking forward to it, and having a journalist tailing me all day would ensure that I was, to use a sporting analogy, on top of my game. We all spent the night at the Finlay home and slept soundly. What a difference twenty-four hours can make in an industrial dispute!

As soon as we got into the car the following morning and tuned to RTÉ's *Morning Ireland*, we were greeted by a familiar voice. Finbarr Masterson was being interviewed about the re-imposition of the 'Westport blockade'. Never a company inclined to indulge in critical self-analysis, Iarnród Éireann had stated as the reason for this latest turn of events that Finbarr had 'intimidated' the Ballina driver. It was ridiculous. The very idea of Finbarr, at 60 years of age, 'intimidating' anyone was a joke. But rather than RTÉ asking Barry Kenny or John Keenan to accept that Iarnród Éireann had misled people with its Tuesday fanfare, Finbarr was being asked to explain his 'intimidation'. Instead, he outlined how he had called the driver concerned and explained the pressure he was under and how continued actions like Tuesday's would undermine his position. He had asked the driver to consider giving him renewed support by not working his trains. The driver, having considered the request, had called management and said that he regretted going into Westport and was not prepared to repeat the exercise the following day. It was as simple as that. I had been told that Finbarr had taken a tough time in some interviews in the previous days, but on this occasion he was superb.

I arrived in Athlone by mid-morning and when I turned into the estate I lived in, I noticed a sporty coupé parked outside my home. I drove up and presented myself to Justine McCarthy as she got out of her car. As I entered my house for the first time since Tuesday morning, I picked up the post. Lying on top of the usual array of bills and junk mail was a loose leaflet entitled, 'What SIPTU Said'. It was a leaflet that we had issued describing the SIPTU position in relation to a number of different disputes. It outlined the hypocrisy of SIPTU's position on this dispute, when viewed against statements the union had made on other occasions. I wondered why someone was dropping one of our leaflets in my letterbox. I turned it over and the puzzle was solved. There, handwritten in large red letters on the back, was the message 'FUCK YOU AND ILDA'. It wasn't the first time I had received this type of intimidation, or the last. Finbarr and I both received threatening hate mail through the post during and after the dispute. Some of it went further than insults and warned us to 'watch our backs'. However, it tended to be from people who didn't have our proper addresses, and it found its way to us because our names were well known to our postmen. This handwritten note was different. It wasn't in an envelope and hadn't been posted. It had actually been dropped into my letterbox, presumably by its 'author'. I showed it to Justine McCarthy, but asked her not to mention it to my wife when we met for lunch later. I didn't want Pauline knowing that it seemed that one of our neighbours — most likely one who worked for Iarnród Éireann — was now resorting to this sort of thing.

It was a peculiar sort of a day after that. I had to write an article for the *Irish Examiner*, and Justine watched and questioned me as I did so. Halfway through, we picked Pauline up and went for lunch before returning in the afternoon to finish the article and prepare for that evening's appearance on *Prime Time*. As I was writing upstairs, I explained that Finbarr would soon arrive to accompany me to Dublin. Justine asked me, tongue in cheek, whether the Finbarr that I was expecting was the same one who was rampaging around the West of Ireland threatening the lives of any SIPTU or NBRU member who dared to come within twenty miles of Westport. I laughed and we spoke about Finbarr for a while, his lifetime of service in the railway and how and why he had found himself in his position. I was busy now and I left my mobile phone downstairs. I was pissed off with it ringing constantly and wanted an hour or two without it frying my brain. It rang and rang and rang. Repeatedly. Justine looked at me and asked me more than once whether I was going to answer it, but my typing was slow and I was busy answering her questions also. The phone could wait. Then Finbarr arrived and came up to our 'office'. I introduced him to Justine by name but didn't outline who she was or what she was doing there. Then I flippantly asked Finbarr how he had managed to get the Ballina driver to go back to Ballina. Finbarr looked at me with a twinkle in his eye and replied, 'Easy — I just called him and told him if he ever came near Westport again, I'd break his two legs.' It was exactly the sort of thing we say to each other just before we burst out laughing and get told what was actually said, but would Justine McCarthy see it like that? Imagine if that little anecdote was to be misrepresented and portrayed as a serious comment in that weekend's *Irish Independent!* As Finbarr settled down and told us what he had really said to the driver concerned, I relaxed, realising that Justine had seen the remark for what it was.

I then went downstairs to iron my shirt for the trip to RTÉ. Justine glanced at my mobile phone and told me that I had missed forty-one calls. Forty-one calls in about two hours. Even by ILDA standards during the dispute, that was remarkable. Something was happening. I switched on the television and went to RTÉ's teletext. There it was — at last, news of an intervention in the dispute, a 'unique joint initiative' by the Labour Court and the LRC. Immediate relief gave way to questions. The Labour Court and the LRC? How did that work? What would they do? How soon? What were the conditions? I answered the next call, and it was a journalist who wanted to know what our response was to the 'unique joint intervention' by the Labour Court and the LRC. I had no statement or terms of reference, so I told him we were considering the position and hung up. Perhaps someone from the Court or Commission had been trying to call me. Perhaps there was a message from them on my phone. I listened to all my messages but they were all from the media or from our members looking for a reaction. I called one of our members. Had he been listening to the news and did he know anything I didn't? The answers were yes and no in that order. Fergus Finlay was my next call. I walked around my back garden talking, listening, while Justine watched me and took notes. She had picked a good day to follow me around! Fergus simply told me to stay calm and say nothing until I knew all the facts. He told me not to get bounced by the media into giving an ill-thought-out or knee-jerk reaction. More calls with questions followed. I had to get a handle on this. I called the LRC but no one would talk to me. The Chairman of the Labour Court was not available. I already smelt rats — big, smelly, diseased ones, with long dragging tails.

Justine McCarthy left, thanking me for my time and telling me that the piece would run on Saturday. It did and it took up a full page and a half in the day's newspaper. The article was fair and true to the events of the day, although Justine diplomatically omitted Finbarr's little joke and her offer to iron my shirt! However, as she left, it was *Prime Time* that was on my mind. The show was going to be very important to us indeed. Iarnród Éireann was taking it so seriously that John Keenan, who was on holiday in France, was flying in especially as no one else could apparently be trusted to do it. We were taking it equally seriously. Throughout all that had occurred, I had been happy with any live media head-to-head I had taken part in, but this show would have by far the biggest audience. It was going to be an important evening. And now, at last, some sort of intervention too. I had an idea. I made an offer that, if *Prime Time* would concentrate its show on this intervention, I would make no comment whatsoever on the topic until I was live on the show. A few minutes later, the researcher called me back and agreed. I was delighted. This allowed me to stop talking to the media and concentrate on preparing for that night's show. It also meant that the interviews that had been conducted with various adversaries over the previous few days — and which I was sure would be used to put me in a very difficult spot — would now seem superfluous to the key discussion on that day's initiative.

As Finbarr and I drove to Dublin, we discussed events and tried to get a handle on what exactly was contained in the initiative. One thing was obvious. This initiative had come as a direct result of the disruption of Dublin Bus services the previous day. No one gave a damn about Westport or Kerry, or even Cork. They had had few or no services for eight weeks and everyone had looked in another direction. One day of disruption in Dublin, however, and the Labour Court and LRC were concocting what we were told was a 'unique joint initiative' to deal with the 'exceptional' circumstances. Lesson learned! Never again would our members around the country suffer while we went easy on Dublin. In any event, we were where we were and I was now looking forward to meeting Vincent Browne and to my live head-to-head with John Keenan.

Some weeks previously, I had arrived at the RTÉ studios to do a radio interview with Philip Boucher-Hayes. It was an in-depth interview that I enjoyed but I had been somewhat surprised to be stopped by RTÉ staff on the way in and congratulated for the stand that we were taking. I was glad of the support and, as we turned into the studios for *Prime Time*, I wondered if we would have another welcoming party this evening. I wasn't to be disappointed but this time those assembled had microphones, cameras and notebooks at the ready. The media had obviously got wind of the fact that we would be on *Prime Time*, and, as I'd had my phone switched off for most of the evening, they came to Donnybrook to get our reaction to the day's intervention. I said very little and headed into the studios. I watched the 9 o'clock news in the greenroom. John Keenan was there too after his flight from France and so was Tim Hastings who had been brought in as an independent expert in the field. It was all cordial enough. I was then shown, for the very first time, a copy of the joint Labour Court/LRC 'initiative'. It quickly told me a number of things. They wanted us back to work by the following Monday 'under protest if necessary' in return for a 'joint investigation' into all the issues in dispute. This joint initiative was presented as having a defined statutory basis, but the detail of its workings was unclear. I immediately made a few calls and convened an emergency meeting of our executive to consider these proposals and any clarification we might subsequently receive. The meeting was arranged for the following Sunday, 13 August. Then it was down to the studio.

The show began with an interview with Liam Tobin in which he told the viewers how wrong we were about everything, how right he was about everything, and how we'd just have to do without wages until we copped ourselves on. He was taken through an ILDA flier and given ample opportunity to rubbish every word of it. Whatever about the content of what he was saying, his bitterness was very clear to me. Obviously the initial idea had been then to cut to me and ask me to respond to Liam

Tobin. However, the day's events meant that the first question related to the ILDA response to the 'unique joint Labour Court/LRC initiative'. I immediately welcomed the initiative, asked why it had taken eight weeks, and said that it contained much of merit but needed clarification on a number of points. I would spend the next day or two seeking such clarification, and had called an emergency meeting of our executive to consider it the following Sunday. The statement contained a demand for us to return to work by the following Monday, 14 August. Vincent Browne quite reasonably wanted to know whether we would return or not. I said I hoped so and that I would work hard to ensure that that was possible. I challenged the company to do the same. I was also pressed on safety issues and on whether our protests should continue while we were considering this matter. I responded that this was the first time in eight weeks that we had something positive to say to our members and that I hoped that those members would allow us space to consider this in depth over the coming days.

Vincent Browne then turned to John Keenan and asked whether it would be possible to 'fudge' some issues to allow a resolution of the dispute. John Keenan — buoyed by weeks of soft interviews — immediately took issue with the interviewer's use of the word 'fudge'. There was no fudge, he said, 'in Iarnród Éireann's safety record'. Then something happened that hadn't happened before. A journalist put it up to John Keenan. As Vincent Browne interrupted to state bluntly that he hadn't asked about Iarnród Éireann's safety record, John Keenen visibly reddened, winced and became uncomfortable. He tried again, mentioning Halcrow Rail and the three-year process. He was sitting directly on my right, and I could almost feel him boiling up. The *Prime Time* presenter wasn't wearing this mantra and interrupted again. That was not what he had asked. Could some issues be fudged to allow a return to work with dignity on all sides? John Keenan again returned to the safety issue, and also stated that 'over 25 per cent' of our members were back at work (in fact, 118 members entered dispute on 19 June 2000, and 106 ended it ten weeks later). Vincent Browne waited his time and asked how come, if everything was so safe, a majority of drivers did not support this agreement across all three unions, asking John Keenan to confirm that two-thirds had not, in fact, supported the agreement. John Keenan responded with figures regarding how many were working it, but Vincent Browne, unlike previous interviewers throughout the dispute, refused to allow the focus of discussion to be changed from something John Keenan was uncomfortable with to union recognition. At this point, when other journalists would have just shut up and allowed the Iarnród Éireann representative to finish his script, Vincent Browne went further, challenging John Keenan and Iarnród Éireann on having contributed to the dispute by forcing through an agreement that only a third of drivers approved of. When John Keenan failed to answer, the *Prime Time* presenter wouldn't let go, and pressed home the key question again and again. When Vincent Browne eventually released John Keenan from his grip and turned to Tim Hastings, the Iarnród Éireann representative was damaged and furious. I couldn't believe it. So often, I had walked away from interviews feeling that the questioning had lacked balance and that Iarnród Éireann had been given an easy ride. Not tonight.

I bumped into Vincent Browne later while I was having my make-up removed, and as we discussed the forthcoming Supreme Court appeal, it was clear that he had done his research. He outlined how he had read the High Court judgment and how he found the logic in it shocking. I couldn't believe this. Not alone a journalist who was prepared to put it up to Iarnród Éireann, but one who did real research too!

Labour Court/LRC Joint Initiative

Over the next few days, we needed to assess this joint Labour Court/LRC initiative carefully. As we did so, a number of issues arose. Firstly, the joint initiative had been made by both agencies 'under the powers vested in them under Section 26 of the Industrial Relations Act 1990'. This posed an immediate problem. Section 26 provides for an investigation of a matter in dispute by the Labour Court only. This may happen following an investigation by the commission or a direct referral to the Labour Court. However, there is absolutely no provision for a 'joint' investigation involving both agencies in this section, or indeed in any other section, in industrial relations law. So why was the LRC added to this investigation? The answer to that was simple and clear to ILDA members. The LRC had, of course, facilitated the entire 'New Deal' from the outset and had even 'supervised' the ballot count. Now we were questioning whether this agreement, brokered by the state agency, contained safety concerns, breached our statutory entitlements regarding Sunday and public-holiday premium payments and was flawed in so many other respects. We had also criticised the LRC for not implementing the code of practice it had written for itself, and for failing to assist with a resolution of the dispute to date. So the LRC was clearly a party to the agreement that provoked the dispute. However, section 26 of the Industrial Relations Act provided for the Labour Court to investigate these matters alone and, in all of the circumstances, this was, in fact, the only appropriate course. But what if the Labour Court were to find in our favour? Wouldn't that impugn the work of the LRC? Of course it would and that is why the LRC, without any statutory basis whatsoever, appended itself to this 'unique joint initiative'. That was bad enough. But to portray the investigation publicly as fully in line with 'the powers vested in them under the Industrial Relations Act 1990' was quite another matter when, in fact, the opposite was the case.

We also wanted to be careful that we didn't buy a pig in a poke. What if, by some miracle, this joint investigation by the Labour Court and the LRC found that the deal brokered by the LRC was flawed in all the ways we had said it was? Would the report have a statutory basis or could Iarnród Éireann then pop up quoting the real provisions of the 1990 Act and point out the anomaly in order to side-step some or all of its findings? These were serious issues. At this point, we had to be careful how we trod, and we had every intention of being careful.

There were also other matters to consider. It was clear that this investigation was strange in that it would not provide for hearings for the parties. Instead, 'all parties with an interest in this dispute will be entitled to make a written submission and in order to allow for the completion of the investigation it is expected that prior to the investigation commencing all the drivers in Iarnród Éireann will return to duty under the new conditions of employment by the start of business on Monday 14 August 2000. Train drivers who maintain that they are in dispute can return to work "under protest" if necessary'. It was also outlined that the investigation would be completed 'within a three month timeframe'.

The most remarkable thing about the joint statement is that the word ILDA, which was now a word familiar and known to practically every citizen in the state, was contained nowhere in the statement. We interpreted this as an example of how sensitive even these two bodies had now become to the issue of 'recognition', to the extent that they felt unable to include in their statement the one word on everybody's lips. It was totally bizarre. However, the most bizarre thing was that ILDA had as yet received no official notification of this 'unique joint initiative'. No phone calls; no faxes; no emails; nothing — just questions from the media who had been issued with it, and demands for responses to points being raised by the other parties who had been given the document. I first saw the document in RTÉ on the evening of 10 August, almost eight hours after every significant reporter and news agency in Ireland had received it, but I still had no copy to take home with me. As I sat down the following morning to begin assessing the initiative properly, I still hadn't got a copy to which I could refer. Contact with the LRC was fruitless. All morning, phone calls went unreturned or were ignored. Eventually I had to write and formally seek a copy of this one-page document. I did so at 3pm and I eventually had a copy faxed to me that evening at 4pm precisely. It was now over twenty-four hours since it had been issued.

The statement itself raised as many questions as it answered. I decided to write again with several reasonable questions, namely:

1. Will this trade union be invited to make written submissions?
2. Will this trade union be invited to an oral hearing?
3. Will this process be open to discussion and/or debate?
4. Can this trade union present independent expert advice on matters such as rail safety?
5. What status will the report to be issued by the proposed investigation have?
6. Will ILDA members have a vote on proposals/recommendations emanating from the proposed investigation?
7. Will bodies unconnected with the railway be asked to make submissions?
8. On the assumption that the investigation will ensure that basic statutory entitlements of employees are fully upheld how will this affect Iarnród Éireann's 'New Deal for Locomotive Drivers'?
9. How will these entitlements be upheld while this investigation is ongoing?

10. Will the nature of this investigation be inquisitorial or adversarial?

11. Will its findings be mandatory or directory?

Reasonable? Well perhaps the 'inquisitorial or adversarial' question might have seemed a bit over the top. Normally of course the nature of such a process would be 'inquisitorial' but every contact that we had had with the LRC to date had been terse. Even getting the statement had been a long-drawn-out process. In any case, Friday evening brought no response. I spent the evening making arrangements for our executive meeting in Tullamore on Sunday. I awoke on Saturday morning fully expecting a fax to be waiting for me, but there was none. All day, the position was the same. Finally, at 9.54pm on Saturday, 12 August, at a time when I might have already been in Tullamore meeting up in advance of our meeting, I received a fax with the number of the sender erased. The only identifying mark on the fax was the legend 'G3' on the bottom of the page. The letter referred to my fax and gave the following answers:

1. As indicated in the Joint Labour Court/LRC initiative of 10 August 2000 written submissions will be taken from all interested parties

2. As stated in the joint initiative of 10th August, parties are free to make written submissions to the investigation

3. The process for the investigation will be determined jointly by the Labour Court and the LRC

4. As indicated in the joint initiative written submissions will be taken from all interested parties on all relevant issues

5. The status of the report of the investigation will be that normally accorded to reports issued by the Labour Court and the LRC

6. This is not an issue for the investigation

7. Please refer to the answer at (1) above

8. & 9. The joint initiative makes it clear that it is expected that all train drivers will return to duty under the new conditions of employment while working under protest if necessary

10. Please refer to the answer at (5) above.

Question 11 received no answer, presumably because it was felt that the issue had been dealt with in other replies. The correspondence was jointly signed by the Chairman of the Labour Court and the Chief Executive of the LRC. Readers can judge for themselves the value of these clarifications and whether they answer the questions that had been put. I certainly found them of little value. Moreover they were disingenuous. For example, look at answer 5. How could this report have the status 'normally accorded to reports issued by the Labour Court and the LRC' when the Labour Court and LRC had never before issued a joint report on anything and had, in fact, themselves trumpeted this investigation as a 'unique joint initiative'. Against that background, what was 'normal'?

The fact that no actual hearings would take place seemed to imply that bodies were anxious to avoid meeting ILDA. We could not be seen to be having our concerns addressed in the normal manner. The fact that dealing with concerns like ours was the sole reason for the existence of these organisations was irrelevant. We were 'the great unwashed', pariahs in the movement, and we were to be treated like that at every turn.

Iarnród Éireann had moved into overdrive. Would we ask our members their views? The company wanted the media to ask us for them. Our members were portrayed as poor deluded souls sucked into the mire by our executive — me in particular — and with no minds of their own. If only we would ask our members, the 'real picture' would emerge of a group of men ready to abandon all at the altar of this pious nonsense. I now know that when the 'social consensus' doesn't like the position taken by a group of workers — be they train drivers or secondary-school teachers — the union members are portrayed as fools led down a path by 'evil people' like myself or some other easy target. The faces, even the issues, might change, but the tactic doesn't.

There was never any question of not asking our members. Of course our members would have a say on this initiative. Our union had always been led from the bottom up, not from the top down. I resolved to answer these annoying questions by our actions over the coming days. We would give our opponents, questioners and observers a lesson on how any union should use democracy to ascertain the 'true' feelings of its members. If the media and Iarnród Éireann wanted the 'true' feelings of ILDA members, that is exactly what they would get.

And so our Executive Committee and the media once again

assembled in the Tullamore Court Hotel on Sunday 13 August 2002. While we considered the burning questions presented by the Labour Court/LRC joint initiative, the media settled down to watch Offaly topple All-Ireland hurling champions Cork at Croke Park. The hotel in Tullamore was buzzing with excitement and it wasn't all about ILDA. Our executive discussed the initiative and the Saturday-night 'clarification'. We were as one. Working under protest would mean working an unsafe agreement. How could we take responsibility for our trains if we knew that they were being worked under unsafe conditions? Peter Rayner had provided us with further advice through the week just past. He had grown annoyed at attempts to smear him and his reputation but, instead of bending the knee and backtracking on his assessment of part-time drivers in particular as unsafe, he was stronger than ever. He outlined to anyone who would listen how he had spoken to other experts in the field, and they were all agreed that part-time drivers were out of the question. So were we, and we weren't about to be responsible for their introduction or implementation.

The manner in which ILDA had been ignored in the issuing of the initiative and the treatment of our questions didn't inspire confidence either. And then there was the 'expectation' that we return to work by Monday. Commentators seemed to believe that the entire initiative was contingent on this 'expectation' being met. To me, expectations and conditions are quite different. The initiative was clearly not conditional on a return to work on 14 August. I didn't expect that the Labour Court and the LRC, having finally issued this initiative, would now withdraw their offer of an investigation whenever a return to work might happen, 14 August or some other time. In any event, as everyone kept telling us, we had to ask our members, and that takes time.

Interestingly, if we had emerged from the Tullamore Court Hotel on 13 August and said that we accepted the initiative and would return to work at 9 o'clock the following morning, nobody would have given a damn whether or not we asked our members' views or how we had reached the decision. If, on the other hand, we had come out and rejected the proposal outright, without asking our members, we would have been pilloried. But as I said, there was never a question in our minds. What we actually said when we emerged from that meeting was that we were convening a Special General Meeting of ILDA members less than twenty-four hours later in Dublin. There our members would have an opportunity to give their views on the initiative, and we would obviously be bound by any decisions they would make. Of course this did not satisfy Iarnród Éireann. The questions just changed. Would the executive be putting proposals; would every member have a vote; and, crucially, would that vote be by secret ballot?

I went home with Finbarr who stayed with me in Athlone that night and we prepared for the next day's meeting. I got a phone call from RTÉ. Would I appear on the panel for *Questions & Answers* on television the following evening, after our meeting? I got the views of our executive members — as I always did when something major came up — and they agreed that I should do it. Another big day beckoned.

Before I arrived at our meeting that Monday afternoon, I made some plans. Firstly, I did interviews where I was asked whether or not we would be affording our members a secret ballot. I knew the answer to that but it was our members' business first and foremost, and so I basically said that people would have to wait and see. Then I got on to our legal people and arranged for a solicitor to attend our meeting. I then drove to Martin King's house and picked up three sets of ballot papers for our members, which Martin had kindly spent the morning preparing, while I was driving or doing interviews. When I eventually arrived at the hotel, we set up registration books and booths. This would be done properly, not because we were being watched, but because we were in the habit of doing things the right way. In previous existences, we had experienced how not to conduct ballots. We knew how to do it properly.

It was clear that the dispute had reached one of its defining moments. It was therefore important not alone to ascertain our members' views on new developments, but also to allow them to reconsider their position relating to the 'New Deal' itself. If — as Iarnród Éireann had been loudly contending — they actually wanted to return to work the 'New Deal', we needed to know that. And so our members arrived to make some vital decisions. Seventy-four locked-out members came to this meeting. It was incredible. The dispute had been begun by 118 members, and 106 would finish it. And here — having had less than twenty-four hours' notice of this Special General Meeting — seventy-four of them had come from three corners of Ireland in the middle of the holiday season. They didn't have one vote. They didn't even have one secret vote. They had three secrets votes, independently verified by a solicitor present specifically for that purpose. The first thing we needed to do was to confirm their views of the 'New Deal'. Obviously if that had changed, there would be no need to go any further. And so Motion One simply asked, 'Do you accept the New Deal for Locomotive Drivers?' Seventy-four drivers went up past the supervising solicitor to vote; seventy-four drivers signed a confirmation that they had been afforded a secret ballot on the motion; and seventy-four drivers — each of them now in his ninth week without wages — said NO, he did not accept the 'New Deal'.

Motion Two asked whether they agreed to return to work under the terms of the Labour Court/LRC investigation. Again, all drivers in attendance went up to vote in the same way; and again the unanimous response was NO. And then there was a third motion, this time on a possible framework for settlement, tabled by the executive. This proposal sought to move the situation forward and cut through a lot of the propaganda used against us in recent weeks. For example, it specifically dealt with recognition by stating emphatically: 'ILDA will not seek to be formally recognised for negotiation purposes as a condition for any return to work or for any settlement of the dispute.' The document went on to outline the industrial relations and safety issues respectively and propose formats for resolving them. In particular, our safety concerns would need to be addressed before we returned to work, but we welcomed the initiative. In essence, we could not return to work while we were responsible for unsafe elements of the agreement. It was a significant move for us. While part-time drivers were totally ruled out, we proposed that a new five-person committee could be set up within the company to monitor safety. This did not happen but the new legislation that established an independent rail-safety body in Ireland for the first time ever is something for which ILDA lobbied long and hard; and it has powers far in excess of what ILDA suggested on that August afternoon in 2000. Members were asked to vote on this proposal. Again seventy-four of them did so in a secret ballot and 100 per cent of them endorsed the view of the ILDA Executive. For us, on the day, this was an incredible outcome. When the results were announced, the room broke into spontaneous applause. I felt vindicated and relieved. For weeks, we had been told by outsiders that our members felt differently from us, but here they were standing side by side with their executive. Again. As I went to announce the results to the waiting media, I was buoyant. Democracy had had its day, and ILDA was as united as ever. And I was off to RTÉ for *Questions & Answers*, in top form.

Most readers will know the format of this show or its BBC equivalent, *Question Time* — a panel facing audience questions on a predetermined range of topics. The topics I was told to prepare for in advance, apart from the rail dispute, included traveller accommodation and road-accident rates in Ireland. I was joined on the panel by Fianna Fáil Minister of State Eamon Ó Cuiv, Fine Gael former leader Alan Dukes and Martin Collins, a representative from the traveller group, Pavee Point. As we assembled in RTÉ's greenroom, conversation was awkward. I was glad to get into the studio and on with the show. Naturally the first question was on the dispute and that discussion took up at least half of the hour-long show. I spoke first and was soundly, but fairly, questioned by the chairman. Minister of State Ó Cuiv began his response by dealing with the question but then went off on so many tangents that he almost got into a row with Vincent Browne. This should have set it up nicely for Alan Dukes to attack the Government's role in events. He didn't. He instead took the easy option and attacked ILDA. In fact, he did so more forcibly than Eamon Ó Cuiv. I couldn't believe my ears. However, if it had been a boxing match, you would have said he didn't lay a glove on me or ILDA despite his best efforts. The Pavee Point representative read an answer that basically told us to go back to work. He followed up, however, with a strong criticism of the media and their treatment of me personally, which drew spontaneous applause from the audience. All in all, it went well. Viewers will be unaware that after the show the audience can move forward to meet the panel. I was amused to see a line of people waiting to speak with me while Alan Dukes and Eamon Ó Cuiv got ready to leave. Every one of them shook hands and said how much they admired ILDA for taking a stand. This was yet another example, albeit a small one, of public reaction to ILDA not equating with the mass media reaction and portrayal.

And so the dispute entered Week Nine. The issues needing

immediate resolution had now been distilled down to safety issues, with a forum now available for investigation of industrial relations issues following any return to work. As I suspected, the Labour Court/LRC initiative had not been withdrawn following our inability to meet their 'expectation' that we return to work by 14 August. Nevertheless, we had still not thought up a manner of dealing with our safety issues in such a way as to enable a return to work to happen in the immediate term. Our members were hurting though. It now seemed that every day another of our members was reaching financial breaking point. At this stage, I didn't mind when a handful of our members began, through sheer financial necessity, to drift back to work. This dispute was now about breaking ILDA and nothing else, and I knew that these men still felt very strong in their beliefs. Going back to work was harder for them than it was for those of us who could stick it out for another while. At this stage, I was determined that there would be no falling out with any member who was starved back. I wondered as the week went on without further intervention how long we could keep our members together. Whatever happened, we could not allow ourselves to be split. We began to assess every member on an almost daily basis and, for the first time, we began to contemplate how much more our members could take. But they had been so strong on the previous Monday, and when I spoke to them now by telephone, that strength was still there. A terrifying thought struck me. What if they were staying out beyond their breaking point, out of loyalty to me or to the executive?

Fergus Finlay and Phil Flynn were still working on possible letters from the CIÉ Chairman to our members. We had an executive meeting scheduled for the Monday 21 August, and Fergus asked if he could come to it. He wanted to speak with our executive. Normally Fergus would be happy to speak with me and allow me to pass on any views he had to the rest of the members. But by now, I had other ideas in my head. Although I didn't fully realise it then, I was coming to the conclusion that the dispute needed to end one way or the other. I didn't see how we could keep a large bulk of our members out past the end of the tenth week of the dispute. The lack of money was now the key issue for our members, and I felt that another week would break a big section of them. That couldn't be allowed to happen. We would finish this united, whatever that meant doing. If it meant going back to work, then it was much better that we do so together, with dignity, than through division and recrimination. But there were still some things we hadn't tried yet. I suspected that some of our members would secretly welcome a proposal from me that we go back. But I knew that others weren't ready for that and would see such a suggestion as something akin to heresy. I also thought we should do even more. The buses were hit again and, despite the predictions of SIPTU and the NBRU, once again we got super support from their members in Dublin Bus. But there was still no further breakthrough.

I was also very concerned about just how blatant the scabbing operation mounted by SIPTU and the NBRU had become on the rail. A press release issued jointly by NBRU General Secretary at the time Peter Bunting — before he defected to ICTU — and SIPTU's Noel Dowling, directed at their members on the buses, chides them for supporting our 'pickets'. It outlines that their support for workers 'on strike for 7 weeks' is understandable but misplaced and it asks them not to support us any further. In the middle of the statement, a single-sentence paragraph reads: 'Our members totalling 245 out of a workforce of 350 [in their dreams] are passing ILDA pickets every day.' Some boast for trade unionists to make!

We had also blocked more level crossings in Dundalk and between Ballinasloe and Athlone. Every day, I was hearing some of our members discuss the possibility of sitting on railway lines, of chaining themselves to tracks or of taking over signal cabins. I didn't think that such actions would work but I knew the sentiments that lay behind the ideas. I felt that Week Ten would see the end of it one way or another.

Week Ten

At the end of Week Nine, one of our members in Connolly — one of the Connolly Three, as they had become known — called me to say that he would be going back to work on Monday. He had several children, a new house and a wife who didn't work outside the home. Financially, Iarnród Éireann and its allies had succeeded in breaking him. I knew that he was hurting, and appreciated his call — his honesty. I asked him for one more week and made him a promise that we would do everything in our power to end it in that week and that we might well all return together thereafter.

He spoke to his wife at home and gave it another week. I am sure that similar discussions were taking place with members around the country. Monday 21 August 2000, was the beginning of that week. We assembled in the Aisling Hotel for our meeting. As normal, the lads travelled from everywhere.

Fergus Finlay attended his first ILDA Executive meeting. It was a tough meeting which began at 8pm and lasted for over five hours. Christy Holbrook was wound up before we even went in. His son Leonard had been working part-time with Iarnród Éireann on the platform in Cork's Kent Station, with three other young lads who had been taken on at the same time. When he had returned from holidays a week before, he had been told that he was no longer required. The other three — whose fathers were not in ILDA — had been kept on. It was a cruel act that hurt Christy deeply. Nevertheless, he had kept going and was in the chair as usual for our meeting. Fergus Finlay still hadn't given up hope of producing a letter that would allow us to go back to work. I had. In my opinion, it had gone on too long and I suspected that Phil Flynn and Fergus Finlay — with all the best intentions in the world — were not going to get the CIÉ Chairman to sign such a letter. I thought that we needed something new and I outlined to the meeting what I had in mind, at least in part. I wanted a sit-in protest. A group of our members would effectively take over a key Iarnród Éireann or CIÉ building or office and maintain a peaceful sit-in protest for as long as it took. Others could rally around outside and, if we were really lucky, we might even get support from other workers in CIÉ and outside. We could issue press statements, conduct interviews and generally bring our protest into another final phase. I outlined that we should be prepared to be arrested and even go to jail if that was what it took. I knew I was prepared for that course myself, and I emphasised that only those similarly disposed should attend the protest. Our executive considered what I was proposing.

I had not been part of the so-called 'flying pickets' or barrier protests. Instead, I had been going around with a microphone in my face while our members did the hard work. I wanted to do this with them. I rationalised that if it failed, they would feel that they had given everything they could, and could therefore face the hard decision — whether or not to go back — in a better frame of mind. I even thought that there was an outside chance it would succeed. I thought that as it changed the focus of our actions away from disruption to services, it might give the media and any of the public who were opposed to us food for thought.

Fergus Finlay was opposed to my idea. He didn't want to see any of us get arrested or jailed, and he asked the members for more time to work on the CIÉ letters. We agreed to give him until close of business on Wednesday 23 August — less than two days — to see if John Lynch would agree a text for those letters. It was after 1am when we left the Aisling for the long road home. I was lucky in that I had only eighty miles to drive. Christy Holbrook and Dave Healy had longer journeys. I hit the sack and actually slept in the next morning. The phone rang all morning, but I ignored it. Around noon, I answered. It was Dave Healy. Had I heard about Christy? He had suffered a heart attack.

Christy now recalls that night vividly — the debate; the long drive; the worry. As he reached his home in Douglas, Co. Cork, it was bright. He felt dizzy and breathless, 'tingly'. And then he was in hospital. Christy Holbrook would never drive another train or attend another meeting of the ILDA Executive. Our president, chairman, was gone.

I was stunned. In so many ways, Christy was our outlet. When meetings became fraught, which was often, he was the one who would crack a joke or wind someone up. He was our release valve. He had a lovely wife — Eleanor — and three children. Four days earlier, following a visit to the Waterford Glass factory, where we had explained our case to some of the workers, and received a donation of £1,500 to help our members, we had stayed at the Holbrooks' mobile home in Ardmore, Co. Waterford. Christy called it our 'Camp David'. Eleanor had turned up the next morning to cook us breakfast and we had left them alone for the weekend. Then there was Monday's meeting and now this. As word spread, all our members were shocked. We were all greatly relieved when it became apparent that Christy was not in immediate life-threatening danger. He was in hospital in a stable condition. I got to speak to him on the phone at some stage that day, and I told him I'd drive down. He lied and said that he'd be out in the morning. He knew I had a sit-in to organise. We carried on.

The Sit-in

I began to prepare for the sit-in — our 'Alamo', as Martin King referred to it when I told him. Most people who knew anything about it thought that we were planning a sit-in at the Connolly Station boardroom. In fact, the CIÉ boardroom at Heuston Station was the only place I ever had in mind. I knew that it would be spacious. It also opened onto a large, green area where our other members, the media and anyone else who wanted to join them could assemble. And it looked down the quays into the city centre, from where, if we got the chance, we could organise marches like the ones earlier in the dispute. Those who were going in knew what to bring — sleeping bags, basic food provisions like teabags, sugar and biscuits, clothes, and toiletries. We needed enough for several days, maybe even weeks. I spoke to Brian Dunphy. I didn't want him coming in with us. He could play a much more important role as our man on the outside. He would liaise with us and deal with the media. Most importantly, he would feed us. We got a large bucket and a rope, and we planned to pull it up and down to Brian with whatever we needed to get in or out. There were other things to plan too. We would need a way of dealing with the media and getting our message across. I knew that the office suite would be well stocked with phones and computers. I packed a number of floppy disks with me, containing my e-mail circulation list. I planned that we would issue press releases through e-mail, and I even wrote out the first one in advance. It outlined the reasoning behind our sit-in.

I wrote this statement the night before the sit-in. I then put my own things together and discussed with Pauline what we were about to do. Every member had done his bit during the dispute in whatever way he could. This was just another of the many actions our members could support. Some actions would suit some members; others wouldn't. I awoke on that beautiful August Wednesday and wondered just where I would be sleeping that night. Heuston? A police station somewhere? Jail even? They were all possibilities.

Finbarr arrived with our member from Ballina, Dessie Gallagher. They had lots of stuff with them. Finbarr had enough provisions to keep a platoon of squaddies alive in a hostile war zone for weeks. Even at this stage, Dessie didn't know where we were going. He knew that it was something new and 'novel' but wasn't in on the details. We headed off for

Dublin early as we had another appointment. I had arranged a meeting with Fianna Fáil's Rory O'Hanlon TD, but the meeting brought nothing positive to bear on the situation.

We headed off to the Aisling Hotel, where the rest of the lads began to arrive. I had decided that we would go in at two minutes before 5 o'clock. We didn't want to be sitting in the middle of office staff for half of the afternoon, but we had to get in before they left and locked up. Just after 4pm, we had the twenty people I had envisaged. In addition to Brian, 'our man on the outside', they were:

Martin Dullaghan – Dundalk
Charlie McMasters – Dundalk
Liam Whyte – Dundalk
Tony Murphy – Dundalk
Peter Clinton – Drogheda
Shane Butler – Drogheda
Martin Rice – Drogheda
John Courtney – Inchicore
Joe Darcy – Inchicore
Gerry Delaney – Inchicore
Anto Halpin – Inchicore
Alan Ward – Inchicore
Mick Hurley – Inchicore
Christy Horan – Inchicore
Hugh McCarthy – Inchicore
Brian O'Keeffe – Waterford
Finbarr Masterson – Westport
Dessie Gallagher – Ballina
Brendan Ogle – Athlone

They had all arrived at the Aisling Hotel with their sleeping bags and other provisions. None of them knew exactly what was planned. I took Martin Dullaghan from Dundalk aside. I picked him because, as a Dundalk driver, his face would not be known around Heuston. I asked him to walk the 150 yards over to the station and enter the small reception office that we needed to get through in order to gain entry to the offices upstairs. There was a security guard in front of a door that led to the stairs to the offices. We needed to ensure that the door was open. If it wasn't, we needed to know how it could be opened. Martin went over alone and knocked on the door to gain entry to the reception room. He went up to the security guard and asked for a train timetable. The unsuspecting guard explained that timetables were available in the concourse only. Martin left and came straight back to the Aisling. The news was good. Perhaps because of the heat of the day, the door behind the security guard was wide open. In addition, he had had no difficulty in inducing the security guard to open the first door into the reception room.

At 4.45 we all left the hotel and assembled in the car park of the Aisling. Here, for the first time, I outlined the full details of what was planned. I told them all that if they didn't want to be a part of it, they could go home — there would be no hard feelings. Nobody left. There was one last piece of business to do. At 4.55, just before close of business on Wednesday evening, I called Fergus Finlay on my mobile phone. I asked whether he had made any progress on the CIÉ letters. He said that he hadn't and began to explain why. It was what I had expected. I told him that I would phone him back in a few minutes.

As I hung up, we were already walking in single file across Kingsbridge towards Heuston Station. Brian Dunphy led the way. When we got to the large Georgian glass window that fronted the office entrance, we ducked down, out of sight, while Brian walked ahead a few yards to the glass-door entrance of the reception room. He knocked on the door and held up a white envelope (empty), giving the impression that he had a letter to hand to the security man. The security man immediately pressed the door release Brian gave us a hand signal and we moved. Mick Hurley was the first in and I was behind him. Mick is a big man and he approached the security guard who was behind a counter. Mick stood at the end of the counter with his arm across the exit point. From there, he directed our members through the door and up the stairs to the office suites above. I was the first man up the stairs. I walked up two flights and turned to see a long, red-carpeted corridor with offices on either side. I had my bag and my sleeping bag. A man walked across the corridor from one office to another and, hearing a noise, turned to see me. He greeted me with a bemused smile, and watched as eighteen more men carrying sleeping bags and various other items breezed past him. I went through the first open door I saw. The office was large, full of office equipment, and empty of people. I sat at a computer and inserted my floppy disk with the news release. It was 5.01 p.m. Two of our members began removing the locks from the door with a screwdriver. We didn't want to be locked into a room at the back of the building. Getting our bearings, two others went looking for the boardroom. They were back in seconds and guided us to our intended destination.

It was as we had expected — a large room with a massive table and luxury chairs all around. This was no drivers' mess room! By pressing a button, the table opened and a large projector/video unit emerged. Through a door on one end were kitchen facilities, including cooking implements, kettles, crockery and cutlery. At the other end of the kitchen, was the entrance to the corridor. We locked the door, now content that we were in the best position. I looked to the other end of the boardroom. There was an office, and in it sat an alarmed-looking CIÉ Chief Executive. He needn't have been alarmed, but in the immediate moments following this 'occupation', the situation must have seemed surreal. He didn't hang about to see what was happening and, as he left his office, we locked the door behind him. We were now in a self-contained three-room boardroom complex, and, within minutes of entering, I was on RTÉ radio doing a live interview with Rachel English. I outlined that we had a constitutional and legal right to protest at the place of our employer during a trade dispute, and asserted that our members were abused workers and not the corrupt holders of Ansbacher accounts or recipients of 'political donations' in brown envelopes. Anyone looking for criminality could look for it in some of Dublin's other fine buildings.

Within minutes, a crowd was assembling down on the green in front of us. Our late-arriving members from Cork and Limerick were joined by other workers and the quickly assembling media. Television cameras came to get pictures of us for the upcoming teatime news shows. I did a series of interviews from the Chief Executive's office while Charlie and Liam hung out a banner with an ILDA slogan on it. Others were figuring out how to work the state-of-the-art video equipment, and we even watched one of Iarnród Éireann's internal management-training videos.

Brian O'Keefe had a radio with him and we could listen to coverage of our 'invasion' on the airwaves. All in all, things had gone extremely smoothly.

Then we had a knock on the door at the kitchen end of the boardroom. It was security and they wanted to speak to somebody. We moved the material we had blocked the door with and opened it. As the lads crowded behind me, a burly security guard asked us to leave. I replied that we were engaged in a peaceful sit-in and that we wouldn't be leaving voluntarily. He was pleasant enough and when he told us we had hurt a security guard while entering, it was obvious he didn't really believe that himself. No one had been hurt or abused. We told him so and he left. We locked ourselves in again.

One of CIÉ's many media gurus, Cyril Ferris, was now outside on the green giving interviews. Peter Cluskey of RTÉ called and told me that Cyril Ferris was simply stating that we were employees and were entitled to this protest. Iarnród Éireann would rather that we were here than on level crossings, and would even ensure that we were properly fed and looked after. I sensed that the company was up to no good. As we settled down, we phoned our families and assured them that we were fine. They had all been following our exploits on television in any case. Then we watched a football match in which Leeds United were playing; some of our members present were Leeds fans. I told them that I wouldn't bother but that I wanted to see the upcoming Celtic v Rangers match the following Sunday! I was prepared for the long haul. Meanwhile, I was engaged in more telephone conversations. I spoke to Fergus Finlay who wasn't very impressed that he had been talking to me on the telephone one minute and we had invaded the CIÉ boardroom the next. I think he knew, however, that 'diplomacy' had failed. In fact, you could say that it had failed for nine-and-a-half weeks now. As darkness began to fall, the media had all been briefed by CIÉ that we would be allowed stay as long as we wished. Understandably, they left, one by one, telling us that they would return in the morning to get the pictures and sounds for another day's news coverage. Some of our members remained downstairs; others went for videos that we could watch overnight; and Brian Dunphy was taking orders for our first meal inside — nineteen portions of fish and chips!

It happened suddenly. Christy Horan entered the kitchen area from where I was making my latest phone call and told me that the shutters had been pulled down on the front of the station and that those outside had spotted gardaí entering the building. It was just after 9 p.m. Now that the media had gone, Iarnród Éireann had decided to call in the heavies. I tried to call Peter Cluskey to get the RTÉ outside broadcast unit back, but Peter had gone home. By the time he called me back, it was too late.

We sat around the large table, all nineteen of us, and waited. Within seconds, there was banging on the door and shouts telling us to open up or they would smash it down. Although we had been very careful not to damage any property, we knew that we would be held responsible for any damage the gardaí did, so I gave the nod and our member nearest the door opened it. Uniformed gardaí poured into the room in a tidal wave of luminous yellow jackets. There were dozens of them. They were accompanied by the stationmaster, John Lane, and a suit. The suit spoke and identified himself as a senior ranking officer. John Lane spoke to say, 'That's them.' (Who did he expect to find?) The garda officer told us that we had no business there and asked us to leave. I said that we were engaged in a trade dispute with our employer; this was the place of business of our employer; and we had a right to conduct a peaceful sit-in protest at this venue in this situation. He responded by saying that we were in breach of the Public Order Act — an act of parliament that had been introduced with assurances that it would not be used against trade unionists involved in disputes like this — and that we would have to leave, voluntarily or otherwise.

I refused to leave voluntarily. He then asked did I speak for all the others. I replied that I spoke for myself only and that it was up to the others what position they took. He then asked each of the other eighteen in turn whether they would leave voluntarily. One member was worried about a family law case that he had upcoming and felt that this might count against him regarding access to his offspring. He, rightly in the circumstances, left at that point. All the others stayed. At this point, the gardaí had formed a circle around us, and stood behind our chairs. The senior garda ordered his officers to remove us. Anto Halpin was sitting closest to the door. A garda asked him to leave, and he refused. They asked again, and he again refused. They told him that he was under arrest and asked him to leave the building. He refused. Eventually they had to carry him bodily out of the room, by his arms and legs. Alan Ward sat beside him. We watched as the same scenario played itself out, and Alan too was bodily removed from the building. And so it continued. One by one, our members were arrested, and, one by one, they either walked out or were carried out of the building. And then — after a considerable time — there were three. Finbarr, Charlie and I were left.

Throughout all of this, a very nice garda had been beside me, asking me to leave. He argued that there were people downstairs taking photographs and that his colleagues and he didn't want to have to carry me out past them. Finbarr was on my right and was next. He too refused to leave and was arrested. He walked out with his head held high. That left Charlie and me, surrounded by a squad of gardaí. He was seated at one end of the table and I was at the other. Charlie was in debate with a garda who asked him to leave, and told him that he knew how we felt and that he — the garda — was only doing his job. With John Lane standing within yards, Charlie said that the garda didn't know what it felt like to be conned out of his conditions of employment by the likes of the stationmaster. John Lane left. Charlie outlined our treatment, isolation, victimisation and abuse at the hands of our employer. I looked down at him and said, 'What do you think we should do, Charlie?'

'Whatever you do, I do,' was the response. As I said I was not leaving voluntarily, the garda behind me told me that I was arrested. When Charlie was also arrested, I said, 'Come on, Charlie. We'll walk out of here together.' With that, I moved around and left the room. As I walked down the stairs I had climbed five hours earlier, I had two gardaí behind me on either side. Charlie was behind us with his two 'minders'. As I reached the bottom of the stairs, I heard one of my escorts whisper to the other, 'Just let him go.'

What did this mean? I thought I had been arrested already? Just at that point, John Lane walked out from a side door in front of me. He was only feet away. I felt myself losing control and the temper welled in me. I turned to one of my guards and asked, 'Am I arrested or not?' When he answered in the negative, I said, 'Well, you'd better arrest me now before you have something serious to arrest me for.' At that, my arm was grabbed, and I was formally arrested and told my rights. John Lane disappeared. We reached the bottom of the steps and turned into the reception room through which we had initially entered. As we left it and walked into the concourse, we saw that all the shutters had been brought down to restrict the view of those outside. Quite a crowd appeared to have gathered, and they banged hard on the shutters as they peered through to see who was being brought out. They called our names and shouted slogans of support. At that point, we were turned to walk across the entire concourse. It was strangely void of members of the public, but many staff members had gathered and stood around in small groups. We were frogmarched past our colleagues who were members of SIPTU and the NBRU, and they applauded us and also called out slogans of encouragement. At this point, my arresting garda was telling me that the gardaí had troubles in their employment too, and he respected what we were involved in but he had a job to do. I responded that I respected his position.

By this time, we were walking up the long platform number 2 in Heuston Station. I could see our transport vehicle at the end of the platform. This was the old police 'paddy wagon'. None of the new gleaming Ford transits for us! That luxury was reserved for the sophisticates of the criminal underworld on their way to Ireland's finest prison facilities. We — tax-paying, law-abiding train drivers — were to get a spin in an old, black paddy wagon with its internal cells. I was getting near it now and, as the last in the line, I could see the lads entering it. Then on my right, I saw two staff members whom I knew. Both were senior staff members — one a ticket checker and one a train guard. They greeted me and one of them grabbed my hand and shook it, saying, 'Fair play to you, Brendan. It's a disgrace what's being done.' I appreciated the support as, to be honest, I was struggling a bit to keep my feelings and emotions in check. I was then at the paddy wagon. At the door was a really tough-looking cop made for this job. He was short, bald and built like a horse. He greeted me roughly, and pushed me into the back of the van. I got the feeling that there would be no apologies or regrets from this guy!

As I entered, the smell of urine hit me immediately. It was rotten. I looked down a dark, narrow corridor with 'cells' on either side. The lads who were already in called, 'Who's that?' As I said my name, they all banged their fists on their doors and shouted, 'Good man, Brendan'. I was put into my cell and locked in. It was tiny — about 2 foot square with no window and a stench of piss. Charlie had somehow managed to get behind me and was now entering the wagon. Someone called, 'Who's that?' When the response came, 'Charlie', we all shouted, 'Good man, Charlie', and banged on our doors in unison. Then the back door shut, and the sirens sounded. We all chatted and shouted to each other as we sped through Dublin, incarcerated in this mobile prison from hell. It felt like we were in there for ages but it was really only for minutes. We had come to a sudden stop, the doors flew open, the sirens went silent, and we were ushered out into a police yard. I didn't know where we were but it transpired that we were at Kevin Street station. As one of the last in the van, I was now one of the first out. I was escorted into the station and we all formed a line to be processed. One by one, our names and details were taken. We were then moved into a room with two gardaí. They asked us to empty our pockets, and they searched us. Then they put us into a big communal cell. One by one, the room filled up with our members. We were in high spirits — running on adrenalin, I suppose. We could also now see outside. Across the yard, a crowd had gathered at the gate. We recognised some of the faces as they waved and, in time, we saw the media, including television cameras, arriving.

I can't be sure how long we were kept there — perhaps a few hours. In the end, we were released and told that, if we attempted to re-enter the boardroom at Heuston, we would be arrested again and taken straight to a special court sitting. I didn't know what to do. We all gathered on the station steps and walked towards the gate together. We were escorted by two gardaí. It was a beautiful balmy night. I was in short sleeves. As we got to the gates, cameras flashed, and journalists shouted out their questions. I did a fairly lengthy interview with RTÉ and Padraig Yeates of *The Irish Times*. None of us knew what to do next. Instinctively, we walked back to Heuston. When we arrived, the gardaí were present in transit vans, watching our every move, but friendly at all times. In any event, we had no way of getting back into the boardroom as the station had been locked up and the boardroom was on the first floor. We all agreed to go home and consider the night's events in the morning. The Dublin lads offered accommodation to their country cousins, and I drove over to Martin King's house, stopping for fish and chips on the way. After the food, we enjoyed a whiskey or two, and I went to bed. Shattered. Major assessments would have to wait until the following day.

The End

If the hopelessness of our situation had not fully dawned on me prior to now, it did on Thursday, 24 August. This was the toughest day I personally had during the dispute. There was no specific media pressure or event. Certainly there was nothing on the scale of some of the more significant media events of recent days and weeks. On this day, the problems were in my head. The events of the previous day had seen the state abuse a piece of legislation never intended for use against trade unionists. Moreover, our clear legal right to protest at the place of our employer during a trade dispute had been ignored completely by the gardaí. To this day, I believe that a political decision was taken to end our sit-in protest before it got up a head of steam. One thing is clear: we were breaking no laws in protesting peacefully in the CIÉ boardroom. Iarnród Éireann's lie to the media that we would be left there as long as we wished was simply a smokescreen to ensure that the media were not present when the police moved in. As if all the forces ranged against us over the previous ten weeks had not been enough, now the civic power was also to be used as a political tool to smash ILDA.

As the day wore on, I reflected on this, on our members' financial position, and on the apparent impossibility of gaining any further concessions through mediators. Could we hold our members for another week — an eleventh week — and, if we did, what hope could we now offer to sustain them during that week, or indeed any longer? I spent most of the day in Dublin, thinking, and talking to our most senior officers. I was still very reluctant to consider going back to work while we were responsible for lunacies such as part-time drivers. But what were we to do? What options had we? The more I thought about it, the more I knew that it was over. I knew from soundings in the various depots that the numbers of ILDA members who would return to work the following week would far outnumber the total who had gone back on the previous nine Mondays combined. I had also given assurances to one or two of them that if we waited another week and nothing materialised, we would go back together. In that single week, Fergus Finlay's and Phil Flynn's best efforts had come to nothing; our sit-in protest had been improperly stopped; and our president had suffered a heart attack. It was a savage price to pay for defending our rights as employees.

In mid-afternoon, I called Pauline at work. We had convened a general meeting of our members for the following day, Friday, 27 August, in Dublin. I told Pauline that I was going to recommend that our members return to work, but that I personally would resign my position with the company and with ILDA. At that moment, I couldn't see how I could again work with the people who had treated us in this way. In addition to the difficulties all of our members had faced, I had also been publicly vilified by my employer. It was a difficult telephone conversation — an emotional one. By the end of it, I was falling to bits for the first time during the dispute. But what I was saying to her, to myself, was not logic but emotion. Brian and Finbarr looked at me, wondering what was going on. Padraig Yeates called me in the middle of this critical self-analysis, poking around in the Flynn/Finlay initiative and telling me that Mary O'Rourke was denying any knowledge of it. I wasn't in the mood for this. By late afternoon, we had decided to drive home to Athlone and prepare for our meeting the following day. I kept my thoughts to myself, arrived in Athlone and went for a few pints with Finbarr, Dessie, Thomas and Tom O'Brien. As the evening wore on, I became more settled in my mind. I had done nothing wrong. I had led this dispute from the front, and at no time had I been dishonest or had I hidden from my responsibilities. I had nothing to be ashamed about and indeed I had much to be proud of. But it was over as far as I was concerned, and tomorrow I would address our members and tell them that. They would expect nothing less, and they deserved nothing less of me. By the time my head hit the pillow — my own pillow for one of the few times in those ten weeks — my mind was clear, and I was almost looking forward to the next day's meeting. I even had an idea about how we could go back to work without shouldering responsibility for unsafe elements of the agreement. It was time for others to take the strain in this fight. Our members had done all they could to maintain a safe railway and protect their conditions. Now others could take up the task, or someone else would pay the price.

Perhaps I should have let Finbarr in on my thoughts that Thursday evening. In the event, I told him the conclusion I had reached as we were driving up to the meeting. It was a peculiar drive. The media wanted to know what course of action we were going to pursue next. It was bizarre that on this occasion the idea that we might actually go back to work didn't seem to dawn on any of them. For ten weeks, Iarnród Éireann and commentators had been predicting that ILDA would fall apart at any time. They had always been wrong. Now the idea that we might actually return together — still united but effectively starved into some sort of submission — was one that seemed to be in the minds of ILDA members only. By the time we reached Kinnegad, Finbarr had accepted the logic of what I was saying. But he was now going through the emotions that had hit me the previous afternoon; he told me that he would not go back himself. I argued that as we had led our members out, led them for ten weeks, in the interests of unity, it fell on us now to lead them back. We were obliged to do so and, in doing so, we would lift the burden on every member when the awful moment came. How could we allow them to go back without us? How could we abandon them at this stage, and how could we stay out while ILDA split down the middle? It was up to us to lead. I called Fergus Finlay, and told him of our decision. I told him my plans for the day and asked him how I might present them to best effect. He thought the scenario that I outlined to him was excellent and couldn't be improved upon in the circumstances. And then he told me what I already knew. He told me that there would be only one question that many in the media would ask — would Brendan Ogle be returning to work too? I told him that I would, but that I was going to have a problem eating humble pie. I remember his reply still: 'Brendan, there is only one good thing about eating humble pie — you get the chance to shit it out again soon afterwards!'

As usual, the media were at the Aisling Hotel for our meeting. I gave no indicator as to my thoughts when entering the meeting. As the media left the room, a difficult few hours began. Some members argued, some agreed, some shouted, some appealed, some cried — literally — and all present wrestled with the conflict tearing their hearts from their bodies. In time, however, the two characteristics that had maintained ILDA intact through all of this madness came to the fore. Logic and the need to maintain unity won the day.

At lunchtime, I went outside to greet the media, and I told them that the meeting had been adjourned and that it would reconvene at the joint offices of the Labour Court and the Labour Relations Commission in the afternoon. The pundits were baffled. Had we been invited to talks? Were we going to stage a sit-in at the offices of these two agencies akin to the Heuston Station one? I wouldn't say anything more and, when they called the Labour Court and the LRC, they were told that those bodies knew nothing of our plans either.

We had agreed to meet outside Lansdowne Road DART station and to march to the Labour Court and LRC as we had in the early weeks of this dispute. I called the Garda Síochána and arranged an escort without difficulty. Most of our members went for lunch in the hotel and they all resisted the temptation to tell the media what we were up to. By now, the lunchtime news shows were speculating as to what was going on. ILDA had been involved in so much for so long that nobody could predict what we had up our sleeves on this occasion. We assembled at the agreed location and began our march. Photographers were running alongside us on the roadway, and interviews were taking place, but still only ILDA members knew what was happening — and we weren't telling, yet. As we turned into the grounds of the Labour Court and LRC, there was a large police presence throughout the area. It was obvious that they were prepared for some type of trouble, but as with all events in which ILDA members had been involved throughout the dispute, they needn't have worried. We climbed the steps and I entered the building with Finbarr Masterson and John Courtney who was standing in for the stricken Christy as president. The media waited outside, alongside our members, watching events through the glass-panel windows. In full view of them all, I went up to the reception desk and asked for the Chairman of the Court and the Chief Executive of the Commission. I didn't even know if they would be present but suspected that, in the circumstances, they would be. In a very short period of time, they emerged, together. Finbarr Flood greeted us warmly, offering a firm handshake. Kieran Mulvey was less warm in his greeting.

The statement that our members had agreed that morning was then read in full to both men and presented to them with safety documents. The statement began:

ILDA SGM PASSES RESPONSIBILITY FOR RAIL SAFETY TO LRC/LABOUR COURT
ILDA members met today, 25 August 2000, at the end of the tenth

week of this most unnecessary dispute.

ILDA members have raised and carried the issue of rail safety at the cost of their own wages for the past ten weeks. We have invested 1,000 weeks' wages in trying to make safety the focus of rail transport in Ireland. We have tried consistently to raise safety issues of the 'New Deal' with our employer, Iarnród Éireann, who has responded by locking us out unless we work an agreement that we believe to be inherently unsafe. We have protested, demonstrated, lobbied, and on numerous occasions tried to explain, in our own words and those of safety expert PG Rayner, the serious safety concerns that caused more than 100 train drivers to refuse to work an unsafe agreement.

The statement went on to outline our attempts over the previous weeks to pursue the issue of the unsafe nature of aspects of the 'New Deal', and to criticise those who had apparently joined forces to oppose us, whether through condemnation or ignoring of means to resolve the dispute. It emphasised that ILDA had not been crushed by this opposition, but that we were 'united, determined and organized in such a manner that we will never be crushed. We have brought Trade Union principles to life again in the railway.'

We stated that we had welcomed the LRC/Labour Court intervention despite concerns about its statutory basis, and that our members had voted unanimously in support of it, while restating their safety concerns, continuing: 'A further initiative intended to address the safety concerns and allow us return to work met with further silence. We protested and were arrested.'

The statement laid the responsibility for safety firmly at the door of the shareholder and management, and said that we, the drivers, refused to carry the burden of it any longer. We would therefore:

return to work on Monday next August 28th at 9 a.m. together. We will be staying together thereafter.... ILDA members will report for work under the LRC/Labour Court expectation and jurisdiction. We will work the disputed agreement under protest and with some relief that rail safety responsibility now passes to the LRC/Labour Court.

Included with the statement were copies of the independent safety reports we had commissioned, and which had formed the basis for our safety position during the dispute, and the statement continued:

> Each week we will provide the LRC/Labour Court with a detailed update of our safety concerns in operation as part of their investigation. We now call on the LRC/Labour Court to expedite their investigation of all issues which gave rise to this dispute. In view of their new and daily responsibility for rail safety, we urge the LRC/Labour Court to commence immediately their investigations into safety aspects of the 'New Deal' and, in the interests of the travelling public and Iarnród Éireann, to report on all matters as quickly as possible.

We urged the Labour Court and LRC to deal with these issues of public safety, and apologised to the travelling public for the disruptions of the previous ten weeks. We also thanked those who had supported us throughout the dispute, and concluded:

> ILDA note assurances from Iarnród Éireann that no victimisation of any Driver will occur. Similar assurances from SIPTU and NBRU do not interest us. The actions of their officials and some members have been quite disgraceful.
>
> Rail safety remains an issue of most serious concern. The LRC/Labour Court is now the custodian of our rail safety concerns. Under their jurisdiction we return to work, 'under protest' and under their stated expectation of us. Submissions on the infringement of our statutory and employment rights will be made to the LRC/Labour Court and within the Iarnród Éireann Grievance Procedures consistent with SI 146/2000.

When we had finished reading the statement, we emerged from the building and gathered our members and the media around us. We read the statement to them, outlining that the work stoppage was over. We then took a number of questions. It was Mark Costigan of Today FM who asked the hard, and obvious, question. Did the statement represent an admission that we had failed? There was no easy answer to that. However, the reality was that the 'New Deal' would now be fully investigated by a unique joint review carried out by the Labour Court and the LRC, aided by independent safety experts from the UK. The undeniable fact is that, if our members had simply capitulated and worked the agreement from the start, that would not have happened.

It remained to be seen what that investigation would bring to bear on events. On that day, however, I just wanted out of there. I think that the media respected that, and we headed off to Jury's Hotel in Ballsbridge for a private gathering. Every member had mixed feelings — pride, relief, and anxiety about going back to work with people, some of whom had behaved disgracefully for the full three months of the dispute, were the dominant feelings. I was interviewed on national radio with Barry Kenny. The interview was balanced. At that moment, we might have felt like the losers, but the stark reality was that all parties were losers, and the losses would continue to be suffered for a considerable time. The only difference with Iarnród Éireann was that it would be the Irish taxpayer and not the managers responsible who would pick up the tab. In a peculiar way, I took satisfaction from the fact that I had lost three months' wages for what I believed in. That is, after all, what the trade union movement was founded upon — workers united, making sacrifices for their common good. That was ILDA summed up in one sentence.

As we drove home, we were all a bit emotional. I had taken a few pints and Finbarr drove. Brian was in the back of the car. I continued to take calls all the way to Athlone from members, family and well-wishers. Two particular calls I received meant a lot. One was from Fine Gael transport spokesman Jim Higgins. He thanked me for my co-operation and availability over the course of the dispute and even congratulated us for the dignified manner in which we had ended the work stoppage. The other was from RTÉ's Peter Cluskey who also thanked me for my availability and co-operation over such a protracted time and wished me well on a personal level as we moved forward. Then on the news we heard an interview with Labour Court Chairman Finbarr Flood. He welcomed our initiative and spoke of his hope that we could now enter a new relationship with the Labour Court, where future difficulties could be avoided. All of these things meant a lot to us because they were things that people didn't have to say at all, but things they chose to say anyway. In other words, they were sincere and they were appreciated as such. Fergus Finlay called to tell us that the ending of the dispute, and the manner of it, was receiving decent coverage across the news media.

I spent the evening with Pauline and our daughter, and the following day, I went down to Pauline's parents' home town of Thurles. That Sunday, in Glasheen's bar, I watched Celtic hammer Rangers 6-2. Things were looking up already!

We were all dreading the return to work. However, in Athlone it wasn't so bad. The ILDA members met outside just before 9 on the fateful day and walked into work together. We were received politely although it wouldn't have taken much to spark off an argument with some of the SIPTU members present. John Keenan called me on my mobile phone to see how things had gone and we spoke affably at length as we had done throughout a lot of the dispute. I told him that I was concerned that I would be singled out or targeted for dismissal. He gave a verbal assurance that that would not happen. Elsewhere our members' experiences were similar. The day passed largely without incident. In Cork, things went particularly well. Our members assembled outside the station and walked towards the door together, where the SIPTU members in Cork had assembled and formed a type of guard of honour. There they applauded our members back into work. SIPTU Cork members are unlike many of the SIPTU members elsewhere. It was they who had placed the first picket in this dispute way back in Week One, they who had ignored all of the pressure to work our trains during the IFI charade, and they who were at the meeting from which Des Geraghty had fled back to Dublin, with his tail very much between his legs. And now it was they who went the extra mile to make the return to work of our members in Cork as painless as possible. Gentlemen, every one of them.

Why the Delay in Accepting the Labour Court/LRC Initiative?

One exception to the media coverage on the day we returned to work had been RTÉ's Eilis Brennan, who asked questions about why we had waited two weeks before accepting the Labour Court/LRC initiative. It was a fair point. However, the questions she posed totally missed the point regarding the nature of the stoppage. By now, readers will have a sense of the scale of what I call 'the conspiracy' against ILDA. For eight weeks, this effectively prevented many parties from offering a solution to the dispute. In that time, however, many well-meaning public figures did offer their services to help. They were so numerous that it would be difficult to mention them all here. Indeed, some would not wish to be mentioned. However, they included the following: Tom Darby — NBRU founder and former General Secretary; the Catholic and Church of Ireland Bishops of Cork; the Lord Mayor of Cork; John Mulvihill — Chairman of Cork County Council; Jim O'Keefe TD; the Killarney Rail Action Group (KRAG).

On each occasion, ILDA accepted the offers of help from each of those named, and others. On each occasion, Iarnród Éireann refused to co-operate with initiatives. And then in Week Eight — less than twenty-four hours after ILDA had received tremendous support from workers in Dublin Bus, bringing increased mayhem to the already grid-locked streets of our capital — we had the first intervention from the state agencies charged by statute with assisting in difficulties such as ours. Even then they did not contact us directly, and provided scant information to ILDA in the following days. We felt entitled to take a somewhat cynical view of their actions and timing, and, initially, we did.

However, that is but the tip of the iceberg and only begins to explain the two-week 'delay'. The truth is, we never believed that the Labour Court/LRC initiative would be worth anything to us in industrial relations terms — even when we decided to end the dispute. How could it be with the LRC unnecessarily appended to it to ensure that the deal brokered wasn't ripped apart as it ought to have been? And we were right. When the report was finally issued, it was, in industrial relations terms, worthless to ILDA. Remove from it all the executive summaries, bluff and bluster, spin and counter-spin, and there you have it — a puff of smoke that condemned Iarnród Éireann for suing us and not much else. It told us to go back to SIPTU and the NBRU, and advised that if we needed help in doing that, the ICTU should help us. For four years, the ICTU had had an opportunity to help, and had chosen not to.

We did hope that the external safety review might be conducted properly, and it was. It found for us on three of our four major safety concerns, including ruling out part-timers driving our trains. It didn't disagree with us on the fourth either. The LRC, predictably, stuck the safety report in the back of the booklet and generally failed to draw any attention to the key safety concerns we had that Sedgwick Wharf found to be valid. The next time you are on a 300-tonne train, with 800 other mortals, hurtling along at 100 mph, you can rest assured that it won't be driven by a part-timer who was checking tickets yesterday, shunting the day before, and sweeping platforms the day before that. It cost us ten weeks' wages, but your safety matters to us — and ours does too!

To return to the delay, however, while the Labour Court and the LRC were waiting to see if we would get support in Dublin, Fergus Finlay was working with ILDA on an initiative to end the dispute, while his friend, Phil Flynn, was dealing with Minister O'Rourke and the Chairman of CIÉ. We were assured that progress was being made, and a final draft was all but agreed. I was talking to our members, preparing them for some of the concepts contained in the letter, some of which would be unpalatable to them. At that time, this Finlay/Flynn initiative was 'the only game in town', and it looked like delivering.

Moreover, the simple fact is that our members were not ready to go back to work on 10 August. They were still fighting and would not have accepted a return to work on the basis outlined, as shown in the results of our secret ballot at the time.

Over two weeks later, it was different. So much had happened in that two-week period. The CIÉ letter didn't materialise now that the 'unique joint initiative' was on the table. In addition, our members had gone from eight weeks without wages to ten weeks without wages. They were now ready to go back. Skint might be the word I'm looking for here. Those who weren't finished yet had been in Heuston Station with me and had seen a state abuse of a piece of public-order legislation to crush a trade dispute.

And finally, crucially, the man who on 10 August was ILDA's President was in hospital by 25 August, having suffered a heart attack. In summary, on 25 August, circumstances dictated that it was over, but that could not have been said two weeks before. If anyone had asked me to outline all that on that most difficult of days, I would have told them. They didn't.

There is one final point that rankles. Fergus Finlay is a friend. He never at any time believed in breakaway unions, and he still doesn't. He was not responsible for ILDA and was only ever a peripheral figure. But he was a peripheral figure who knew us, and knew me. And he knew enough to know that the company portrayal of us was wrong, and that much of the media portrayal of us was also wrong, and that our issues were, in fact, worthy of serious consideration. When things went wrong and when everybody else who could have helped sat on their hands, he did what friends do — he tried to help. We left Killarney on Wednesday, 9 August, and drove to Dublin to meet with Fergus Finlay to discuss his initiative — the CIÉ letter. It was a long meeting that continued into the night at his home. The LRC/Labour Court intervention had not occurred at that time. None of us knew that it was imminent. The following day, while I was meeting Justine McCarthy, Fergus was working on his initiative. The other people who, we were told, were parties to this initiative were Minister O'Rourke and the CIÉ Chairman, John Lynch. It was all in process before the Labour Court/LRC initiative was announced. Here, however, is a piece of text from the Labour Court/LRC report into the dispute (published on 18 December 2000). It is included under the heading 'Attempts at mediation':

> A variety of individuals and organisations offered to assist in finding a basis for the resolution of the dispute. Many of those who offered had no connection with or experience in industrial relations matters. Later in the dispute a prominent person [Fergus Finlay], described by the ILDA as a friend of its Executive Secretary [me] became involved in providing assistance to that organisation. It appears that through this source some indirect communication was established with senior management of the C.I.E. group. Some initiative was canvassed through this contact but again nothing materialised. This latter involvement occurred in the period after 17 August 2000 when the Court and the Commission announced their offer to engage in the present investigation provided the drivers resumed work under the terms of the 'New Deal' agreement. There can be little doubt that these interventions kept open in the minds of ILDA members the unrealistic possibility that a solution could be found through unofficial channels and on terms other than those laid down. Undoubtedly this delayed the acceptance on their part that the dispute could only be resolved through the formal channels. In the view of the Court and the Commission there can be little doubt that this had the effect of prolonging the dispute unnecessarily.

In other words, the Labour Court and the Labour Relations Commission — who did nothing but ignore their statutory obligations for a full eight weeks — were actually laying the blame for prolonging the dispute at the door of those who had tried to fill that unnecessary void! It should also be noted that the Labour Court and LRC intervened on 10 August 2000, not 17 August as their own report wrongly states (another 'administrative error', perhaps). In fact, the Finlay/Flynn initiative did not occur after the Labour Court/LRC initiative, but before it, and it is oversimplistic to say that 'nothing materialised'. The letter simply needed the signature of the CIÉ Chairman to end the dispute. What was objectionable in that letter to any other party? Why was it not signed? And how can we or Fergus Finlay be blamed for John Lynch's failure to sign it?

If the court, and more particularly the LRC, had been as interested from the outset in solving the dispute as they were after it in apportioning blame to those who tried to help, much of the difficulty could have been avoided in the first place. ILDA, Iarnród Éireann, SIPTU and the NBRU aren't the only ones who need to learn lessons from their failures in the summer of 2000.

A GOOD MAN DONE BAD

There remain a few areas of the ILDA story yet to be told before I conclude. Firstly, there is the Supreme Court appeal of our recognition claim to be an 'excepted body'. There is also the decision of ILDA members to join with the ATGWU, and the deposing of that union's Irish colossus, Mick O'Reilly, taking us up to the present day.

However, first there are a few loose ends. As the clock moved forward from the seismic events of the summer of 2000, it appeared that many in Iarnród Éireann were unable to do likewise. Individual personal relationships between ILDA members and some members of SIPTU and the NBRU were terribly damaged by events. Throughout the dispute, we were often unaware of exactly what trains other working drivers had been driving. Some had blatantly done our work, and openly flaunted their behaviour. Others had performed their own duties only and had steadfastly declined each management effort to induce them to drive trains that would otherwise have been driven by ILDA members. And then there were others who liked us to believe that they had done nothing other than their own work but who had, in fact, done quite a bit more besides. When we returned to work, however, there was no shortage of people prepared to tell us everything. It transpired that there had been a lot less principle and a lot more scabbing than we would have liked, and those actions, and our knowledge of them, didn't help the 'healing process'.

In addition, the work environment to which we returned was different from the one that had been promised. For ten weeks, we had been told that we should return to 'enjoy the benefits of the "New Deal"'. Foremost among these 'benefits' was a five-day week — like most other workers in this country. However, when we returned, we discovered that not alone were our members required to work conditions they didn't agree for five days a week, but they were actually still required to work six- and seven-day weeks. Nothing had changed at all. Some members were quite prepared to work the extra days. They saw it as a way of clearing debts that had accumulated during the dispute. Others though — myself included, and the majority of the executive — took the view that they had been told throughout the dispute how wonderful this five-day week was, and that is what they now wanted. They refused to work any rest days whatsoever. ILDA needed to adopt a policy that suited all of our members, and we did so. Rest-day working would be voluntary as far as ILDA was concerned. If you wanted to work rest days, that was your choice; but if you wanted to 'enjoy the benefits' of the promised five-day week, that was your right also. Iarnród Éireann, however, disagreed.

Many of our members found themselves rostered to work rest days that they didn't want to work. When they didn't show up, they were disciplined and actually threatened with the sack. It made no sense. Iarnród Éireann referred to the need to provide a service seven days a week, seemingly oblivious to the fact that this latest crisis had been created through their own foolishness in introducing a deal that they didn't have the staff to implement. They also failed to answer one simple question — how would sacking a man who would drive trains five days a week help to provide a service seven days a week? In the event, the Labour Court decided the issue. In a case that became a test case, in the name of an ILDA member, the Labour Court decided that our members should work rest days where they were 'reasonably available to do so'. That seemed entirely logical and suited us fine. Where our members were 'reasonably available', they worked rest days, and where they were not 'reasonably available', they didn't. Nobody was sacked and many enjoyed their rest days while watching with a mixture of amusement and derision as some of the most vocal SIPTU and NBRU members during the dispute — people who had spent weeks lecturing us about how great it was to have time off — worked every rest day they could.

Another bone of contention for us was Iarnród Éireann's refusal to pay the loss-of-earnings payments owed to our members if those members declined to work all the rest days the company wanted.

I became very familiar with the Labour Court. As Iarnród Éireann managers flexed their muscles, we referred case after case to the Labour Court. Despite our lack of recognition, we used every piece of legislation available to us. We studied the various acts, statutory instruments, codes of practice and procedures, and became adept in their use. In particular, case after case was referred to the Labour Court under section 20(1) of the Industrial Relations Act 1969. 'Section 20s', as they are known, are generally not favoured by trade union officials, because they provide direct access to the court without any prior conciliation or discussion. In addition, they are binding only on the person referring the case, although it is unlikely that Iarnród Éireann would get away in civil law with acting against a worker who had been supported by a Labour Court recommendation. For that reason, companies tend to implement court recommendations whether binding in the strictest sense or not. In the case of ILDA, we had no access to the internal processes that often resolve issues before they even become issues, and we certainly couldn't rely on help from the LRC. On occasion, the Rights Commissioners helped with certain defined issues, but generally it was a 'section 20' or nothing. Each case was for high stakes with — uniquely in Iarnród Éireann — our members' jobs often dependent on the outcome. So this high-wire style of industrial relations was often the only avenue our members had to third-party assistance. Given the stakes, it was therefore important that we won the argument on whatever questions came before the Labour Court, and in 90 per cent of the cases argued, we did. It was quite a strike rate, but each detailed submission had to be written by me, and the work involved was colossal. It is all part of a day's work for paid union officials, but for me it was a real chore, eating into time that I would otherwise have spent doing other things.

On 25 August 2000, Iarnród Éireann had issued a news release — one of many similar statements issued during the course of the dispute — stating that ILDA drivers would be welcomed back to work and 'would not face victimisation of any kind from the company'. Overall, however, Iarnród Éireann did not honour that very public commitment. For example, a member of SIPTU was guilty of speeding by 15 to 20 miles per hour on at least five occasions but was still driving locomotives afterwards. However, a decision was taken to sack an ILDA member accused of speeding by just 4 miles an hour, on a class of locomotive — 201 class — that has defective speedometers. Another member of the recognised trade unions broke a set of level-crossing gates and was back up driving the next day. An ILDA member in Inchicore has been removed from mainline driving duties for over three years now, having broken a similar set of gates outside Waterford. Since 2000, Iarnród Éireann has issued decisions that three ILDA members be sacked for various offences. In that timeframe, no driver member of the recognised trade unions — a majority of drivers — has been sacked. The following example should be enough to portray the true picture.

Iarnród Éireann workers are located in so many different areas that often it is impossible to have on-site leisure or recreation facilities. However, in recent years, the company has entered into agreements with organisations providing these services to the wider community, whereby employees can use facilities in leisure centres at reduced rates that are deducted from their wages. Not long after our return to work, management displayed a notice in the drivers' rest room in Inchicore, seeking names of employees interested in using a gymnasium and sauna at a north Dublin leisure centre. Two ILDA members applied. When they didn't hear anything back from the centre, one of them called, only to be told that his application for the gymnasium had been 'rejected'. He was stunned, but discovered the following day that his fellow ILDA member was in the same position. All other applicant employees, however, had been accepted. When both ILDA members confronted the gymnasium about their rejected applications, an embarrassed manager told him that they had been excluded from the scheme by management. The reason? Their membership of ILDA. That was in 2000. Then in the summer of 2002, the same thing happened in Westport. Sixteen employees joined the local scheme and two of them were ILDA members. A short time later, both received phone calls from the stationmaster in Westport, outlining that they were excluded from the scheme as a result of their membership of ILDA. When they sought confirmation of this in writing, letters were willingly supplied, stating that this facility was not available to members of ILDA. The scheme subsequently collapsed through lack of numbers.

The Supreme Court Appeal

Our Supreme Court appeal of the recognition issue couldn't come quickly enough. In November 2000 — three months after the end of the dispute — our appeal was considered by the highest court in the land. The stakes were very high and, after all the events that had gone before, my biggest concern was whether or not our case would get a fair hearing. After all, if the Supreme Court now found that ILDA had been entitled to be recognised as an excepted body and negotiated with under the terms of section 55 of the Railways Act 1924, where did that leave Iarnród Éireann? Where did it leave the 'New Deal'? Why had there been an unnecessary three month lock-out, and how would Iarnród Éireann pay for its decision to press ahead the work changes, with such disastrous effects, before the Supreme Court had had a chance to adjudicate on recognition? We would certainly be demanding costs, loss and damage from our employer, and others, if that new scenario emerged, and that would be in addition to, and separate from, the incredible impact that such a decision would have on industrial relations within the company. Would the Supreme Court make a decision that provided for such an amazing, and costly, outcome?

Before the appeal, our legal team explained to us some of the workings of the Supreme Court. The court is made up of up to seven sitting judges in any given case. Each judge may make their own decision and issue their own separate judgment, and the case can be decided by either a majority decision or a unanimous verdict of the sitting justices. In our case, we had five sitting judges. They were Mr Justice Fennelly, Mr Justice Murphy, Mr Justice Murray, Ms Justice Denham and Ms Justice McGuinness. The Supreme Court is situated in the very centre of Dublin's main Four Courts building. It is a single, large building that many walk past without ever knowing that the country's highest court is sitting just yards away. Our appeal hearing lasted two days, and Brian Dunphy, Finbarr Masterson and I sat through the case in its entirety. Other ILDA members popped in and out at different times also. Although the protagonists were the same as they had been in the High Court, the issue in dispute was now much more confined. Having initially threatened to appeal the decision of the High Court that the eleven individual ILDA members had not been responsible in law for conspiracy to cause service disruptions in Athlone and Cork in July 1999, Iarnród Éireann had eventually decided to save itself further embarrassment and accept that element of the High Court judgment. Therefore, the issue before the Supreme Court was our appeal of the High Court declaration that 'Iarnród Éireann cannot lawfully conduct negotiations for the fixing of pay, hours of duty and other conditions of service of locomotive drivers'. We wanted the Supreme Court to confirm that:

- ILDA was a trade union registered under the Trade Union Act 1871
- ILDA was an excepted body within the meaning of the Trade Union Act 1941
- ILDA was a trade union representative of railway employees within the meaning of section 55 of the Railways Act 1924.

We also wanted:

a declaration that the plaintiff (Iarnród Éireann) is required to reach agreement with the Irish Locomotive Drivers Association together with other Trade Unions representative of railway employees within the meaning of Section 55 of the Railways Act 1924 in order to amend the agreement relating to rates of pay, hours of duty and other conditions of service of locomotive drivers, made about the month of May 1994 with the Trade Unions representative of such railway employees.

In other words, we wanted the Supreme Court to render the 'New Deal' null and void!

We found the Supreme Court to be a very different place from the High Court. For two days, all five judges effectively debated the arguments put and points of law at issue with counsel for both sides. The debate was intense and fascinating throughout. It was open, transparent and direct, and could be viewed by any citizen entering the courtroom. At times, the argument would swing one way, only for it apparently to swing back to the other side minutes later. Complex legislation was discussed and debated, line by line, as each point at issue arose. For much of the two days, we thought we had it in the bag. The reasoning of the High Court judgment was ripped apart by Ireland's most senior judges. It became clear that they didn't agree that our old rule 5, which had theoretically allowed membership of ILDA to those employed in companies other than Iarnród Éireann, was enough to deny us 'excepted body' status. All of Mr Justice O'Neill's reasoning on the excepted body issue had been based on rule 5, and it was clear to us during the hearing that the Supreme Court didn't support his view on that key issue. Although we had subsequently changed this rule, it was the rules as considered by the High Court that were under appeal, which meant that our much-talked-about rule change after the High Court had been unnecessary and academic. Nevertheless, we were pleased to see that the Supreme Court did not support the view of the High Court on this matter.

Similarly, one by one, each tenet of Iarnród Éireann's case seemed to fall away before our eyes. As Peter Charleton argued that we were bound by contract to be members of either SIPTU or the NBRU, Mr Justice Fennelly retorted that surely such a contractual compulsion would be unconstitutional and that the constitutional right of each citizen to associate, and disassociate, in any organisation or trade union had been well tested and proven. Next up was Iarnród Éireann's argument that agreements reached under section 55 of the Railways Act 1924 were binding on all employees, and therefore ILDA 'could not satisfy the statutory condition that they negotiate on behalf of no other employees'. That didn't seem to hold water either. We simply wanted to negotiate for ILDA members. It was not for us to decide the binding nature, or otherwise, of what we might negotiate. Put simply, this argument was stretching logic and the English language beyond its elasticity. We weren't going to lose on that one either. And then what we thought was another key moment arrived. Peter Charleton had seen each of his arguments challenged, one by one, by one judge or another, very often with others nodding or offering their assent. He was left with the argument that it would be extraordinary if all of the collective negotiations in the state's rail company were to be regulated by a narrow section of legislation dating back to 1924. Surely that couldn't be right? As Mr Justice Murphy responded that, extraordinary or not, it did appear that section 55 of the Railways Act 1924 did provide for a resolution to this problem and a statutory basis for recognition of ILDA, I almost stood up in the court and cheered. Brian and Finbarr also thought that that was it. Didn't this mean that we were covered by section 55? Certainly if we were a union holding a negotiating licence, or an excepted body, we were covered. We weren't the holders of a negotiating licence, but all of Iarnród Éireann's arguments that we were not an excepted body seemed to have been demolished before our eyes. Did this mean we had it?

Then something truly extraordinary happened. Mr Justice Murphy asked Peter Charleton what import he put on the words 'carries on negotiations for fixing wages…' in the definition of an excepted body contained in the Trade Union Act 1941. Peter Charleton said that he put no import on that wording whatsoever, and looked at the judge as if he didn't know what he was talking about. Mr Justice Murphy then asked whether it was a fact that ILDA was not 'carrying on' negotiations and whether this meant that we could not be an 'excepted body' until negotiations had begun, which patently they had not. Peter Charleton — counsel for Iarnród Éireann — seemed to think this was some kind of trap, and initially refused to take the bait. He began to argue his own points again, but Mr Justice Murphy persisted. He outlined clearly that he didn't agree with any of Iarnród Éireann's arguments to date but that it seemed to him that this 'carrying on' point held the key for the company. Would the company not make that argument? I couldn't believe my ears. Here we were sitting in the Supreme Court, listening to a justice tell Iarnród Éireann how to win the case. This was truly bizarre. There was no doubt that it was valid practice of the Law. But was it justice? Just as I thought that things couldn't get any worse, the truly unbelievable happened. Mr Justice Murphy formally asked Peter Charleton whether he would like to put that argument to the court. Iarnród Éireann's counsel still declined the offer, but when Mr Justice Murphy persisted, he eventually, almost reluctantly, said that Iarnród Éireann would agree that the phrase 'carries on' held the whole key to the case, and as ILDA didn't 'carry on' negotiations — in the present tense — with Iarnród Éireann, it could not be an excepted body.

We looked at each other totally bemused. As Finbarr whispered to me, 'He's giving it to them', I felt in my heart that the game was over. The best brains the Irish legal system had to offer had finally managed to find, in pages and pages of legislation, two words that they could interpret in the required manner — that is, two words that could keep ILDA out of negotiations and save Iarnród Éireann from a nightmare scenario costing the company millions and condemning to the dustbin its new collective agreements with its pet unions. The only positive thing that can be said about it was that it was open and transparent and happened before our eyes.

John Rogers got to his feet and began our argument. He put forward a powerful case. However, nobody had anticipated the new 'point of law' that Mr Justice Murphy would pluck from the legislation. It was also clear to me that it would be difficult to convince someone that something was wrong when they, in fact, had thought the concept up themselves to begin with. As John Rogers sat down, around lunchtime on the second day of the hearing, and we left the court to await judgment, I think I knew that we had lost it. It wasn't even that Iarnród Éireann had won it — the company's legal team had been given it wrapped up in shiny paper with ribbons on top. Think football match. Think Liverpool v Manchester United in the FA Cup Final. Think of both teams trying so hard to score the winning goal. Thinks of posts being hit, balls being cleared off goal lines, wonderful saves from goalkeepers, and still the teams cannot be split. And then think of the referee taking the ball, walking forward and kicking it into the net to score the winning goal for one team or the other!

At least they didn't take long to put us out of our misery. Christmas and the New Year were quickly followed by a trip to the court for the Supreme Court Judgment, on 25 January 2001. We sat down and awaited a lengthy but inevitable judgment. The five judges came in, and, one by one, they all muttered something about agreeing with Mr Justice Fennelly. Then Mr Justice Fennelly said a few words about his finding that we were not an excepted body, but also amending the High Court declaration. The judges got up and left. It was over in about two minutes. What did this mean? The smiles and handshakes on the other side of the courtroom told us that we had lost, but what of the specifics? What was the significance of the amendment to the High Court declaration? We left the court and were immediately surrounded by journalists. I didn't know what to say, so I said that we would have to consider the judgment in full. Donal Spring emerged and took us to a quiet part of the building. We were soon joined by John Rogers and Cathy Maguire.

In time, a full copy of the judgment appeared and we read it. As we did so, my spirits lifted. This made some sort of sense, even if it was on a purely literal level. And a number of matters were cleared up. As we had suspected, our rule change was superfluous as Mr Justice O'Neill's argument that we couldn't be an excepted body because of rule 5 was judged to be 'ill-founded'. Neither could we now be found to be contractually obliged to be members of SIPTU or the NBRU. The judgment confirmed specifically that 'trade union membership is not compulsory and, although the court was not addressed on the constitutional implications of the interpretation of the section, it can hardly be doubted that it cannot be made so by law'.

This was all a great improvement on the High Court judgment. But then, inevitably and as expected, came the key issue. The Supreme Court found that until we 'carried on' negotiations with Iarnród Éireann, we could not be deemed to be an excepted body. As we didn't hold a negotiating licence or 'carry on' negotiations, we could not be covered by the relevant act or statute. In other words, Iarnród Éireann could decide to deem us an excepted body by beginning negotiations with us, and we would then fall fully within the parameters of section 55 of the Railways Act 1924. If Iarnród Éireann didn't do so, we would need to get a negotiating licence. It was that simple in the end. And logical — in a literal, if not a practical, sense.

The judges were even direct enough to outline explicitly the strange manner in which this decision had been reached. One paragraph reads:

At this point it is important to note that the definition of an excepted body is one which '*carries on* negotiations for fixing wages....' [court's emphasis], whereas, as in this case, it cannot actually carry on such negotiations where the employer refuses to negotiate. No argument based on this point was advanced by the respondents, though it was raised by the Court during the hearing. The Court must, nonetheless, interpret that statute in what it conceives to be the manner required by law and cannot adopt an erroneous interpretation because none of the parties relies on the *correct one* [my emphasis].

Finally, the Supreme Court amended the High Court declaration that claimed that it would be 'unlawful' for Iarnród Éireann to negotiate with ILDA to make it lawful, and simply stated that, as things stood, we were not an excepted body. The fact that every argument put by Iarnród Éireann had failed did not prevent our employer from seeking costs. In the event, no award of costs was made.

As the day progressed, I tried to convey in media interviews the full significance of the judgment and the key legal points decided. As with the High Court, many of the key issues had fallen in our favour. It didn't matter to the pundits though. They thought in terms of winners and losers and, once again, ILDA had lost. I had an altercation on the lunchtime national news with RTÉ's Richard Downes as he wasn't inclined to allow me to go into the full detail of the judgment. He just knew that Iarnród Éireann had 'won' and we had 'lost', so he simply asked whether or not we would now join SIPTU or the NBRU who held negotiating licences. I accepted that ILDA could not now progress independently against a background where Iarnród Éireann would inevitably refuse to designate ILDA an excepted body. The company would rather run the risk of more mayhem than use its newly acquired option to designate us an excepted body.

However, Richard had a point. In order to fall within the terms of the judgment, we would need to ally ourselves to a union holding a negotiating licence, as even if every train driver in Ireland joined us, we could still not reach the 1,000 threshold necessary to procure our own in the conventional manner. Readers will recall that joining ASLEF was not an option as that union did not have a licence either. But there were still more players in the field than SIPTU or the NBRU. They, in fact, chose not to put themselves in the field at all.

Moving On

Given what we had heard in the Supreme Court itself, the judgment and the reasons presented for it didn't come as a major surprise to us. The positive effect of this was that, as soon as the judgment had been issued, we were ready to assess what we needed to do to move our position on. Theoretically, there were two possibilities. However, as Iarnród Éireann was not about to exercise the option of designating ILDA an excepted body, in practice there was only one option. ILDA members had to be represented in any further collective agreements affecting train drivers and we believed that the Supreme Court did not leave it open to Iarnród

Éireann to conclude further such agreements that excluded representation for our members if we had a negotiating licence. Therefore, ILDA now needed to move on from being an independent separate entity seeking recognition, to being part of a wider organisation or movement that was fully licensed and covered by all relevant legislation, particularly the relevant provisions of the Railways Act 1924.

We decided to enter into that process with as open a mind as possible. That included entering talks with our adversaries in SIPTU and the NBRU, as well as with any other unions who would be interested in representing our members. Indeed, we went further. The Labour Court/LRC report had pointed to the ICTU as a body from whom we should seek help in trying to resolve the representation issue. And so we swallowed our pride and contacted ICTU. It was a big thing for ILDA to do. ICTU's failure for four years to honour a commitment to deal with our problems relating to 1994 had contributed to the situation that had led to ILDA's being formed. Then we received more documentation under the Freedom of Information Act. A note from one senior civil servant to another, dated 2 May 2000, let another ICTU cat out of the bag. It told us:

> Mr. Peter Rigney of ICTU asked on 10 April that we amend section 55 of the Railway Act 1924 by adding 'with a negotiating licence' after trade union....

This was in light of the High Court judgment in our case. ICTU had formally requested that the law be changed to prevent a group of Irish workers and trade unionists from achieving representation with their employer. And the Labour Court/LRC thought that ICTU could help us!

Anyway, we met them on Friday 19 January 2001. The meeting took place in their Parnell Square headquarters, and ICTU was represented by Assistant General Secretary Tom Wall, Hugh Geraghty of the ICTU/CIÉ group of unions and Peter Rigney himself. I went along with John Courtney, Finbarr Masterson and Brian Dunphy. At the outset, we raised the subject of our disappointment with ICTU's past actions. However, the ICTU representatives thought that it would not be helpful to go into those matters at the meeting. The meeting lasted about an hour and was tense, but businesslike. We outlined — to the surprise of the ICTU representatives — that we were prepared to enter into discussions with any trade union in seeking representation of our members, and that this included the NBRU and SIPTU. We told them that we had already begun talks with two other unions but we asked them to facilitate a talks process with SIPTU and the NBRU, and we laid down just one condition. The talks would be about representation of ILDA members as a united group of workers — in other words, all of our members would be joining one union. A ten-week lock-out and a High Court action had not broken ILDA and we weren't about to break now either. ICTU had expected this stipulation and willingly agreed to it. We left, and it was agreed that Tom Wall and I would liaise on details of meetings to follow. However, far from this heralding a new and better relationship between ILDA and ICTU, our problems with ICTU were actually only just beginning.

As had been the case throughout most phases of our progression, John Keenan and I were in close contact on this new ICTU involvement. Indeed, he was co-operating fully and was prepared to facilitate my attendance at any meetings that might be set up — it was clearly in the company's interests that he do so. I had a number of telephone conversations with Tom Wall in the middle weeks of February as he attempted to set up separate meetings between ILDA and ICTU's largest affiliate, SIPTU, and the NBRU. We had scheduled our AGM for 25 February, and we were determined to put any decision that needed to be put to our members at that meeting. In fact, we had first advised ICTU of this position as early as 20 January 2001. Following this, we were advised that ICTU had outlined to SIPTU and the NBRU that it would facilitate separate meetings with ILDA (even though the NBRU is not affiliated to ICTU), and that both unions had 'somewhat reluctantly' accepted that position. But despite this clear understanding, no meetings had taken place by the time of our AGM.

It was as well we weren't simply sitting on our hands and waiting for ICTU's help to move the situation forwards. In fact, we were already in discussions with two other unions about a possible tie-up. The first of these was the AEEU trade union. This is the UK's biggest trade union and also has an active Irish region. It was already recognised by Iarnród Éireann and represented some craft workers in the maintenance area. In addition, it represented all of the locomotive drivers employed by Translink in Northern Ireland. In fact, as far back as the autumn of 1999, Christy Holbrook and I had met with the AEEU's Regional Secretary, Peter Williamson, and some AEEU representatives from the famous Harland and Wolff shipyards in Belfast. It had been a good meeting and it resulted in a further meeting between our executive, Peter Williamson and an AEEU official from London, Michael Murdoch. Events then seemed to take us over and we moved on, but we had been impressed by the people we had met and the trade union ethos they had espoused.

Following the Supreme Court judgment, it now seemed appropriate that we re-institute contact with the AEEU, and we did. By this time, the union had a new official, Brian Gormley, with whom I met on a number of occasions. We then had a further meeting with a large AEEU delegation in the Ballymascanlon Hotel outside Dundalk in the lead-up to our AGM. All of these meetings went well. As it happened, the AEEU had had its own problems with ICTU, having been suspended, later expelled, from ICTU, following a row with the TEEU over the representation of electricians. The AEEU representatives were also fully aware of the possible response of Iarnród Éireann to any request that they extend their member base within Iarnród Éireann to locomotive drivers, and seemed willing and well capable of fighting, and winning, any battle that might lie ahead. Overall, it seemed that, at our AGM, we would have a position to put to our members regarding the AEEU.

The other union with which we were in discussion was the ATGWU. This was the second largest affiliate of ICTU but, apart from that, there would be several other potential benefits to our members in joining that union. The ATGWU was already recognised by Iarnród Éireann for its representation of craft workers and, under the leadership of Regional Secretary Mick O'Reilly, it had, in recent times, taken strong and principled stands on a wide range of issues, particularly social-partnership agreements. I had first met Mick O'Reilly during the preceding summer lock-out, when a number of elected representatives I had met with advised us at the Buswell's Hotel meeting, and elsewhere, to join the ATGWU in order to achieve recognition. Indeed, it seemed that commentators and legislators alike all felt that the ATGWU seemed like a natural home for ILDA members. While we had got on quite well at the time, the reality was that Mick O'Reilly felt that a tie-up in the middle of a dispute of that nature was always going to be difficult. Although I didn't know it then, Mick O'Reilly had what could most diplomatically be described as a difficult relationship with the London-based ATGWU General Secretary, Bill Morris. Nevertheless, I knew that Mick was privately following with interest developments regarding ILDA. I had met a colleague of his, Denis Rohan, in Athlone, and he always seemed interested in getting ILDA members into the ATGWU. I also knew that Mick had been spotted by an Iarnród Éireann manager outside the Supreme Court on the day we received that judgment. And so it was natural that, when we were conducting any review of how we should move forward, we would revisit the possibility of joining the ATGWU.

Such talks as did take place were positive, but no more so than those with the AEEU. The ATGWU offered to accept our members' individual applications and — as with the AEEU — to form a branch for train drivers, as provided for in its rules. In addition, the rules allowed fundraising for branch activities over and above our subscriptions to the union. This was a key difference from the AEEU whose rules didn't allow for such a measure. ILDA had already held one member conference, in Horse and Jockey, and hoped to hold more; fundraising for such activities was important to us.

By and large, however, there was very little that separated these two unions. Accordingly, both were invited to send an official to address our members at our AGM on 25 February 2001. On 23 February, however, I received a call from a clearly put-out Brian Gormley of the AEEU. The AEEU was in the process of merging with the MSF trade union (who represented management). This was a matter of some concern to Irish members of the AEEU but was favoured strongly by the London leadership. Against that background, Brian told me that Gerry Shanahan — an MSF official — had somehow communicated to the office of the AEEU General Secretary, Ken Jackson, that any decision by the AEEU to accept ILDA members might have implications for the proposed merger. Brian outlined that word had come back down to him, through Peter Williamson, that further progress for ILDA would be impossible until this matter was clarified. Accordingly, the AEEU would be unable to send an official to our AGM two days later.

And so, decision day arrived. Our executive considered the position and, in the afternoon, Mick O'Reilly addressed a meeting of ILDA members in our old haunt in Dublin's Aisling Hotel. When he left, a proposal to ballot our members on joining the ATGWU was put to the meeting and accepted. We would spend a week balloting. In the meantime, Finbarr Masterson and I met with Mick O'Reilly and ATGWU brief Alan Turner. The issue of outstanding legal costs arose, and we met to discuss that and the positive nature of the Supreme Court judgment regarding recognition following any tie-up. We demonstrated to Alan Turner that we had paid IR£65,000 in respect of these costs, and that we would endeavour to pay more if possible (it should be remembered that these costs represented ILDA's own costs only, as no award of costs had ever been made against ILDA to Iarnród Éireann). Moreover, we would be joining whatever union we joined as individuals, and ILDA, at least in the immediate term, would continue to exist as a separate entity.

As ICTU had not assisted us in putting any position to our members at our AGM, it was with some surprise that I received a letter from ICTU, dated 28 February — three days after our meeting — proposing meetings with SIPTU and the NBRU. I believe that it would have been reasonable to tell them where to go. But I didn't. Our members could, in theory, reject the proposal on which they were voting, so all options needed to remain open. Accordingly, I agreed that we would attend meetings with SIPTU and the NBRU. I contacted John Keenan who arranged for a number of our members to be released from duty to attend these meetings. They were scheduled to take place on the morning and afternoon of Saturday 3 March 2001.

However, on Friday afternoon, ICTU's Tom Wall called again. He said that SIPTU and the NBRU insisted on meeting us together or not at all. They didn't even trust each other enough to have separate meetings with us! I made more phone calls to our members and also to John Keenan, who seemed to be as exasperated by this behaviour as we were. In the end, it was no deal. I again outlined to Tom Wall our consistent position that we would meet each separately or not at all. For the record, I outlined our position in a letter to Tom Wall. In the letter, I pointed out that ILDA had, at least since 20 January, been available to meet with any trade union that had a position or proposals to put to us. The letter continued:

> ILDA have been engaged in a process aimed at re-integrating our members into the bargaining structures within Iarnród Éireann as members of an autonomous group representing Locomotive Drivers. Our actions have been fully in accordance with the findings of the Labour Court/LRC in their report into the ongoing rail dispute. Nowhere in the text of that report is the role for ICTU limited to re-integration of our members into the 'authorised trade union structure for the category'. It may well be that an ICTU affiliate representing Locomotive Drivers desires to impose such strictures, but the Labour Court/LRC report clearly does not.

I went on to remind Tom Wall that we had always intended to put our final position to our members at our AGM, and that, although this had been understood by all parties, including ICTU, neither SIPTU nor the NBRU had, by that date, provided any position for consideration by ILDA members. Although no meeting with SIPTU and the NBRU had been proposed by ICTU until three days after our AGM, we had still been prepared to attend. However, now I had been advised that both unions insisted on meeting ILDA together, or not at all, and further that they had no 'definitive or concrete' proposals to bring to such a meeting. Having stated that our members had a constitutional right to choose which trade union they joined, and that they were considering the proposals put to them at the AGM, I said that a statement would be made on 5 March, regarding those proposals. I concluded:

> I wish to thank you, and your colleagues in the ICTU, for your help in reaching this position. I wish to assure you that one of our primary aims is to discuss a basis upon which all unions representing Locomotive Drivers can work together in the interests of the grade, Iarnród Éireann and the travelling public. Any assistance you can give in that regard would be most welcome.

Had our members rejected the opportunity to join the ATGWU, we would have continued to talk to the AEEU and ICTU. In fact, every member who voted — ninety-eight of them — voted to join. On 5 March

2001, we held a press conference in Wynn's Hotel in Dublin where we announced that our members would be joining the ATGWU as individuals, and that the ATGWU would establish a train drivers' branch. Simultaneously, the ATGWU issued a news release welcoming our decision.

The day after we joined the ATGWU, SIPTU, in an act of gross duplicity given its refusal to take the opportunity open to it to make progress with ILDA in the preceding weeks, complained to ICTU about the ATGWU taking us as members, and actually claimed fifty-six ILDA members as its 'members in arrears'.

A New Beginning?

On 5 March, I spent the lunchtime period on news programmes, heralding a new dawn, and the ATGWU link was getting a warm reception from the media personnel to whom I spoke. However, that afternoon, I got a phone call from Peter Cluskey, who told me that he had been talking to Iarnród Éireann and that the company was describing the ATGWU link as a 'stunt'. We had joined Ireland's second largest union, an ICTU affiliate, a licence holder and a union already recognised by Iarnród Éireann. We were now clearly covered by the provisions of the Railways Act 1924, and yet our employer was still playing hardball, even after all that both sides had been through.

Peter Cluskey wanted me to do an interview for that evening's news programmes. His surprise was considerably greater than mine. For weeks, I had been intimately aware that SIPTU and the NBRU were not engaging with ILDA and were, in fact, showing no willingness to represent our members. Moreover, I was aware of the interference that had put a spanner in the works regarding the AEEU. And then something else had happened. Within hours of our statement that we had joined the ATGWU, Mick O'Reilly had received a disturbing phone call from one of his members — an ATGWU shop steward in the CIÉ works in Inchicore. This man had outlined that he would consider leaving the ATGWU because ILDA members were joining. I had suspected Iarnród Éireann's hand immediately. So, Peter Cluskey's call and its contents did not surprise me in the slightest. By the time, I had reached RTÉ, however, I was hearing that officials in Mary O'Rourke's department were not happy with the speed and nature of Iarnród Éireann's response to developments. Apparently, noises were being made and Iarnród Éireann was being urged to consider the possible benefits of this move. It was to be one of Mary O'Rourke's last direct independent involvements in ILDA affairs. Throughout all that was to follow, Taoiseach Bertie Ahern seemed to take personal control of events.

These could have been viewed as mere teething problems in any other circumstances. However, given what had gone before, Iarnród Éireann's approach and the Taoiseach's growing interest seemed to me to be somewhat unusual. There were other factors too of which I was not aware. The complaint to Mick O'Reilly from his shop steward was only the tip of the iceberg. I began to realise that there were difficulties in that union of which I had been hitherto oblivious. In two conversations with Andrew Turner, he had made reference to Mick's difficulties with the General Secretary, Bill Morris. Little pieces about this difficult relationship also started to appear in some press coverage. As time wore on, letters started to arrive from London HQ, seeking explanations from Mick about why he had taken ILDA members in — as if it was unusual for a regional secretary to recruit members to his union. I raised it with Mick and he outlined differences with Bill Morris. However, I didn't understand the full scale of the chasm that existed between the leadership of the Irish region and TGWU HQ. And more particularly, I didn't appreciate how those with knowledge of that chasm would be prepared to exploit it to damage ILDA and ultimately bring the career of Mick O'Reilly crashing to its knees. Mick didn't know these things either. He considered many of those who were about to do him damage to be good colleagues or people with whom he had a good working relationship — friends even. He knows better now.

We began looking for recognition with a series of letters from Mick to Iarnród Éireann. Recognition was flatly denied. We would either have to fight for it or go back to court with our Supreme Court judgment in hand. In the meantime, ICTU was trying to set up meetings to consider SIPTU's complaint, but it was all taking time, and time was something that we didn't have. Weeks after we joined the ATGWU, Iarnród Éireann sacked an ILDA member in Limerick. We would have to move quickly. We looked at the situation tactically. If we went to court to pursue recognition with our new negotiating licence, it could takes months, longer even. Would the union sanction such a course? Would we get an injunction to stop Iarnród Éireann proceeding with any further changes or actions against our members in the meantime? These were judgements we needed to make. It was a course that held great attraction for me. I wanted to drag ICTU's inter-union transfer procedures through the courts and test their constitutionality and their viability in relation to article 11 of the European Convention of Human Rights. On the other hand, we sensed a change within our employment at grassroots level. Despite the posturing of their officials, we knew that most SIPTU and NBRU members now saw no reason to deny representation to their colleagues in ILDA. Moreover, any new dispute would not be a lock-out predicated on disputed work changes that they had accepted, but would be a simple recognition dispute with official pickets. We knew that most Iarnród Éireann workers would not pass official pickets and would support our action. It could be over very quickly indeed. With Iarnród Éireann applying more and more pressure on our members on every issue, from rest day working to more roster changes and disciplinary matters, we decided in all of the circumstances to go for the quick, sharp option — an official strike.

Once our members had voted for strike action, which they did unanimously in the required secret ballot, it fell to the Branch Executive to decide tactics. While the Irish Regional Committee of the ATGWU was endorsing a proposed strike by its new ILDA members, we were planning the most effective means of conducting the action. We had always felt that industrial action should be planned to have the maximum effect on the employer and the minimum effect on members. Workers in dispute need to put the employer on the back foot to force a solution. An employer who is not suffering as a result of a dispute is unlikely to be in much of a hurry to want to settle it. However, this was the first time that ILDA members had been involved in a dispute where we had the luxury of planning tactics — including the timing and nature of the dispute — to suit ourselves.

We decided that the work stoppages would have to take place on working days and not at weekends. This was not a dispute where we were simply seeking, by some token action, to send a message to our employer regarding our strength or frustration. Iarnród Éireann already knew all about our frustrations and our strength. This was a recognition dispute that would have to be won and lost, and where no punches would be pulled. It was decided that a series of one-day stoppages on working days, beginning in May 2001, would be best. Many of our members were still feeling the financial repercussions of the previous summer's industrial carnage, so an all-out dispute was out of the question. However, we were also conscious that single-day stoppages each week might not have had the desired impact to bring things to a head quickly, and six days between stoppages would give management a lot of time to recover and plan between actions. And so we decided on a series of rolling one-day stoppages, affecting different locations on different days. We effectively got a map of the network and split it into three areas. Members in each area would strike on one day per week for three weeks. If the dispute was not resolved by then, we would reconsider and either continue or escalate our action. This plan had many attractive features. Firstly, it would give us three days of strike action per week, while each member would lose only one day's pay. That meant three days' publicity, and all the pressure on the company that goes with that, for the loss of one day's pay per member. In addition, each day's action in each area would disrupt services in such a manner as to have a negative effect on the day before and after that action also, with trains being out of position and drivers' rosters being affected. As we put the plan in place, we were confident that it would have the desired impact. Nevertheless, both SIPTU and the NBRU foolishly put themselves out on a limb by predicting that most, or even all, of their members would ignore our pickets. Management seemed to take these assurances at face value, and I believe that management's political paymasters did also.

However, I had given them a 'get out' option before any strike took place. On 19 April 2001, I had written a 'briefing note' to Minister O'Rourke. The letter, on ATGWU headed notepaper contained a clear message regarding the ongoing industrial relations difficulties affecting ILDA members. Prior to our return to work following the lock-out, we had been assured that our grievances would be dealt with on a 'fast-tracked' basis if we returned to work. However, by the following April, not a single grievance in respect of a single member had been processed by

Irish Rail. Our members had referred their grievances to the LRC and that body had issued fifty-six invitations to conciliation, none of which had been accepted by our employer. Moreover, Iarnród Éireann had changed its own grievance and disciplinary procedures, to exclude the chosen colleague of drivers facing disciplinary charges. And the company had also refused to provide the ATGWU with copies of proposed changes to work patterns. The list of our grievances was finally topped by the company's refusal to treat with the ATGWU with respect of locomotive drivers. It was all laid out in my letter to the minister, which concluded:

> Accordingly I wish to advise that this union is to hold an emergency meeting of its Branch Committee on 22 April 2001 to consider what is now a total breakdown of industrial relations with respect to our members. Following the grave difficulties of 2000 this union and its members have worked extremely hard to rebuild relationships with our colleagues and management.... [T]he continued alienation and isolation of our members from all normal and democratic industrial relations processes and procedures cannot be sustained.
>
> Whatever decisions our Branch Committee take next Sunday will be taken with a view to protecting our members' entitlements, restoring their right to normal industrial relations processes and continuing to improve relations between staff employed by Iarnród Éireann.

That letter had received no response. The inevitable result was that management received two weeks' strike notice to begin with immediate effect from 22 April.

Apart from efforts by John Keenan to persuade Mick O'Reilly not to go ahead with it, generally nobody did anything meaningful to stop the strike. Why should they when SIPTU and the NBRU had told all interested parties that our action would be totally ineffective and that their members would pass our pickets? Mick and the ATGWU, however, were more inclined to listen to our assessments of the probable impact of our action. And so, on Tuesday 8 May, our first proper strike action began. Train services in Dublin and other key areas were devastated. Even the DART almost stopped as SIPTU and NBRU members in all grades refused to put their principles aside. How could the unions continue to argue that, if we got recognition, their members would strike, when their members were supporting our strike action for recognition? How could the company and government sustain their decision not to treat with us now in these changed circumstances? We now had them on an even playing field at last, and so they went for the only weakness they could find. That weakness didn't lie within ILDA or even the railway at all. It lay in the relationship between Mick O'Reilly and Bill Morris.

Licensing of Trade Unions

As outlined elsewhere, the licensing of trade unions in Ireland is not a phenomenon that is reflected in the UK or, indeed, elsewhere in Europe. In Britain, unlike Ireland, any trade union gaining a specified level of membership in an industry or employment is entitled under statute to be recognised by an employer. Not so in Ireland. Indeed, Irish trade unions now seem to have accepted their lot in not having a statutory basis for trade union recognition. All they now do is simply pay occasional lip service to the idea at times such as the imposition of new national pay agreements. The fact, however, that they cannot claim recognition simply by weight of numbers does not mitigate their requirement to hold negotiating licences, reach specific membership thresholds and lodge considerable sums of money (IR£20,000) with the High Court simply in order to exist in this country. Similarly, unions based in the UK, which do not need negotiating licences there, do require them to operate in Ireland. Moreover, they are given to them only if very specific requirements are met.

The primary requirement that needs to be met is a statutory requirement and it relates to the entitlement of Irish members of a British union to have autonomous decision-making authority relating to matters solely affecting that Irish membership. The statute(s) concerned are contained in section 17 of the Trade Union Act 1975, subsections (1) and (2). They read:

> 17.—(1) Notwithstanding Part II of the Act of 1941 and section 2 of the Act of 1971, a body of persons which is a trade union under the law of another country and has its headquarters control situated in that country shall not hold or be granted a negotiation licence under that Part unless, in addition to fulfilling the relevant conditions

specified in section 7 of the Act of 1941 and section 2 of the Act of 1971, it fulfils the condition specified in subsection (2).

(2) The condition referred to in subsection (1) is that the trade union concerned has a committee of management or other controlling authority every member of which is resident in the State or Northern Ireland and which is empowered by the rules of that trade union to make decisions in matters of an industrial or political nature which arise out of and are in connection with the economic or political condition of the State or Northern Ireland, are of direct concern to members of the trade union resident in the State or Northern Ireland and do not affect members not so resident.

In other words, a British union like the TGWU cannot hold a negotiating licence in Ireland unless it provides for all decisions of an 'industrial or political nature' that concern members in Ireland only to be decided upon solely by a committee of management or controlling authority, every member of which is resident in the Republic or in Northern Ireland.

In the case of the ATGWU, that committee of management is the Irish Regional Committee which accepted individual ILDA members into the union and, further, endorsed our industrial action of May 2001. These provisions are, of course, necessarily reflected in the constitution of the Irish Congress of Trade Unions. In fact, the second article of the ICTU constitution states at subsection (ii):

The Trade Unions shall provide that decisions on all matters of an industrial or political nature which arise out of and are in connection with the internal economic and political conditions of Ireland and are of direct concern to Irish members only, shall be considered and decided upon by Irish members provided that the decisions shall have due regard to and shall not prejudice the position of members outside Ireland. A delegate conference of Irish members, or an Irish committee elected by the Irish membership, shall make such decisions.

So there we have it — a clear statutory requirement that Irish members of a British union decide on matters affecting the Irish membership only, copper-fastened by the very constitution of ICTU itself.

The Shafting of Mick O'Reilly

The pressure in the dispute began to mount on Tuesday 8 May, in the form of a number of media interviews given by Mick O'Reilly. The first of these was with Eamon Dunphy. Mick had always had a good relationship with Eamon Dunphy in previous discussions. However, from the interview, it was plain that, in the interviewer's head, Mick had crossed a line by taking in 'Ogle' and ILDA. It was sickening to listen to but Mick performed very well indeed. In any event, he had another media performance to prepare for that evening — a much more important one.

RTÉ's *Prime Time* had decided to feature the strike on the show that evening. Mick would be interviewed in studio, along with John Keenan, SIPTU's Des Geraghty, and Gerry Flynn of the *Irish Independent*. It was a remarkable piece of television, in which Des Geraghty, a man with many advisors of his own, launched a personal attack on Mick's advisor, Marty Whelan, that was as vindictive as it was irrelevant to the issue in dispute. Des Geraghty later went on to ask Mick to call off the strike on the basis that he, Des Geraghty, would open talks with Mick if he did so! It was shocking stuff from a man obviously embarrassed by the support his own members, contrary to leadership urgings, had given us.

The following day, Wednesday 9 May 2001, is a day I will not forget quickly. It began with a number of telephone conversations where I ascertained that our strike action had been almost 100 per cent effective in the two areas covered to date. I myself was to experience some of the unity among members of all three unions when my SIPTU colleagues in Athlone supported us to a man, even to the point of joining us on picket duty. A SIPTU member even called the Gerry Ryan Show in my presence to correct a number of facts contained in an interview that Gerry Ryan had aired with a reporter from the *Irish Examiner*. The facts he wanted to correct included the assertion that SIPTU members had been 'intimidated' into supporting the ILDA/ATGWU action. He wasn't put on the air.

I left the Athlone picket to travel to Dublin with my colleague and friend, Tom O'Brien. Earlier in the day, Mick had called me to say that

Iarnród Éireann had issued legal papers to the union, claiming that our ballot had not been properly conducted; our notice of strike action was deficient; and that the company was entitled to damages from the union for our action. These legal papers had not been served on the 'committee of management every member of which is resident in the state or northern Ireland', as required by section 17 of the 1975 Trade Union Act, but had, in fact, been sent to the London-based General Secretary of the TGWU, Bill Morris. Perhaps Iarnród Éireann's in-house solicitors were not aware of the provisions of the Trade Union Act 1975.

I gathered all my material on the ballot and, as we drove to Dublin to meet Mick, his solicitor, Andrew Turner, and barrister, Oisín Quinn, I reflected on this legal threat from the company. It didn't add up. Iarnród Éireann knew full well that the statutory strike notice required was one full week. We had given two. Moreover, we in ILDA were careful to the point of paranoia about how we conducted our ballots. Not only was every ballot we conducted a secret ballot with results provided to members at the first opportunity, as required in law, but we also habitually collected signatures from every member balloted, affirming that they had received a secret vote, free from interference; and we had counts independently verified, invariably by a member of the Garda Síochána. Finally, Iarnród Éireann had made a case that we were obliged to ballot ATGWU members not in the ILDA Branch — in other words, not involved in the dispute. However, not only were we not obliged to ballot members not involved in the dispute, but the act specifically outlawed any attempt by us to draw workers not affected into a dispute that related solely to our members. I felt that Iarnród Éireann should know that we had our backs well covered on this matter, and the unanimous nature of the ballot result left little room for doubt regarding the intentions of our members. So what was going on? Did the addressee of the legal correspondence hold the key to the answer to that question?

In any event, our afternoon meeting with Mick and his legal people went very much as expected. In due course, a formal legal opinion was provided that took the view that Iarnród Éireann's proposed action was 'ill-founded'. But it went further than that. It also gave the ATGWU a full armoury of legal ammunition to use — based around the Supreme Court judgment — to ensure the quick achievement of representation of our members. What was unknown to us at the time, however, was that there were people within that organisation who didn't want such an armoury.

After a very satisfactory meeting, I was introduced to a senior lay member of the union, Jackie McKay. Jackie was the elected chairman of the Irish Regional Committee — the body identified in the 1975 act and under the ICTU constitution which had the power to decide on all of these matters affecting our members. That body was to meet the following day in Dublin, and Jackie had come down from his native Belfast a day early. Mick was in RTÉ's Dáil studio, doing a live interview for the teatime news. Together we walked over to Leinster House and, while Mick went in for the interview, Jackie, Tom O'Brien and I waited across the road in Buswell's Hotel, the hotel most used by members of the Oireachtas to meet with each other and their associates. That evening it was packed, and we tried, without success, to hear Mick's interview on the television in the bar. After Mick had finished speaking, the footage cut to Taoiseach Bertie Ahern speaking on the floor of the house. I knew he was talking about us but what was he saying? I couldn't hear with all the chatter around me. I was soon to be told though.

Just as we got back to the ATGWU office, my mobile phone rang. It was Jim Higgins of Fine Gael, and he outlined how the Taoiseach had been pinned down during question time in the Dáil and had gone on the attack. He had attacked the ATGWU, Mick and me personally. I have since got a transcript of what took place in the Dáil that day. In fairness to the Taoiseach, he was subjected to the most rigorous questioning by various members of the opposition including Deputy Higgins, Fine Gael leader Michael Noonan, Labour leader Ruairí Quinn, Green Party leader Trevor Sergeant, and Socialist member Joe Higgins. It is only fair that his comments, attitude and approach be seen in that light. Nevertheless, it is clear from what he said, and what he didn't say, that, as far as the Taoiseach was concerned, the Supreme Court judgment that upheld our constitutional right to join a union of our choosing might as well never have happened. A host of statements such as the following would imply that Mr Ahern believes in one holy and apostolic trade union only — SIPTU — and will not permit worship at the feet of false gods like the ATGWU, constitutional rights or not:

'I will not support the actions of the ATGWU, which are in breach of an agreement between CIÉ, the Congress of Trade Unions and SIPTU.'

'It was not foreseen that members of ILDA, who created such difficulties last year, would move into the ATGWU. That fact, which has arisen only in the past two months, was not anticipated by ICTU, SIPTU, the company or the Minister.'

'The key element is that the ATGWU is in breach of the negotiated agreement with the ICTU. Mr. Ogle and his colleagues tried one way and failed. They are now trying another way, but will fail again.'

I could go on to refute point after point made by the Taoiseach, about ILDA, the ATGWU and me personally. From a personal point of view, suffice it to say that I was very upset on the day, and felt under siege. In retrospect, I suppose I should feel honoured to be the only train driver named by the Taoiseach on the floor of the Dáil since the state came into being. However, by far the most concerning aspect of Bertie Ahern's diatribe was that he, on the record, on the floor of the house, stated seven times that the ATGWU was in breach of ICTU procedures. Who decided that? ICTU had not even met by then to consider the SIPTU 'members in arrears' complaint, still less the actual strike. How then could the Taoiseach who had never been a trade unionist, still less a member of the ICTU Executive, tell the Dáil on seven occasions on 9 May that we were in breach of ICTU rules? Had Bertie Ahern been briefed behind the scenes by someone in ICTU about the ICTU position? If that were the case, any subsequent ICTU 'investigation' would simply be a charade that had been predetermined.

Be that as it may, at the very moment when the Taoiseach was speaking in the house, ICTU General Secretary Peter Cassells was in meetings about the strike — meetings that didn't involve ILDA or the Irish region of the ATGWU at all. Given the provisions of the ICTU constitution, as outlined earlier, one might have expected that any concerns ICTU might have had with the strike action would have been raised with the 'Irish committee elected by the Irish membership', identified in article 2 of its own constitution. Similarly, one might have expected that any concerns that the TGWU in London might have had about a few train driver members in Ireland would have been aired with those train drivers or their elected committee. My experience is that one seldom gets what one expects or is entitled to in the Irish trade union movement, and that was certainly true in this case

We left Mick shortly after the conversation with Jim Higgins. Mick was preparing for the Regional Committee meeting the following day, and then he was meeting some of the committee members who were starting to arrive at a local hotel in advance of the meeting. Tom O'Brien and I decided to hit the road back to Athlone. Given that we had spent most of the day with Mick, I was somewhat surprised when he called us within an hour of our leaving him. He was furious. He had gone to the hotel to meet the Regional Committee members for a drink. There he had met Ray Collins, Bill Morris' right-hand man in London HQ, who had been sent over to 'supervise' the following day's meeting. It was a gross interference in the autonomous affairs of the region. But there was worse to come. Ray Collins told Mick that he had spent the afternoon in a meeting with ICTU General Secretary Peter Cassells, discussing ILDA and the strike, and that Peter Cassells had presented him with unspecified information that he would be reporting back to Bill Morris with. I immediately realised that Mick was in trouble. I also immediately realised that ICTU was now complicit in whatever might follow, by its actions in meeting Ray Collins and giving him information without the assent or even knowledge of the 'Irish Committee elected by the Irish membership' of the ATGWU.

I spent the early part of the following day at home, assessing media reportage, talking to our members who were now on strike in the west, and studying the detail of Bertie Ahern's Dáil speech. In the early afternoon, I would have to travel to Dublin for our meeting with ICTU. I spoke to Mick by phone before he went in to the Regional Committee meeting. He had calmed down overnight but was still furious. However, his committee members had been just as incensed as he was and he felt safe surrounded by them and his colleague and friend, Ben Kearney, the soon-to-retire Republic of Ireland Secretary of the ATGWU.

Around midday, I heard a news report that there had been an intervention in the dispute. The National Implementation Body had issued a statement calling on the Labour Court to intervene, and the Labour Court had agreed. Then Mick called. He had the statement and he read it to me. He was enthusiastic about it, but I had lots of questions not least of which was: 'What the hell is the National Implementation Body?

The National Implementation Body (NIB) is a 'high-level' three-person group formed as part of social partnership agreements. It is in place to ensure that glitches in social partnership agreements or matters of concern to the parties to such an agreement can be dealt with by recourse to the combined font of infinite wisdom its three members can bring to any problem. Those three members were IBEC head Turlough O'Sullivan; a senior civil servant from the Department of the Taoiseach, Dermot McCarthy; and ICTU General Secretary Peter Cassells. So there was a direct link between Peter Cassells and Bertie Ahern's department, through the NIB.

I asked Mick not to say anything public on the initiative until we got to Dublin. In particular, I stressed that, under rule, it was for our members to decide the next step. However, I knew that Mick felt under enormous pressure. This was a man worried by what was emerging around him. And with good reason too. Finbarr Masterson and I listened to the news. Mick's voice came over the airwaves and he said that he welcomed the initiative and thought that it could solve the dispute, but that the ultimate decision fell to our members. That put all of the pressure onto our members, but that was fine too. The only problem was that those members who heard the interview now started to ring me asking me about the statement. When I explained that I hadn't actually got it yet, they wanted to know why Mick had 'accepted' it. I needed to be in Dublin.

When I got close to the ATGWU's Abbey Street offices, I phoned and was told that there was a large media presence in and around the front of the building. I didn't want to be questioned on an initiative that I hadn't seen yet, so Finbarr parked the car at the rear and I entered through that entrance. The building was a hive of activity. Union officials and staff mingled with media personnel and advisors. I went to Mick's office on the second floor and was soon joined there by Mick and Jimmy Kelly. Jimmy was a member of the executive and had given media interviews supporting the ILDA members. Mick produced the NIB statement and I studied it, reading it slowly a couple of times. The statement called on the Labour Court to investigate the dispute under the powers vested in it by section 43 (functions of the Labour Court relating to codes of practice) of the Industrial Relations Act 1990 — Bertie Ahern's Thatcherite charter. The legislations states:

Functions of Labour Court relating to codes of practice.

43.—(1) The Court may on the application of one or more parties concerned give its opinion as to the interpretation of a code of practice, provided that in the case of an application by one party notice of the application has been given by that party to the other party.

(2) The Court may investigate a complaint that there has been a breach of a code of practice provided that the complaint has been referred to the Court by a party directly involved and that the complaint has first been considered by the Commission in accordance with section 26.

(3) Where the Court has investigated such a complaint, it may make a recommendation setting forth its opinion in the matter and, where appropriate, its view as to the action which a party in breach of the code should take or cease from taking in order to ensure compliance with the code.

Whether or not the National Implementation Body was entitled to be deemed a party who could refer this to the court became a moot point. Who was going to say it wasn't? Only someone who didn't want the strike to stop at this point would do so. Government did. The NIB did. Iarnród Éireann did. The public did. And it was clear that powers within the ATGWU did. I was under pressure now. ILDA was under pressure. Was this a time for us to assert the independence of our members under union rule just over two months after we had joined the union? I read on. The investigation would be 'for the purpose of recommending on the fairness, or otherwise of the procedures employed in Iarnród Éireann in respect of the disciplinary cases in dispute, with reference to the code of practice on grievance and disciplinary procedures.'

The media were at the door. They wanted the ILDA perspective.

They knew that Finbarr and I were in the building. We needed time to study the statement. As it happened, I had a copy of section 43 of the 1990 act with me. We studied it in light of the statement. We didn't get bogged down on whether or not the NIB was entitled to refer this to the court at all. It had and the court had accepted the referral. It was now our call. The Labour Court usually gives recommendations that are often binding on one or other of the parties. This was just an 'opinion'. Opinions aren't binding. This was good. Moreover, what was referred to was not a general review of procedures, but a specific review of the procedures employed in respect of the disciplinary cases in dispute. This was also good. Everyone knew that it was the failure to recognise the ATGWU for representation purposes in eight individual cases in dispute that was at issue here. If we were entitled to represent those eight, how could we not be entitled to represent others? The abuses in these eight cases were at the extreme end of what was going on with our members generally. And these were the specific cases in dispute now to be investigated by the Labour Court. Finbarr and I were happy with all of this. But there was not a word about recognition. Not a hint even. That was the key to all the problems. Mick explained that ICTU would deal with that and that the ICTU meeting at 5pm would be a start. He had talked to SIPTU and believed that it might be possible to do a deal. He had already agreed with SIPTU that we would not make a submission today but that both unions would tell ICTU that they would try to resolve the matter between themselves. Only if they failed would ICTU be asked to decide on the formal SIPTU complaint. And Mick had things that SIPTU wanted in other areas where there was difficulty between the two unions. He had spoken to Jack O'Connor of SIPTU, and Mick and Jack got on well. At least between those two, the portents seemed good.

I don't know what we would have decided if London hadn't been poking their noses into our business in the Irish region — if Mick hadn't been under pressure. As it was, I simply said that we would have an ILDA meeting to make our decision at the weekend, but that any future action was 'postponed' pending those deliberations. Mick was happy with that and informed the media. I spoke to an RTÉ reporter myself and made positive noises. As we left to take the short walk to ICTU, the 'Morris cloud' seemed to lift from over the building. Ray Collins was already on his way back to London. Now we could concentrate on ICTU.

There was a large media presence assembled outside the ICTU building as we walked up along Parnell Square. I was pictured entering with Mick and Jimmy Kelly. We were greeted by Tom Wall and taken into a room that housed the 'disputes committee'. Noel Dowling and Brendan Hayes were there for SIPTU, accompanied by Paul Cullen, a train driver from Connolly. From the outset, it was clear that this was SIPTU's domain. Noel Dowling read a SIPTU submission about the ATGWU 'breaching' a 'spheres of influence agreement' between the two unions. There was no signed agreement. But in the ICTU world, that wouldn't matter. Mick explained that both unions had agreed that they would ask the disputes committee not to make a decision yet and, for that reason, we would not make our submission now. He said that SIPTU and the ATGWU would see if they could resolve this matter amicably themselves. Noel Dowling agreed. The 'disputes committee' nodded sagely. We all got up and left.

Afterwards we had a pint in Abbey Street. Marty Whelan joined us. It was a happy meeting. I looked up and saw Peter Cassells on the news talking about us. He said that we would not be allowed to renegotiate the 'New Deal' following this impending settlement of the latest industrial dispute involving ILDA. Who had raised that? It didn't smell right to me. To some it looked like a victory, or close to a victory. And, on the surface, the raw material needed to resolve all outstanding issues — recognition, disciplinary, grievance — seemed to be available if all of the parties involved wanted to use it. But did they? There was something that I couldn't quite put my finger on.

Saturday's ILDA meeting came and we agreed to give the Labour Court and the bi-laterals with SIPTU a chance. I began working on our submission to the court. The hearing would be on Friday 8 June 2001, and it would need to be a very detailed submission. Mick began to lobby for a 'no' vote in the upcoming referendum on the Nice Treaty on expansion of the European Union. He believed that the treaty infringed Irish 'neutrality'. By co-incidence, the vote would be on 7 June, and the result would be known on 8 June, the day of our Labour Court hearing.

Sometime in the intervening weeks, Mick called me and told me that Margaret Prosser was in his Belfast office and would also be coming down to Dublin. She hadn't spoken to him. Margaret Prosser was the London-based Assistant General Secretary of the TGWU. If Ray Collins was Bill Morris' right-hand man, then Margaret Prosser was the female equivalent. She was looking into files, talking to people behind closed doors — to everyone, it seemed, except Mick — carrying out an 'investigation'. This was bad, very bad. Mick carried on, always cheerful, always helpful, always himself. Mick is a trade unionist, not a bureaucrat. Some people think that they are not working unless they are bogged down in papers, minutes, files, emails and faxes. Mick isn't one of those people. He works by dealing with people, members — not pieces of paper. Margaret Prosser was only interested in pieces of paper.

At that point, Mick and I were working very closely together. We didn't discuss the 'investigation' much at all though. There didn't seem to be any need to. Mick knew that he had great support within the region and that he hadn't done anything wrong. In particular, he knew that he hadn't done anything dishonest. He lives in an ordinary house in an ordinary part of Dublin and lives, and has always lived, a modest life. He would much rather have a pint on a Friday night with the lads he worked on the shop floor with twenty-five years ago than enter the social merry-go-round that many senior trade unionists can find themselves intoxicated by. It's part of the reason why he has never lost his 'edge'. It's hard to tear strips off people, especially powerful people, with whom you were drinking wine and eating canapés the previous weekend.

While this 'investigation' was ongoing, Mick was engaged in talks with SIPTU. These talks took place over several Saturday afternoons in Liberty Hall. Mick was accompanied by Ben Kearney, and Jack O'Connor was joined by Noel Dowling and another SIPTU official, John Fay, on at least one occasion. As reported to me, the talks never really got going.

While all of this was going on, I wrote our Labour Court submission for the 8 June hearing. It was hugely detailed. I emailed it to Mick who looked over it and got it made up for court. He was going to attend the hearing with me. On 8 June, we met at the Abbey Street office and were driving over to the court when he got a phone call. The first tallies in the Nice referendum were coming in and indicated that the referendum could be lost. Mick was euphoric.

The Labour Court hearing took place under the chairmanship of Caroline Jenkinson. At the outset, something strange happened. John Keenan questioned the validity of our membership of the ATGWU. Mick responded by saying that he was head of the Irish Region and could assure the court that there was no question over our membership. John Keenan said that the General Secretary in London believed otherwise. Something was going on.

I won't get bogged down here with the hearing and its aftermath. In essence, the Labour Court, having listened to our submission, gave an opinion that totally ignored the procedures applied in each individual case at issue, and instead considered the procedures as a document — a piece of paper — and not as something that had been applied in practice. The court found that the written procedures were fine. We agreed. We had never had any problem with the agreed procedures in Iarnród Éireann. Our problem was the failure to apply those procedures in the case of ILDA members. The court's terms of reference called for an investigation into the 'disciplinary cases in dispute', not just the procedures. But the court offered no opinion on the 'cases'. Our submission might as well have been pages of blank paper.

The Labour Court delivered its opinion on 25 July 2001. By then, Mick O'Reilly had been removed from office and we were told by our union that any help we needed on any issue thereafter would need to be approved by Bill Morris in London.

After the Labour Court and confirmation that the Irish electorate had rejected the Nice Treaty, Mick had flown out to Lanzarote for a family holiday. It was while Mick was on holiday that the ICTU disputes committee decided to hear the SIPTU complaint. I didn't like that. In any event, I went with Ben Kearney and John Bolger, another ATGWU official. Ben made a submission on part of SIPTU's complaint but not on the non-existent spheres-of-influence agreement. Before reading the submission, he pointed out to the committee that it was a submission from 'our ILDA members'. Gerry Shanahan was on the three-man committee. This was the same Gerry Shanahan who had intervened to try to ensure that we didn't get to join the AEEU union a few months earlier. Now he would deliberate on whether or not we could stay in the ATGWU.

I knew that it was a waste of time. Of course, they would find against us. SIPTU had claimed that we were in breach of a 'spheres-of-influence' agreement between the two unions. No such agreement existed. The last time somebody had tried to put one together, they had failed. It wouldn't matter. ICTU would find us in breach of an agreement that didn't exist, because SIPTU demanded it. But just to make sure, John Keenan — as our employer — wrote to ICTU to say that he wouldn't deal with us anyway. SIPTU used John Keenan's letter during the hearing to paint a picture of industrial mayhem if they lost. And then, when ICTU made the inevitable decision in favour of SIPTU, that we had breached the non-existent agreement, John Keenan hailed it as the reason why he could not recognise the ATWGU's ILDA members.

Mick flew back from Lanzarote on the night of 19 June 2001. He had a meeting in Belfast the following afternoon. At 2.20 the phone rang. It was Valerie, Mick's secretary. She said that Mick wanted to speak to me urgently. Mick's voice came over the phone: 'Hello, Brendan. Listen I've been suspended. I have to leave the building. I'm not allowed to talk to anyone in the union. Your new Regional Secretary is called Jimmy Elsby. I'll talk to you when I can.'

The strange events of the previous weeks all fell into place now that this piece of the jigsaw was available. What I had been witnessing for weeks was the choreography that precedes a beheading. After 4pm our executive member from Dundalk, Kevin Connolly, called. He asked me whether it was true that Mick had been suspended. He had received a call from a friend who had just been talking to Mick's colleague, Brendan Hodgers, in Dundalk. He had been told that Mick was suspended and that the ILDA members were about to be expelled from the union. I didn't know what to make of this. I decided not to take any chances. If we were expelled, it would be wrong. We would then have to fight to get back into a union that had wrongly expelled us. That would be an untenable position to be in and we needed to prevent that from happening. I tried to get Donal Spring without success. I then spoke to a solicitor friend of mine, Ann Gallagher, who went to work for us. I continued to listen and wait. By midnight, I had given up, and I went to bed.

I got Mick very early indeed the following morning. I told him that I had heard that the ATGWU was going to expel our members, and that I intended to act to prevent that from happening. Meanwhile, Anne Gallagher had drawn up a strongly worded letter addressed to Jimmy Elsby. It stated that our members were in compliance with all union rules and, as such, the union would be acting contrary to its own rules if it attempted to expel any of them. This would place our members in a vulnerable position with their employer. In those circumstances, we would initiate immediate legal proceedings against the union should it attempt to usurp our rights as members. The letter was immediately faxed, emailed and posted to Jimmy Elsby. It has protected our position as members of the ATWGU ever since.

Mick O'Reilly has a book to write. He has led a remarkable life and has been through so much personally and professionally that I really hope he takes the time to catalogue all the details of these events and how they affected him. I will not do so here.

I hope that my role was as a friend of Mick's — an ally. Ultimately every charge against him and his number two, Eugene McGlone, as they related to ILDA, was dismissed. Initially, Bill Morris went through a ridiculous disciplinary process that lasted over a year and cost tens of thousands of pounds in members' money. Bill Morris, the accuser, himself judged Mick and Eugene guilty when the charade finally ended. Mick and Eugene appealed to a three-man committee of Bill Morris' peers. By the time they got around to making a decision, Margaret Prosser had gone and Bill Morris had announced his retirement. Both men were offered jobs back with their old salaries and conditions, all back pay that they had lost to be repaid, and all charges in respect of ILDA were summarily dismissed. To save face, their old jobs would be advertised and they couldn't apply for new positions for twelve months.

THE WORKERS' POLICEMAN

There are those who have asked – or who seem to expect – that I would have become embittered towards Iarnród Éireann or their individual managers given all the events outlined in this book. Indeed there are some who wondered how I could have returned to work for them at all after the vitriol of the 2000 lock out. While remembering the detail of events and the role played by the various personalities bitterness is not my predominant reaction to them. The main protagonist for Iarnród Éireann was always John Keenan. At this stage I know John quite well. We have discussed all these events from our differing perspectives thoroughly and bluntly. Little if anything in this book will come as a surprise to him. I have what I consider to be a pragmatic – but some would say old-fashioned – view of employers and worker representative bodies. Although the relationship between employers and unions is a complex one in the final analysis it boils down to this. Employers are duty-bound to get as much work out of their employees for as little as possible. Unions are there to ensure the best pay and terms and conditions for their members for as little a sacrifice as possible. I know who's doing the better job in Iarnród Éireann. In achieving their aims management will necessarily have to confront unions and vice versa. At least if they are both behaving as they should be they will. In doing so it will not be a picnic for those involved and I am, and always was, aware of this. But the ILDA dispute stood out because it was different in so many ways. One of the major differences was in the extent to which management went to destroy us. In taking High Court action against us management crossed a line. At that stage families were also under attack and that made the difficulties personal. The trumped up nature of the charges and the fact that the action was over a dispute that had been the inevitable result of management – and not ILDA – actions all made the High Court action a very damaging nonsense. Iarnród Éireann went too far and the Labour Court and even the LRC roundly condemned them for this action at the appropriate time. John Keenan has conceded that he played a major part in this strategy. As an industrial relations strategy it was a disaster sewing the seeds for much of the bitterness that followed.

John has also told meetings of various staff members that the personalised attacks on me through the media were a necessary but not very nice part of the Iarnrod Éireann strategy during the disputes that took place. He has told these meetings that he knows that the Brendan Ogle portrayed at that time to the public bears no resemblance to the real person. To be honest, I can accept much of what was done in PR terms. I can't say that John Keenan was responsible for the more salacious attacks on me behind the scenes, and he seemed genuinely shocked when I raised those matters with him. Neither is it his fault when someone like Eamon Dunphy decides to let some steam off on an easy target and goes over the top. Overall, the personalised nature of much of the media coverage was designed to break me, but it didn't. Yesterday's chip paper.

Iarnrod Éireann did make mistakes though. Big ones. At every stage, management is too inclined to respond immediately to difficulties with the harsh word, the tough act, the stringent position. I suspect that when Iarnrod Éireann bosses initially took proceedings to sue us, they thought we'd break before it ever got to court. Instead, we mounted a counter-claim and got a highly respected legal team to fight them every inch of the way. It became too late for anyone to turn back. Then they locked us out of work, thinking that our members would scramble back after a couple of days. After all, the normal talk from unions these days is how it is nigh impossible to mount a sustained campaign of industrial action, given the 'modern financial circumstances' (mortgages, loans etc.) faced by their members. But to everyone's shock and horror, ILDA members didn't crack. Even worse, we fought an aggressive rearguard action and lasted the pace beyond their worst nightmares. What could they do but keep going as they clocked up losses measured in millions (€19.6 million for the summer 2000 lock out to be precise)? And then, when we joined the ATGWU, they responded publicly within hours, backing themselves, and us, into another corner that resulted in another dispute and the ultimate removal of Mick O'Reilly. That chapter of the ILDA dispute is unfinished business and the scars of the injustice done to Mick O'Reilly and Eugene McGlone remain.

However, with regard to ILDA and Iarnrod Éireann here's an idea. How about the next time there is a problem — and there will be a next time — both sides sit down and think before they open up on each other? How about actually thinking through all the positions and options and looking for a solution rather than an altercation? And how about treating each other with the same respect in public as is normally afforded in private? You never know — it might help.

Government Ministers

And so what of the others parties involved? At a political level, what we experienced initially from two government departments was a failure to govern, to lead, to help, and to use all available avenues to resolve ongoing difficulties — in short, a failure to do everything we elect our political leaders to do. Mary Harney's failure to act on her own statutory instrument — our interpretation of which was ultimately upheld by the Labour Court and LRC — was a disgrace. Mary O'Rourke actually called to my house looking for a vote in the May 2002 general election campaign. I'd just moved and she didn't expect to see me standing at the door. In my kitchen, I told her that, as minister for five years, her behaviour regarding ILDA had been a disgrace. I accused her of letting SIPTU and others effectively determine the policy of her department as it related to us, and I pointed out that I knew that her public utterances regarding the High Court judgment where at odds with advice she had received from her most senior civil servants. It didn't go down too well. She accused me of spoiling her holidays — 'you and your ILDA' — and she left as hurriedly as she could. I don't think she'll be back looking for my vote again.

It's a pity about Mary O'Rourke, because in so many other ways, she was a breath of fresh air as Minister for Transport. I believe she was genuinely shocked by an accident almost on her doorstep — in

Knockcroghery, Co. Roscommon in 1996 — where scores of passengers narrowly escaped injury or worse when their train derailed because of the state of the track, and fortunately fell against a raised bank rather than down a falling one. Thereafter, she ploughed more money than could ever have been imagined into the safety of the rail network — admittedly at a time when the country was riding high on the back of the now-dead Celtic Tiger — to provide passengers and workers alike with a much safer network. I have no doubt that lives have been saved as a result. She also fulfilled our wishes by setting up an independent statutory rail safety authority, for the first time ever. This was long overdue, much needed and not at all popular with many in Iarnrod Éireann management. However, the Department of Public Enterprise and Transport should not allow itself to be used as a vehicle to allow big unions to settle scores with little ones at taxpayers' expense. In adopting SIPTU's position towards ILDA so aggressively and apparently unquestioningly, Minister O'Rourke allowed that to happen. It was wrong and not in the interests of taxpayers. Which brings me to Bertie Ahern and his Dáil attack. All that can be said about that attack is that it says more about Bertie Ahern than it ever does about Mick O'Reilly and me.

The Labour Court and the LRC

As regards the Labour Court and the LRC, I believe that those who argue that we should be proud to have such 'sophisticated industrial relations machinery' are, on balance, correct. In our case, however, the role of the LRC was not sophisticated. It was, in turn, ham-fisted, insincere, biased, corrosive, petulant and immensely damaging. Far from fulfilling its statutory functions without fear or favour, the LRC behaved disgracefully from the moment it made an invitation to conciliation into an 'administrative error' to the time finally when it appended itself to an investigation that needed to investigate the LRC itself as much as anything or anybody else. It is my view that by its behaviour, the LRC diminished itself and its reputation as the initial source of impartial conciliation in industrial disputes between warring parties. The Labour Court, for its part, can take little credit, in my opinion, for the manner of the announcement of its investigation, and its agreement to allow the LRC a role in it. Similarly the Labour Court investigation into the May 2001 dispute and the eight individual cases involved was not handled in the manner that might have been expected or required by its terms of reference. Nevertheless, I have had many positive experiences with and in the Labour Court, as have our members. Chairman Finbarr Flood began to earn my respect with his conciliatory words on the day the 2000 lock out ended, and by his words and actions has continued to do so since. The odd scrape aside, I have similar respect for his aides, Kevin Duffy and Caroline Jenkinson. Even ordinary Labour Court members such as former SIPTU Vice-President Jimmy Somers have surprised us with their fairness during key hearings, even if Labour Court recommendations tend to be very ambiguous at times. We in ILDA are rightly proud of the quality of our submissions to the Labour Court and of our success rate. Section 20s are industrial relations by high wire and, as it is often the only third party avenue open to us, and often our members' jobs have depended on it, we need to be up to the job and to get a fair hearing. I have found myself now arguing section 20 referrals before the court on many, many occasions and have always been treated with respect and fairness during the hearings. If only I could say the same for everyone else we in ILDA have had to deal with. If I have one final criticism, it is that more imagination should have been used to resolve the overall ILDA problem for once and for all. We have always looked for imaginative solutions to the recognition issue, and will continue to do so, but sometimes we need help. Too often that help has not been forthcoming, and so the overall problem identified by the Labour Court — the undesirability of having ILDA drivers outside the collective bargaining procedures in Iarnrod Éireann — remains unresolved. Simply and blandly telling us to rejoin SIPTU is not putting a lot of thought into a solution.

The Irish Trade Union Movement

To some readers who have never been involved in the minutiae of trade union organisation in Ireland, this book may come as something of a shock. Did you think that trade union members decided union policy and that their officials dutifully carried out their wishes? Did you believe that the old adage 'the members are the union' still held true? Did you believe that it was for workers — and not for their employer — to choose what trade union they should be a member of, or whether or not they should be a member of a union? Did you believe that trade unions would fight any employer suing workers in the High Court tooth and nail, or that they would encourage their members to desist from doing the work of other employees in dispute? And finally, did you believe that the Irish Congress of Trade Unions would be a bastion of justice for any union member with a complaint, would fiercely protect the constitutional right of citizens to associate or dissociate and would insist on the full implementation of Article 11 and 11.1 of the European Convention of Human Rights, which allows for citizens to form and join unions of their choosing for the protection of their rights? And finally, did you believe that Irish trade unionists could expect the Irish Congress of Trade Unions to use its rules, its constitution and all available legislation to ensure that Irish workers and their representatives could not be 'taken out' by overseas-based bureaucrats acting out of personal enmity, political bias or a combination of both?

I hope that you now know better. The Irish Trade Union movement is as much a policeman of workers as it is a representative of them. It is what employers and government rely upon to keep workers in their place as much as it is a thorn in their sides. Cut through the regular dollops of bluff and bluster from ICTU or SIPTU worthies — or other spokespersons for the trade union 'establishment' — on your radios and televisions, and what you find is a movement without policy, lacking in action and which is becoming increasingly irrelevant to the majority of workers in this country. This is a movement that has meekly accepted right wing legislation such as the Industrial Relations Act 1990 and has, in fact, embraced it as a tool in the policing of its own members. It is a movement that has ceased to insist, in any meaningful way, on a legislative basis for trade union representation. It is a movement that postures and threatens — often loudly but remember the old adage about empty vessels — while it assesses which way the wind of public opinion is blowing on issues such as the deregulation of public services, before deciding to act and how. In short, it is a movement of followers and conformists as opposed to one filled with leaders or alternative thinkers.

In fact, alternative thinking or challenging the orthodoxy decreed from above is the one thing likely to get a rank-and-file union member into trouble. A certain amount of timid questioning may be tolerated but, as ILDA members found before ILDA was even dreamt of, push beyond that and suspicion leads to censure which leads to alienation, which ultimately leads to naked antagonism. In the annals of modern Irish trade unionism the word 'solidarity' should be replaced in all literature, badges and banners with a simple word — 'meekness'. My dictionary tells me that 'meek' means 'quiet, ready to do what other people say'. I cannot think of a word that better describes the type of worker who is most cherished in today's Irish trade union establishment. I don't know about the 'meek' inheriting the earth, but they have certainly inherited — or taken control of — a once proud movement. To be other than 'meek' is to be described and treated as a 'revolutionary'. ILDA members were described and treated as 'revolutionaries'. We were thought of as dangerous, driven élitists, almost subversive in some people's eyes. And why? Because we refused to accept a ready-up in 1994, and a cover-up of a ready-up from 1994 to 1998, and because, in 1998, in frustration at both of these events, we committed the 'crime' of forming our own union. We were not the first to fight a wrong within our unions. There are many dedicated members of various unions who do so often. What was different about ILDA was that we decided we had had enough after four years of stonewalling and we left to form our own union. We stopped being meek and became pro-active in defence of our members' terms and conditions of employment. Is that a crime in modern Ireland? Can the trade union movement not make room for — let alone, encourage — the levels of commitment and dedication to the representation of our members that we displayed? Can we not have exactly that — a 'movement', with people, personalities, issues and models of organisation and representation moving, evolving and changing constantly to keep things fresh and dynamic? ILDA is proof positive that this is not allowed. Things must be constant, stable, certain and predictable at all times. Anything that challenges that must be crushed.

Of course, the 'meekness' of the movement has brought it close to government and employers' groups. For their good behaviour, unions have been rewarded by government and the media for playing their part in the social and economic projects of our day. They have gone from being the *enfant terrible* to being the nice boy next door who it is safe to bring home for tea — or to Farmleigh for a state banquet. Since 1997, we have had tripartite national agreements that have involved government, employers and unions. The first was called the 'Programme for National Recovery' (PNR). This was needed because our economy was on the brink of collapse. And so the unions agreed to stay quiet while their partners — those with Charvet shirts and Ansbacher accounts — shut hospital wards, allowed schools to fall apart and basically cut and withdrew money from all our public services. In short, they stopped spending — except on themselves, of course. Inevitably, an economic recovery arrived, and with it much praise for the unions who, in the 'public interest', had not looked for pay rises for their members. Then the three-year agreement ended, and the unions entered a new agreement, the 'Programme for Economic and Social Progress' (PESP). Then another three years passed before they entered the 'Programme for Competitiveness and Work' (PCW), and then Partnership 2000 (P2000), and then the 'Programme for Prosperity and Fairness' (PPF).

As the names imply, the economy had turned. The Minister for Finance had billions of pounds of budget surpluses and it seemed it would never end. Certainly the unions didn't want it to end. In fact, so eager were they that the newly christened Celtic Tiger should continue to roar that they didn't even demand a fair share of the cake for their members. High levels of foreign direct investment — thanks to the lowest corporation tax rates available in the European Union — brought new jobs, skills and revenue pouring into Ireland. It got to the stage where unemployment had been effectively eliminated and employers had a labour shortage to contend with. One might have thought that this was just the time for the unions to demand large pay increases for their members in the ongoing spate of national agreements. But that is not what happened. Because, we were told, such demands would have brought us back to the days of the 1980s. So we continued to get paltry increases that had the bad look taken off them slightly by falling income tax rates — falling from the punitive rates of the Haughey era, that is.

And then it all went sour again. The Tiger died. Ireland now had more millionaires than ever before and white collar crime and corporate tax evasions were almost accepted practices. The government had spent all their excess money. But on what? The hospitals that were falling apart in the 1980s are now worse than ever; and children are still educated in rat-invested prefabricated huts masquerading as schools; and many working people can't afford places to live, and those who can, spend hours on overcrowded roads, travelling to work and home; and the socially disadvantaged are still forgotten, ignored and disenfranchised on the edges of our cities and towns where crime runs rampant and there aren't enough police to do anything about it because we can't afford them. Those spin doctors are damned expensive you know! In short, the rich got richer and the poor fell further and further behind. When the country was poor, our unions didn't demand big pay increases for their members because Ireland Inc. couldn't pay; when it was rich, they didn't demand them either in case we became poor again; and then when we became poor again anyway, they didn't demand them because, once again, they decreed that we couldn't afford it.

I think it's clear who's winning this game!

Workers responded by avoiding unions and their charms in record numbers. The number of workers in membership of a union, as a percentage of the overall workforce, was down to 39 per cent in 2001 across the public and private sectors. That is a fall from a peak of 55.34 per cent in 1980. Steadily, year by year during the partnership years when Ireland's trade union leaders enjoyed all the trappings of power and influence that partnership with employers and government gave them, workers voted with their feet. 1987 (PNR) 45.56 per cent level of unionisation. 1990 (PESP) 43.96 per cent level of unionisation. 1994 (PCW) 41.80 per cent level of unionisation. 1998 (P2000) 38.90 per cent level of unionisation. 2001 39.00 per cent level of unionisation. And then what did they call the new agreement reached in 2003? 'Sustaining Progress'. You really couldn't make this up. Union penetration below 40 per cent and falling! If the unions continue to 'sustain' this level of 'progress', there'll be no members left at all in thirty years.

The picture is even worse than that illustrated above. Union membership levels are actually collated from union member returns that include retired and unemployed members. Take those away and the number of active members is even lower. Moreover, the greatest preponderance of actual membership is in the public sector — in the companies like Iarnrod Éireann where your employer effectively recruits you as a member of the union when you take up employment, and then if you want to leave — for example to join ILDA — your employer takes you to the High Court and argues that you can't. Given that the majority of trade union members in the public sector were, in fact, effectively conscripted into their union by their employer — in many cases, as an unconstitutional condition of their employment — it is no wonder that the average member doesn't give a damn, and doesn't attend meetings or conferences or take any active part in their union at all. Moreover, the employer takes money from workers' wages before they get it, and presents it to the unions that the employer insists the workers join. And nobody is allowed to see anything wrong with this relationship!

So we move on to the private sector — the sector where employers don't present thousands of conscripts to their favourite unions, and where the unions actually have to recruit for themselves. 'Recruit' is an old-fashioned word in the Irish trade union movement. Not for us the radical organising models used so effectively by unions in the US, which require shoe leather, meetings with prospective members, arguments and exchange of ideas, and building and organising from the bottom up. In Ireland, as two prominent academics and commentators correctly observed:

> The resurgence of national pay bargaining from 1987 to date has thus underscored a tradition in which union governance and decision-making has always been vested in mainly national organisations and in union branches acting for the most part as agents of national policy.
> – William K. Roche and Jacqueline Ashmore, 'Irish Unions: Testing the Limits of Social Partnership' in Peter Fairbrother and Gerald Griffin, eds, *Changing Prospects for Trade Unionism: Comparisons Between Six Countries*, Continuum, London & New York, 2002

In other words, our trade union movement is organised from the top down and not from the bottom up, and the local branches and members simply carry out the policies handed down to them from on high. But how does that work in a private sector employment where you have no members but are trying to find them? Where are the minions to spread the gospel? There isn't much point in pontificating from on high when there is no one to pontificate to. So instead, our unions try to recruit the employer! Where efforts are made to recruit in the private sector, they invariably take the form of meetings between union gurus and the employer, to see if an agreement can be reached where the employer will encourage or otherwise persuade prospective or actual employees to join the union. And why would an employer want to do that? Certainly not through a wish to see employees joining a body that is a proud protector of workers' rights, terms and conditions. In short, would you want to join a union that your employer is encouraging you to join; and if you did join, could you trust that union to act in your best interests?

Thus, it should come as no big surprise to learn that less than 20 per cent of private sector employees are in trade unions — not even 1 in 5 workers. In my own town of Athlone, SIPTU tried to reach such an agreement with international pharmaceutical company Élan. When Élan, which has a no-union policy but sophisticated in-house works committees and complaints procedures, raised concerns about continuity of production, SIPTU's response was to signal its willingness to enter a binding third-party disputes mechanism. That's a no-strike clause to you and me. Even so, Élan said 'thanks, but no thanks', and SIPTU slipped away back to those nice, helpful public sector employers.

So, unions continue to focus primarily on the public sector to maintain their membership levels and bureaucracies. But deregulation in the public sector is changing workplaces that for generations have provided the unions' bread and butter. This often ideologically driven deregulation creates massive difficulties for unions seeking to maintain, let alone increase, membership levels. If a market — any market — is open to free competition, how can unions ensure that all entrants to that market will be as obliging in providing a steady stream of recruits to them as companies such as CIÉ, Bord na Mona or Aer Rianta. have been?

There are answers to these problems, of course, but these answers will put the unions on an inevitable collision course with their 'partners' in government and IBEC. So instead of falling out with their 'partners', the unions stick their heads in the sand. Instead of going proudly forth and ploughing new furrows, unions such as SIPTU, IMPACT, AEEU or TEEU squabble over who owns what members. They jealously guard existing members and will use any tool available to ward off 'poachers'. Until 2001, ICTU had a rule whereby an affiliate union could not take a member of another affiliate unless 80 per cent of the entire grade, group or category of workers involved agreed to move also. So IMPACT couldn't recruit Aer Lingus cabin crew in membership of SIPTU unless 80 per cent of them agreed to transfer. The fact that 79 per cent of the cabin crew might have been totally browned off with SIPTU didn't matter. And, as far as ICTU was concerned, its rules were more important than the constitutional rights of each individual cabin crew member to associate with or dissociate from any union or body of their choosing. So a row broke out about whether or not IMPACT had 80 per cent. A barrister who was called in to sort it out became concerned about the constitutional difficulties, and fears were raised that IMPACT or some cabin crew members might trot off to High Court, citing constitutional rights, and bring the whole house of cards tumbling down. So a deal was struck, and IMPACT won. The almost impossible target of 80 per cent had been met and the cabin crew left SIPTU for IMPACT.

However, then the ICTU conference came along and the almost impossible was made impossible. The bar was raised even higher — all the way to the ceiling, in fact. From 2001 not only must 80% per cent of the grade, group or category concerned want to transfer from one affiliate to another but they must also get – wait for it - the permission of the union they want to leave to do so. If you are a member of a union in ICTU and you want to leave to join another union in ICTU, you must get 80 per cent of your colleagues to agree to move with you, and you must then beg your union's permission to let you go — to free you from your chains. At the conference, one or two delegates pointed out that some members get dissatisfied with their union from time to time and might have complaints. New ICTU General Secretary David Begg had the solution. ICTU would establish a complaints procedure to hear complaints from members about their union (some of us thought that ICTU already had one of those and that it didn't work in our case, but we must have missed something somewhere). This complaints procedure would take him some time to put it in place but it would happen. So the conference delegates agreed the 80% and the 'please sir, can I leave' amendment to the rules. Now, over two years later, the 2003 conference is over and – despite further passed motions calling for it to be set up - the newly promised complaints procedure still isn't in place.

Another interesting thing occurred to me when I was watching coverage of the ICTU conference in June 2003 — the age profile of the delegates. When Pat Rabbitte was canvassing for his ultimately successful bid to become Labour Party leader in 2002, as he toured the branches, he was struck by the dearth of young people in the party. The trade union movement is the same. And there's a reason for it — falling membership, retired members still on membership lists, no new national active recruiting campaigns in new industries in this changing world. It's also the inevitable consequence of the practice of smothering dissenting voices and 'dealing with' dissenters. Young people entering the workforce are now better educated than ever. Do the union leaders really think that they will want to join organisations that want their money but not their opinions, their membership but not their energy? Why would these young employees choose to join bodies that want to shackle their freshness, their radicalism, their new and fresh way of looking at sometimes very old, sometimes very new, problems? The unions will tell you that they are learning, but the evidence suggests otherwise.

SIPTU hasn't learned from the problems that led to the emergence of ILDA. Since we left, ballots have still been conducted in circumstances that have been questioned, including the recent ballot for the vacant position of General Secretary. SIPTU representatives in Dublin Airport were asked to sign blank cheques for the branch account and, when they refused, were suspended from their positions being re-instated only when they fought their case against their own union in the High Court. Bus workers who put pickets outside Liberty Hall to protest at a grievance were expelled from the union and left at the mercy of their employer, with no protection. A member in Iarnrod Éireann was denied shift rotation despite the fact that Iarnrod Éireann management (John Keenan, in fact) and a Rights Commissioner's decision said that he should have — his own union said that he couldn't. To be fair, the union leaders aren't generally bad people. On the contrary, many of them have given a lifetime of service to the movement and some of their members. But they seem to have lost the plot totally. They have become complacent and have lost their edge, their direction and even, in our experience, their grounding in the principles of the movement. When unions work with management, government, the media and forces of the state to persecute 130 train drivers — whatever differences or arguments we have — it's time for a rethink and a return to basics.

However, if by now you're ready to tear up your union card or throw that application form your boss gave to you in the bin, hold on a minute. From the ashes, hope emerges, as it often does.

The ATGWU

The process within the ATGWU that was initially used to remove Mick O'Reilly and Eugene McGlone was instituted for the first time in their cases. A 'precautionary suspension' is a phenomenon that unions would not tolerate if applied to their members by many employers, especially when coupled with charges as spurious as those used against Mick O'Reilly and Eugene McGlone. It was, however, an integral part of a new procedure drawn up by Bill Morris for use against his own officials, and at the start it seemed to work well from his perspective. Although affording workers natural justice and due process must not have been foremost in his mind when he devised the procedure, it successfully — from his point of view and that of other 'interested parties' — removed Mick O'Reilly and Eugene McGlone from office and kept them silent for a considerable period while Margaret Prosser went looking for 'evidence' to justify the suspensions. And it is also true to say that by the time actual disciplinary hearings began and the stitch-up started to unravel, most of the media interest had long since vanished. In those circumstances, Bill Morris can be forgiven for feeling that this procedure could be a useful tool for use against other 'difficult' employees into the future.

Another TGWU official with difficulties of his own at that time was the National Secretary of the Automotive Group, Tony Woodley. He had been a member and official of the union for over thirty years and had represented workers in the automotive section almost from the outset. He had literally given his working life to the representation of T&G members. But the British car industry had fallen on hard times from the late 1970s onwards, with imports from Europe and the Far East eating into markets and changing the industry forever. Where industry survived at all, new work practices and increased productivity levels were always needed to keep pace with competition. The Rover Group had once been the jewel in the crown of the British automotive industry but even it had floundered, and eventually it was taken over by the German company BMW. Even though it was no longer British-owned, Rover continued to ensure that mass production in the car industry continued in the industrial heartland of the West Midlands where Liverpool-born Tony Woodley worked with management and union members alike to try to keep the industry alive.

When BMW decided to pull out of Rover, therefore, it came as a hammer blow to Tony Woodley and all of those employed in the industry — 20,000 direct jobs with approximately another 100,000 related jobs could be affected. It was time for careful consideration of the options available. One option was for a group of venture capitalists, who called themselves Phoenix, to take over some, or all, of the group. However Phoenix did not intend to engage in mass produced car manufacture, but planned instead to specialise in producing high quality cars aimed at a more select market. Tony Woodley didn't believe that the industry couldn't be saved as it was. He couldn't accept that a group of workers and a craft that had shown itself so willing to accommodate change to maintain competitiveness could not meet the new challenges, and he engaged in a plan to effect a buy-out by some of the old management team. Many in union head office, however, saw it differently. They didn't believe that mass production of cars could be maintained in the West Midlands and they saw the Phoenix development as 'the only show in town'. They also took the extremely political — some would say pragmatic — view that if the industry was to close, it was better to close now than perhaps to wait for another year when Tony Blair's Labour Party would be going before the electorate seeking another term in office, and votes could be lost. Tony Woodley knew that there were tensions and that not everybody in head office shared his confidence that a successful management buy-out could be effected. However, on one of his few days off during the period, he was shocked to receive a phone call at home from Bill Morris, who instructed him to open immediate dialogue with Phoenix. When Tony Woodley argued the case for a buy-out, the general secretary asked whether his authority was being questioned. Tony Woodley knew all about what had happened to Mick O'Reilly and Eugene McGlone and began to fear for his own job. Indeed, soon afterwards he heard that a file was being prepared on him in head office.

Would the General Secretary move against this respected officer? Why not? He had already done so in Ireland and the experience might have emboldened him.

Tony Woodley found this situation a strange one. He had done nothing wrong and was working in the members' interests at all times. He was in constant discussion with them and, in any event, they would be the final arbiters of any deal. In common with the vast majority of other officers in the union, he didn't like the new internal disciplinary procedures. To him they seemed more redolent of a non-unionised employment where workers' rights are not always top of the agenda, than of an employment made up of workers acting in solidarity, moving forward for the common good and that of the wider membership. So he decided to challenge the establishment in the most effective way possible — through the ballot box. Having successfully concluded a management buy-out at Rover that kept the industry alive, he threw his hat into the ring for the position of assistant general secretary. He, like all candidates, made the usual arguments for a return of power to the grassroots, coupled with the typical fodder of any union election — worker rights, representation, taxation, social service maintenance and provision. But there was one issue on which he could put clear water between himself and the rest of the candidates. He pledged to change the new procedures that could be used against officers at the first opportunity and also argued the case for the Irish officers. Most of the officers, privately terrified that a similar fate could befall them, supported Tony Woodley. His campaign was so effective that he romped home to become the second most senior figure in the union.

However, there was more to come. Bill Morris would not outlast Margaret Prosser in office by long. Soon a peerage would be on its way to him, and an election for his replacement would be underway. Tony Woodley decided to keep going, and entered the race. His election as assistant general secretary had shocked the union establishment who had a year and a half to mount an effective campaign against him. One of his opponents for the position of general secretary was, appropriately enough, the man who had been planted by Bill Morris in Belfast to replace Mick O'Reilly — Jimmy Elsby. The latter had now been in Ireland two years and had tried to build a union free of the influence of Mick O'Reilly and

Eugene McGlone. However, Tony Woodley actively campaigned on a pledge to undo the injustice meted out to both men. He was the only candidate to do so effectively, and those who supported the Irish men campaigned for his election and a return to union democracy. Tony Woodley was also familiar with the ILDA dimension. In fact, he had sought to introduce us to Mick O'Reilly four years earlier through his good friend, and ours, then ASLEF General Secretary Mick Rix. ILDA members, like many others, were again asked to support the Woodley candidature.

At the end of May 2003, the election result was announced. Tony Woodley had romped home again with 67,000 votes — 22,000 ahead of his nearest competitor, Jack Dromey. Jimmy Elsby didn't fare at all well. He came fourth in a four-horse race, with a meagre 13,000 votes. The grassroots activist had risen to the top of Britain's Transport and General Workers' Union and was set to replace Bill Morris as General Secretary in October 2003. His election has rocked the union establishment, just as Derek Simpson's as general secretary of that other giant union, AMICUS, had months earlier. Following the election, Bill Morris moved within hours to appoint Mick O'Reilly's one-time friend Brendan Hodgers to O'Reilly's old position, despite fierce opposition from Tony Woodley. Eugene McGlone's job was also filled in this way. It seemed that even after a humiliating electoral defeat, the soon-to-depart regime was still preoccupied with Mick O'Reilly and Eugene McGlone. Nevertheless, this is one union where regime change is now a certainty — the democratically expressed will of the members. Tony Woodley has a massive programme of work ahead of him. One of his first tasks will be to rejuvenate the floundering Irish region and return it to the members. From the ashes, hope arrives.

Conclusion

For ILDA members, these events have provided some light also. Since Mick O'Reilly's removal, the ATGWU has continued to take our money but refused to represent us collectively. The union has refused to act on its own legal advice which lays a path to full representation for our members. Some of the efforts to which that body has gone not to represent us border on the ridiculous, but that is for another day. At one point, ILDA was actually prepared to ballot our members on joining the NBRU. In the context of no representation, a ban on recruitment from our own union, and falling membership prior to Tony Woodley's election, it had seemed to some like 'the least worst option'. It was also surely an opportunity for the NBRU. It was a test of all those pleas that we would be welcomed back to the bargaining procedures within Iarnrod Éireann. But the NBRU dropped the ball. Caught between some of its members seeing developments as an opportunity to vent their spleen against our members, and the reality that our bulk membership would suddenly catapult that union to centre stage on rail issues, with lots more clout — and responsibility — the NBRU panicked and withdrew an initial assurance that all our members would be welcomed. Instead, its officials would select which of our members could join, omitting whom they liked. They missed a historic opportunity to step out of SIPTU's shadow in the railway and to add to their industrial muscle — and at a crucial time too — and we had a lucky escape. The episode did, however, demonstrate how ILDA is constantly trying to move forward and resolve ongoing difficulties, while others are happy for things to remain the same.

In life, however, things seldom remain the same. I am 35 years old now, married with two young children, and am older and wiser than I was when these events began. The same would go for my colleagues in ILDA and the many friends we have made. As this chapter closes, so too, I hope, will an episode from which the Irish trade union movement can take no credit at all. Our members continue to struggle without collective representation in their employment despite our clear legal rights, not to mention our rights as members of the ATGWU. We continue to believe in our entitlement to equal treatment with our colleagues in other unions, and our unity and support for each other remains. But it lives now in an environment of renewed hope. Issues will arise that will need to be resolved affecting our members again — that much is certain. It is to be hoped that, when they do, all parties involved will approach them with an increased sense of dedication towards problem-solving rather than problem-creation.

As a trade unionist, I also hope that the movement takes time to reflect on its actions and approach to ILDA and indeed to reflect on its wider future and role in society and in the workplace. It needs to welcome argument and dissent, rather than run from it; it needs actively to push forward to recruit in new areas of the workplace — particularly the private sector; it needs once again to find its roots among the working classes, the socially disadvantaged and those most in need in our society; and it needs to start to bridge the gap between rich and poor in society. Unless it does these things, it will continue to become increasingly irrelevant to working people and will soon cease to live in any meaningful way. If that happens, it will have been killed not by employers or enemies of the movement, but by the inertia of its own leaders — the guardians of a movement that needs once again to find its soul.

Step by Step

Step by step the longest march
Can be won can be won,
Many stones can form an arch
Singly none singly none,
And by union what we will
Can be accomplished still,
Drops of water turn a mill
Singly none singly none.

Lyrics: nineteenth century Mining Union rulebook
Music: Pete Seeger

INDEX